Lecture Notes in Artificial Intelligence   6057

Edited by R. Goebel, J. Siekmann, and W. Wahlster

Subseries of Lecture Notes in Computer Science

Peter McBurney   Iyad Rahwan
Simon Parsons   Nicolas Maudet (Eds.)

Argumentation in Multi-Agent Systems

6th International Workshop, ArgMAS 2009
Budapest, Hungary, May 12, 2009
Revised Selected and Invited Papers

 Springer

Series Editors

Randy Goebel, University of Alberta, Edmonton, Canada
Jörg Siekmann, University of Saarland, Saarbrücken, Germany
Wolfgang Wahlster, DFKI and University of Saarland, Saarbrücken, Germany

Volume Editors

Peter McBurney
University of Liverpool, Department of Computer Science
Liverpool, L69 3BX, UK
E-mail: mcburney@liverpool.ac.uk

Iyad Rahwan
The British University in Dubai, Faculty of Informatics
P.O. Box 502216, Dubai, UAE
and
University of Edinburgh, School of Informatics
Edinburgh EH8 9AB, UK
E-mail: irahwan@acm.org

Simon Parsons
City University of New York, Brooklyn College
Department of Computer and Information Science
2900 Bedford Avenue, Brooklyn, NY 11210, USA
E-mail: parsons@sci.brooklyn.cuny.edu

Nicolas Maudet
Université Paris 9 Dauphine, LAMSADE
75775 Paris Cedex 16, France
E-mail: maudet@lamsade.dauphine.fr

Library of Congress Control Number: 2010925494

CR Subject Classification (1998): I.2, I.2.11, C.2.4, F.4.1, H.4, H.3

LNCS Sublibrary: SL 7 – Artificial Intelligence

ISSN	0302-9743
ISBN-10	3-642-12804-1 Springer Berlin Heidelberg New York
ISBN-13	978-3-642-12804-2 Springer Berlin Heidelberg New York

springer.com

© Springer-Verlag Berlin Heidelberg 2010
Printed in Germany

Typesetting: Camera-ready by author, data conversion by Scientific Publishing Services, Chennai, India
Printed on acid-free paper   06/3180

Preface

This volume contains revised versions of the papers presented at the sixth edition of the International Workshop on Argumentation in Multi-Agent Systems, (ArgMAS 2009), held in Budapest, Hungary, in association with the 8th International Conference on Autonomous Agents and Multi-Agent Systems (AAMAS 2009) in May 2009. Previous ArgMAS workshops have been held in New York City, USA (2004), Utrecht, The Netherlands (2005), Hakodate, Japan (2006), Honolulu, USA (2007) and Estoril, Portugal (2008). The event has now clearly established itself on the international calendar among researchers in computational argument and dialectics.

A brief word to explain these topics is in order. Different agents within a multi-agent system (MAS) potentially have differential access to information and different capabilities, different beliefs, different preferences and desires, and different goals. A key aspect of the scientific and engineering study of multi-agent systems therefore has been the development of methods and procedures for identifying, assessing, reconciling, arbitrating between, managing, and mitigating such differences. Market mechanisms and voting procedures are two methods for dealing with these differences. Argumentation is another. Argumentation can be understood as the formal interaction of different arguments for and against some conclusion (e.g., a proposition, an action intention, a preference, etc.). An agent may use argumentation techniques to perform individual reasoning for itself alone, in order to resolve conflicting evidence or to decide between conflicting goals it may have. Two or more agents may also jointly use dialectical argumentation to identify, express, and reconcile differences between themselves, by means of interactions such as negotiation, persuasion, inquiry, and joint deliberation.

In recent years, formal theories of argument and argument interaction have been proposed and studied, and this has led to the study of computational models of argument. The ArgMAS series of workshops has focused on computational argumentation within the context of agent reasoning and multi-agent systems. The ArgMAS workshops are of interest to anyone studying or applying: default reasoning in autonomous agents; single-agent reasoning and planning under uncertainty; strategic single-agent reasoning in the context of potential competitor actions; and the rational resolution of the different beliefs and intentions of multiple agents within multi-agent systems. There are close links between these topics and other topics within the discipline of autonomous agents and multi-agent systems, particularly: agent communications languages and protocols; game theory; AI planning; logic programming; and human–agent interaction.

The papers in this volume were selected for inclusion in the ArgMAS 2009 workshop following a peer-review process undertaken by anonymous reviewers, resulting in 15 papers being selected for inclusion in the workshop. We thank all authors who made submissions to ArgMAS 2009, and we thank the members of the Program Committee for their efforts in reviewing the papers submitted. One innovation adopted at the 2009 workshop was the use of official pre-chosen respondents to offer short, prepared critiques to a number of the papers presented at the workshop. This innovation was borrowed from conferences in philosophy, where it is standard, and we found it worked very well. The comments of respondents, who each knew of their assignment ahead of time and so could make a careful reading of their assigned paper, better focused the discussions at the workshop, and led to improvements in the quality of the revised papers later published here. This volume also contains a paper from the invited keynote speaker at the workshop, prominent argumentation-theorist Douglas Walton of the University of Windsor, Canada. His talk presented and his paper reports on his current research exploring the burden of proof in deliberation dialogs. We were honored by Professor Walton's participation, and we thank him for giving the keynote address.

As in collections of papers at previous ArgMAS workshops, we have also invited several papers from the main AAMAS Conference of relevance to argumentation in multi-agent systems. There are three invited papers here: a paper by Guido Boella and colleagues, entitled, "Dynamics in argumentation with single extensions: attack refinement and the grounded extension"; a paper by Paul Doran and colleagues, entitled, "Using ontology modularization for efficient negotiation over ontology correspondences in MAS"; and, thirdly, a paper by Yuqing Tang and colleagues, entitled, "A model for integrating dialogue and the execution of joint plans."

We hope that you enjoy reading this collection.

February 2010   Peter McBurney
                                                          Iyad Rahwan
                                                          Simon Parsons
                                                          Nicolas Maudet

Organization

Program Chairs

Peter McBurney	University of Liverpool, UK
Iyad Rahwan	British University in Dubai, UAE
	(Fellow) University of Edinburgh, UK
Simon Parsons	Brooklyn College, City University of New York, USA
Nicolas Maudet	Université Paris Dauphine, France

ArgMAS Steering Committee

Antonis Kakas	University of Cyprus, Cyprus
Nicolas Maudet	Université Paris Dauphine, France
Peter McBurney	University of Liverpool, UK
Pavlos Moraitis	Paris Descartes University, France
Simon Parsons	Brooklyn College, City University of New York, USA
Iyad Rahwan	British University in Dubai, UAE
	(Fellow) University of Edinburgh, UK
Chris Reed	University of Dundee, UK

Program Committee

Leila Amgoud	IRIT, France
Katie Atkinson	University of Liverpool, UK
Trevor Bench-Capon	University of Liverpool, UK
Jamal Bentahar	Laval University, Canada
Elizabeth Black	Oxford University, UK
Guido Boella	Università di Torino, Italy
Brahim Chaib-draa	Laval University, Canada
Carlos Chesnevar	Universitat de Lleida, Spain
Frank Dignum	Utrecht University, The Netherlands
Yannis Dimopoulos	University of Cyprus, Cyprus
Sylvie Doutre	IRIT, Toulouse, France
Paul Dunne	University of Liverpool, UK
Rogier van Eijk	Utrecht University, The Netherlands
Anthony Hunter	University College, London, UK
Antonis Kakas	University of Cyprus, Cyprus
Nikos Karacapilidis	University of Patras, Greece

Nicolas Maudet   Université Paris Dauphine, France
Peter McBurney   University of Liverpool, UK
Jarred McGinnis   Royal Holloway, University of London, UK
Sanjay Modgil   King's College London, UK
Pavlos Moraitis   Paris Descartes University, France
Tim Norman   University of Aberdeen, UK
Nir Oren   King's College London, UK
Fabio Paglieri   ISTC-CNR, Rome, Italy
Simon Parsons   City University of New York, USA
Enric Plaza   Spanish Scientific Research Council, Spain
Henri Prade   IRIT, Toulouse, France
Henry Prakken   Utrecht University, The Netherlands
Alun Preece   University of Aberdeen, UK
Iyad Rahwan   British University in Dubai, UAE
                           (Fellow) University of Edinburgh, UK
Sarvapali Ramchurn   University of Southampton, UK
Chris Reed   University of Dundee, UK
Michael Rovatsos   University of Edinburgh, UK
Hajime Sawamura   Niigata University, Japan
Guillermo Simari   Universidad Nacional del Sur, Argentina
Elizabeth Sklar   City University of New York, USA
Francesca Toni   Imperial College, London, UK
Leon van der Torre   University of Luxembourg, Luxembourg
Paolo Torroni   Università di Bologna, Italy
Bart Verheij   Maastricht University, The Netherlands
Gerard Vreeswijk   Utrecht University, The Netherlands
Douglas Walton   University of Winnipeg, Canada
Simon Wells   University of Dundee, UK
Michael Wooldridge   University of Liverpool, UK

Table of Contents

Part IV: Applications and Emotions

Burden of Proof in Deliberation Dialogs

Douglas Walton

University of Windsor, Windsor ON N9B 3Y1, Canada
dwalton@uwindsor.ca

Abstract. The literature in argumentation and artificial intelligence has distinguished five types of burden of proof in persuasion dialogs, but there appears to have been no serious investigation so far on how burdens of proof should be modeled in deliberation dialogs. The work in this paper is directed toward filling that gap by extending existing formal models of deliberation dialog to analyze four examples of deliberation dialog where burden of proof is at issue or poses an interesting problem. The examples are used to show (1) that the eight stages in the formal model of Hitchcock, McBurney and Parsons (2007) need to be divided into three more general stages, an opening stage, an argumentation stage and a closing stage, (2) that deliberation dialog shifts to persuasion dialog during the argumentation stage, and (3) that burden of proof is only operative during the argumentation stage. What is shown in general is that deliberation is, in the typical type of case, a mixed dialog in which there is a shift to persuasion dialog in the middle.

Both in argumentation studies as an interdisciplinary domain and in artificial intelligence, the type of dialog that has been most intensively studied so far is that of persuasion dialog. In this type of dialog, there is some claim at issue, and the object of the dialog is to prove or disprove that claim. Deliberation has a different kind of goal. It is to solve a problem about what course of action to take. The problem statement is not a proposition, but a question, called a governing question by McBurney, Hitchcock and Parsons (2007). Examples of these questions are: 'Where should we go to dinner ?' and 'How can we provide all Americans with health care insurance?'. The goal of a deliberation is to find a solution to a common problem. Unlike persuasion dialog, there are no winners and losers. Everyone wins if the dialog is successful. Does burden of proof have a place in this type of dialog? It seems so, because arguments go back and forth in a deliberation dialog, and once an argument is brought forward, like 'Ricardo's is the best place to go for dinner, because their food is organic', it requires evidence to back it up if it is challenged. It appears then that understanding how burden of proof works in it is an important step in the study of deliberation dialog as a form of group decision-making.

There is a growing literature on burden of proof in argumentation (Kauffeld, 2003) and in work on formal dialog models in artificial intelligence (Prakken, Reed and Walton, 2005; Prakken and Sartor, 2006, 2007, 2009; Gordon, Prakken

P. McBurney et al. (Eds.): ArgMAS 2009, LNAI 6057, pp. 1–22, 2010.
© Springer-Verlag Berlin Heidelberg 2010

and Walton, 2007). Importantly, this work has distinguished several types of burdens in persuasion dialog, as opposed to the widely accepted traditional assumption that there is a single concept of burden of proof. There is also a recent literature on formal models of deliberation dialog (Tang and Parsons, 2006; McBurney, Hitchcock and Parsons, 2007). However, there appears to be no serious investigation so far on the special problem of how burden of proof should be modeled in deliberation dialog.

The work in this paper is directed toward filling that gap by extending existing formal models of deliberation dialog to analyze four examples of deliberation dialog where burden of proof poses a problem. Based on analysis of the argumentation in these examples, a working hypothesis is put forward. It is that burden of proof only becomes relevant when deliberation dialog shifts, at the beginning of the argumentation stage, to a persuasion dialog. The hypothesis is that the shift can be classified as an embedding of one type of dialog into another, meaning that the goal of the first type of dialog continues to be supported once the transition to the second type of dialog has been made (Walton and Krabbe, 1995, p. 102). In other instances, it is well known that a shift can be illicit, where the advent of the second dialog interferes with the fulfillment of the goal of the first one. It has also been shown that such shifts can be associated with fallacies, as well as other logical and communicative problems (Walton, 2007, chapter 6).

1   Types of Dialog

A dialog is defined as an ordered 3-tuple $\langle O, A, C \rangle$ where O is the opening stage, A is the argumentation stage, and C is the closing stage (Gordon and Walton, 2009, 5). Dialog rules define what types of moves are allowed (Walton and Krabbe, 1995). At the opening stage, the participants agree to take part in some type of dialog that has a collective goal. Each party has an individual goal and the dialog itself has a collective goal. The initial situation is framed at the opening stage, and the dialog moves through the opening stage toward the closing stage. The type of dialog is determined by its initial situation, the collective goal of the dialog shared by both participants, and each individual participant's goal. The global burden of proof is set at the opening stage, but during the argumentation stage, as particular arguments are put forward and replied to, there is a local burden of proof for each argument that can change. This local burden of proof can shift from one side to the other during the argumentation stage as arguments are put forward and critically questioned. Once the argumentation has reached the closing stage, the outcome is determined by judging whether one side or the other has met its global burden of proof, according the requirements for burden of proof set at the opening stage.

During the argumentation stage of a dialog, two parties (in the simplest case) take turns making moves that take the form of speech acts, like asking a question, making an assertion, or putting forward an argument. Dialog rules define what types of moves are allowed (Walton and Krabbe, 1995). As each party makes a move statements are inserted into or retracted from his/her commitment store.

The six basic types of dialog previously recognized in the argumentation literature are persuasion dialog, inquiry, negotiation dialog, information-seeking dialog, deliberation, and eristic dialog. Discovery dialog has been added in new list of the properties of the basic types of dialog in Table 1.

Table 1. Seven Basic Types of Dialog

TYPE OF DIALOG	INITIAL SITUATION	PARTICIPANT'S GOAL	GOAL OF DIALOG
Persuasion	Conflict of Opinions	Persuade Other Party	Resolve or Clarify Issue
Inquiry	Need to Have Proof	Find and Verify Evidence	Prove (Disprove) Hypothesis
Discovery	Need to Find an Explanation of Facts	Find and Defend a Suitable Hypothesis	Choose Best Hypothesis for Testing
Negotiation	Conflict of Interests	Get What You Most Want	Reasonable Settlement Both Can Live With
Information-Seeking	Need Information	Acquire or Give Information	Exchange Information
Deliberation	Dilemma or Practical Choice	Co-ordinate Goals and Actions	Decide Best Available Course of Action
Eristic	Personal Conflict	Verbally Hit Out at Opponent	Reveal Deeper Basis of Conflict

On the account given by (McBurney and Parsons, 2001, 4), the properties of discovery dialog and inquiry dialog are different. In inquiry dialog, the proposition that is to be proved true is designated at the opening stage, whereas in discovery dialog the hypotheses to be tested are only formulated during the argumentation stage. A discovery dialog moves through ten stages (McBurney and Parsons, 2001, 5) called open dialog, discuss purpose, share knowledge, discuss mechanisms, infer consequences, discuss criteria, assess consequences, discuss tests, propose conclusions, and close dialog.

Persuasion dialog can be classified as a truth-directed type of dialog, as opposed to deliberation dialog, which is not aimed at finding the truth of the matter being discussed, but at arriving at a decision on what to do, given a need to take action. While persuasion dialog is centrally adversarial, deliberation is a collaborative type of dialog in which parties collectively steer actions towards a common goal by agreeing on a proposal that can solve a problem affecting all of the parties concerned, taking all their interests into account. It may seem initially that we can distinguish between the two types of dialog by saying that deliberation is about actions and persuasion dialog is about the truth and falsity of propositions. However, both deliberation and persuasion dialogs can be about actions, and hence the dividing line between the two types of dialog is not so simple. To determine in a particular case whether an argument in a text of discourse can better be seen as part of a persuasion dialog or a deliberation type of dialog, one has to arrive at a determination of what the goals of the dialog and the goals of the participants are supposed to be. The starting point of a deliberation dialog is a problem to be solved, whereas in a persuasion dialog the starting point is a claim that has to be proved (Walton et al., 2009). The goal of a deliberation dialog is not persuasion. It is to solve the problem posed at the starting point. Deliberation dialog is also different from negotiation dialog, because negotiation deals with competing interests, and its central role is to resolve a conflict of interests by arriving in a compromise that both parties can live with. In contrast, in a deliberation dialog the participants evaluate proposed courses of action according to standards that may be contrary to their personal interests.

During a sequence of argumentation there can be a dialectical shift from one type of dialog to another (Walton and Krabbe, 1995, 100-116). For example suppose in a debate in a legislative assembly on whether to pass a bill to install a new dam, the participants will want to find out things like how the dam needs to be constructed, what its ecological consequences will be, and what it will cost to build it. To answer these questions they might consult experts in engineering and ecology. Here there has been a shift from the original deliberation dialog on whether to build the dam to an information-seeking dialog. In some shifts there is an interruption of the first dialog when the shift occurs, so that the advent of the second dialog is an easily visible break from the line of argumentation in the first dialog. In other cases, the dialog seems to flow smoothly along over the shift so that the second dialog fits nicely into the first. This second type of case, called a dialectical embedding (Walton and Krabbe, 1995, p. 102), is said to occur where there is a productive functional relationship between the two dialogs so that the argumentation in the second dialog enhances the quality of the argumentation in the first. The special concern of this paper is with dialectical embedding of persuasion dialog in deliberation.

Deliberation dialog begins with a problem, and the goal of the dialog is to find a solution to the problem, usually some action to take, typically in a collaborative, not an adversarial context. This process often involves a brainstorming phase in which ideas are put forward that are not yet formulated as proposals that the person who put the idea forward has a commitment to defend. Arguments for and against these ideas can be gathered, with every party providing pro and con arguments for all the alternatives on the table. During this brainstorming phase, parties will put forward con as well as pro arguments for the ideas put forward by other parties. Only later in the deliberation, after the brainstorming phase do parties propose and defend specific solutions. It is during this phase, as we will contend below, that the deliberation dialog shifts to a persuasion dialog.

2   Burdens of Proof in Persuasion Dialog in Law

In law, there is a fundamental distinction between two main types of burden of proof (Prakken and Sartor, 2009). One is the setting of the global burden of proof at the opening stage, called the burden of persuasion. It does not change during the argumentation stage, and is the device used to determine which side has won at the closing stage. The other is the local setting of burden of proof at the argumentation stage, often called the burden of production in law. This burden can shift back and forth as the argumentation proceeds. For example, if one side puts forward a strong argument, the other side must meet the local burden to respond to that argument by criticizing in or presenting a counter-argument, or otherwise the strong argument will hold, helping to fulfill the burden of persuasion of its proponent.

In everyday conversational argumentation, the burden of proof in the case might be more problematic to pin down. In the kinds of examples often used to illustrate arguments and fallacies in critical thinking courses, for example, the given argument may be merely a fragment, and not enough about the context of the discussion may be known in order to determine which side should properly be said to have the burden of proof.

There are also other burdens of proof that can be identified in legal argumentation. Prakken and Sartor (2009, 225) explain the difference between burden of persuasion, burden of production and tactical burden of proof as follows. The burden of persuasion specifies which party has to prove its ultimate statement to be proved to the degree required by its proof standard. The failure to prove the statement results in the loss of the proceeding as a whole for that side. The burden of production specifies which party has to offer evidence to support a claim one has made at some particular point in the proceeding. If the evidence put forward does not meet the proof standard for this burden, "the issue is decided as a matter of law against the burdened party, while otherwise the issue is decided in the final stage by the trier of fact according to the burden of persuasion"(2009, 243). Both the burden of persuasion and burden of production are assigned as a matter of law. The tactical burden of proof is not. It is decided by the party himself, by assessing the risk of losing on that issue if he presents no further evidence. The tactical burden of proof is fulfilled at a given point during the argumentation stage if, when you add up all your arguments at that point, they are sufficient to fulfill your burden of persuasion. In this paper, burden of production and tactical burden of proof are subsumed under the general category of local burden of proof.

In law, in a criminal case, only the prosecution side has the burden of persuasion, and this burden is fixed during the whole trial. In contrast, in a civil case, each side has a burden of persuasion, and each side has to prove its thesis by the standard of the preponderance of evidence. Four standards are formally modeled in the Carneades dialog system (Gordon and Walton, 2009). In Carneades, there are two sides, and there can be pro and contra arguments put forward by each side during the argumentation stage.

- The standard of scintilla of evidence is met if and only if there is one argument supporting the claim.
- The preponderance of the evidence standard is met if and only if the scintilla of evidence standard is met and the weight of evidence for the claim is greater than the weight against it.
- The clear and convincing evidence standard is met if and only if the preponderance of the evidence standard is met and the weight of the pro arguments exceeds that of the con arguments by some specified threshold.
- The beyond reasonable doubt standard is met if and only if the clear and convincing evidence standard is met and the weight of the con arguments is below some specified threshold.

These standards can apply to the burden of persuasion set at the opening stage, or to arguments put forward during the argumentation stage. In either instance, note that the burden of persuasion is fixed at the opening stage, in contrast to the local burden, which is only operative during the argumentation stage. The local burden requires that when a participant makes an assertion, or makes a claim of any sort, he is required to give sufficient evidence of the right kind to support the claim, to the appropriate standard of proof. If s/he fails to fulfill this requirement, the argument is not strong enough to fulfill its required burden.

3   Three Examples

The first example was a debate in a Rhode Island Assembly on whether or not to bring in no-fault insurance, fully described in Lascher (1999), and cited in more abbreviated form as an example of deliberation dialog in (Walton, 1998, p. 169). One side proposed bringing in a new system of no-fault insurance in Rhode Island, arguing that insurance rates were too high, and that paying the premiums had become burdensome. The goal of both sides was presumably to lower insurance rates if possible. The opposed side argued that the proposed no-fault system would unfairly make good drivers pay for bad drivers, and would fail to lower insurance premiums.

This example initially appears to be one of a deliberation dialog in which two groups engaged in discussion with each other are arguing from what they take to be their common commitments. The point of disagreement is that each side is doubtful that the proposals for action put forward by the other side will fulfill the central goal both agree on. This case looks like deliberation, because there were two sides, for and against, and each used practical reasoning to support its side, often by employing argumentation from consequences. The no-fault side argued, for example, that the change to no-fault insurance would reduce costs of coverage. The opposed side argued, for example, that no-fault unfairly makes good drivers pay for bad drivers. In this case, each side put forward some general or global action that it advocated. The no-fault side advocated changing to a no-fault system. The opposed side argued for retaining the status quo.

The second example is also argumentation based on a practical need to take action, and therefore also appears to be a case of deliberation dialog (Wigmore, 1935, 440).

For example, if A, as he arrives at his destination and steps out of his car to the crowded sidewalk, sees a purse lying there, picks it up, and looks around to see who may have dropped it, suppose that M steps up to him, and claims it as his own. At first A is in doubt; hence, inaction as to surrendering it. Then he says to M, "Prove your ownership." Suppose that M makes a statement that is unconvincing; A is still in doubt, hence continued inaction. But suppose that M describes exactly the contents of the purse; then conviction comes to A, and he hands the purse to M.

In this example, A does not act on the basis of any legal notion or theory of burden of proof, according to Wigmore's analysis. A's decision is an instinctive one of requiring M to remove his doubt before he hands over the purse. As long as A's doubt remains in place, M does not get the purse. According to Wigmore (1935, 439), doubt and conviction are the two contrasting states of mind of a person who is confronted with a choice of actions. Doubt leads to inaction, whereas conviction leads to action.

The third example concerns a problem that has recently arisen concerning the importation of active pharmaceutical ingredients from overseas. One example cited concerned imported heparin[1] that was contaminated and that claimed the lives of patients taking pharmaceuticals in which this drug was an ingredient. An energy and commerce committee asked Congress to grant it powers to order recalls of drug products, to block suspicious imports from gaining access to the U.S., and to require foreign firms to divulge data in inspections. One committee member expressed the problem by saying that according to current practice, the Federal Drug Administration (FDA) must show at the border that imported active pharmaceutical ingredients are unsafe. Instead of the burden being on the FDA to prove that the shipment is unsafe, he suggested, it would be better if the company importing the shipment had the obligation to prove that it is safe.[2] How could this case be analyzed as an instance of deliberation dialog in which there is argumentation on two sides of an issue and burden of proof is involved? Finally, there is a fourth example that needs to be treated at more length because it is especially controversial and problematic.

4   The Precautionary Principle

The precautionary principle was introduced in Europe in the nineteen seventies to give the environmental risk managers regulatory authority to stop environmental contamination without waiting for conclusive scientific evidence of harm to the environment. It is controversial how the principle should be defined, but a rough definition that provides a beginning point for discussion can be framed as

---

[1] Heparin is a highly sulfated glycosaminoglycan widely used as an anticoagulant.

[2] This example is a paraphrase of a case described in Joseph Woodcock, "Burden of Proof of Safety Must Fall on Drug Manufacturers", Validation Times, May, 2008, 1-7. Found on Dec. 22, 2008 at
http://findarticles.com/p/mi_hb5677/is_5_10/ai_n29445559

follows: if an action or policy might cause severe or irreversible harm to the public or the environment, in the absence of conclusive scientific evidence that harm would not ensue, the burden of proof falls on the side that advocates taking the action. Note that this definition links the precautionary principle to the notion of burden of proof. It is meant to be applied to the formation of environmental policy in cases like massive deforestation and mitigation of global warming, where the burden of proof is ruled to lie with the advocate.

An early application of the principle was to the prohibition of the purging of ship bilge contents into the oceans (Freestone and Hey, 1996). Because of lack of scientific data on the effects of the purging of bilge contents on the oceans, scientific risk assessment of the practice was not possible. The application of the precautionary principle gave regulatory officials the authority to prohibit the practice without waiting for scientific evidence that it could prove harmful to the environment.

Among criticisms of the precautionary principle is the argument that its application could create an impossible burden of proof for marketing new food products or ingredients (Hathcock, 2000, 225). According to this criticism, excessive precaution can lead to paralysis of action resulting from unjustified fear. Some examples cited are the outbreak of cholera resulting from fear of chlorinated water, and the reluctance to permit food fortification with folic acid to reduce the incidence of birth defects for fear of masking vitamin B12 deficiency (Hathcock, 2000, 255). What is especially interesting is that both defenses and criticisms of the precautionary principle link it closely to the concept of burden of proof.

The precautionary principle was adopted by the U.N. general assembly in 1982, and was implemented in an international treaty by the Montreal Protocol in 1987. According to the Rio Declaration of 1992, "where there are threats of serious or irreversible damage, lack of full scientific certainty shall not be used as a reason for postponing cost-effective measures to prevent environmental degradation". In some countries, like the U.S., the precautionary principle is designated as an approach rather than a principle, meaning that it does not have legal status. In other countries, and in the European Union, it has the legal status of a principle, meaning that is it is compulsory for a court to make rulings in cases by applying it (Recuerda, 2008).

Critics have argued that the precautionary principle can be used to stop the use of any new food products, because safety cannot be proved with certainty in any case of a new product (Hathcock, 2000, 258). There is also the problem of judging how serious a harm has to be and how likely it is, before the principle can be applied. The principle was originally meant to give regulatory authority to stop environmental contamination, but once made into law, as Bailey (1999, 3) pointed out, it could conceivably be applied to all kinds of activities. Applying the principle to other areas, for example, inventors would have to prove that their inventions would never do harm before they could be marketed to the public (Bailey, 1999, 4).

One of the problems with implementing the precautionary principle is that there are open questions about the standard of proof that should be applied to the side advocating the action or policy question. It would seem that, since the principle is supposed to be applied under conditions of lack of full scientific certainty, a high standard of certainty, like beyond reasonable doubt, would not be appropriate. On the other hand, there are the questions of how serious and widespread the harm needs to be, and how it can be shown that it is irreversible, before the principle should be applied. There is also the question of how it should be judged how much evidence should be given by the advocate of the action to match the perceived seriousness and likelihood of the harm. The principle needs standards of proof for both sides, but the standards of proof that should be required might be expected to vary from case to case.

5   The Formal Structure of Deliberation Dialog

Deliberation always begins with the formulation of a problem about which action to take in a given set of circumstances. The problem is formulated in a governing question of the kind 'What should we do now?' The first stage of the dialog comprises both the formulation of the governing question and the circulation of the information about the given circumstances of the decision to be made among all the members of the group. Knowledge of the circumstances is continually being updated and circulated during a typical deliberation dialog, but the collection of data is typically limited by costs, and in particular by the cost of delaying arriving at a decision on what to do. There is always a tradeoff between arriving in a timely decision on what to do, and the improvement of the deliberation that would be made by collecting more relevant information about the circumstances. This opening stage comprises the first two stages represented in the formal model of deliberation dialog of McBurney, Hitchcock and Parsons (2007, 100) called *open, inform, propose, consider, revise, recommend, confirm,* and *close.*

Open: A governing question, like "Where shall we go for dinner this evening?", expressing a need take action in a given set of circumstances, is raised.
Inform: This stage includes information about facts, goals, values, constraints on possible actions, evaluation criteria for proposals.
Propose: Proposals cite possible action-options relevant to the governing question.
Consider: This stage concerns examining arguments for and against proposals.
Revise: Goals, constraints, perspectives, and action-options can be revised in light of information coming in and arguments for and against proposals.
Recommend: Based on information and arguments, proposals are recommended for acceptance or non-acceptance by each participant.
Confirm: The participants confirm acceptance of the optimal proposal according to some procedure. For example, all participants must do so before the dialog terminates.
Close: Termination of the dialog, once the optimal proposal has been confirmed.

An important property of deliberation dialog (McBurney, Hitchcock and Parsons, 2007, 98) is that a proposal may be optimal for the deliberating group but suboptimal for any individual participant. Another feature is that in a proper deliberation dialog each participant must share his/her individual goals and interests, as well as information about the given circumstances. The goal of deliberation dialog is for the participants to collectively decide on what is the optimal course of action for the group.

It is important to note that the temporal progress of a real deliberation is not the same as the normative model of the argumentation that should ideally take place in it. The bringing in of information is not restricted only to the opening stage in real instances.

Deliberation needs to proceed under conditions of uncertainty and lack of knowledge about a complex situation that is constantly changing. For this reason, information about the changing situation needs to be continually updated. An important skill of deliberation is to adapt an initial plan of action to new information that comes in reporting changes in the existing circumstances. There is typically feedback in which the agents who are involved in the deliberation may see the consequences of the actions they have already carried out, and need to modify their plans and proposals by updating in light of the new information. For this reason, deliberation dialog needs to be seen as having an information-seeking dialog embedded into it. It is constantly shifting from looking at the arguments for and against a proposal and taking into account the new information about the changing factual circumstances of the case being considered. At the opening stage, the *inform* function is employed to collect a database of information concerning the circumstances of the given situation, but later additions and deletions to it need to be made during the argumentation stage.

The opening stage also has a brainstorming phase in which ideas are put forward, but not yet as firm proposals that the participant who voiced the proposal is committed to defending. Nor is he committed to attacking opposed proposals at this point. At this stage, a participant may bring out weak points in a proposal he has articulated, and find strong points in a proposal someone else has voiced. But then at the *revise* phase, there is a shift. At this point, when a party puts forward a proposal, he is advocating it as the best solution to the problem posed in the opening stage. Thus at this point, we are no longer in the opening stage. We are now in the argumentation stage. The argumentation stage also includes the *recommend* phase, but the last two phases in the McBurnery, Hitchcock and Parsons model, the *confirm* and *close* phases, are parts of the closing stage of the deliberation dialog.

Now we have divided the eight phases of the McBurney, Hitchcock and Parsons model into three more general stages, there is a problem that arises. In the middle stage, the argumentation stage, each party defends the proposal he or she has advocated as solving the problem set at the opening stage, and attacks the alternative proposals put forward by other parties. In this stage, has there been a shift to a persuasion dialog, even though later on, at the closing stage, the discussion will shift back to a deliberation dialog? Reconsidering the examples might help to answer this question.

6   Analysis of the No-Fault Insurance Example

There are two basic types of persuasion dialog, depending on how the burden of proof is allocated (Walton and Krabbe, 1995). In a dispute (symmetrical persuasion dialog) each side has a thesis to be proved. For example, White (a theist) has to prove that God exists while Black (an atheist) has to prove that God does not exist. In a dissent, one party has a thesis to be proved while the other, in order to win, needs only to cast doubt on the first party's attempts to prove her thesis, so that her burden of proof is not met. For example, White (a theist) has to prove that God exists while Black (an agnostic) needs only to cast doubt on White's attempt to prove her thesis, so that her burden of proof is not met. Thus the following propositions follow.

- In a dispute, both sides have a burden of proof. One side has to prove A and the other has to prove not-A.
- In a dissent, one side has to prove A while the other only needs to cast doubt on the attempts of the first side to prove A.
- It follows that the standard of proof needed to win must be set at the opening stage.
- In persuasion dialog, burden of proof must be set at the opening stage.

At first sight, the way the burden of proof needs to be organized in the no-fault insurance example seems comparable to a persuasion dialog.

To see whether it is, let us examine some features of the no-fault insurance example. In this example the burden of proof seems initially to be set in a clear way that is unproblematic. Each side has a proposal. The proposal of the one side is the opposite of that of the other. This suggests a dispute about what action to take. One side proposed bringing in a new system of no-fault insurance, while the opposed side was against the no-fault system. This case shows how serious problems of burden of proof can arise during the argumentation stage. Consider the example dialog in table 2.

From such examples, we can see that the speech act of making a proposal is very much like the speech act of putting forward an argument in a persuasion dialog, and involves the same problems arising from disputes about burden of proof. The proposal itself can be seen as a claim put forward, with a local burden of proof comparable to that attached to the speech act of putting forward an argument in a persuasion dialog.

The making of a proposal advocates a proposition for action that needs to be supported, if questioned or attacked, by putting forward other propositions that are offered as reasons in favor of accepting the proposal. On the analysis advocated here, these other propositions are linked to the proposition that is the proposal by practical reasoning, including related schemes like argumentation from consequences. Both sides share the common goal of lowering the insurance rates if possible, but the disagreement is about the best way to carry out the goal. One side has put forward a proposal to bring in a new system of no-fault insurance, while the other side argues against this proposal. We are not told

Table 2. Argumentation in Dialog Format in the No-fault Insurance Example

	No-fault Side	Opposed Side
1	I propose a no fault-system.	On what grounds?
2	The insurance rates are too high under the existing system.	How can you prove that a no-fault system would lower the rates?
3	How can you prove that a no-fault system would not lower the rates?	It's up to you to prove that a no-fault system would lower the rates.
4	No, it's not.	Yes, it is.
5	You made the claim that a no-fault system would not lower the rates.	No I didn't. Where did I say that?
6	Your argument depends on that claim.	Not really, I just know that the rates are too high under the existing system.
7	Unless you can prove that a no-fault system would not lower the rates, your argument fails.	No, you need to prove that a no-fault system will lower the rates.
8	OK, but my reason is that it would lower the rates.	Well then, prove that this claim is not true.

whether the other side has a different proposal of its own to put forward. It may be that they have no new proposal and are simply arguing for sticking with the old system until a better one can be found, or perhaps for modifying the old system in some way.

What can we say about the role of burden of proof in such a case? In the way the cases are described above, it would appear that the side who has proposed bringing in the new system of no-fault insurance would have to make a strong enough case for their proposal to show that it is significantly better than the alternative of sticking with the old system. For example if they put forward a series of arguments showing that the new proposal was only marginally better than the existing system, that might not be regarded as a sufficient reason for making the change to the new system, or regarding it is worth doing. To convince the audience that the new proposal is the best way to move forward in reducing insurance rates, they would have to provide reasons sufficient to show that the new system has advantages over the old system that are significantly worthwhile enough to warrant the cost of making the change. But this conservatism is just another argument from negative consequences (the negative consequence of added costs).

Does each side have a burden of proof to fulfill, set at the opening stage of the deliberation dialog, or can a side win the dialog merely by proving that its proposal is stronger than all the alternative ones, even if it is only slightly stronger? Some might say that this question depends on how the burden of proof was set at the opening stage of the deliberation dialog. Was the deliberation set up in such a way that only the no-fault side has a positive burden to prove its proposal is acceptable, while the opposed side can be allowed not to prove any proposal that it has advocated?

However, a different answer to the question can be given. The answer is that in a deliberation dialog, proposals are put forward only during the argumentation stage. If this is right, burden of proof is set and is operative only during the argumentation stage. If this is so, the question is raised whether burden of proof only comes into play during the argumentation stage. The next question raised is whether the argumentation stage consists of a persuasion dialog. Only when proposals are put forward, during the argumentation stage, does burden of proof come into play. If this approach is right, it suggests that the deliberation has shifted to a persuasion interval during the argumentation stage. These questions can be investigated by taking a closer look at the argumentation used during the argumentation stage of the no-fault insurance example.

Much of the argumentation in the no-fault insurance example fits the argumentation schemes for practical reasoning and argument from consequences (highly characteristic of deliberation). The argumentation scheme in such a case is that for practical reasoning (Atkinson, Bench-Capon and McBurney, 2006). The simplest form of practical reasoning, called practical inference, is represented by the following scheme (Walton, Reed and Macagno, 2008, 323).

Instrumental Practical Reasoning

MAJOR PREMISE: I (an agent) have a goal G.
MINOR PREMISE: Carrying out this action A is a means to realize G.
CONCLUSION: Therefore, I ought (practically speaking) to carry out this action A.

Below is the set of critical questions matching the scheme for instrumental practical reasoning (Walton, Reed and Macagno, 2008, 323).

CQ_1 What other goals do I have that should be considered that might conflict with G?

CQ_2 What alternative actions to my bringing about A that would also bring about G should be considered?

CQ_3 Among bringing about A and these alternative actions, which is arguably the most efficient?

CQ_4 What grounds are there for arguing that it is practically possible for me to bring about A?

CQ_5 What consequences of my bringing about A should also be taken into account?

The last critical question is very often called the side effects question. It concerns potential negative consequences of a proposed course of actions. Just asking about consequences of a course of action being contemplated could be enough to cast an argument based on practical reasoning into doubt.

The basic scheme for practical reasoning is instrumental, but a value-based scheme has been formulated by Atkinson, Bench-Capon and McBurney (2005, pp. 2-3).

Value-based Practical Reasoning

- In the current circumstances R
- we should perform action A
- to achieve New Circumstances S
- which will realize some goal G
- which will promote some value V.

According to this way of defining the scheme, values are seen as reasons that can support goals. The scheme for value-based practical reasoning can be classified as a composite of instrumental practical reasoning and argument from values.

In the account of schemes given in (Walton, Macagno and Reed, 2008), argument from values is seen as a distinct type of argument in its own right.

Argument from Positive Value

PREMISE 1: Value V is *positive* as judged by agent A (value judgment).

PREMISE 2: The fact that value V is *positive* affects the interpretation and therefore the evaluation of goal G of agent A (If value V is *good*, it supports commitment to goal G).

CONCLUSION: V is a reason for retaining commitment to goal G.

Argument from Negative Value

PREMISE 1: Value V is *negative* as judged by agent A (value judgment).

PREMISE 2: The fact that value V is *negative* affects the interpretation and therefore the evaluation of goal G of agent A (If value V is *bad*, it goes against commitment to goal G).

CONCLUSION: V is a reason for retracting commitment to goal G.

How practical reasoning and argument from values are used by the no-fault side in the no-fault insurance example is shown in the Araucaria diagram in figure 1. How practical reasoning and argument from values are used by the opposed side in the no-fault insurance example is shown in the Araucaria diagram in figure 2.

Finally, we need to see that one other argument is involved in the deliberations in the no-fault insurance example. One side argues that the no-fault system would have bad consequences by making good drivers pay for bad drivers. The opposed side argues that a no-fault system would fail to lower insurance premiums. Both sides agree that lowering insurance premiums is a good thing, and is even the goal both sides are striving for.

To argue that a no-fault system would fail to lower insurance premiums is to argue that such a system would fail to have good consequences. Such an argument is an attack on the practical reasoning of the other side that can be seen as a form of attacking an argument by alleging that it does not have the good consequences it was thought to have. Argument from consequences can take either one of the two following forms.

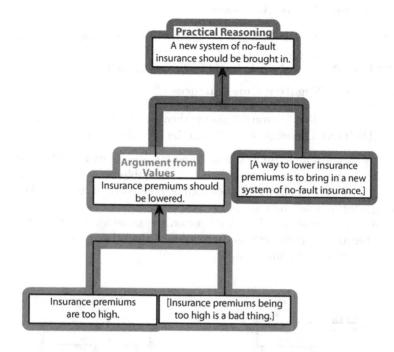

Fig. 1. Practical Reasoning and Argument From Values Used by the No-fault Side in the No-fault Example

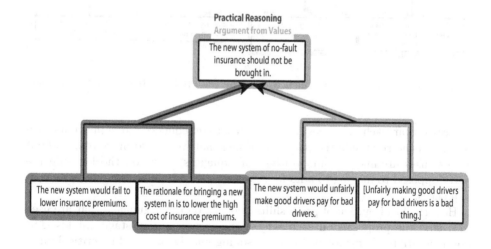

Fig. 2. Practical Reasoning and Argument From Values Used by the Opposed Side in the No-fault Example

Argument from Positive Consequences

PREMISE: If A is brought about, good consequences will plausibly occur.

CONCLUSION: Therefore A should be brought about.

Argument from Negative Consequences

PREMISE: If A is brought about, then bad consequences will occur.

CONCLUSION: Therefore A should not be brought about.

Figure 3 shows how argument from consequences is used by both sides in the no-fault insurance deliberation dialog. The double-headed arrow represents refutation, a relationship in which one claim is used to attack another. The statement in the top box on the right is the proposal of the one side that we should move to a no-fault system. The statement on the same level to the left, shown in the darkened box, is the opposed proposal of the other side, saying that we should not move to a no-fault system.

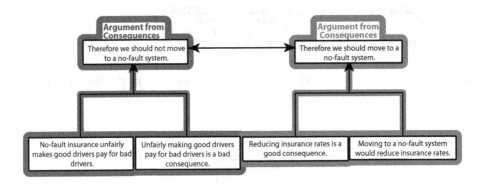

Fig. 3. Argument from Consequences Used by Both Sides in the No-fault Example

Notice that each side uses argument from consequences to support its proposal. On the right side the party proposing that we should move to a no-fault system uses argument from positive consequences, while on the left side the party opposed to moving to a no-fault system uses argument from negative consequences.

How the local burden of proof shifts depends on the arguments that are used to defend the proposals on each side as the argumentation stage unfolds. The argumentation scheme for practical reasoning may be attacked by critical questions that raise doubts, or by counter-arguments. It may also be supported by arguments like argument from values and argument from negative consequences. As the burden of proof dialog above shows, this local burden of proof shifts back and forth during the dialog, depending on the moves and counter-moves made. However, even though the conclusions of the arguments are actions, or at least statements to the effect that certain states of affairs should be brought about or not, it looks like they are arguments that we can analyze and evaluate within the structure of persuasion dialog.

7   Analysis of the Wigmore, FDA and Precautionary Principle Examples

We now turn to the second example, Wigmore's example of the man finding a purse in the street. An explanation of how burden of proof operates in the case can be given by seeing the argumentation as a sequence of dialog. This dialog structure is shown in table 3.

Table 3. Dialog Structure of Deliberation in Wigmore's Purse Example

Round	A	M	A's Commitment
1	A sees purse. What to do?	M claims purse.	Doubt
2	Asks for proof of ownership.	Unconvincing argument.	Doubt
3	A hangs on to purse.	M describes contents [convincing argument].	Conviction [doubt overcome].
4	A hands purse to M.	Dialog concluded.	BoP fulfilled.

As the sequence of dialog represented in table 3 shows, the key factor is how A's commitment to M's argumentation changes during the sequence of moves. When M first claims the purse and A asks for proof of ownership, A is in a state of doubt. Even when an unconvincing argument is presented to him, A remains in a state of doubt. It is only at the third move, when M describes the contents of the purse, that A's doubt is removed. Thus the mechanism whereby the burden of proof is fulfilled, and A is convinced to hand over the purse to M, is the convincing argument presented by M. The reason the burden of proof is fulfilled is because the argument presented by M meets or supersedes the standard of proof required for A to come to accept the proposition that M is the owner of the purse. This sequence can be analyzed as an instance of a persuasion dialog. The proponent claims to own the purse and has the burden of proof. The person who found the purse is the respondent. They are not deliberating about whether or not to give the proponent the purse, but are taking part in a persuasion dialog about whether or not the proponent owns the purse.

We now turn to the third example. According to one analysis, burden of proof is obviously very important in the right kind of argumentation that should be required to resolve the issue and solve of the problem. According to exponents of this analysis, the example shows that setting the global burden of proof at the opening stage is an important step in solving a problem with deliberation dialog. This decision would imply that there needs to be a classification of

different types of deliberations that distinguishes between ordinary deliberations, like those cited in the previous examples, and special deliberations in
cases where public policy decisions need to be made about widely important
matters like environmental issues where the anticipated outcome may be at a
high level in relation to its impact on public safety and where the decision may
have potentially irreversible consequences. These could perhaps be classified as
public danger cases. The proposal that appears to be put forward by advocates
of the precautionary principle is that public danger cases need to be treated as
a special species of deliberation dialogs in which the burden of proof is set to an
especially high standard of proof right at the outset, i.e. at the opening stage.

According to a second analysis, the deliberation dialog in this case is actually
about the issue of setting the burden of proof in a controversial case. On this
analysis, the case is an odd one, because the governing question is: on which
side should the burden of proof be placed, the FDA or the manufacturers of the
pharmaceutical ingredients? Since the dispute itself is about burden of proof, this
case does not show that burden of proof in a deliberation type of dialog should be
set at the opening stage. It would appear that according to the advocates of the
precautionary principle, the burden of proof to be set in cases of environmental
deliberation where the anticipated harm may be a high level should be set at
the opening stage. According to this analysis, there is no need to create a special
class of deliberation dialogs of the danger type, because if there are serious and
widespread consequences that are potentially irreversible, amounting to creating
risk of serious public harm, these consequences can be taken into account during
the persuasion dialog in argumentation stage. During this stage, argumentation
schemes, like practical reasoning and argumentation from negative consequences,
will bring out factors of serious and widespread public consequences that are
potentially irreversible. Thus, for example, if there is great danger of irreversible
harm to the environment from a particular proposal that has been advocated in
environmental deliberations, negative argument from consequences can be used
to attack this proposal.

This decision about how to deal with the precautionary principle in terms of
formal systems of deliberation by dialogical assignments of burden of proof has
implications for the criticisms of the principle that it could be applied generally
to stop the marketing of any new food products. For those who advocate setting
special burdens of proof at the opening stage, the issue becomes one of determining whether a given case, like that of making public decisions on the safety of
new food products, can be globally classified as a danger case for not. For those
who advocate dealing with the burden of proof locally at the argumentation
stage in all cases, the problem is one of weighing safety against matters of which
side has greater access to the evidence, matters of setting reasonable standards
of proof for safety under conditions of uncertainty, and balancing these factors
against the value of allowing the introduction of new food products that might
have valuable public benefits.

8   Conclusions

As suggested by the analyses of the examples above, burden of proof becomes relevant only during the argumentation stage. It is during this stage, when proposals are put forward, and attacked by arguments like argument from negative consequences and argument from negative values, that the need to differentially impose burden of proof becomes operative. For these reasons, it is argued here that no burden of proof should be set at the opening stage of a deliberation dialog. When competing proposals are brought forward during the argumentation stage, the one to be accepted at the closing stage is the one most strongly supported by the evidence brought forward during the argumentation stage. This criterion corresponds to the proof standard called "best choice" by Gordon and Karacapilidis (1997, 15). A choice is said to meet this standard if no other alternative currently has the better arguments. As noted by Atkinson and Bench-Capon (2007, 108), of the five standards of proof set by Gordon and Karacapilidis, the best choice and the "no better alternative" standards apply to deliberation, as contrasted with the other three standards, scintilla of evidence, preponderance of evidence and beyond a reasonable doubt, that apply to persuasion dialog and matters of fact, as opposed to actions. However, it is argued here that the best choice standard of proof is the one a successful proposal needs to meet during the argumentation stage, except at points where a move in the dialog indicates that a different standard is appropriate. This standard is that of the standard of the preponderance of the evidence that is used in persuasion dialog, in that both adopt the standard of a successful proposal (claim) as the one that has more weight supporting it than any other proposal (claim).

In a persuasion dialog, global burden of proof is defined as a set $\{P, T, S\}$ where P is a participant, T is the thesis to be proved by a participant and S is the standard of proof required to make that proof successful at the closing stage. Burden of proof in a deliberation dialog defining the standard of proof required to be met to secure victory for a proposal only comes into play during the argumentation stage of the deliberation, once a shift to persuasion dialog has been made. The standard appropriate for proving it will generally be that of the preponderance of the evidence. To determine whether this standard is met, the argumentation for each of the competing proposals has to be weighed in a comparative manner so that some are judged stronger than others. If there is one that is the strongest, that is the proposal to be accepted, according to the preponderance of the evidence standard set during the argumentation stage.

Support for this approach can be found in a remark of McBurney and Parsons (2001, 420) to the effect that in a deliberation dialog, the course of action adopted by the participants may only emerge during the course of the dialog itself, i.e. during what is called above in this paper the argumentation stage of the dialog. It is a corollary of this approach that burden of proof in deliberation dialog is operative only at the argumentation stage and works in the same way local burden of proof operates in a persuasion dialog. Once a party has put forward a proposal, he is obliged to defend it, or he can be required to retract it if he is unable to offer a suitable defense.

It is concluded that the burden of proof should not be set more highly against one side than the other in a deliberation dialog, even in the special type of case where serious harm to the public is at stake. The distinction between such a case and the normal case of a deliberation does not need to be drawn at the opening stage, and can be handled perfectly well during the argumentation stage, as shown by the four examples analyzed above. On this model, a deliberation always has the burden of proof set equally during the argumentation stage, so that each side, whatever proposal it puts forward to solve the problem posed by the governing question, has to support its proposal by an argument shown to be stronger than that put forward by the competing side, in order to prove that its proposal is the one that should be accepted. When some evidence of serious irreversible harm to the public is shown to be a possible outcome of a proposal that has been put forward during the argumentation stage, this evidence now becomes a strong argument against the proposal. These factors of serious harm arising as negative consequences of a proposal being considered come out in the argumentation stage, as shown very well in the analyses of the examples presented above using argumentation schemes and other tools widely used in persuasion dialogs.

According to this analysis, in such cases, there is a local burden of proof on both sides during the argumentation stage, but the burdens are distributed unequally. The opponent who alleges that there is serious irreversible harm to the public as a consequence of the proposal put forward by the proponent has to use argument from negative consequences. Because the opponent has put forward this argument, in order to make it plausible, he has to fulfill a local burden of proof to give some evidence to support it. At minimum, his argument has to meet the standard of scintilla of evidence to have any worth in shifting the burden of proof to the proponent's side. Once the burden has shifted, the proponent has to give some evidence of safety to a threshold depending on three factors.

- The first factor is how serious the harm is.
- The second factor is how likely to harm is to occur.
- The third factor is what benefits there may be of the positive action that might be weighed against the alleged harm.

For example, to illustrate the third factor, the proposed action may involve the saving of human lives. This kind of argumentation does involve burden of proof because there is a balance between the two sides. When the opponent puts forward even a small bit of evidence there may be serious irreversible harm to the public as a result of implementing the proponents proposal, the proponent must respond by meeting higher standard in giving an argument for safety based on the three factors cited above. Such matters of burden of proof come into play only during the argumentation stage, once there has been a shift to persuasion dialog. This kind of argumentation can be represented adequately by the use of the schemes for practical reasoning, argument from values and argument from consequences, as shown in the example treated above.

Acknowledgment

The work in this paper was supported by a research grant from the Social Sciences and Humanities Research Council of Canada. I would like to thank Katie Atkinson and Tom Gordon for trenchant comments that were extremely helpful in making revisions.

References

1. Atkinson, K., Bench-Capon, T.J.M., McBurney, P.: A Dialogue Game Protocol for Multi-Agent Argument over Proposals for Action. Autonomous Agents and Multi-Agent Systems 11(2), 153–171 (2005)
2. Atkinson, K., Bench-Capon, T.J.M., McBurney, P.: Computational Representation of Practical Argument. Synthese 152, 157–206 (2006)
3. Atkinson, K., Bench-Capon, T.: Argumentation and Standards of Proof. In: Winkels, R. (ed.) Proceedings of the Eleventh International Conference on AI and Law (ICAIL 2007), pp. 107–116. ACM Press, New York (2007)
4. Bailey, R.: Precautionary Tale (April 1999),
   http://www.reason.com/news/show/30977.html
5. Bench-Capon, T.J.M.: Persuasion in Practical Argument Using Value-based Argumentation Frameworks. Journal of Logic and Computation 13, 429–448 (2003)
6. Freestone, D., Hey, E.: Origins and Developments of the Precautionary Principle. In: Freestone, D., Hey, E. (eds.) The Precautionary Principle and International Law, pp. 3–15. Kluwer Law International, The Hague (1996)
7. Gordon, T.F., Karacapilidis, N.: The Zero Argumentation Framework. In: Branting, L.K. (ed.) Proceedings of the Sixth International Conference on AI and Law, pp. 10–18. ACM Press, New York (1997)
8. Gordon, T.F., Prakken, H., Walton, D.: The Carneades Model of Argument and Burden of Proof. Artificial Intelligence 171, 875–896 (2007)
9. Gordon, T.F., Walton, D.: Proof Burdens and Standards. In: Rahwan, I., Simari, G. (eds.) Argumentation in Artificial Intelligence. Springer, Heidelberg (2009)
10. Hathcock, J.N.: The Precautionary Principle - an Impossible Burden of Proof for New Products. Ag. Bio. Forum. 3, 255–258 (2000)
11. Kauffeld, F.: The Ordinary Practice of Presuming and Presumption with Special Attention to Veracity and Burden of Proof. In: van Eemeren, F.H., Blair, J.A., Willard, C.A., Snoek Henkemans, A.F. (eds.) Anyone Who Has a View: Theoretical Contributions to the Study of Argumentation, pp. 136–146. Kluwer, Dordrecht (2003)
12. Lascher, E.L.: The Politics of Automobile Insurance Reform: Ideas, Institutions, and Public Policy in North America. Georgetown University Press, Washington (1999)
13. McBurney, P., Parsons, S.: Chance Discovery Using Dialectical Argumentation. In: Terano, T., Nishida, T., Namatame, A., Tsumoto, S., Ohsawa, Y., Washio, T. (eds.) JSAI-WS 2001. LNCS (LNAI), vol. 2253, pp. 414–424. Springer, Heidelberg (2001)
14. McBurney, P., Hitchcock, D., Parsons, S.: The Eightfold Way of Deliberation Dialogue. International Journal of Intelligent Systems 22, 95–132 (2007)
15. Girela, M.A.R.: Dangerous Interpretations of the Precautionary Principle and the Foundational Values of the European Food Law: Risk versus Risk. Journal of Food Law and Policy 4 (2008)

16. Prakken, H.: Formal Systems for Persuasion Dialogue. The Knowledge Engineering Review 21, 163–188 (2006)
17. Prakken, H., Reed, C., Walton, D.: Dialogues about the Burden of Proof. In: Proceedings of the Tenth International Conference on Artificial Intelligence and Law, pp. 115–124. ACM, New York (2005)
18. Prakken, H., Sartor, G.: Presumptions and Burdens of Proof. Legal Knowledge and Information Systems: JURIX 2006. In: van Engers, T.M. (ed.) The Nineteenth Annual Conference, pp. 21–30. IOS Press, Amsterdam (2006)
19. Prakken, H., Sartor, G.: Formalising Arguments about the Burden of Persuasion. In: Proceedings of the Eleventh International Conference on Artificial Intelligence and Law, pp. 97–106. ACM Press, New York (2007)
20. Prakken, H., Sartor, G.: A Logical Analysis of Burdens of Proof. In: Kapitein, H., Prakken, H., Verheij, B. (eds.) Legal Evidence and Proof: Statistics, Stories, Logic, Applied Legal Philosophy Series. Ashgate Publishing, Aldershot, pp. 223–253 (2009)
21. Reed, C., Rowe, G.: Araucaria: Software for Argument Analysis, Diagramming and Representation. International Journal on Artificial Intelligence Tools 14, 961–980 (2004)
22. Tang, Y., Parsons, S.: Argumentation-Based Multi-agent Dialogues for Deliberation. In: Parsons, S., Maudet, N., Moraitis, P., Rahwan, I. (eds.) ArgMAS 2005. LNCS (LNAI), vol. 4049, pp. 229–244. Springer, Heidelberg (2006)
23. Walton, D.: Dialog Theory for Critical Argumentation. John Benjamins, Amsterdam (2007)
24. Walton, D.: How to Make and Defend a Proposal in Deliberation Dialogue. Artificial Intelligence and Law 14, 177–239 (2006)
25. Walton, D., Krabbe, E.C.W.: Commitment in Dialogue. State University of New York Press, Albany (1995)
26. Walton, D., Atkinson, K., Bench-Capon, T.J.M., Wyner, A., Cartwright, D.: Argumentation in the Framework of Deliberation Dialogue. In: Bjola, C., Kornprobst, M. (eds.) Argumentation and Global Governance (2009)
27. Walton, D., Reed, C., Macagno, F.: Argumentation Schemes. Cambridge University Press, Cambridge (2008)
28. Wigmore, J.H.: A Student's Textbook of the Law of Evidence. The Foundation Press, Chicago (1935)

A Generative Dialogue System for Arguing about Plans in Situation Calculus

Alexandros Belesiotis[1], Michael Rovatsos[1], and Iyad Rahwan[1,2]

[1] School of Informatics, The University of Edinburgh,
Edinburgh EH8 9LE, UK
{A.Belesiotis,Michael.Rovatsos}@ed.ac.uk
[2] Faculty of Informatics, The British University in Dubai,
P.O. Box 502216, Dubai, UAE
irahwan@acm.org

Abstract. This paper presents an argumentation mechanism for reconciling conflicts between planning agents related to plan proposals, which are caused by inconsistencies between basic beliefs regarding the state of the world or the specification of the planning operators.

We introduce simple and efficient argument moves that enable discussion about planning steps, and show how these can be integrated into an existing protocol for belief argumentation. The resulting protocol is provably sound with regard to the defeasible semantics of the resulting agreements. We show how argument generation can be treated, for the specific task of argumentation about plans, by replacing the burden of finding proofs in a knowledge base by guided search.

1 Introduction

In recent years, argumentation [1] has attracted much attention as a technique for resolving conflicts between agents, mainly due to its strong logical foundation and its suitability for use in multiagent situations.

One area in which argumentation has been recently employed is that of collaborative practical decision making [2,3,4], e.g. deciding on task allocation in teamwork frameworks [5]. In this case, it can be imagined that different agents come up with proposals for joint action, such as multiagent plans, and discuss such plans with their teammates in order to reach agreement. The need for conflict resolution may arise from the agents having different viewpoints due to locality of sensing, different fundamental assumptions about the domain, or simply because different agents may have conducted different inferences and therefore their beliefs may not be aligned.

In cooperative distributed problem solving [6] (e.g. frameworks like GPGP [7]), conflicts are normally resolved by merging agents' different views. However, this is only feasible if agents use highly structured knowledge bases that contain only knowledge relevant to the task in hand. In more general agent designs (where agents have arbitrary beliefs about the world), detecting conflicts when merging beliefs is computationally complex and, in some cases, completely unnecessary

P. McBurney et al. (Eds.): ArgMAS 2009, LNAI 6057, pp. 23–41, 2010.

and wasteful. Efficiency can be increased by identifying conflicts that are related to plans that are currently being debated, and resolving only disagreements that affect the viability of concrete plan proposals.

In this paper, we propose a method that aims to tackle precisely this problem. Based on the observation that logical theories of planning are highly structured and fairly simple, we devise an argumentation protocol that allows agents to discuss plan proposals and to identify reasons for potential disagreements that originate in differences regarding beliefs about the planning domain. We provide an algorithm and explain how the proposed protocol can be used to guide the search for relevant disagreements in a focused way. We also show that it is easy to integrate our argument moves with conventional belief argumentation protocols, and discuss useful properties of the resulting framework for reasoning about plans. An overview of the process is described in Figure 1. In this paper we do not focus on the process of planning itself, but on how structured argumentation-based dialogue can be employed as the means for identification of disagreements regarding plans.

The paper advances the state-of-the-art in multiagent planning in two ways. Firstly, we present the first dialogue protocol that is specifically designed to enable agents to detect and resolve disagreements about a plan generated via

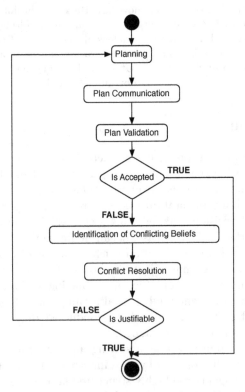

Fig. 1. Outline of how the employed protocol can be used to identify and resolve conflicts about plans

conventional planning algorithms. This contrasts with other approaches [8,3] which are concerned with the process of planning itself. The second contribution of this paper is to show that the dialogue generation process can be simplified by exploiting the structure of the planning problem to systematically discover disagreements over only the beliefs relevant to the plan structure. In particular, in contrast to general protocols [2] which allow very expressive dialogues about goals, intentions, etc, but come with no clear bounds on the length of dialogues, we give exact upper bounds on the number of messages exchanged before disagreements are identified.

The remainder of this paper is structured as follows: Section 2 introduces the argumentation and planning background required for the development of our framework. Section 3 introduces the suggested protocol, followed by an example illustrating the protocol. Section 5 provides an analysis of protocol properties, and in Section 6 we present an algorithm for argument generation. Section 7 concludes.

2   Preliminaries

2.1   Planning Framework

Our planning framework follows the *situation calculus* framework [9], a logical language designed for representing dynamic domains. Three disjoint sorts are supported. The sort *action* represents actions, the sort *situation* represents situations and the sort *object* all the rest. S_0 is a constant symbol representing the initial situation. The binary function symbol $do : action \times situation \rightarrow situation$ denotes the successor situation after performing an action. $Poss : action \times situation$ is a binary predicate symbol representing whether an action is applicable in a situation. The binary predicate symbol $\sqsubset: situation \times situation$ defines an ordering relation over situations, where $s \sqsubset s'$ denotes that s is a proper subsequence of s'. Symbols whose value change in different situations are called fluents (relational or functional), and they have an argument of sort situation as their final argument.

Each agent maintains the representation of the domain as a *Basic Action Theory*, as proposed by Reiter [10]. A basic action theory $\mathcal{D}$ has the form:

$$\mathcal{D} = \Sigma \cup \mathcal{D}_{ss} \cup \mathcal{D}_{ap} \cup \mathcal{D}_{una} \cup \mathcal{D}_{S_0} .$$

Σ is a set of fundamental domain-independent axioms providing the basic properties for situations. Successor state axioms $\mathcal{D}_{ss}$ are introduced for each relational or functional fluent in the domain, and specify the conditions that govern its value in a situation. The conditions under which an action can be performed are specified by the action precondition axioms, $\mathcal{D}_{ap}$. $\mathcal{D}_{una}$ contains the unique names axioms for actions. $\mathcal{D}_{S_0}$ is a set of first-order sentences that represent the initial state of the world.

We follow the following convention: Variables begin with a lower case letter and are universally quantified with maximum scope, unless stated otherwise. Constants begin with an upper-case letter.

Each Successor State axiom (A_{ss}) describes the conditions that should hold in situation s so that a relational or functional fluent takes a certain value in the situation $do(a, s)$, which follows from the application of action a in s. For relational and functional fluents respectively, they have the following form:

$$F(x_1, ..., x_n, do(a, s)) \equiv \Phi_F(x_1, ..., x_n, a, s)$$

$$f(x_1, ..., x_n, do(a, s)) = y \equiv \Phi_f(x_1, ..., x_n, y, a, s)$$

Action Precondition axioms (A_{ap}) specify the preconditions of actions:

$$Poss(A(x_1, ..., x_n), s) \equiv \Pi_A(x_1, ..., x_n, s)$$

A plan in the situation calculus is treated as an executable situation that satisfies a goal statement.

Definition 1. *Given a basic action theory $\mathcal{D}$, a plan in the situation calculus for a goal sentence G is a variable-free situation term s_π iff $\mathcal{D} \models executable(s_\pi) \wedge G(s_\pi)$, where $executable(s_\pi) \stackrel{\text{def}}{=} (\forall a, s^*).do(a, s^*) \sqsubseteq s_\pi \supset Poss(a, s^*)$.*

Definition 2. *A planning problem $\mathcal{P}$ is a tuple $\langle \mathcal{D}, G \rangle$, where $\mathcal{D}$ is a basic action theory denoting the planning domain and G is a fluent sentence specifying the goal.*

A consequence of the definition of a plan and the foundational axioms for situations is that $executable(do(a, s)) \equiv executable(s) \wedge Poss(a, s)$. This enables the transformation of the definition of a plan. For the remainder of the paper plans will follow the following definition.

Definition 3. *A plan $\pi = A_1; A_2; ...; A_n$ is a solution to a planning problem $\mathcal{P}$ iff $\mathcal{D} \models Poss(A_1, S_0) \wedge do(A_1, S_0) = S_1 \wedge Poss(A_2, S_1) \wedge do(A_2, S_1) = S_2 \wedge ... \wedge Poss(A_n, S_{n-1}) \wedge do(A_n, S_{n-1}) = S_n \wedge G(S_n).$*

This definition asserts that the actions in the plan can be performed in sequence, and that after preforming the final action the goal sentence G will be true.

In classical AI planning, domain knowledge is assumed to be conflict-free. In a multiagent setting, however, there are cases where agents have mutually conflicting beliefs. In order to find a plan that satisfies all parties, the agents need to solve a planning problem involving conflicting knowledge.

Assume two agents i and $-i$ each of which has an (internally consistent) domain knowledge $\mathcal{D}_i/\mathcal{D}_{-i}$. A planning problem $\mathcal{P}$ is said to be *potentially conflicted* among agents i and $-i$, if there exist statements in $\mathcal{D}_i$ that conflict with statements in $\mathcal{D}_{-i}$.[1]

Assuming that the goal has been agreed upon, then due to the contradictory beliefs of the agents, it can be challenging to discover a plan that satisfies both i and $-i$, since from each agent's local perspective, the plan needs to solve a different planning problem: i is looking for a solution to $\mathcal{P}_i = \langle \mathcal{D}_i, G \rangle$, whereas

---

[1] This paper assumes two-player situations; in case of more than two agents, our results carry over assuming dialogues are conducted between all pairs to reach agreement.

agent $-i$ wants to solve $\mathcal{P}_{-i} = \langle \mathcal{D}_{-i}, G \rangle$. An *acceptable plan* that can be agreed upon by two agents i and $-i$ is therefore defined as follows:

Definition 4. *Given the domain representations for the two agents $\mathcal{D}_i$ and $\mathcal{D}_{-i}$, and a common goal G, a plan is acceptable if and only if it is a solution to both planning problems $\mathcal{P}_i = \langle \mathcal{D}_i, G \rangle$ and $\mathcal{P}_{-i} = \langle \mathcal{D}_{-i}, G \rangle$.*

With this, the purpose of our argumentation protocol can be specified as follows: *for a potentially conflicted planning problem $\mathcal{P}$ between two agents and an initial proposed plan π, determine whether this plan is acceptable.*

2.2 Argumentation Framework

Argumentation is a mechanism that can be used for the resolution of conflicts. Our basic argumentation framework follows [1]:

Definition 5. *An argumentation system is a structure $\mathcal{H} = \langle \mathcal{A}, \rightarrow \rangle$ where $\mathcal{A}$ is a set of arguments and $\rightarrow \subseteq \mathcal{A} \times \mathcal{A}$ is a binary attack relation between arguments. The following additional definitions on sets of arguments are useful:*

1. *A set of arguments $S \subseteq \mathcal{A}$ is* conflict-free *iff $(\nexists A, B \in S).A \rightarrow B$*
2. *An argument $A \in \mathcal{A}$ is* acceptable *with respect to a set $S \subseteq \mathcal{A}$ of arguments iff $(\forall B \in \mathcal{A}).(B \rightarrow A \Rightarrow [(\exists C \in S).C \rightarrow B])$*
3. *A set of arguments $S \subseteq \mathcal{A}$ is called* admissible *if it is conflict-free and if each argument in S is acceptable with respect to S*
4. *A* preferred extension *of an argumentation framework is a maximal (with respect to set inclusion) admissible set of the argumentation framework.*
5. *S is a* stable extension *of an argumentation framework, if S is conflict-free and $(\forall A \notin S).[(\exists B \in S).(B \rightarrow A)]$*

Further refinements that we use below include (i) *credulous preferred semantics*, which require an argument to be part of at least one preferred extension to be considered acceptable, and (ii) *sceptical preferred semantics*, which require that the argument is contained in all preferred extensions of the argumentation framework.

To apply these notions in a logic-based framework, we define arguments based on an inference procedure $\vdash$ in a knowledge base, and reinterpret the attack relation:

Definition 6. *Arguments for agent i are pairs $A = \langle H, h \rangle$, where $H \subseteq \mathcal{D}_i$, and*

i. *H is consistent (i.e. $H \nvdash \bot$),*
ii. *$H \vdash h$,*
iii. *H is minimal (no subset of H satisfies both* i. *and* ii.*).*

H is called the support of the argument and h its conclusion.

If an argument follows the aforementioned definition then we can refer to it as being a *valid* argument.

Definition 7. *An argument $A_1 = \langle H_1, h_1 \rangle$ attacks an argument $A_2 = \langle H_2, h_2 \rangle$, denoted $A_1 \rightarrow A_2$, if either $\exists \phi$ in H_2 such that $h_1 \equiv \neg\phi$, or $h_1 = (F \equiv \Psi)$, $\phi = (F \equiv \Phi)$ and $\Phi \not\equiv \Psi$.*

The attack relation considers contradictory beliefs and formulas providing different definitions of the same symbol. Reasoning about dynamic domains is based on the axioms representing the domain. It is essential that the domain theory does not include different axioms regarding the same fluent.

3   Dialogue Protocol

We suggest a protocol that is a *two-party immediate response dispute* (TPI-dispute) type protocol and builds on [11,12]. It extends the protocol presented in [11] to include planning-related argument moves (for proposing a plan, attacking a plan and attacking the attackers of a plan).

In the protocol described in [11], the dialogue moves COUNTER, BACKUP and RETRACT may be employed to progress the dialogue by attacking the other party's most recent argument, or by returning to an earlier point in the dialogue and providing an alternative attack. Rules are provided formulating the conditions under which the moves can be used, depending on the "current" state of the dispute and the arguments that are available to each agent. We have adapted this protocol so that the applicability of moves can be evaluated only with respect to the state of the dialogue. This is necessary for our system as agents do not know all the possible arguments that can be created from their beliefs. Instead they construct candidate responses before making their next move.

Planning-related moves are provided as instantiations of TPI-dispute moves, through further restrictions on the preconditions and the form of the exchanged argument. These restrictions also depend on the state of the dialogue.

3.1   TPI-Disputes

In order to discover if an argument to follow a plan is acceptable (and therefore if a plan is acceptable), the agents engage in an argumentation game. The agent proposing the plan, initiates the game, and plays the role of the proponent PRO, leaving the role of opponent OPP to the other party. The proponent agent is responsible for constructing arguments in favour of the plan, while the opponent is attempting to attack the validity of the plan. The game progresses with the agents exchanging arguments attacking the previous argument of their rival. The proponent attempts to create an admissible set containing the initial argument, which in this case proposes a plan believed to achieve the shared objective. The following definitions follow [11].

Definition 8. *Let $\mathcal{H} = \langle \mathcal{A}, \rightarrow \rangle$ be an argumentation system with $\mathcal{A} = \mathcal{A}_{PRO} \cup \mathcal{A}_{OPP}$ the union of the arguments that can be constructed by the proponent and the opponent. A dispute tree for some argument X in $\mathcal{A}_{PRO}$, denoted by $\mathcal{T}_A^{\mathcal{H}}$, is a tree with root X whose vertices and edges are subsets of $\mathcal{A}$ and $\rightarrow$, respectively.*

Note that the edges in a dispute tree are directed from vertices to their parent node. A *dispute line* is a path in the dispute tree, and is of the form

$$t = v_k \to ... \to v_1 \to v_0 = X$$

A dispute line is called *open/closed* if the agent who has to make the following move is able/unable to construct an argument following Definition 6. A closed dispute line for some argument X is a *failing defence of* X if the leaf node argument move has been made by the opponent. On the contrary, if the final argument has been raised by the proponent the dispute line is considered a *failing attack of* X.

A TPI-dispute for some argument X of a system $\mathcal{H}$ is a sequence of moves

$$M = \langle \mu_1, \mu_2, ..., \mu_i, ... \rangle$$

The agents have a finite repertoire of available move types. The moves available to the proponent are COUNTER^{PRO} and RETRACT^{PRO}, whereas the moves available to the opponent are COUNTER^{OPP} and BACKUP^{OPP}. Whether it is possible for an agent to perform a move is decided depending on move preconditions and the current state of the dispute. The state of the dispute after the kth move, with ($k \geq 0$), is described by the following tuple:

$$\sigma_k = \langle T_k, v_k, CS_k^{PRO}, CS_k^{OPP}, P_k, Q_k \rangle$$

T_k is the dispute tree after move k. The last argument proposed is denoted by v_k. CS_k^{PRO}/CS_k^{OPP} contain the proponent's/opponent's commitments. P_k contains arguments that are presented as a subset of the admissible set, and Q_k contains sets that have been shown not to be a subset of an admissible set. The initial state of the dispute for some argument X is

$$\sigma_0 = \langle \langle X \rangle, X, \{X\}, \{\}, \{X\}, \emptyset \rangle.$$

Turntaking in the dialogue is determined by the running index of the current move. The current player is *OPP* if the index of the current move k is odd, and *PRO* otherwise. If the current player has a legal move available, then the dispute is active; if not, then it terminates. When a dialogue terminates, the winner can be determined using the number of moves, $|M|$. If $|M|$ is odd/even, then the proponent/opponent wins the argument, respectively.

The repertoire of moves available to the agents and their applicability will be presented in terms of preconditions and effects related to the state of the dispute before the moves are applied.

If k is odd, the opponent may attack the most recent argument presented by the proponent by putting forward argument Y, using the $\mu_k = COUNTER_k^{OPP}(Y)$ move.

$$\mu_k = COUNTER_k^{OPP}(Y)$$

Preconditions:
- Y is a valid argument;
- $Y \to v_{k-1}$;
- $Y \notin CS_{k-1}^{OPP}$;
- $Y \notin CS_{k-1}^{PRO}$;
- $(\nexists Z \in CS_{k-1}^{PRO}). Z \to Y$.

Effects:
- $T_k := T_{k-1} + \langle Y, v_{k-1} \rangle$;
- $v_k := Y$;
- $CS_k^{PRO} := CS_{k-1}^{PRO}$;
- $CS_k^{OPP} := CS_{k-1}^{OPP} \cup Y$;
- $P_k := P_{k-1}$;
- $Q_k := Q_{k-1}$.

The definition of this move asserts that in order to respond to the most recent argument put forward by the proponent, the opponent must construct a valid argument, according to Definition 6, that attacks the proponent's previous argument v_{k-1}. The opponent cannot reuse arguments that have already been presented by her or by the proponent, or any arguments that can be attacked by arguments previously proposed by the proponent. This dialogue move affects the state of the dialogue by including the new argument in the dispute tree as the most recently presented argument, as well as in the opponent's commitments.

A variation of the counter available to the proponent is defined in a similar fashion.

$$\mu_k = COUNTER_k^{PRO}(Y)$$

Preconditions:
- Y is a valid argument;
- $Y \rightarrow v_{k-1}$;
- $Y \notin CS_{k-1}^{PRO}$;
- $(\nexists \, Z \in CS_{k-1}^{PRO}).\, Z \rightarrow Y$.

Effects:
- $T_k := T_{k-1} + \langle Y, v_{k-1} \rangle$;
- $v_k := Y$;
- $CS_k^{PRO} := CS_{k-1}^{PRO} \cup Y$;
- $CS_k^{OPP} := CS_{k-1}^{OPP}$;
- $P_k := P_{k-1} \cup Y$;
- $Q_k := Q_{k-1}$.

The proponent, when using the counter move, cannot repeat arguments or state arguments that contradict her commitments. This move progresses the dispute by adding Y to the dispute tree, the proponent's commitments, and to the subset of the admissible set that the proponent is attempting to construct.

The backup move can be used by the opponent if a counter move responding to the proponent's most recent argument is not possible. This move returns to the most recent point in the dispute, in which the opponent can proceed with an alternative attack. This point is represented by j, which must be even and $0 \le j \le k - 3$.

$$\mu_k = BACKUP_k^{OPP}(j, Y)$$

Preconditions:
- Cannot construct a valid argument that attacks v_{k-1};
- For each r in $\{j+2, j+4, \ldots, k-3\}$, no argument Y' exists that
  - Y' is a valid argument;
  - $Y' \rightarrow v_r$;
  - $Y' \notin CS_r^{OPP} \cup \{v_{r+1}, v_{r+3}, \ldots, v_{k-2}\}$;
  - $Y' \notin CS_r^{PRO} \cup \{v_{r+2}, v_{r+4} \ldots, v_{k-3}\}$;
  - $(\nexists \, Z \in CS_r^{PRO} \cup \{v_r, v_{r+2}, \ldots, v_{k-3}\}).\, Z \rightarrow Y'$.
- Y is a valid argument;
- $Y \rightarrow v_j$;
- $Y \notin CS_j^{OPP} \cup \{v_{j+1}, v_{j+3}, \ldots, v_{k-2}\}$;
- $Y \notin CS_j^{PRO} \cup \{v_{j+2}, v_{j+4} \ldots, v_{k-3}\}$;
- $(\nexists \, Z \in CS_j^{PRO} \cup \{v_j, v_{j+2}, \ldots, v_{k-3}\}).\, Z \rightarrow Y$.

Effects:

- $T_k := T_{k-1} + \langle Y, v_j \rangle$;
- $v_k := Y$;
- $CS_k^{PRO} := CS_{k-1}^{PRO}$;
- $CS_k^{OPP} := CS_j^{OPP} \cup Y \cup \{v_{j+1}, v_{j+3}, \ldots, v_{k-2}\}$;
- $P_k := P_{k-1}$;
- $Q_k := Q_{k-1}$.

This move can be used by the opponent to attack the argument presented by the proponent in move μ_j, if there do not exist any more recent points in which the opponent can mount an alternative attack. The argument Y must not have been repeated by the proponent or the opponent, and it must not be attacked by any arguments presented by the proponent.

The following move can be used by the proponent in order to retract and provide an alternative justification for X, if the opponent has shown that P_k is not part of an admissible set. By retracting, PRO attempts to construct a different admissible set containing X.

$$\boxed{\mu_k = RETRACT_k^{PRO}}$$

Preconditions:

- PRO cannot attack u_{k-1};
- $P_k \neq \{X\}$.

Effects:

- $T_k := \langle X \rangle$;
- $v_k := X$;
- $CS_k^{PRO} := CS_0^{PRO}$;
- $CS_k^{OPP} := CS_0^{OPP}$;
- $P_k := P_0$;
- $Q_k := Q_{k-1} \cup \{P_{k-1}\}$.

According to [11], if there exists a terminated TPI-dispute over an argument X in the argument system $\mathcal{H}$ that is a successful defence of X (i.e. k is even), then at least one preferred extension of $\mathcal{A}$ contains X, and X is said to be credulously accepted in $\mathcal{H}$.

To define sceptical acceptance semantics, Dunne and Bench-Capon [11] use the notion of an *x-augmented system* $\mathcal{H}_a$ which is formed for an argument system $\mathcal{H}(\mathcal{A}, \rightarrow)$ and $X \in \mathcal{A}$, by introducing a new argument X_a and an attack $\langle X, X_a \rangle$. For an argument system $\mathcal{H}(\mathcal{A}, \rightarrow)$, in which every preferred extension is a stable extension, an argument $X \in \mathcal{A}$ is sceptically accepted (i.e. is part of every preferred extension) in $\mathcal{H}$, if and only if there is a dispute M, providing a successful rebuttal of X_a in the x-augmented system $\mathcal{H}_a$.

3.2   Arguments in Situation Calculus

Dialogue about plans may be broken down to two distinct levels. The *Plan Level Dispute* (PLD) involves arguments regarding future states of the world, explaining the agents' views on how the proposed plan will affect the environment. The *Domain Level Dispute* (DLD) involves arguments about the planning domain, and involve beliefs about the initial state of the world or the specification of the planning operators. All PLD and DLD arguments need to follow Definition 6 and attack the most recent argument proposed by the other party, according to the preconditions of the dialogue moves. In order for the following argument types to be instantiated into arguments respecting Definition 6, the conditions for using each argument type need to be followed.

Plan Level Dispute. The argument game is initiated through a plan *Proposal* argument. The agent that introduces this argument plays the role of the proponent. The proposed plan is considered to be acceptable with respect to the proponent's beliefs:

Proposal (P), for $\pi = A_1; A_2; \ldots; A_n$

o *Argument:*
$\{Poss(A_1, S_0), S_1 = do(A_1, S_0), \ldots, Poss(A_n, S_{n-1}), S_n = do(A_n, S_{n-1}), G(S_n)\}$
$\vdash Poss(A_1, S_0) \wedge S_1 = do(A_1, S_0) \wedge \ldots \wedge Poss(A_n, S_{n-1}) \wedge S_n = do(A_n, S_{n-1}) \wedge G(S_n)$

Invalid Action arguments show that a certain action in the plan cannot be applied in the relevant situation. The support of such arguments contains the relevant Action Precondition axiom and a statement, $\neg \Pi_A(S)$, describing that the conditions that make the action applicable are not satisfied in the situation in which the action needs to be performed.

Invalid Action (IA)

o *Preconditions:*
- $Poss(A, S) \in H_{v_{k-1}}$, where $H_{v_{k-1}}$ contains the support for v_{k-1}
o *Argument:*
$\{\neg \Pi_A(S), Poss(A(x_1, \ldots, x_n), s) \equiv \Pi_A(x_1, x_2 \ldots, x_n, s)\} \vdash \neg Poss(A, S)$

Statement does Not Hold in S arguments can be used to attack statements $\Phi(S)$ regarding a future situation. Support is provided as one step regression [10]. They explain that a series of (relational or functional fluent and non-fluent) terms which appear in $\Phi(S)$, take values that assert that $\Phi(S)$ is not satisfied. As support, such arguments use the relevant successor state axioms, in order to describe the conditions in the previous situation that led specific fluents to take certain values that make the statement $\Phi(S)$ to be false.

Statement does Not Hold in S (NHS)

o *Preconditions:*
- $\Phi(S) \in H_{v_{k-1}}$
- $S \neq S_0$
o *Argument:*
$\{\{A_{ss_i}\}_{i \in \{1..n\}}, \{(\neg)F_i(S')\}_{i \in \{1..m\}}, \{(\neg)(f_i(S') = y_i)\}_{i \in \{1..k\}}, \{Y_i\}_{i \in \{1..l\}},$
$S = do(A, S')\} \vdash \neg \Phi(S)$

The notation $(\neg)$ means that the symbol $\neg$ may or may not be present. $A_{ss}^{F_i}/A_{ss}^{f_i}$ denotes the relevant Successor State axioms, F/f relational/functional fluents, Y non-fluent symbols, and $\{\Psi_i\}_{i \in \{1..n\}}$ denotes a sequence of n statements of the form Ψ.

Domain Level Dispute. Ultimately, PLDs identify disagreements about the domain. These disagreements may involve differences in the operator specification, conflicting initial situation beliefs, or contradicting situation-less statements. To resolve such disagreements, agents proceed to the domain level phase of the dialogue.

Statement does Not Hold Initially arguments explain why a statement regarding initial situation beliefs is incorrect. The justification is based on formulas regarding initial state beliefs of relevant situation-less beliefs.

Statement does Not Hold Initially (NHI)

- *Preconditions:* $\Phi(S_0) \in H_{v_{k-1}}$
- *Argument:* $\{\Phi'_1(S_0), \ldots, \Phi'_n(S_0)\} \vdash \neg\Phi(S_0)$

Situation-less Statement does Not Hold arguments explain why a statement regarding non-fluent facts is not correct. The justification is based on other non-fluent formulae.

Situation-less Statement does Not Hold (NH)

- *Preconditions:* $\Phi \in H_{v_{k-1}}$
- *Argument:* $\{\Phi'_1, \Phi'_2, \ldots, \Phi'_n\} \vdash \neg\Phi$

Invalid Successor State axiom arguments can be used to attack statements regarding the effects of actions. They explain that a proposed successor state axiom is wrong as it does not match the correct axiom.

Invalid Successor State axiom (ISS)

- *Preconditions:*
    - $F(x_1, x_2, \ldots, x_n, do(a, s)) \equiv \Phi_F(x_1, x_2, \ldots, x_n, a, s) \in H_{v_{k-1}}$ or
      $f(x_1, x_2, \ldots, x_n, do(a, s)) = y \equiv \Phi_f(x_1, x_2, \ldots, x_n, y, a, s) \in H_{v_{k-1}}$
    - $\Phi'_F(x_1, x_2, \ldots, x_n, a, s) \not\equiv \Phi_F(x_1, x_2, \ldots, x_n, a, s)$ or
      $\Phi'_f(x_1, x_2, \ldots, x_n, y, a, s) \not\equiv \Phi_f(x_1, x_2, \ldots, x_n, y, a, s)$
- *Argument for relational fluents:*
    $\{(F(x_1, x_2, \ldots, x_n, do(a, s)) \equiv \Phi'_F(x_1, x_2, \ldots, x_n, a, s)\} \vdash$
    $\quad F(x_1, x_2, \ldots, x_n, do(a, s)) \equiv \Phi'_F(x_1, x_2, \ldots, x_n, a, s))$
- *Argument for functional fluents:*
    $\{f(x_1, x_2, \ldots, x_n, do(a, s)) = y \equiv \Phi'_f(x_1, x_2, \ldots, x_n, y, a, s)\} \vdash$
    $\quad f(x_1, x_2, \ldots, x_n, do(a, s)) = y \equiv \Phi'_f(x_1, x_2, \ldots, x_n, a, s)$

Invalid Action Precondition axiom arguments can attack statements regarding the preconditions of planning operators.

Invalid Action Precondition axiom (IAP)

- *Preconditions:*
    - $Poss(A, s) \equiv \Pi_A(x_1, x_2 \ldots, x_n, s) \in H_{v_{k-1}}$
    - $\Pi'_A(x_1, x_2 \ldots, x_n, s) \not\equiv \Pi_A(x_1, x_2 \ldots, x_n, s)$
- *Argument:*
    $\{Poss(A, s) \equiv \Pi'_A(x_1, x_2 \ldots, x_n, s)\} \vdash Poss(A, s) \equiv \Pi'_A(x_1, x_2 \ldots, x_n, s)$

If the opponent cannot make any valid DLD attacks, and cannot backup to attempt an alternative attack, then the dispute is a failing attack. Therefore, the plan proposal that initiated the dispute as well as the arguments that the proponent employed to support it are acceptable.

4   Parcel World Domain Example

In this section, we present a simple example, revealing the key aspects of how the framework works. Two agents need to decide on a plan that will get an object processed. Agent A is the delivery agent, and is able to move($\Uparrow$, $\Downarrow$, $\Rightarrow$, $\Leftarrow$), *pickup* and *deliver* parcels. Agent B is the processing agent and can only *process* deliveries. Actions *pickup* and *deliver* have no preconditions, but produce conditional effects depending on the position of the object. The *process* action requires B to hold the object. Agents have conflicting beliefs about the position of the object. The shared objective of the two agents is to process the object. The "view" of the initial state of the world for agents A and B is described in Figure 2.

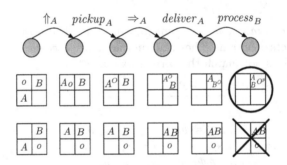

Fig. 2. How a plan affects the environment according to each agent's beliefs in the Parcel World Domain example

Agent A constructs a plan and makes a proposal. B validates the plan and discovers that the final action of the plan is inapplicable. Figure 2 describes the state of the world after each action in the plan for the two agents. Figure 3 describes the argumentation-based dialogue regarding the validity of the plan and the beliefs supporting it. If A convinces B, the plan will be followed; otherwise, replanning will be required. The dialogue shows that B will attack the proposal, because she believes that she will not have the object in the situation that the process action will be performed. A disagrees and bases her next argument on statements about the previous situation, explaining that B will have the object, since it will be delivered to her. The messages show that each *NHS* argument is supported by statements regarding a situation closer to the initial situation. Eventually, an initial situation belief disagreement is identified. Resolution can be attempted through belief argumentation.

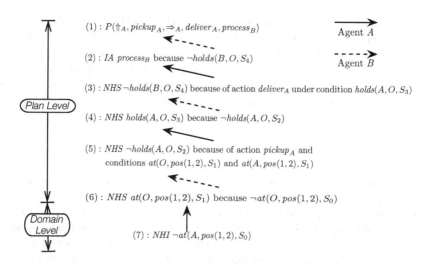

$$(1): P(\Uparrow_A, pickup_A, \Rightarrow_A, deliver_A, process_B)$$

Agent A

$$(2): IA\ process_B\ \text{because}\ \neg holds(B, O, S_4)$$

Agent B

$$(3): NHS\ \neg holds(B, O, S_4)\ \text{because of action}\ deliver_A\ \text{under condition}\ holds(A, O, S_3)$$

Plan Level

$$(4): NHS\ holds(A, O, S_3)\ \text{because}\ \neg holds(A, O, S_2)$$

$$(5): NHS\ \neg holds(A, O, S_2)\ \text{because of action}\ pickup_A\ \text{and}$$
$$\text{conditions}\ at(O, pos(1, 2), S_1)\ \text{and}\ at(A, pos(1, 2), S_1)$$

$$(6): NHS\ at(O, pos(1, 2), S_1)\ \text{because}\ \neg at(O, pos(1, 2), S_0)$$

Domain Level

$$(7): NHI\ \neg at(A, pos(1, 2), S_0)$$

Fig. 3. Messages exchanged by the agents in the Parcel World Domain example

5   Protocol Properties

In this section, we will present some properties of the dialogue. In order to do so, the introduction of assumptions is necessary.

5.1   Assumptions

We consider the beliefs of each agent to be independently consistent. So there cannot be contradictory statements following from an agent's beliefs. We consider cooperative agents, which are truthful with respect to the facts that they introduce to the dialogue. They can employ statements that follow from their beliefs or appear in the other party's commitments. We also assume that the agents are trying to achieve a common goal, i.e. all plans that are discussed have to achieve this predefined goal.[2]

We consider the agents to have a confident assertion attitude and a sceptical acceptance attitude. Agents with a confident assertion attitude will present any valid argument they can construct. Sceptical acceptance attitude ensures that only claims of acceptable arguments will be accepted. Agent attitudes are necessary because protocols usually define preconditions that make some argument moves available to an agent, but do not prescribe which of the available moves an agent will actually perform. By assuming underlying attitudes we can predict what these moves will be. The effects of different agent attitudes on dialogues have been studied in [13].

We follow the Causal Completeness Assumption, which ensures that all the effects of the planning operators are explicitly enumerated in the Successor State

---

[2] Note that other protocols could be used for goal negotiation prior to the use of the protocols we suggest, if necessary.

axioms. This assumption is employed to treat the *ramification problem* in the same way treated in [10]. Therefore, there are no side effects of any action that are not listed explicitly through the Successor State axioms. In other words, there is no distinction between direct and indirect action effects (if this was the case, a standard planner would not be able to construct a plan in every case, since only direct effects would be considered during planning; see [8] for planning under defeasible knowledge).

5.2 Properties

The following properties explain that the proposed protocol produces sound results. Completeness has to do with the construction of the proposals, and is closely related to the planning problem. In this paper we do not focus on planning. We consider agents that construct proposals through conventional planning methods [14]. The protocol enables the exchange of proposals for any plans that can be expressed in Situation Calculus and follow the relevant definitions.

Proposition 1. *If a plan is acceptable to both agents, no argument attacking the proponent's proposal argument will be raised by the opponent.*

Proof. From the specification of the arguments and the dialogue moves, the opponent can attack a 'Proposal' argument (P) either by raising an 'Invalid Action' (IA) or a 'Not holds in Situation S' (NHS) argument. An attack can be made if OPP believes that either an action a proposed by the proponent is not applicable, $\mathcal{D}_{OPP} \models \neg Poss(A, S)$, or the plan does not achieve the goal, $\mathcal{D}_{OPP} \models \neg G(S_n)$. This contradicts the claim that the plan is acceptable to the opponent, according to Definition 4.   □

The following proposition identifies bounds on the length of Plan Level Dispute (PLD) sub-dialogues, showing that it is linear in the number of actions in the plan.

Proposition 2. *If the plan is not acceptable, a finite number of PLD arguments will be exchanged. The length of the PLD $|M_p|$ will always be $|M_p| \leq n+1$, where n is the number of actions in the plan.*

Proof. The PLD dispute is formed by a sequence of arguments, initiated by P. A PLD sequence is terminated either if a Domain Level Dispute (DLD) argument is raised or if one of the agents is unable to perform a counter move (resulting in either retraction, backup, or dialogue termination). We will show that if the plan is not acceptable with respect to the opponent's beliefs, then a finite sequence of COUNTER moves will be made, until a DLD argument is raised, terminating the PLD. The intuition guiding this proof is that until the dispute focuses on domain beliefs, agents can always perform a valid COUNTER move, which is supported by statements regarding a situation closer to S_0.

From the definition of an acceptable plan, if the plan is not acceptable to the opponent, we can infer that OPP will either believe that one of the proposed actions is not applicable in the relevant situation, $\mathcal{D}_{OPP} \models \neg Poss(A, S)$, or that the plan does not achieve the goal, $\mathcal{D}_{OPP} \vDash \neg G(S_n)$. In the second case, the disagreement lies in a statement of the form $\Phi(S)$. In the first case, using the relevant Action Precondition axiom, OPP can infer the required support for constructing a IA argument of the form $\{\neg \Pi_A(S), Poss(A(x_1, \ldots, x_n), s) \equiv \Pi_A(x_1, x_2 \ldots, x_n, s)\} \vdash \neg Poss(A, S)$. If the proponent disagrees with the presented Action Precondition Axiom, then an 'Invalid Action Precondition Axiom' (IAP) argument can be raised terminating the PLD. If this is not the case, then the disagreement lies on whether $\Pi_A(S)$ or $\neg\Pi_A(S)$ is true. Again the disagreement lies in a statement of the form $\Phi(S)$.

We will focus on disagreements on statements of the form $\Phi(S)$. In such cases, agent i presented an argument which included the sentence $\Phi(S)$, but the other agent $-i$ disagrees with this statement (i.e. $\mathcal{D}_i \vDash \Phi(S)$ and $\mathcal{D}_{-i} \vDash \neg\Phi(S)$). If $S \neq S_0$, and the disagreement is about a non-fluent statement responsible for $\neg\Phi(S)$ (in both cases DLD moves can be constructed terminating the PLD), agent $-i$ may employ the relevant Successor State axiom to show that some relational or functional fluents ($F(S)$ or $f(S)$) take particular values in S that make $\Phi(S)$ false. To construct the necessary support, $-i$ identifies the conditions, which are specified in each relevant Successor State axiom (either $\Phi_F(S')$ or $\Phi_f(S')$), which hold in the previous situation S'.

Since the agents disagree about $\Phi(S)$, they would disagree also on some statements regarding the conditions in the previous state or on whether the employed axioms are correct. If the second is the case, agent i would introduce an 'Invalid Successor State axiom' argument, initiating a DLD. In the first case, disagreement lies again on a statement $\Phi(S')$.

Therefore, if a DLD argument is not introduced, the agent that needs to make the next move can always come up with a NHS argument attacking a statement the previous argument put forward by the other party. The statements mentioned in the support of this argument (and can be attacked by a PLD argument) refer to situation S', the fluents that are in the claim of the argument refer to S, and $S = do(A, S')$. Each attack made by a NHS argument is justified by statements regarding a situation closer to the initial situation. Therefore, since NHS arguments cannot attack statements regarding the initial situation, the maximum length of a sequence of consecutive NHS statements is n, if the argument initiating the sequence attacks a statement referring to situation s_n. Moreover, from the specification of the argument types, 'Proposal' and the 'Invalid Action' arguments can only appear once in a sequence of COUNTER moves. Therefore, the amount of consecutive PLD arguments can be at most $n + 1$. Such a sequence, will always result in a DLD argument, since agents are always able to construct either a PLD or a DLD argument when presented with a PLD argument. All arguments in a PLD argument sequence will be unique, since they refer to statements regarding different situations.   □

Proposition 3. *The proponent will present a successful (credulous) defence of the plan proposal if and only if either (i) the plan is acceptable with respect to the opponent's beliefs, or (ii) if the dispute terminates as a failing attack of the plan proposal argument.*

Proof. If the plan is acceptable, then no argument will be raised against the plan proposal argument (Proposition 1). *PRO* wins the dispute.

If the dispute terminates as a failing attack of the plan proposal argument, then the final argument is presented by the proponent. Therefore, the length of the dialogue is odd, and *PRO* wins the dispute.

If the plan is not acceptable with respect to the opponent's beliefs, and the dispute terminates as a failing defence of the plan proposal argument, then the opponent would have presented an argument that the proponent could not counter, or backup. This will be the final move of the dispute, making the number of moves even. Therefore, the opponent would win the dispute.   □

Proposition 4. *If the dispute for a Proposal argument terminates as a failing attack after move k, then the plan will be acceptable with respect to the set of beliefs* $D_{acc} = D_{OPP} \backslash \{\Phi(S_0) | (\exists \langle H, h \rangle \in P_k) . [(\exists \Phi'(S_0) \in H \cup \{h\}) . \Phi(S_0) \wedge \Phi'(S_0) \vdash \perp]\} \cup \{\Phi(S_0) | (\exists \langle H, h \rangle \in P_k) . [(\exists \Phi'(S_0) \in H \cup \{h\})]\}$

Proof. Since all runs are failing attacks, P_k is the set of the acceptable arguments the proponent presented during the dialogue. In addition, a Domain Level Dispute phase would have been initiated for every domain belief that is not shared among the agents and is relevant to the plan. Let D_{OPP}^{conf} be the set of all the statements from the domain beliefs of the opponent that conflict with statements appearing in an argument in P_k. These are the beliefs that were responsible for OPP not accepting the plan initially.

The plan will be acceptable with the set containing all statements appearing in P_k and all statements in D_{OPP} that do not conflict with the statements from P_k. By excluding all statements that were used to construct the arguments attacking the plan, and the arguments that supported these, we have excluded all the statements that are responsible for the arguments that were employed by the opponent. Therefore, no other arguments attacking the plan can be constructed using the opponent's remaining beliefs, since if this was the case, the opponent would have constructed them in move k continuing the dialogue (since we consider agents with confident assertion attitude).   □

6   Argument Generation

In order for the protocol to be effective, the agents need efficient mechanisms for argument generation. In general, argument generation is a complex task. Even with the assumptions that i) the agents' knowledge bases are propositional and ii) conflict-free, argument generation is co-NP-complete, since it is as complex as finding a proof in propositional logic (a further analysis can be found in [13]). Moreover, the support of such arguments will chain back to beliefs about the initial situation, resulting in extensive proofs, if there are no heuristics to restrict them. In this section, we will provide an algorithm for argument generation related to plans and will explain how this algorithm guides the search through the agents beliefs. The algorithm is based on the evaluation of the executability of all the actions in the plan, and on the projection of the actions' effects, in order

switch *Type of received argument v_{k-1}* **do**

case P

if $Poss(A, S) \in H_{v_{k-1}}$ and $\mathcal{D}_i \vDash \neg Poss(A, S)$ **then return** IA for action A
and relevant A_{ap};
if $\mathcal{D}_i \vDash \neg G(S_n)$ **then return** NH or NHS argument for the relevant fluent(s)
and A_{ss} that explain $\neg G(S_n)$;

case IA

if $A_{ap} \in H_{v_{k-1}}$ and $A_{ap} \notin \mathcal{D}_i$ **then return** IAP argument for correct A_{ap};
if $\Phi(S) \in H_{v_{k-1}}$ and $\mathcal{D}_i \vDash \neg \Phi(S)$ **then return** NH, NHI or NHS argument
for the relevant fluent(s) and A_{ss} that explain $\neg\Phi(S)$;

case NHS

if $A_{ss} \in H_{v_{k-1}}$ and $A_{ss} \notin \mathcal{D}_i$ **then return** ISS argument for correct A_{ss};
if $\Phi(S) \in H_{v_{k-1}}$ and $\mathcal{D}_i \vDash \neg\Phi(S)$ **then return** NH, NHI or NHS argument
for the relevant fluent(s) and A_{ss} that explain $\neg\Phi(S)$;

case NHI **if** $\Phi(S_0) \in H_{v_{k-1}}$ and $\mathcal{D}_i \vDash \neg\Phi(S_0)$ **then return** NH/NHI argument
for $\neg\Phi(S_0)$;

case NH **if** $\Phi \in H_{v_{k-1}}$ and $\mathcal{D}_i \vDash \neg\Phi$ **then return** NH argument against Φ;

case ISS **return** ISS argument for correct A_{ss};

case IAP **return** IAP argument for correct A_{ap};

return no move;

Algorithm 1. Argument generation algorithm

to evaluate the values of statements in the resulting situations. The complexity of these processes is related to the expressive power of the employed planning formalism [15].

The proponent constructs the initial plan proposal argument by bootstrapping a plan from her beliefs. After being presented with an argument, agents search for valid attackers. The task of argument generation can be performed by searching through the plan projection data. The search is guided by the type of the received argument. The constructed argument must follow the specification of the employed dialogue move, for example the rules regarding repetition of arguments.

If the agent receives a plan proposal, it can attack it if she identifies that according to her beliefs an action is not possible to be performed, using a IA argument, or if she believes that the plan does not succeed in achieving the goal. Differences of opinion regarding the operator specification (i.e. Successor State axioms or Action Precondition axioms) can be identified through the introduction of ISS or IAP arguments. Arguments supported by statements of the form $\Phi(S)$ that the agent believes to be incorrect (the validity of which may be evaluated through projection), can be attacked by NH, NHI or NHS arguments. In order to construct such arguments, the agent needs to identify the symbols that appear in $\Phi(S)$ and are responsible for $\Phi(S)$ to be false. If S is not S_0, then the agent needs to construct a proof, explaining that the necessary conditions hold in the previous situation, so that these symbols have certain values in the resulting situation that falsify $\Phi(S)$. In this case a NHS argument can be constructed.

If S is S_0, then the statement is about the initial situation and the agent can respond with a *NHI* argument. Finally, if the statement is false because of non-fluent statements, a *NH* argument can be employed.

Argument generation for the DLD subdialogues will need to be based on logical proofs, since it involves unstructured initial world beliefs. In this case, a large subset of the agent's beliefs are no longer relevant, since for DLD argument generation, only beliefs regarding the initial state of the world should be considered. All beliefs regarding the operator specification and the planning theory are irrelevant. This greatly reduces the set of the statements the agents have to search over when constructing a DLD argument. Moreover, if argument generation is implemented in propositional logic, the first order representation for all statements needs to be translated to propositional logic. The size of a propositional representation is exponentially larger in the worst case than the size of a corresponding first-order representation. This means that the propositional representation is considerably smaller without the operator specification and the planning theory axioms, i.e. a naive inclusion of planning axioms in propositional logic would be completely intractable for any real-world domain.

7 Conclusion

In this paper, we presented a novel dialogue protocol that allows cooperating agents to jointly evaluate plan proposals and to identify relevant conflicts in agents' beliefs. Moreover, we proposed efficient search-based algorithms for argument generation based on the specific characteristics of the planning domain.

Our approach is influenced by recent work on argumentation for practical reasoning and deliberation [2,3,4] and planning over defeasible knowledge [8]. While related to this work, we maintain a closer relation to classical AI planning, as no assumptions are made regarding plan generation and therefore any efficient planner can be employed for this task.

In the future we would like to investigate different strategies for argument selection, in cases where the opponent has a choice over various *IA* or *NHS* moves. In addition, our research can be complemented with heuristics for planning under uncertainty, considering multiagent planning among cooperative agents with different beliefs. It would be interesting to extend our protocol to include moves that enable distributed planning, especially in cases in which there is no agent that can construct a plan alone.

References

1. Dung, P.M.: On the acceptability of arguments and its fundamental role in non-monotonic reasoning, logic programming and n-person games. Artificial Intelligence 77(2), 321–357 (1995)
2. Atkinson, K., Bench-Capon, T.: Practical reasoning as presumptive argumentation using action based alternating transition systems. Artificial Intelligence 171(10-15), 855–874 (2007)

3. Rahwan, I., Amgoud, L.: An argumentation based approach for practical reasoning. In: Proceedings of AAMAS 2006, pp. 347–354. ACM, New York (2006)
4. Tang, Y., Parsons, S.: Argumentation-based dialogues for deliberation. In: Proceedings of AAMAS 2005, pp. 552–559. ACM, USA (2005)
5. Pynadath, D.V., Tambe, M.: The Communicative Multiagent Team Decision Problem: Analyzing Teamwork Theories and Models. Journal of Artificial Intelligence Research 16, 389–423 (2002)
6. Durfee, E.: Distributed Problem Solving and Planning. In: Weiß, G. (ed.) Multiagent Systems. A Modern Approach to Distributed Artificial Intelligence, pp. 121–164. MIT Press, USA (1999)
7. Lesser, V., Decker, K., Carver, N., Garvey, A., Neiman, D., Prasad, M., Wagner, T.: Evolution of the GPGP domain-independent coordination framework. Technical Report 98-05, Computer Science Department, UMASS (1998)
8. Garcia, D., Garcia, A., Simari, G.: Planning and defeasible reasoning. In: Proceedings of AAMAS 2007. ACM, USA (2007)
9. McCarthy, J., Hayes, P.J.: Some philosophical problems from the standpoint of artificial intelligence. Machine Intelligence 4 (1969)
10. Reiter, R.: Knowledge in Action: Logical Foundations for Specifying and Implementing Dynamical Systems. MIT Press, Cambridge (2001)
11. Dunne, P.E., Bench-Capon, T.: Two party immediate response disputes: properties and efficiency. Artificial Intelligence 149(2), 221–250 (2003)
12. Vreeswijk, G., Prakken, H.: Credulous and sceptical argument games for preferred semantics. In: Brewka, G., Moniz Pereira, L., Ojeda-Aciego, M., de Guzmán, I.P. (eds.) JELIA 2000. LNCS (LNAI), vol. 1919, pp. 239–253. Springer, Heidelberg (2000)
13. Parsons, S., Wooldridge, M.J., Amgoud, L.: An analysis of formal inter-agent dialogues. In: Proceedings of AAMAS 2002, pp. 394–401. ACM, USA (2002)
14. Nau, D., Ghallab, M., Traverso, P.: Automated Planning: Theory & Practice. Morgan Kaufmann Publishers Inc., San Francisco (2004)
15. Nebel, B.: On the compilability and expressive power of propositional planning formalisms. Journal of Artificial Intelligence Research 12, 271–315 (2000)

Dominant Decisions by Argumentation Agents

Paul-Amaury Matt, Francesca Toni, and Juan R. Vaccari

Department of Computing, Imperial College London, UK
{pmatt,f.toni,juan.vaccari08}@imperial.ac.uk

Abstract. We introduce a special family of (assumption-based argumentation) frameworks for reasoning about the benefits of decisions. These frameworks can be used for representing the knowledge of intelligent agents that can autonomously choose the "best" decisions, given subjective needs and preferences of decision-makers they "represent". We understand "best" decisions as *dominant* ones, giving more benefits than any other decisions. Dominant decisions correspond, within the family of argumentation frameworks considered, to *admissible arguments*. We also propose the use of *degrees of admissibility* of arguments as a heuristic to assess subjectively the value of decisions and rank them from "best" (dominant) to "worst". We extend this method to provide notion of *relative value of decisions* where preferences over benefits are taken into account. Finally, we show how our techniques can be successfully applied to the problem of selecting satellite images to monitor oil spills, to support electronic marketplaces for earth observation products.

1 Introduction

This paper presents two methods for evaluating and ranking (respectively) decisions using assumption-based argumentation (ABA) frameworks [4,13,14]. These ABA frameworks can be used for representing the knowledge of intelligent agents that autonomously make the best decision, e.g. by choosing the "best" items/ services available in a service-oriented architecture, as envisaged in [34]. We define a notion of *dominance* to characterise "best" items, and show that these items are those that correspond, within the family of argumentation frameworks considered, to *admissible arguments* as defined in [4,13]. Intuitively, the method relies upon comparing the "value" of different items by "arguing" about the benefits they provide. The reason why an item provides a benefit is explained logically (by means of arguments). ABA allows to study collections of logically constructed arguments based upon assumptions. As we shall see, ABA frameworks are particularly adequate for representing and reasoning about the benefits of items as well as for providing explanations to users.

In practice, decision-makers do not always choose top-quality ("best") items, but often choose items which fit their budget and have highest quality/price ratio. In this context, it is useful to assess numerically the quality or relative quality of items. We propose a novel criterion (or "semantics", as understood in argumentation) for choosing sets of assumptions and arguments. This criterion assigns

P. McBurney et al. (Eds.): ArgMAS 2009, LNAI 6057, pp. 42–59, 2010.

degrees of admissibility to sets of assumptions, measuring the fraction of counter-attacked arguments against the given sets. We show that this criterion allows to rank items rather than simply classifying items as good (dominant/admissible) or bad (non-dominant/non-admissible). We also propose a generalisation of the formula for degrees of admissibility of decisions to take numerically into account the customer's preferences over benefits or goals, thus giving the *relative "value" of decisions*. Overall, we thus propose three argumentation-based methods for comparing decisions: conventional admissibility, degrees of admissibility, and relative "value" of decisions. In decision-theoretic terms, our work can be classified as providing three methods for solving problems of decision making under certainty.

Our methods are defined for simple decision frameworks. We believe that these frameworks have nonetheless wide applicability. In particular, they are suitable to support decision-making in electronic marketplaces. These allow internet users to meet business organisations, to discover, select and purchase their goods or services. Motivated by our involvement in the ARGUGRID project[1], one of our goals and aspirations for this work is to propose tools for supporting users during the selection phase of this business process and, notably, to empower the user with expert insight on specific categories of goods and services. We demonstrate the potential of our approach by dealing with the problem of selecting satellite images to monitor oil spills, to support electronic marketplaces for earth observation products.

The paper is organised as follows. We briefly introduce ABA in section 2. In section 3 we describe the kind of decision problems we consider in this paper and the notion of dominance to characterise the "best" decisions amongst a set of possible ones. In section 4 we propose a special family of ABA frameworks suitable for representing and reasoning about the benefits of decisions. We also prove that, within the family of frameworks considered, the notion of dominance is equivalent to the semantics of admissibility in argumentation. Section 5 discusses the use of degrees of admissibility as a low complexity heuristic for assessing the "value" of decisions and for ranking them from "best" to "worst". In section 6, the notion of dominance and the heuristic are applied to the industrial procurement of satellite images in the case of oil spills. We discuss related work (from decision theory and argumentation-based decision making) in section 7 and finally conclude in section 8.

2   Background: Assumption-Based Argumentation

Here we provide essential background on assumption-based argumentation (ABA), more details can be found in [4,13,10,14].

An *ABA framework* is a quadruple $\langle \mathcal{L}, \mathcal{R}, \mathcal{A}, \mathcal{C} \rangle$ where

- $\mathcal{L}$ is a set of sentences, referred to as *language*
- $\mathcal{R}$ is a set of *(inference) rules* of the form $\frac{p_1,\ldots,p_n}{q}$ for $n \geq 0$, where $p_1,\ldots,p_n \in \mathcal{L}$ are called the premises and $q \in \mathcal{L}$ is called the conclusion of the rule

---

[1] www.argugrid.eu

- $\mathcal{A} \subseteq \mathcal{L}$, referred to as the set of *assumptions*
- $\mathcal{C} : \mathcal{A} \to \mathcal{L}$, referred to as the *contrary* mapping

As in [13,10], we will restrict attention to *flat* ABA frameworks, such that if $l \in \mathcal{A}$, then there exists no rule of the form $\frac{p_1 \dots p_n}{l} \in \mathcal{R}$ for any $n \geq 0$.

Arguments are deductions of conclusions supported by assumptions. Arguments can be represented as trees having conclusions as their roots and assumptions as their leaves [14]. These trees can be computed in a forward or backward manner. If computed backwards, an *argument* $A \vdash p$ with conclusion $p \in \mathcal{L}$ and supported by the set of assumptions $A \subseteq \mathcal{A}$ is a finite sequence of multisets of sentences $S_1, \dots, S_m$, where $S_1 = \{p\}$, $S_m = A$, and for every $1 \leq i < m$, where σ is the sentence occurrence in S_i selected by a given selection function:

1. if $\sigma \notin A$ then $S_{i+1} = S_i - \{\sigma\} \cup S$ for some inference rule of the form $\frac{S}{\sigma} \in \mathcal{R}$
2. if $\sigma \in A$ then $S_{i+1} = S_i$

This backward computation of arguments is employed within all computational tools for ABA (e.g. see [20]).

Given two sets of assumptions A and B, we say that the set A *attacks* B if and only if there exists an argument $A' \vdash p$ for $A' \subseteq A$ whose conclusion is the contrary of some assumption $b \in B$, or, formally, when there exists $b \in B$ such that $p = \mathcal{C}(b)$. In other words, A attacks B if a subset of A supports an argument that "contradicts" an assumption in B.

This notion of attack is a binary relation over sets of assumptions which can be represented by a set of pairs *attacks* $\subseteq \mathcal{A} \times \mathcal{A}$. Properties of sets of assumptions, aimed at sanctioning them (and the arguments they support) as "acceptable", can be defined based on such a relationship. "Acceptable" sets of assumptions represent the rational arguments that intelligent agents may use to support their opinions.

In the literature, several notions of "acceptability", referred to as extension-based *semantics*, have been defined and studied [12,4,13,10]. In this paper we are concerned with the semantics of *admissibility*. Formally, given a set of assumptions $A \subseteq \mathcal{A}$

- A is *conflict-free* if and only if A does not attack itself
- A is *admissible* if and only if A is conflict-free and attacks every B that attacks A

The language of an ABA framework may contain sentences representing properties of interest for an agent such as goals, beliefs and possible actions or decisions [33,11]. The set of inference rules gives a logical structure to the language. The inference rules are used to model either known or observed facts and construct arguments to support claims. Assumptions play the role of beliefs which are not directly observable or known, but are useful in building arguments. Arguments are justified claims, but they do not have the value of proofs as they are disputable, so agents need semantics such as admissibility to elaborate rational opinions.

3   Dominant Decisions

We will consider simple decision-making settings where a user/agent needs to decide which element of a given (finite) set to choose. This set can be thought of as consisting of mutually exclusive items. Different items will typically bring the user/agent different benefits (or goals), according to the features of these items as well as some general beliefs of the user/agent concerning how these features affect the benefits. Formally, in this paper a *decision framework* is a tuple (D, G, F, B) where

- D is a (finite) set of (mutually exclusive) *decisions*
- G is a (finite) set of *benefits/goals* that the user wishes to achieve
- F is a (finite) set of *features* that items may exhibit
- B is a (finite) set of *beliefs* concerning (i) the features that items actually exhibit and (ii) the achievement of goals, given (some) features

B can be seen as a set of beliefs on which to base opinions regarding the value of items towards achieving benefits. We will assume that B is a set of implications of the form:

$$(i)\ d \rightarrow f$$
$$(ii)\ f_1, \ldots, f_n, sg_1, \ldots, sg_m \rightarrow g \quad (n, m \geq 0, n + m > 0)$$

where $d \in D$, $f, f_i \in F$ (for $i = 1, \ldots, n$), $g, sg_j \in G \cup SG$ (for $j = 1, \ldots, m$) with SG a given set of *sub-goals*, $SG \cap G = \{\}$.[2] An implication $d \rightarrow f \in B$ stands for "item d has feature f". An implication $f_1, \ldots, f_n, sg_1, \ldots, sg_m \rightarrow g \in B$ stands for "features $f_1, \ldots, f_n$ and the achievement of sub-goals $sg_1, \ldots, sg_m$ guarantee the achievement of (goal or sub-goal) g". The first kind of implication is specific to given available decisions, whereas the second kind is generic and represents beliefs that would hold even for different available decisions.

As we will discuss in section 6, although simple, our decision frameworks can be used to represent realistic, industrial applications, e.g. a wide range of e-procurement problems. Note that decision frameworks may accompany or be obtained from influence diagrams [7], that are widely used representation tools to support decision-making.

Until section 6, we will use, for illustration purposes, a toy scenario whereby a user/agent needs to choose accommodation in London that is close to Imperial College (represented as *near*) and reasonably priced (represented as *cheap*), and considers as options a hotel (referred to as *jh*), Imperial college student halls (referred to as *ic*), both in South Kensington, and the Ritz hotel (referred to as *ritz*), in Piccadilly. This scenario can be represented by a decision problem with

- $D = \{jh, ic, ritz\}$
- $G = \{cheap, near\}$

---

[2] Note that we do not include SG explicitly as a component of the decision framework, since this can be drawn from the other components, namely SG is the set of all sentences occurring in B but not in $D \cup F \cup G$.

- $F = \{price = 50\pounds, price = 70\pounds, price = 200\pounds,$
  $inSouthKen, inPiccadilly\}$
- $B = \{ic \rightarrow price = 50\pounds,\ jh \rightarrow price = 70\pounds,\ ritz \rightarrow price = 200\pounds,$
  $ic \rightarrow inSouthKen,\ jh \rightarrow inSouthKen,\ ritz \rightarrow inPiccadilly,$
  $price \leq 50\pounds \rightarrow cheap,\ inSouthKen \rightarrow near,$
  $price = 50\pounds \rightarrow price \leq 50\pounds,$
  $price = 70\pounds \rightarrow price > 50\pounds,\ price = 200\pounds \rightarrow price > 50\pounds\}$

The set of sub-goals underlying this decision problem is $SG = \{price \leq 50\pounds,$ $price > 50\pounds\}$.

In order to determine the "value" of an item one shall first find out which benefits the item provides.

Definition 1 (γ–value of an item). *The* value *of an item $d \in D$ is given by*

$$\gamma(d) = \{g \in G \mid B \cup \{d\} \vdash_{MP} g\}$$

where $\vdash_{MP}$ stands for repeated applications of the modus ponens inference rule for $\rightarrow$.[3]

In our toy scenario, $\gamma(ic) = \{cheap, near\}$, $\gamma(jh) = \{near\}$ and $\gamma(ritz) = \{\}$.

If the value of an item d is bigger (in the sense of set inclusion) than the value of any other item, then the item d basically provides all benefits that can be achieved by any other item and is undoubtedly "best". We call any such item "dominant".

Definition 2 (Dominance). *An item $d \in D$ is dominant if and only if $\gamma(d) \supseteq \gamma(d')$ for every $d' \in D - \{d\}$.*

In our toy scenario, ic is a dominant item/choice, since its value includes both goals in G. No other item is dominant.

Note that other notions of dominance are possible, for example considering the number of benefits given by decisions. We plan to explore other such notions in the future.

4   A Family of ABA Frameworks for Comparing Decisions

We introduce a family of ABA frameworks $\langle \mathcal{L}, \mathcal{R}, \mathcal{A}, \mathcal{C} \rangle$ for comparing decisions, given a simple decision framework (D, G, F, B) (with set of sub-goals SG) as outlined in section 3. For every item $d \in D$, feature $f \in F$ and benefit $g \in G$, let us introduce the following sentences in $\mathcal{L}$:

- f^d, standing for "item d has feature f"
- g^d, standing for "benefit or sub-goal g is provided by item d"
- $M(\neg g^d)$, standing for "item d cannot provide benefit g"
- $\neg d$, standing for "the user does not choose item d"

---

[3] The modus ponens inference rule amounts to deriving c from $a \rightarrow c$ and a, for any set (conjunction) of sentences a and sentence c.

For example, the sentence $near^{ritz}$ stands for "the $ritz$ hotel is close to Imperial College", the sentence $price = 50\pounds^{jh}$ stands for "the jh hotel costs $50\pounds$ per night", and the sentence $\neg ic$ stands for "the user does not choose ic".

Given these sentences, we formally define $\langle \mathcal{L}, \mathcal{R}, \mathcal{A}, \mathcal{C} \rangle$ as follows:

- the language
$$\mathcal{L} = D \cup \{\neg d \mid d \in D\} \cup \{f^d \mid f \in F, \, d \in D\} \cup$$
$$\{g^d, M(\neg g^d) \mid (g, d) \in G \cup SG \times D\}$$

- the inference rules $\mathcal{R}$ consist of all the rules of the form
  - $\frac{d}{f^d}$ if $d \rightarrow f \in B$, for $d \in D$ and $f \in F$
  - $\frac{d, f_1^d, \dots, f_n^d, sg_1^d, \dots, sg_m^d}{g^d}$ if $f_1, \dots, f_n, sg_1, \dots, sg_m \rightarrow g \in B$, for $f_i \in F$, $sg_j \in SG$, $g \in SG \cup G$
  - $\frac{g^{d'}, M(\neg g^d)}{\neg d}$ for every benefit $g \in G$ and pair of distinct items $d, d' \in D$
- the assumptions
$$\mathcal{A} = D \cup \{M(\neg g^d) \mid (g, d) \in G \times D\}$$

- the contrary mapping $\mathcal{C} : \mathcal{A} \rightarrow \mathcal{L}$, defined, for all $a \in \mathcal{A}$, as
$$\mathcal{C}(a) = \begin{cases} \neg d \text{ if } a = d \\ g^d \text{ if } a = M(\neg g^d) \end{cases}$$

The first two types of inference rules in $\mathcal{R}$ can be automatically obtained from B in the given decision framework. In our toy scenario, these include

$$\frac{ic}{price = 50\pounds^{ic}} \qquad \frac{jh}{inSouthKen^{jh}}$$

$$\frac{jh, inSouthKen^{jh}}{near^{jh}} \qquad \frac{ic, price \leq 50\pounds^{ic}}{cheap^{ic}}$$

These rules allow the generation of arguments of the form

$$\boxed{\{d\} \vdash g^d}$$

playing the role of expert proofs that a given item d allows to achieve a benefit g. Examples of these arguments in our toy scenario are $\{ic\} \vdash cheap$ and $\{jh\} \vdash near$.

The third type of rules allow to express reasons for not taking decisions, motivated by other decisions fulfilling goals that the current decision can be assumed not to fulfil. Examples of these rules in our toy scenario include

$$\frac{cheap^{ic}, M(\neg cheap^{ritz})}{\neg ritz} \qquad \frac{near^{jh}, M(\neg near^{ic})}{\neg ic}$$

Reasons for not choosing particular items are arguments of the form

$$\boxed{\{d', M(\neg g^d)\} \vdash \neg d}$$

for any d' giving benefit g (namely such that an argument $\{d'\} \vdash g^{d'}$ exists). In our toy scenario, these arguments include $\{ic, M(\neg cheap^{ritz})\} \vdash \neg ritz$ (since $\{ic\} \vdash cheap^{ic}$).

The processing of all these arguments allows us to compare the value of all items in a rigorous and automated fashion. Indeed, given the ABA framework corresponding to a decision framework as detailed above, the dominant items, providing the largest number of benefits as defined in section 3, can be characterised by the semantics of admissibility for the ABA framework, as given by theorem 1 below. In the remainder of the paper we will assume as given a decision framework (D, G, F, B) and the corresponding ABA framework $\langle \mathcal{L}, \mathcal{R}, \mathcal{A}, \mathcal{C} \rangle$.

The proof of theorem 1 relies upon the following lemma:

Lemma 1. *Given an item $d \in D$, there is an argument $\{d\} \vdash g^d$ (with respect to $\langle \mathcal{L}, \mathcal{R}, \mathcal{A}, \mathcal{C} \rangle$) if and only if $g \in \gamma(d)$ (with respect to (D, G, F, B)).*

This directly follows from the fact that $\{d\} \vdash g^d$ if and only if $\{d\} \vdash_{MP} g$.

Theorem 1 (Dominance & admissibility). *Given an item $d \in D$, $\{d\}$ is admissible (with respect to $\langle \mathcal{L}, \mathcal{R}, \mathcal{A}, \mathcal{C} \rangle$) if and only if d is dominant (with respect to (D, G, F, B)).*

Proof. $\Rightarrow$: By contradiction, assume that d is not dominant. Then, by definition of dominance, $\exists d' \neq d$ such that $\gamma(d) \not\supseteq \gamma(d')$. Thus, $\exists g \in \gamma(d')$ such that $g \notin \gamma(d)$. By lemma 1 and by construction of the ABA framework, $\exists g \in \gamma(d')$ means that there exists an argument $\{d', M(\neg g^d)\} \vdash \neg d$ attacking $\{d\}$[4], given that $\mathcal{C}(d) = \neg d$. Since $\{d\}$ is admissible, $\{d\}$ counter-attacks $\{d', M(\neg g^d)\}$. $\{d\}$ does not attack $\{d'\}$ because the only way to attack $\{d'\}$ is by arguments with support containing $M(\neg g^{d'})$ and some other d^*, trivially not contained in $\{d\}$. By elimination, $\{d\}$ attacks $M(\neg g^d)$. Since $\mathcal{C}(M(\neg g^d)) = g^d$, by lemma 1, there exists an argument $\{d\} \vdash g^d$. Therefore, again by lemma 1, $g \in \gamma(d)$, which is absurd. By contradiction, d is dominant.

$\Leftarrow$: $\{d\}$ is necessarily conflict-free since there is no argument supported solely by $\{d\}$ for $\mathcal{C}(d) = \neg d$. Let $X \vdash \neg d$ be an arbitrary argument attacking $\{d\}$. By construction of the ABA framework, there must exist a benefit g such that $M(\neg g^d) \in X$ and a decision $d' \in X$ such that $\{d'\} \vdash g^{d'}$. By lemma 1, $g \in \gamma(d')$. By dominance of d, $g \in \gamma(d)$ too. Again by lemma 1, $\{d\} \vdash g^d$, which attacks $M(\neg g^d) \in X$. Thus, $\{d\}$ counter-attacks X. Since X was chosen arbitrarily, $\{d\}$ is an admissible set of assumptions.

Therefore, argumentation agents can check whether an item d is the "best" or dominant by testing whether (the singleton set consisting of) this item is admissible. For our toy scenario, the only dominant item is ic, since $\{ic\}$ is the only admissible set consisting of a single decision. Any software able to compute admissible sets of assumptions for an ABA framework can be used to identify dominant items. In particular, the CaSAPI ABA engine [20] can be used for this purpose.

---

[4] An argument attacks a set of assumption if and only if the conclusion of the argument is the contrary of an assumption in the set. If an argument attacks a set of assumptions, then the support of the argument attacks the set of assumptions too.

5   Degrees of Admissibility

This section builds upon the previous theorem 1 and aims at obtaining a way of ranking items rather than simply classifying items as good (dominant/admissible) or bad (non-dominant/admissible). The idea is to assess *degrees of admissibility* instead of simply checking *admissibility*. In practice, decision-makers do not always choose items of highest quality, but more often choose those which fit their budget and have highest quality/price ratio. In this context, it becomes necessary to assess numerically the quality or relative quality of items. For example, consider a variant of our toy scenario where the beliefs about *cheap* in B are replaced by:

$price \leq 70\pounds \rightarrow cheap,$
$price = 50\pounds \rightarrow price \leq 70\pounds, \; price = 70\pounds \rightarrow price \leq 70\pounds,$
$price = 200\pounds \rightarrow price > 70\pounds$

Then, both $\{ic\}$ and $\{jh\}$ are dominant, but ic has a better quality/price ratio. If we consider one further goal *luxury*, and add

- to G: *luxury*
- to F: *4star*
- to B: $jh \rightarrow 4star$, $4star \rightarrow luxury$

then the only dominant/admissible decision is jh, but ic may have a better quality/price ratio still.

In order to generalise the notion of admissibility, we introduce a scale of degrees of admissibility for sets of assumptions ranging from 0 to 1. Admissible sets correspond to those with a degree of 1. Sets which are not conflict-free have a degree of 0. Sets which are conflict-free but do not counter-attack all arguments attacking them have a degree comprised between 0 and 1.

For these sets, one can use the fraction of counter-attacked arguments as degree of admissibility. This measure is intuitively appealing, as the higher this fraction for a decision d, the more benefits d provides.

Definition 3 (α-degree of admissibility). *Given an ABA framework $\langle \mathcal{L}, \mathcal{R}, \mathcal{A}, \mathcal{C} \rangle$ and $A \subseteq \mathcal{A}$, let $X_A = \{B \mid B \text{ attacks } A\}$. Then, the degree of admissibility of A is given by*[5]

$$\alpha(A) = \begin{cases} 1 \text{ if there are no attacks against } A \text{ (namely } X_A = \{\}) \\ 0 \text{ if } A \text{ is not conflict-free (namely } A' \in X_A \text{ for some } A' \subseteq A) \\ \frac{|\{B \mid B \in X_A \text{ and } A \text{ attacks } B\}|}{|X_A|} \text{ otherwise} \end{cases}$$

Note that $\alpha(A) = 0$ if (and only if) either A attacks itself or A attacks none of the arguments attacking it. In the revised toy scenario of this section, $\alpha(\{jh\}) = 1$, $\alpha(\{ic\}) = 2/3$ and $\alpha(\{ritz\}) = 0$. Note that, in the specific decision-making setting studied in this paper, (the set of assumptions consisting of) any decision

---

[5] Here, $|S|$ stands for the cardinality of set S.

is necessarily conflict-free, and the case of $\alpha(\{d\}) = 0$ is "reserved" for non-dominant decisions d fulfilling no goals (and thus attacking no arguments in $X_{\{d\}}$).

Trivially, A is admissible if and only if $\alpha(A) = 1$. Thus, for $\langle \mathcal{L}, \mathcal{R}, \mathcal{A}, \mathcal{C} \rangle$ the ABA framework corresponding to a decision framework (D, G, F, B), directly from theorem 1 we have:

Corollary 1 (dominance & (degrees of) admissibility). *For every item* $d \in D$, *the following three propositions are equivalent:*

- $\{d\}$ *is admissible*
- d *is dominant*
- $\alpha(\{d\}) = 1$

In the case of decision frameworks, degrees of admissibility are quite simple to compute. For a given item $d \in D$, we are interested in the arguments that attack d and those supported by $\{d\}$ which counter-attack them. There exist as many attacks against d as there are arguments supporting sentences of the form $g^{d'}$, where $d' \in D$ is an item distinct from d. Let us then introduce the following notations

- $T_{d,g} = \begin{cases} 1 & \text{if there exists an argument supporting } g^d \\ 0 & \text{otherwise} \end{cases}$
- $T_g = \sum_{d \in D} T_{d,g}$
- $T_d = \sum_{g \in G} T_{d,g}$
- $T = \sum_{g \in G} T_g$

Theorem 2 (Degree of admissibility of a decision). *Given a decision framework* (D, G, F, D) *and* $d \in D$:

$$\alpha(\{d\}) = \begin{cases} 1 \; \text{if } T - T_d = 0 \\ \frac{\sum_{g \in G} T_{d,g} * (T_g - T_{d,g})}{T - T_d} & \text{otherwise} \end{cases}$$

Proof. $\{d\}$ is definitely conflict-free. The number of arguments attacking d is given by the sum

$$\sum_{g \in G} \sum_{d' \in D - \{d\}} T_{d',g} = \sum_{g \in G} (T_g - T_{d,g}) = T - T_d$$

Assume $T - T_d \neq 0$. The only way to counter-attack these arguments is to attack their assumption of the form $M(\neg g^d)$. Clearly, each attacking argument supported by $\{M(\neg g^d)\}$ is in turn counter-attacked on the condition that there exists at least one argument supported by $\{d\}$ and supporting g^d. Consequently, the number of counter-attacks is

$$\sum_{g \in G} \sum_{d' \in D - \{d\}} T_{d,g} * T_{d',g}$$

This last expression can be slightly simplified as

$$\sum_{g \in G} T_{d,g} * (T_g - T_{d,g})$$

Thus, by definition of α, the theorem holds.

Assume $T - T_d = 0$. Then, for every g and every $d' \neq d$, $T_{d',g} = 0$ and $\gamma(d') = \{\}$, which is trivially contained in $\gamma(d)$. Thus d is dominant and, by corollary 1, $\alpha(\{d\}) = 1$ and the theorem holds.

Note that the computation of the values $T_{d,g}$ and thus of degrees of admissibility for decisions simply requires the implementation of a program able to test the existence of arguments supporting goals in an ABA framework. Such programs are understandably rather simple to develop (see the next section 6 for a discussion concerning implementation).

By definition of degree of admissibility, if an item does not provide any benefit at all, its degree is that of a non-conflict-free set, namely 0. The more benefits can be achieved with an item, the higher its admissibility degree. Therefore, the notion of degree of admissibility can be seen as playing the role of a relative utility function to make inter-item comparisons. This role is even clearer if we consider "weights". Indeed, decision makers may attach various degrees of importance to their goals. For example, in our toy scenario, the user may think that location is more important than luxury. In ABA, attacks or counter-attacks have no strength. In practice, however, we may want that certain attacks have more impact than others because they relate to more important issues. We show how to modify the formula for degrees of admissibility so as to incorporate the importance of the customer's goals and more accurately reflect her/his true preferences. Thus, instead of assigning the same importance to all benefits in G, we introduce weights $w(g) > 0$ for all $g \in G$, representing the importance or level of priority of benefit g. Note that these weights can be any and need not sum up to one. The previously established formula for the degree of admissibility as given in theorem 2 can be naturally generalised to the following

Definition 4 (Relative value of a decision). *Given $d \in D$, the relative value of d is given by*

$$\alpha^*(d) = \frac{\sum_{g \in G} w(g) * T_{d,g} * (T_g - T_{d,g})}{\sum_{g \in G} w(g) * (T_g - T_{d,g})} \tag{1}$$

In our toy scenario, assume $w(cheap) = 2$, $w(near) = 3$ and $w(luxury) = 1$. Then, $\alpha^*(jh) = 5/6$, $\alpha^*(ic) = 1$ and $\alpha^*(ritz) = 0$.

Note that, if there exists some constant $\lambda > 0$ such that for all $g \in G$ the importance of the goal g is $w(g) = \lambda$, then for every item $d \in D$ it is clear that $\alpha^*(d) = \alpha(d)$, i.e. the notion of relative value of an item collapses with the one of degree of admissibility. Thus, we may say that the notion of relative value of an item generalises in the mathematical sense the notions of admissibility and dominance of the item. In a nutshell, α^* measures how close an item d is to satisfy the property of dominance.

6   Supporting e-Marketplaces

Electronic marketplaces allow internet users to meet business organisations, to discover, select and purchase their goods, products or services. We have implemented the methods for decision-making described in this paper (dominance=admissibility and degrees of admissibility) and have tested them on an e-market place application, for the selection of *earth observation* products, namely images generated by satellites. Earth observation satellites are specifically designed to observe earth from orbit, and intended for environmental monitoring, meteorology, and maps making. The availability of satellites with different characteristics (type of sensors, types of orbits, etc.) and the pecularities of the images needed by users add complexity to the problem of selecting earth observation products.

The specific earth observation problem described in this section is the problem of selecting satellite images to monitor oil spills. This problem has been proposed by GMV S.A.[6], building upon their extensive field experience. The full problem is described in [32]. In this section we concentrate on dealing with a fragment of this problem, in order to focus on the representation of this kind of problems in terms of a decision framework (D, G, F, B) as understood in this paper. Using the general-purpose method described in section 4, this decision framework can then be mapped onto an argumentation framework to which the methods of sections 4 and 5 can be applied.

We consider two satellites, referred to as *sat*1 and *sat*2, available for choosing images needed to observe a given oil spill. Thus,

$$D = \{sat1, sat2\}.$$

The required satellite must accomplish several goals such as timing and quality of images for the particular oil spill setting. We are going to focus on one such goal, namely (a required) radiometric resolution (*radiometric_resolution*). Thus,

$$G = \{radiometric\_resolution\}.$$

We define B incrementally, as the union of several sets of implications.

In order to accomplish the required radiometric resolution, the selected satellite must be able to distinguish differences of intensity in the images. The differences can be expressed in terms of color emission, temperature, radiation reflection or altitude. These can all be seen as sub-goals.

$$B1 = \{\ color\_emission \rightarrow radiometric\_resolution,$$
$$temperature \rightarrow radiometric\_resolution,$$
$$radiation\_reflection \rightarrow radiometric\_resolution,$$
$$altitude \rightarrow radiometric\_resolution\}$$

To detect differences in terms of color emission the observation must be performed during the day (*day*); there must be no obstacles (*no_obstacle*) such as

---

[6] http://www.gmv.com

rain, clouds, haze, or snow; the colours of the object to be detected and the background must be distinguishable (*colors_distinguishable*); and the satellite must possess a panchromatic sensor (*panchromatic_sensor*).

$$B2 = \{day, no\_obstacle, colors\_distinguishable, panchromatic\_sensor$$
$$\rightarrow color\_emission\}$$

To detect differences in terms of temperature the object and the background must have different temperatures and the satellite must possess an infrared radiometer.

$$B3 = \{temperature\_distinguishable, infrared\_radiometer \rightarrow temperature\}$$

To detect differences in terms of radiation reflection first of all the satellite must possess a synthetic aperture radar. Then the object must reflect and the background absorbe the signal emitted by the satellite or the object must absorbe and the background reflect the signal. The object reflects the signal if it has a riddled surface and the riddles are small (up to 5 centimeters). The background reflects the signal if the background is riddled and the riddles are big (larger than 5 centimeters). The object absorbs the signal if the object surface is smooth or if the surface is riddled and the riddles are small (up to 5 centimeters). The background absorbs the signal if the background surface is smooth or if the surface is riddled and the riddles are small (up to 5 centimeters).

$$B4 = \{ \ object\_riddled, object\_riddles\_big \rightarrow object\_reflection$$
$$background\_riddled, background\_riddles\_big \rightarrow background\_reflection$$
$$object\_smooth \rightarrow object\_absorption$$
$$object\_riddled, object\_riddles\_small \rightarrow object\_absorption$$
$$background\_smooth \rightarrow background\_absorb$$
$$background\_riddled, background\_riddles\_small \rightarrow background\_absorb\}$$

To detect differences in terms of altitude the object and background must be at significantly different altitudes.

$$B5 = \{altitude\_distinguishable, radar\_altimeter \rightarrow altitude\}$$

We also have information about the satellites: *sat1* possesses an infrared radiometer and a panchromatic sensor. It also counts with a radar altimeter. The temporal resolution for this satellite is high. The information for *sat2* is that it has a panchromatic sensor and a medium temporal resolution.

$$B6 = \{ \ sat1 \rightarrow infrared_radiometer,$$
$$sat1 \rightarrow panchromatic_sensor,$$
$$sat1 \rightarrow radar\_altimeter,$$
$$sat1 \rightarrow temporal_resolution_high$$
$$sat2 \rightarrow panchromatic\_sensor,$$
$$sat2 \rightarrow radar\_altimeter,$$
$$sat2 \rightarrow temporal\_resolution\_medium\}$$

To complete the presentation of B, we need to provide information about the environment and the characteristics of the image the user is interested in. In the specific case considered, the images must be obtained during the day, there are no obstacles in the sky, the object to capture is big and has a smooth surface and the background is riddled and those riddles are big.

$$B7 = \{ \to day, \to no\_obstacle,$$
$$\to object\_smooth, \to background\_riddled,$$
$$\to background\_riddles\_big, \to object\_big\}$$

The set B for the decision framework is then defined as:[7]

$$B = B1 \cup B2 \cup B3 \cup B4 \cup B5 \cup B6 \cup B7.$$

The set of features for this decision framework is

$$F = \{ panchromatic\_sensor, infrared\_radiometer, radar\_altimeter,$$
$$temporal\_resolution\_high, temporal\_resolution\_medium\}.$$

This decision framework can be directly translated onto the corresponding ABA framework. As an example, this would include rules:

$$\frac{radiometric\_resolution^{sat1}, M(\neg radiometric\_resolution^{sat2})}{\neg sat2}$$
$$\frac{radiometric\_resolution^{sat2}, M(\neg radiometric\_resolution^{sat1})}{\neg sat1}$$

We have encoded the ABA framework as an input to CaSAPI [20][8] to obtain admissible (and thus dominant) decisions. For the simple fragment considered here, this dominant item is $sat1$, appropriately computed by CaSAPI.

We have also tried the degrees of admissibility method using a Ruby-on-Rails web-service prototype[9]. The results showed a degree of admissibility of 1.0 for $sat1$ and a degree of admissibility of 0 for $sat2$. The Ruby-on-Rails web-service prototype consists of a core Ruby engine able to construct backward arguments and compute degrees of admissibility, embedded into Rails allowing to use the server via a web interface.

---

[7] Note that the information in $B7$ is not strictly speaking in the format of implication beliefs as given in section 3. We could pre-compile $B7$ into the rest of B, unfolding them away from implications. We have chosen not to here because decision frameworks (and the correwsponding ABA frameworks) can be easily extended to include this "information facts" without altering any of the results in the paper.

[8] CaSAPI can be downloaded from http://www.doc.ic.ac.uk/~dg00/casapi.html. The CaSAPI file for the application described in this section can be found at http://homepage.mac.com/paulmatt/homepage/eBusiness/page3.html.

[9] This is available at http://homepage.mac.com/paulmatt/homepage/eBusiness/page3.html

We have also implemented solutions to the full oil spill problem, with 5 satellites (ERS, RADARSAT, SPOT, IKONOS, METOP), 27 implications (for reasoning about images), 57 implications in total for also describing the equipment on the satellites and the scenario of exploitation, and 3 goals (radiometric, spatial and temporal image resolution). The full ABA and Ruby-on-Rails formulations can be downloaded from

http://homepage.mac.com/paulmatt/homepage/eBusiness/page3.html

7 Related Work

The present work can be classified in decision-theoretic terms [15,35,19] as a problem of decision making under certainty. Indeed, the beliefs involved in our problem correspond to features and are by consequence controllable unknowns (secondary decisions). In this problem, argumentation is used for reasoning about the relative value of different items. In decision-theoretic terms, argumentation is used as a model to compute a utility function which is too complex to be given a simple analytical expression in closed form. Note that, broadly speaking, such limitations of classical Decision Theory have lead some authors to develop a number of qualitative approaches to Decision Theory, such as e.g. [28,5,9]. In this paper, we focus on using argumentation as a form of qualitative Decision Theory.

Argumentation has already been proposed for decision making, under strict uncertainty (no probabilistic information is available to the decision maker) [17,18,1,2] and also for decision under risk (some probabilistic information is known) [29,21,27,3]. Argumentation has also been used to support practical reasoning [30,31] and decision support systems [16,24,25]. Differently from all these approaches, in this paper we have focused on using *standard* Dung-style argumentation [12] as instantiated in ABA and showing the suitability of an existing semantics (admissibility) for argumentation (which fundamentally plays the same role as a decision criterion in Decision Theory) in a practical application: our theorem 1 guarantees the suitability of the notion of admissibility for studying choice problems in (simple, but realistic) decision frameworks. [11] also links a semantics for argumentation to a decision-theoretic criterion (Wald's minimax criterion) in a context of decision making under strict uncertainty.

The idea of using degrees of admissibility finds its origins in the notion of graduality [6]. Graduality has been introduced to generalise the classical notion of acceptability in argumentation from [12]. Degrees of acceptability have been recently used to play the role of measure of argument strength [22] and to be mathematically connected to the value of special two-person zero-sum games of strategy with imperfect information [35]. In that work, however, the strength of an argument does not simply correspond to the admissibility of an extension embracing that argument, but rather the expected value of the admissibility of an extension randomly chosen by a proponent of that argument, relative to the one chosen randomly by an opponent.

Some argumentation-based approaches (to decision-making as well as other applications) rely upon inducing preferences amongst sets of arguments from preferences on individual arguments (e.g. see [8]). Our computation of degrees of admissibility can be seen as a means to compute preferences amongst arguments "from first principle", solely based upon the arguments capability to counter-attack (as many as possible) attacking arguments.

Our decision-making approach, described in section 3, relies upon a definition of "value" of decisions, in terms of the benefits brought forward by them. Correspondingly, in the ABA framework given in section 4, arguments can be seen as supporting "values", as in value-based argumentation for decision-making [26]. However, values are not explicit in our ABA frameworks. As future work, it would be interesting to capture our simple ABA frameworks for dominat decisions as instances of value-based argumentation.

8   Conclusion

Electronic marketplaces are not only changing the way items (goods, products and services) are being offered and made available, they are also rendering the task of comparing the value of items more complex than it used to be. The need for intelligent and expert knowledge-based agents supporting both sellers and buyers in this new economy is growing fast. This paper has proposed argumentation-based agent architecture for addressing the problem of comparing items. We have emphasised the suitability of assumption-based argumentation and introduced a family of assumption-based argumentation frameworks for analysing decision problems. In these problems, decisions represent items. These frameworks can be directly deployed by (suitable) agents within an e-marketplace setting.

We have proved theoretically that, within this family of frameworks, the semantics of admissibility is equivalent to the concept of dominance for items. Building upon this theoretical result, we have proposed degrees of admissibility as an intuitive heuristic for comparing the value of items. The original formula for the degree of admissibility of an item has then been generalised so as to take numerically into account the customer's preferences over benefits or goals. The formula obtained allows to rank subjectively the value customisable items from best to worst.

Our techniques are supported at the implementation level by two systems: the general-purpose ABA system CaSAPI and a decision-making specific Ruby-on-Rails web service prototype.

We have illustrated an application of our techniques (and systems) to the procurement of earth observation products. These techniques have also been applied to an industrial procurement problem in support of companies in the complex task of purchasing electronic ordering systems [23]. Both applications require feeding an argumentation agent with expert knowledge used to support the choice of (earth observation or e-ordering) products. The main difference between our methods and the methods currently used by industrial experts in the application areas considered lies in the amount of effort the buyer needs to put in the task of specifying the inputs to the problem. With the industrial methods, the decision-maker needs to specify the decision framework and assess the overall importance of each individual feature and grade their benefits numerically. In our approach, the decision-maker only needs to specify the decision framework (if the third method, computing the relative value, is used, the decision-maker also needs to specify numerically its preferences over the ultimate goals that can be achieved, but these are few and easy to assess). Consequently, we believe that our approach empowers the decision-maker with expert knowledge, allowing to concentrate energy on the specification and weighting of goals. In this context, the use of ABA is beneficial, with respect to the use of abstract argumentation, in that it affords a finer level of granularity in the representation.

Our preliminary experimentation with e-procurement is encouraging. We plan to further this experimentation to provide a more thorough evaluation, e.g. to assess scalability of our approach.

The use of argumentation to determine dominance allows users to be presented with explanatory information as to the reasons of the dominance (in comparison with other items concerning the relative benefits). We believe that this is an important feature of our approach when agents attempt to persuade one another (for example, if the seller of an item is told that its item is dominated by some other, then it may decide to change the specification of its item in order to persuade the buyer to change its mind). We plan to investigate this direction in the future.

We have focused on problems of decision making under certainty. Argumentation could be fruitfully used also to deal with uncertainty, e.g. as in [17,18,1,2]. We plan to study a suitable extension of our approach to cope with uncertainty in the future.

Acknowledgements

This work was funded by the Sixth Framework IST programme of the EC, under the 035200 ARGUGRID project. The authors would like to thank Jose Barba for useful discussions on the earth observation scenario.

References

1. Amgoud, L.: A unified setting for inference and decision: An argumentation-based approach. In: 21st Conference on Uncertainty in Artificial Intelligence (UAI 2005), pp. 26–33 (2005)
2. Amgoud, L., Prade, H.: Making decisions from weighted arguments. In: Decision theory and multi-agent planning, pp. 1–14. Springer, Heidelberg (2006)
3. Amgoud, L., Prade, H.: Using arguments for making decisions: A possibilistic logic approach. In: 20th Conference of Uncertainty in Artificial Intelligence (UAI 2004), pp. 10–17 (2004)
4. Bondarenko, A., Dung, P.M., Kowalski, R.A., Toni, F.: An abstract, argumentation-theoretic approach to default reasoning. Artificial Intelligence 93(1-2), 63–101 (1997)
5. Bonet, B., Geffner, H.: Arguing for decisions: A qualitative model of decision making. In: Proceedings of the 12th Conference on Uncertainty in Artificial Intelligence (UAI 1996), pp. 98–105 (1996)

6. Cayrol, C., Lagasquie-Schiex, M.-C.: Graduality in argumentation. J. Artif. Intell. Res (JAIR) 23, 245–297 (2005)
7. Clemen, R.T., Reilly, T.: Making Hard Decisions with DecisionTools Suite. Duxbury Resource Center (2004)
8. Dimopoulos, Y., Moraitis, P., Amgoud, L.: Theoretical and computational properties of preference-based argumentation. In: ECAI, pp. 463–467 (2008)
9. Dubois, D., Fargier, H., Perny, P.: Qualitative decision theory with preference relations and comparative uncertainty: An axiomatic approach. Artificial Intelligence 148, 219–260 (2003)
10. Dung, P.M., Mancarella, P., Toni, F.: Computing ideal sceptical argumentation. Artificial Intelligence 171(10-15), 642–674 (2007)
11. Dung, P.M., Thang, P.M., Toni, F.: Towards argumentation-based contract negotiation. In: 2nd International Conference on Computational Models of Argument (COMMA 2008). IOS Press, Amsterdam (2008)
12. Dung, P.M.: On the acceptability of arguments and its fundamental role in nonmonotonic reasoning, logic programming, and n-person games. Artificial Intelligence 77(2), 257–321 (1995)
13. Dung, P.M., Kowalski, R.A., Toni, F.: Dialectic proof procedures for assumption-based, admissible argumentation. Artificial Intelligence 170(2), 114–159 (2006)
14. Dung, P.M., Kowalski, R.A., Toni, F.: Assumption-based argumentation. In: Rahwan, I., Simari, G. (eds.) Argumentation in AI: The Book. Springer, Heidelberg (2009)
15. Fishburn, P.C.: Decision and Value Theory. John Wiley and Sons, Inc., New York (1964)
16. Fox, J., Johns, N., Lyons, C., Rahmanzadeh, A., Thomson, R., Wilson, P.: PROforma: a general technology for clinical decision support systems. Computer Methods and Programs in Biomedicine 54(10-15), 59–67 (1997)
17. Fox, J., Krause, P., Elvang-Gøransson, M.: Argumentation as a general framework for uncertain reasoning. In: Heckerman, D., Mamdani, A. (eds.) Proceedings of the 9th Conference on Uncertainty in Artificial Intelligence, pp. 428–434. Morgan Kaufmann Publishers, San Francisco (1993)
18. Fox, J., Parsons, S.: On using arguments for reasoning about actions and values. In: Doyle, J., Thomason, R.H. (eds.) Working Papers of the AAAI Spring Symposium on Qualitative Preferences in Deliberation and Practical Reasoning, pp. 55–63 (1997)
19. French, S.: Decision theory: an introduction to the mathematics of rationality. Ellis Horwood (1987)
20. Gaertner, D., Toni, F.: Hybrid argumentation and its properties. In: Besnard, P., Doutre, S., Hunter, A. (eds.) Proceedings of the Second International Conference on Computational Models of Argument (COMMA 2008). IOS Press, Amsterdam (2008)
21. Krause, P., Ambler, S., Elvang-Gøransson, M., Fox, J.: A logic of argumentation for reasoning under uncertainty. Computational Intelligence 11, 113–131 (1995)
22. Matt, P.-A., Toni, F.: A game-theoretic measure of argument strength for abstract argumentation. In: Hölldobler, S., Lutz, C., Wansing, H. (eds.) JELIA 2008. LNCS (LNAI), vol. 5293, pp. 285–297. Springer, Heidelberg (2008)
23. Matt, P.-A., Toni, F., Stournaras, T., Dimitrelos, D.: Argumentation-based agents for e-procurement. In: 7th International Conference on Autonomous Agents and Multiagent Systems (2008)
24. Modgil, S., Hammond, P.: Decision support tools for clinical trial design. Artificial Intelligence in Medicine 27(2), 181–200 (2003)

25. Morge, M., Mancarella, P.: The hedgehog and the fox. An argumentation-based decision support system. In: Rahwan, I., Parsons, S., Reed, C. (eds.) ArgMAS 2007. LNCS (LNAI), vol. 4946, pp. 114–131. Springer, Heidelberg (2008)
26. Nawwab, F.S., Bench-Capon, T.J.M., Dunne, P.E.: A methodology for action-selection using value-based argumentation. In: Besnard, P., Doutre, S., Hunter, A. (eds.) Proceedings of the Second International Conference on Computational Models of Argument (COMMA 2008), pp. 264–275. IOS Press, Amsterdam (2008)
27. Parsons, S.: Normative argumentation and qualitative probability. In: Nonnengart, A., Kruse, R., Ohlbach, H.J., Gabbay, D.M. (eds.) FAPR 1997 and ECSQARU 1997. LNCS, vol. 1244, pp. 466–480. Springer, Heidelberg (1997)
28. Pearl, J.: From conditional oughts to qualitative decision theory. In: 9th Conference on Uncertainty in Artificial Intelligence (UAI 1993), pp. 12–20 (1993)
29. Poole, D.: Probabilistic horn abduction and bayesian networks. Artificial Intelligence 64(1), 81–129 (1993)
30. Prakken, H.: Combining sceptical epistemic reasoning with credulous practical reasoning. IOS Press, Amsterdam (2003)
31. Rahwan, I., Amgoud, L.: An argumentation-based approach for practical reasoning. In: International Joint Conference on Autonomous Agents and Multiagent Systems (AAMAS), pp. 347–354 (2006)
32. Stournaras, T. (ed.): E-business application scenario - (ARGUGRID) Deliverable D.1.2 (2007)
33. Toni, F.: Assumption-based argumentation for selection and composition of services. In: Sadri, F., Satoh, K. (eds.) CLIMA VIII 2007. LNCS (LNAI), vol. 5056, pp. 231–247. Springer, Heidelberg (2008)
34. Toni, F.: Argumentative kgp agents for service composition. In: Proc. AITA 2008, Architectures for Intelligent Theory-Based Agents, AAAI Spring Symposium. Stanford University, Stanford (2008)
35. von Neumann, J., Morgenstern, O.: Theory of Games and Economic Behavior. Princeton University Press, Princeton (1944)

A Model for Integrating Dialogue and the Execution of Joint Plans

Yuqing Tang[1], Timothy J. Norman[2], and Simon Parsons[1,3]

[1] Dept. of Computer Science, Graduate Center, City University of New York
365 Fifth Avenue, New York, NY 10016, USA
ytang@gc.cuny.edu
[2] Dept of Computing Science, The University of Aberdeen
Aberdeen, AB24 3UE, UK
t.j.norman@abdn.ac.uk
[3] Dept of Computer & Information Science, Brooklyn College, City University of New York,
2900 Bedford Avenue, Brooklyn, NY 11210 USA
parsons@sci.brooklyn.cuny.edu

Abstract. Coming up with a plan for a team that operates in a non-deterministic environment is a complex process, and the problem is further complicated by the need for team members to communicate while the plan is being executed. Such communication is required, for example, to make sure that information critical to the plan is passed in time for it to be useful. In this paper we present a model for constructing joint plans for a team of agents that takes into account their communication needs. The model builds on recent developments in symbolic non-deterministic planning, ideas that have not previously been applied to this problem.

1 Introduction

One of the fundamental problems in multiagent systems is how to get a team of agents to coordinate their behavior. While there are situations in which agents can do this without needing to communicate [13], in general coordination requires communication. Another important part of coordination is having the agents decide what to do. Since [2], the process of deciding what to do is considered to break down into two parts — deciding what goals to achieve, what [2] calls *deliberation*, and then deciding how those goals might best be achieved, which is usually described as *planning*. In this paper we are interested in the planning part of the process. We assume the existence of a set of goals to be achieved, in a form such as a set of joint intentions [10].

We are also greatly concerned with communication. Much recent work on agent communication uses argumentation-based dialogue [17], and the long term goal of our work is to extend existing work on multiagent planning by developing models by which a team of agents can, in the course of an argumentation-based dialogue — by which we mean a process during which agents put forward suggested partial plans backed by reasons, as in [23] — develop a plan for the team. We want this to be done in a way that respects the non-deterministic nature of the world, and which yields efficient implementation. This paper takes several steps towards this goal.

P. McBurney et al. (Eds.): ArgMAS 2009, LNAI 6057, pp. 60–78, 2010.

In particular, this paper gives a mechanism, albeit a centralized mechanism, by which a multiagent team can construct plans that take into account the need to communicate to ensure that the plan is executed correctly [18]. By developing a representation language that is an extension of languages used in non-deterministic planning, our approach can make use of new techniques from model-checking to provide efficient implementations. The extension incorporates the elements necessary to take multiple agents, and the necessary communication, into account. The use of a symbolic model makes it possible to turn the plan construction process into an argumentation-based dialogue in the future.

Building our approach on top of work in planning has advantages beyond ease and efficiency of implementation. By appropriating the underlying formal models, we can easily acquire suitable formal guarantees for the planning model that we construct. It is straightforward, for example, to show that given an adequate description of the world, any plan that our planning process will construct is both a feasible and, in a specific sense an optimal, way to achieve the goals of the plan.

2   Representation Language

We use a state-space model as a basis for our formalization. This model is an adaptation of a model commonly used in non-deterministic planning [8]. *States* are objects that capture some aspect of a system, and *actions* are transitions between states. States and actions together define a *state-space*. When action effects are non-deterministic [8] then what one seeks for any state-space is a *policy*: i.e. a state-action mapping that specifies which actions one should take in a given state. We define a non-deterministic domain to be a tuple $\mathcal{M} = \langle \mathcal{P}, \mathcal{S}, \mathcal{A}, \mathcal{R} \rangle$ where:

- $\mathcal{P} = \mathcal{P}_S \cup \mathcal{P}_A$ is a finite set of propositions;
- $\mathcal{S} \subseteq 2^{\mathcal{P}_S}$ is the set of all possible states;
- $\mathcal{A} \subseteq 2^{\mathcal{P}_A}$ is the finite set of actions; and
- $\mathcal{R} \subseteq \mathcal{S} \times \mathcal{A} \times \mathcal{S}$ is the state-transition relation.

A propositional language $\mathcal{L}$ with quantification can be defined by allowing standard connectives $\wedge, \vee, \rightarrow, \neg$ and quantifiers $\exists, \forall$ over the proposition variables. The resulting language is a logic of quantified boolean formulae (QBF) [3]. A *symbol renaming operation*, which we use below, can be defined on $\mathcal{L}$, denoted by $\mathcal{L}[\mathcal{P}/\mathcal{P}']$, which means that a new language is obtained by substituting the symbols of $\mathcal{P}$ with the symbols of $\mathcal{P}'$ where $\mathcal{P}'$ contains the same set of propositions as $\mathcal{P}$ but uses different symbol names (notice that $|\mathcal{P}'| = |\mathcal{P}|$). Similarly for a formula $\xi \in \mathcal{L}$, if $\boldsymbol{x}$ is a vector of propositional variables for $\mathcal{P}$, then a variable renaming operation can be defined by $\xi[\boldsymbol{x}/\boldsymbol{x}']$ which means that all the appearances of variables $\boldsymbol{x} = x_1 x_2 \ldots x_n$ are substituted by $\boldsymbol{x}' = x_1' x_2' \ldots x_n'$ which is a vector of the corresponding variables or constants in $\mathcal{P}'$. In QBF, propositional variables can be universally and existentially quantified: if $\phi[\boldsymbol{x}]$ is a QBF formula with propositional variable vector $\boldsymbol{x}$ and x_i is one of its variables, the existential quantification of x_i in ϕ is defined as $\exists x_i \phi[\boldsymbol{x}] = \phi[\boldsymbol{x}][x_i/FALSE] \vee \phi[\boldsymbol{x}][x_i/TRUE]$; the universal quantification of x_i in ϕ is defined as $\forall x_i \phi[\mathbf{x}] = \phi[\boldsymbol{x}][x_i/FALSE] \wedge \phi[\boldsymbol{x}][x_i/TRUE]$. Here $FALSE$ and $TRUE$ are two propositional constants representing "true" and "false" in the logic. The introduction of quantification doesn't increase the expressive power of propositional logic but

Table 1. The mapping between set operators and QBF operators

Set operator	QBF operator
$X_1 \cap X_2$	$\xi(X_1) \wedge \xi(X_2)$
$X_1 \cup X_2$	$\xi(X_1) \vee \xi(X_2)$
$X_1 \setminus X_2$	$\xi(X_1) \wedge \neg\xi(X_2)$
$x \in X$	$\xi(x) \rightarrow \xi(X)$
$X_1 \subseteq X_2$	$\xi(X_1) \rightarrow \xi(X_2)$

allows us to write concise expressions whose quantification-free versions have exponential sizes [12].

Based on the two disjoint sets of propositions, $\mathcal{P}_S$ and $\mathcal{P}_A$, two sub-languages $\mathcal{L}_S$ and $\mathcal{L}_A$ for states and actions can be defined respectively. A state $s = \{p_1, p_2, \ldots, p_k\}$, $s \subseteq \mathcal{P}_S$, means that the propositions $p_1, p_2, \ldots, p_k$ are true in state s and all other propositions in $\mathcal{P}_S$ are false — we therefore make a form of closed-world assumption. In other words, each state s is explicitly encoded by a conjunction composed of all proposition symbols in $\mathcal{P}_S$ in either positive or negative form

$$\psi = \bigwedge_{p_i \in s} p_i \wedge \bigwedge_{p_j \notin s} \neg p_j$$

We denote that a formula γ is true in state s by $s \models \gamma$. Then a set of states can be characterized by a formula $\gamma \in \mathcal{L}_S$, with the set denoted by $S(\gamma)$, where $S(\gamma) = \{s | s \models \gamma\}$.[1] Actions are encoded in a similar way to states. Action $a = \{p_1, p_2, \ldots, p_l\}$, $a \subseteq \mathcal{P}_A$ means that propositions $p_1, \ldots, p_l$ are true and all other formula in $\mathcal{P}_A$ are false. We denote that a formula α is true in an action a by $a \models \alpha$, and a set of actions can be characterized by a formula $\alpha \in \mathcal{L}_A$ with the set denoted by $A(\alpha) = \{a | a \models \alpha\}$. Given a set of states S, and a set of actions A, the corresponding formulae in $\mathcal{L}$ are denoted by $\xi(S)$ and $\xi(A)$ respectively. With these notions we can have a mapping between the set operations on states and the boolean operations on formulae as shown in Table 1 when X_1 and X_2 are interpreted as two sets of states. Similarly for actions, we can have the same operation mapping in Table 1 when X_1 and X_2 are interpreted as two sets of actions.

With states and actions defined, the state-transition relationship can then be specified by a set SR of triples: $SR = \{\langle \gamma, \alpha, \gamma' \rangle\}$ where $\gamma, \gamma' \in \mathcal{L}_S$ and $a \in \mathcal{L}_A$. Each triple $\langle \gamma, \alpha, \gamma' \rangle$ corresponds to a transition $R_{\langle \gamma, a, \gamma' \rangle} = \{\langle s, a, s' \rangle | s \models \gamma, a \models \alpha, s' \models \gamma'\}$, and together:

$$\mathcal{R}_{SR} = \bigcup_{\langle \gamma, \alpha, \gamma' \rangle \in SR} R_{\langle \gamma, \alpha, \gamma' \rangle}.$$

Using the renaming operation, we can extend the state and action language $\mathcal{L} = \mathcal{L}_S \cup \mathcal{L}_A$ to be $\mathcal{L} = \mathcal{L}_S \cup \mathcal{L}_A \cup \mathcal{L}_{S'}$ where $\mathcal{L}_{S'} = \mathcal{L}_S[\mathcal{P}/\mathcal{P}']$. $\mathcal{P}_S$ is for the current state, $\mathcal{P}_A$

---

[1] Note that $S(p_1 \wedge p_2 \wedge \ldots \wedge p_k) \neq \{s\}$ where $s = \{p_1, p_2, \ldots, p_k\}$ because S_γ doesn't make the closed world assumption; that is, we don't assume that the unspecified propositions are false when using a formula $\gamma \in \mathcal{L}$ to specify the set of states $S(\gamma)$.

is for the action, and $\mathcal{P}_{S'}$ is for the next state in the representation of a state transition. Now a triple $\langle \gamma, \alpha, \gamma' \rangle$ can be rewritten by one formula in $\mathcal{L}$ as $\gamma \wedge \alpha \wedge \gamma'$ where $\gamma \in \mathcal{L}_S$, $\alpha \in \mathcal{L}_A$ and $\gamma' \in \mathcal{L}_{S'}$. Correspondingly, a state transition $r = \langle s, a, s' \rangle$ is said to satisfy a formula $\delta = \gamma \wedge \alpha \wedge \gamma'$, denoted by $r \models \delta$, if $s \models \gamma$, and $a \models a$, and $s' \models \gamma'$. A set of state transitions R can be characterized by a formulae $\delta = \xi(R)$ and the corresponding set of state transitions $R(\delta) = \{r | r \models \delta\}$. We can capture the meaning of δ more easily if we expand δ into a disjunction, $\delta = \bigvee_i (\gamma_i \wedge \alpha_i \wedge \gamma_i')$, in which each state transition is explicitly encoded as a conjunction. It conforms to the mapping between the set operations on state transitions and boolean operations on the formulae in Table 1 by interpreting X_1 and X_2 with two sets of state transitions.

3 Policies

The state-space model described above gives us a way of describing the world in which an agent finds itself, and the actions it can undertake. We can then turn to considering what the output of the planning process will be. We call this output a *policy*, and we consider it to simply be a set of state-action pairs,

$$\pi = \{\langle s_i, a_i \rangle\}$$

where $s_i \in \mathcal{S}$ and $a_i \in \mathcal{A}(s)$ with

$$\mathcal{A}(s) = \{a | \exists \langle s, a, s' \rangle \in \mathcal{R}\}$$

that is the set of actions that are applicable in s. A policy π is a *deterministic policy*, if for a given state s, there is no more than one action is specified by π, otherwise it is a *non-deterministic policy*. What we are calling a policy is the state-action table used in [8]. It is also related to what the literature on MDPs calls a policy [1], but we allow a policy to only specify actions for a subset of all possible states.

A policy can be specified by a set of pairs composed of a formula, $\gamma \in \mathcal{L}_S$, and an action, $\alpha \in \mathcal{L}_A$: $SA = \{\langle \gamma, \alpha \rangle\}$. Each pair $\langle \gamma, \alpha \rangle$ corresponds to a policy segment: $\pi_{\langle \gamma, \alpha \rangle} = \{\langle s, a \rangle | s \models \gamma \text{ and } a \models \alpha\}$, and together

$$\pi_{SA} = \bigcup_{\langle \gamma, \alpha \rangle \in SA} \pi_{\langle \gamma, \alpha \rangle}$$

A state-action pair $\langle s, a \rangle$ is said to satisfy a formula of the form $\gamma \wedge \alpha$ where $\gamma \in \mathcal{L}_S$ and $\alpha \in \mathcal{L}_A$, denoted by $\langle s, a \rangle \models \gamma \wedge \alpha$. We can characterize a set π of state-action pairs, namely a policy, by a formula of the form $\tau = \bigvee_i \gamma_i \wedge \alpha_i$ and its equivalents. We denote this by $\pi(\tau) = \{\langle s, a \rangle | \langle s, a \rangle \models \tau\}$. In the same way that we represent state transitions as propositions, we can have a propositional representation $\xi(SA)$ for a set SA of state-action pairs, and the mapping between the set operations on policies and boolean operations on the formulae given in Table 1 applies if we interpret X_1 and X_2 as two sets of state-action pairs. We can represent the constraint $\mathcal{A}(s)$ by a formula in $\mathcal{L}$: $\xi(\mathcal{A}(S(\gamma)) = \exists x' \xi(R(S, A, S')) \wedge \gamma$ where x' is the vector of variables for S' and $\xi(R(S, A, S'))$ is the formula representation of the state transition relation in the system. Then we can conjoin the formula $\xi(\mathcal{A}(S(\gamma)))$ to each policy expression of the form $\gamma \wedge \alpha$ to be $\gamma \wedge \alpha \wedge \xi(\mathcal{A}(S(\gamma)))$. For simplicity, we will omit the formula component $\xi(\mathcal{A}(S(\gamma)))$ in the representation of policy below.

The space of all policies is denoted by Π. The set of states in a policy π is $S_\pi = \{s | \langle s, a \rangle \in \pi\}$. Adapting from [8], we have the following definition:

Definition 1. *An* execution structure *induced by the policy π from a set of initial states I is a directed graph $\Sigma_\pi(I) = (V_\pi, E_\pi)$ which can be recursively defined as*

- *if $s \in I$, then $s \in V_\pi$, and*
- *if $s \in V_\pi$ and there exists a state-action pair $\langle s, a \rangle \in \pi$ such that $\langle s, a, s' \rangle \in \mathcal{R}$, then $s' \in V_\pi$ and $a : \langle s, s' \rangle \in E_\pi$ where the action a is the label of the edge.*

Definition 2. *An* execution path *of a policy π from a set of states I is a possibly infinite sequence $s_0, s_1, s_2, \ldots$ of states in the execution structure $\Sigma_\pi(I) = \langle V_\pi, E_\pi \rangle$ such that for all states s_i in the sequence:*

- *either s_i is the last state of the sequence, in which case s_i is a* terminal state *of $\Sigma_\pi(I)$, or*
- *$\langle s_i, s_{i+1} \rangle \in E_\pi$.*

A state s' is said to be *reachable* from s in the execution structure Σ_π if there is a path from s to s' in Σ_π. Σ_π is an *acyclic execution* iff all its execution paths are finite.

These ideas then give us a way to classify policies:

Definition 3. *Given a set of initial states I and a set of goal states G for a nondeterministic domain $\mathcal{M} = \langle \mathcal{P}, \mathcal{S}, \mathcal{A}, \mathcal{R} \rangle$, let π be a policy for $\mathcal{M}$ with execution structure $\Sigma_\pi(I)$, then*

- *π is a* weak solution *to achieve G iff for any state $s_0 \in I$ there is some terminal state s' of $\Sigma_\pi(I)$ such that $s' \in G$ and it is reachable from s_0;*
- *π is a* strong solution *to achieve G iff $\Sigma_\pi(I)$ is acyclic and all terminal states of $\Sigma_\pi(I)$ are also in G;*
- *π is a* strong cyclic solution *to achieve G iff from any state s_0 in $\Sigma_\pi(I)$ some terminal state s is reachable and all the terminate states of $\Sigma_\pi(I)$ are in G.*

With a weak solution policy, we have a path to the goal in a finite number of steps, but no guarantee that in a non-deterministic world the goal will be achieved; with a strong solution policy, we have a guarantee that the goal can be achieved in a finite number of steps despite actions being non-deterministic if the state space is acyclic; and with a strong cyclic solution, we are guaranteed that the goal will be achieved even in the face of non-determinism and cycles in the state-space so long as the cycle can be broken non-deterministically.

4   Joint Policies

To describe the behavior of a team, we need to prescribe more structure over the actions available to an agent. We assume that there is a set of n agents labeled by $\mathcal{T} =$

Table 2. Joint operations

Representation	Meaning
$joint(a_i)$	$\{a \in \mathcal{A} \mid a \models a_i\}$
$joint(a)$	$\bigcap_{a_k \in a} joint(a_k)$
$joint(s_i)$	$\{s \in \mathcal{S} \mid s \models s_i\}$
$joint(s)$	$\bigcap_{s_k \in s} joint(s_k)$
$joint(R_i)$	$\{\langle s, a, s' \rangle \mid \langle s_i, a_i, s_i' \rangle \in R_i,$ and $s \in joint(s_i), a \in joint(a_i), s' \in joint(s_i')\}$
$joint(\pi_i)$	$\{\langle s, a \rangle \mid \langle s_i, a_i \rangle \in \pi_i,$ and $s \in joint(s_i), a \in joint(a_i)\}$
$joint(S_i)$	$\bigcup_{s_i \in S_i} joint(s_i)$
$joint(\{\langle s_i, s_i' \rangle\})$	$\{\langle joint(s_i), joint(s_i') \rangle\}$
$joint(\Sigma_{\pi_i})$	$\langle joint(V_{\pi_i}), joint(E_{\pi_i}) \rangle$
$joint(\{R_i\})$	$\bigcap_i joint(R_i)$
$joint(\{\pi_i\})$	$\bigcap_i joint(\pi_i)$

$\{T_1, T_2, \ldots, T_n\}$ in the system. We call the actions in the set $\mathcal{A}$ *joint actions* of these agents. Each action $a \in \mathcal{A}$ is a tuple of actions of individual agents, so $a = [a_1, \ldots, a_n]$. That is each action $a \in \mathcal{A}$ can be further decomposed into n actions $a_i \in \mathcal{A}_i$ of individual agents T_i. Each $\mathcal{A}_i$ is defined to be a subset $\mathcal{P}_{\mathcal{A}_i}$ of the propositions in $\mathcal{P}_{\mathcal{A}}$. By overloading the notion, we also denote $a \models a_i$ if agent T_i's action is a_i in a joint action a. In total, we have:

$$\mathcal{A} = \prod_i \mathcal{A}_i$$

Similarly, each state $s \in \mathcal{S}$ is a tuple of states combined from the perception of individual agents, so $s = [s_1, \ldots, s_n]$. That is each state $s \in \mathcal{S}$ can be further decomposed into n states $s_i \in \mathcal{S}_i$ of individual agents T_i. Each $\mathcal{S}_i$ is defined to be a subset $\mathcal{P}_{\mathcal{S}_i}$ of the propositions in $\mathcal{P}_{\mathcal{S}}$. By overloading this notion, we also denote $s \models s_i$ if agent T_i's perception of a (joint) state s is in s_i.

Overall, we have:

$$\mathcal{S} = \prod_i \mathcal{S}_i$$

Given these ideas, we can generate the set of join(t) and projection operations on an agent T_i's actions, states and state transitions as shown in Tables 2 and 3 respectively. Join, or joint, operations combine the states and actions that concern individual agents into the states and actions that concern a set of agents, while projection operations extract states and actions of individual agents from those of a set of agents.

An additional formula $\beta \in \mathcal{L}$ can be introduced to constrain possible combinations so that $\mathcal{A}(\beta) = \{a \in \mathcal{A} \mid a \models \beta\}$. For example, this constraint:

$$\beta = \bigwedge_{i=1}^{n} \bigwedge_{j \neq i} a_i \rightarrow \tau_j$$

Table 3. Projection operations

Representation	Meaning
$proj_i(a)$	$\{a_i \in \mathcal{A}_i \mid a \models a_i\}$
$proj_i(s)$	$\{s_i \in \mathcal{S}_i \mid s \models s_i\}$
$proj_i(R)$	$\{\langle s_i, a_i, s_i' \rangle \mid \langle s, a, s' \rangle \in R, \text{ and } s_i \in proj_i(s), a_i \in proj_i(a), s' \in proj_i(s')\}$
$proj_i(\pi)$	$\{\langle s_i, a_i \rangle \mid \langle s, a \rangle \in \pi, \text{ and } s_i \in proj_i(s), a_i \in proj_i(a)\}$
$proj_i(S)$	$\bigcup_{s_k \in S} proj_i(s_k)$
$proj_i(\{\langle s, s' \rangle\})$	$\bigcup_{s_k \in S}\{\langle proj_i(s), proj_i(s') \rangle\}$
$proj_i(\Sigma_{\pi_i})$	$\langle proj_i(V_{\pi_i}), proj_i(E_{\pi_i}) \rangle$

where τ_j is a special symbol for an empty action, captures a situation in which agents are not allowed to carry out actions concurrently. The corresponding constrained joint state transition relationship is:

$$joint(\{\mathcal{R}_i\}, \beta) = \{\langle s, a, s' \rangle \mid \langle s, a, s' \rangle \in joint(\{\mathcal{R}_i\}), \text{ and } a \models \beta, s \models \beta\}$$

and the corresponding constrained joint policy is:

$$joint(\{\pi_i\}, \beta) = \{\langle s, a, s' \rangle \mid \langle s, a \rangle \in joint(\{\pi_i\}), \text{ and } a \models \beta, s \models \beta\}$$

It is should be noted that in practice we need to be careful exactly how we specify formulae like the constraints β since they can adversely affect the complexity of reducing the the formulae into a form in which they can be fed into the BDD implementation. We will discuss this briefly in Section 8.

5   Policy and Communication

At this point we have a language that is sufficiently rich to construct plans that just involve the physical actions that agents carry out. However, we want to create plans that include communications that permit the necessary sharing of information, so we need to add a dialogue model to the model we already have. As the basis of the dialogue model, we will use the same kind of state space model as we use for the world model. To distinguish the two state transition models, we will denote the models and their elements with subscripts. We write $_{|D}$ to denote elements of the dialogue model, for example, $M_{|D}$ denotes the state transition model for a dialogue and $\mathcal{S}_{|D}$ denotes the states of a dialogue. We write $_{|W}$ to denote elements of the world model, for example, $M_{|W}$ denotes the external world model and $\mathcal{S}_{|W}$ the states of the world. However, when the model is obvious from the context, we will omit the subscripts.

As before, we assume that, in the dialogue, there is a set of n agents which we label as $T_1, T_2, \ldots, T_n$ where each agent T_i has a model of the world

$$\mathcal{M}_{i|W} = \langle \mathcal{P}_{i|W}, \mathcal{S}_{i|W}, \mathcal{A}_{i|W}, \mathcal{R}_{i|W} \rangle$$

for which it has a policy $\pi_{i|W} = \{\langle s_i, a_i \rangle\}$. Given this, a dialogue model is then a state transition system $\mathcal{M}_{|D} = \langle \mathcal{P}_{|D}, \mathcal{S}_{|D}, \mathcal{A}_{|D}, \mathcal{R}_{|D} \rangle$ for which there is a policy for conducting dialogues $\pi_{|D}$. The dialogue language $\mathcal{P}_{|D}$ contains elements from language

$$EXEC(s, a) = \{s' | \langle s, a, s' \rangle \in \mathcal{R}\}$$
$$StatesOf(\pi) = \{s | \langle s, a \rangle \in \pi\}$$
$$GetAction(s, \pi) = \{a | \langle s, a \rangle \in \pi\}$$
$$ComputeWeakPreImage(S) = \{\langle s, a \rangle | Exec(s, a) \wedge S \neq \emptyset\}$$
$$ComputeStrongPreImage(S) = \{\langle s, a \rangle | \emptyset \neq Exec(s, a) \subseteq S\}$$
$$ComputeNextImage(S) = \{s' | Exec(s, a) \wedge S\}$$
$$PrunStates(\pi, S) = \{\langle s, a \rangle \in \pi | s \notin S\}$$

Fig. 1. Operations on transition relations and policies

Table 4. The mapping between set representation and QBF implementation of some transition relation and policy functions

Set representation	QBF implementation
$EXEC(s, a)$	$\xi(s) \wedge \xi(a) \wedge \xi(\mathcal{R})[\boldsymbol{x}'/\boldsymbol{x}]$
$StatesOf(\pi)$	$\exists \boldsymbol{a} \xi(\pi)$
$GetAction(s, \pi)$	$\xi(s) \wedge \xi(\pi)$
$ComputeWeakPreImage(S)$	$\exists \boldsymbol{x}' \xi(S)[\boldsymbol{x}/\boldsymbol{x}'] \wedge \xi(\mathcal{R})$
$ComputeStrongPreImage(S)$	$\forall \boldsymbol{x}'(\xi(\mathcal{R}) \rightarrow \xi(S)[\boldsymbol{x}/\boldsymbol{x}']) \wedge \exists \boldsymbol{x}' \xi(\mathcal{R})$
$ComputeNextImage(S)$	$\exists \boldsymbol{x} \xi(S) \wedge \xi(\mathcal{R})$
$PrunStates(\pi, S)$	$\xi(\pi) \wedge \neg \xi(S)$

$\mathcal{P}_{i|W}$ that individual agents use to describe the world, along with auxiliary language elements such as a proposition to mark the differences between two world states. The dialogue information is induced from $\mathcal{P}_D$. The set of dialogue acts $\mathcal{A}_{|D}$ are those available to the agents. How these dialogues change the information state will be specified by the dialogue state transition relationship of these dialogue acts: $\mathcal{R}_{|D} \subseteq \mathcal{S}_{|D} \times \mathcal{A}_{|D} \times \mathcal{S}_{|D}$. Depending on the specific dialogue, we may distinguish a set of initial dialogue states $I_{|D} \subseteq \mathcal{S}_{|D}$ and a set of goal dialogue states $G_{|D} \subseteq \mathcal{S}_{|D}$ (see [19] for an example).

Definition 4. *Agent T_i's behavior model is a joint model that combines its external world $\langle \mathcal{M}_{i|W}, \pi_{i|W} \rangle$ and its dialogue model $\langle \mathcal{M}_i, \pi_i \rangle = \langle \mathcal{M}_{i|D}, \pi_{i|D} \rangle$ defined as:*

$$\langle \mathcal{M}_i, \pi_i \rangle = \langle joint(\mathcal{M}_{i|W}, \mathcal{M}_{i|D}), joint(\pi_{i|W}, \pi_{i|D}) \rangle.$$

The whole system behavior model is $joint_{\{T_i\}}(\{\langle \mathcal{M}_i, \pi_i \rangle\})$.

As before, a policy for a dialogue, $\pi_{|D} = \{\langle s_{|D}, a_{|D} \rangle\}$, specifies what dialogue action should be taken in a given dialogue state to reach the goal states $G_{|D}$ from the initial states $I_{|D}$ at the least expected cost. To distinguish such policies from the policies that govern an agent's actions in the world, we call the policies that govern an agent's actions in a dialogue a *conversation policy* and a policy that governs an agent's actions in the world a *world policy*.

Before we go on to give the description of the algorithm for executing world and conversation policies, we need to take a look at some properties that capture the interaction between the execution of actions in the world and communication between team members.

Definition 5. *A state-action pair* $\langle s, a \rangle \in \pi_{|W}$ *is called* totally autonomous, *if for every agent* T_i *there is no other* $\langle s'_i, a'_i \rangle \in proj_i(\pi_{|W})$ *such that* $\langle s_i, a_i \rangle \in proj_i(\langle s, a \rangle)$, *and* $s_i = s'_i$ *but* $a_i \neq a'_i$. *A team policy* $\pi_{|W}$ *is called totally autonomous if all its constituent joint state-action pairs are totally autonomous.*

In other words, action-state pairs are totally autonomous if for every agent involved there is no confusion about which action it should take, and when a team policy is totally autonomous an individual agent can choose what it should do based only on local information about the world.

Algorithm 1. Execution of world and conversation policies

1: **procedure** $ExecPolicy(\mathcal{M}_{|W}, \pi_{|W}, \mathcal{M}_{|D}, \pi_{|D})$ {
   (1) $\mathcal{M}_{|W}$: Joint external world model ,
   (2) $\pi_{|W}$: Joint external world policy ,
   (3) $\mathcal{M}_{|D}$: Joint dialogue model ,
   (4) $\pi_{|D}$: Joint dialogue policy }
2: $\mathcal{M}_{i|W} \leftarrow proj_i(\mathcal{M}_{|W})$
3: $\pi_{i|W} \leftarrow proj_i(\pi_{|W})$
4: $\mathcal{M}_{i|D} \leftarrow proj_i(\mathcal{M}_{|D})$
5: $\pi_{i|D} \leftarrow proj_i(\pi_{|D})$
6: $s_{i|W} \leftarrow SenseCurrentState()$
7: $s_{i|D} \leftarrow ReceiveCommunication() \wedge ComputeDialState(s_{i|W} \wedge \pi_{i|W})$
8: **while** $s_{i|W} \in StatesOf(\pi_{i|W}) \vee s_{i|D} \in StatesOf(\pi_{i|D})$ **do**
9:   **if** $|joint(GetAction(s_{i|W}, \pi_{i|W}))| > 1$ **then**
10:     $WorldSA \leftarrow ComputeJointSA(s_{i|D})$
11:     **if** $|WorldSA| = 1$ **then**
12:       $a_{i|W} \leftarrow proj_i(GetAction(WorldSA))$
13:       $Execute(a_{i|W})$
14:     **else**
15:       $a_{i|D} \leftarrow GetAction(s_{i|D}, \pi_{i|D})$
16:       **if** $a_{i|D} \neq \emptyset$ **then**
17:         $Execute(a_{i|D})$ {Communicate to resolve the ambiguity about which action to select}
18:       **else**
19:         $WorldSA \leftarrow RetrieveExternalDecision(WolrdSA)$ {Communication cannot help, ask for external decision}
20:         $s_{i|D} \leftarrow ComputeDialState(WorldSA)$ {Update the external decision into the information state}
21:       **end if**
22:     **end if**
23:   **else**
24:     $a_{i|W} \leftarrow GetAction(s_{i|W}, \pi_{i|W})$
25:     $Execute(a_{i|W})$
26:   **end if**
27:   $s_{i|W} \leftarrow SenseCurrentState()$
28:   $s_{i|D} \leftarrow ReceiveCommunication() \wedge ComputeDialState(s_{i|W} \wedge \pi_{i|W})$
29: **end while**
30: **end procedure**

Definition 6. *A state-action pair $\langle s, a \rangle \in \pi_{|W}$ is called* state communication sufficient, *if there is no other state-action pair $\langle s', a' \rangle \in \pi_{|W}$ such that $s = s'$ but $a \neq a'$. A team policy $\pi_{|W}$ is called a* state communication sufficient *if all its joint state-action pairs are state communication sufficient.*

If a team policy is state communication sufficient it is equivalent to a deterministic joint policy and each individual agent can choose correctly what it should do based only on knowledge of the global state. In other words, with sufficient communication about the global state, each agent knows exactly what to do.

Definition 7. *A state-action pair $\langle s, a \rangle \in \pi_{|W}$ is called a* state and action communication sufficient, *if there is another $\langle s', a' \rangle \in \pi_{|W}$ such that $s = s'$ but $a \neq a'$. A team policy $\pi_{|W}$ is called* state and action communication sufficient *if some of its joint state-action pairs are state and action communication sufficient*

If a team policy is state and action communication sufficient, then it equivalent to a non-deterministic joint policy. In this case, individual agents need to decide what to do during policy execution by picking among the set of all possible actions given by the joint policy, and need to communicate with one another to come to a decision.

Definition 8. *A policy π is called a* out of usage *in a state s if there is no $\langle s, a \rangle \in \pi$.*

If the agents have an out of usage policy they need to replan.

A procedure to execute a combined world policy and conversation policy is given in Algorithm 1. It is adapted from the corresponding procedure in [8] with the addition of steps to execute the conversation policy. It uses the transition operations defined in Figure 1 and assumes that the these operators, as well as the $joint$ and $proj_i$ operations, operate on the world and the dialogue transition model according to the symbols $|W$ and $|D$ respectively. $ComputeDialState$, $ComputeJointSA$ and $Retrieve$ $ExternalDecision$ are application dependent, and define how the dialogue is related to the external world model, as in Section 6. In essence the procedure steps through the world policy, executing the steps of a communication policy when communication is required.

6 Generating Policies

Given the general model of dialogue defined in Section 5, we can define a specific conversation policy which will ensure that the correct information is exchanged during world policy execution. In this section we describe an algorithm for generating policies that combine world policies and conversation policies.

We start by assuming that each agent T_i maintains a model of the external world $\mathcal{M}_{i|W}$ and its finite propositional language $\mathcal{P}_{i|W}$ will depend on the application. T_i's dialogue model $\mathcal{M}_{i|D}$ is based on a propositional language

$$\mathcal{P}_{i,S|D} = \mathcal{P}_{S|W} \cup \mathcal{P}_{A|W} \cup \mathcal{P}_{AL} \cup \mathcal{P}_{CM}$$

where $\mathcal{P}_{AL}$ contains a boolean variable for every variable in $\mathcal{P}_{S|W} \cup \mathcal{P}_{A|W}$ to indicate its validity in dialogue state, $\mathcal{P}_{CM}$ contains a boolean variable for every variable in $\mathcal{P}_{S_i|W} \cup \mathcal{P}_{A_i|W}$ of the agent T_i's (the information T_i can effectively known) to indicate whether its value has been communicated in dialogue state, $j = 1 \ldots N$ and N is the number of agents in the system, and

$$\mathcal{P}_{i,A|D} = \{tell(i, j, x_k, v)\}$$

where $j = 1 \ldots N$, $x_k \in \mathcal{P}_{i|W}$ and $v = \{0, 1\}$. $tell(i, j, x_k, v)$ means that T_i tells T_j that the boolean variable x_k representing some bit of the state and action information is in the value v. We denote variables in $\mathcal{P}_{S_i|D}$ by $x_{i,j,k}$, $lx_{i,j,k}$ and $cx_{i,j,k}$ for T_i's information about T_j on state variable k, about its validity and whether it has been communicated to T_j, and those in $\mathcal{P}_{A_i|D}$ by $y_{i,j,l}$, $ly_{i,j,l}$ and $cy_{i,j,l}$ for T_i's information about T_j on action variable l, its validity and whether it has been communicated to T_j where $j = 1, \ldots, N$, $k = 1 \ldots K = |\mathcal{P}_{S_j}|$ and $l = 1 \ldots L = |\mathcal{P}_{A_j}|$. In total, we have $3N * N * (K + L)$ variables for the dialogue system of the whole team[2].

The mapping between agent T_i's current state and its information state in the dialogue can be described by the (connection) conditions β. For example,

$$\beta(s_{i|W}, s_{i|D}) = \bigwedge_{j=1}^{N} \bigwedge_{k=1}^{K} [vx_{i,j,k} \rightarrow (x_{i,j,k} \leftrightarrow x'_{i,j,k})]$$

where $x_{i,i,k} \in \mathcal{P}_{S_i|W}$ and $x'_{i,i,k} \in \mathcal{P}_{i|D}$. More complex mappings can be defined using representation languages such as a restricted linear time logic or a computation tree logic, representations that are used in the symbolic model checking literature [5].

Similarly, there is a mapping between agent T_i's next action decision and its information state in the dialogue. This mapping can be described by the β condition, for example,

$$\beta(a_{i|W}, s_{i|D}) = \bigwedge_{j=1}^{N} \bigwedge_{l=1}^{L} [vy_{i,j,l} \rightarrow (y_{i,j,l} \leftrightarrow y'_{i,j,l})]$$

where $y_{i,i,l} \in \mathcal{P}_{A_i|W}$ and $y'_{i,i,l} \in \mathcal{P}_{i|D}$. Please note that the above two β conditions depend on the validity variables in the dialogue information states. These validity variables will be initialized by

$$\nu_0(s_{i|D}) = \bigwedge_{k=1}^{K} [vx_{i,i,k}] \wedge \bigwedge_{l=1}^{L} [vy_{i,i,l}].$$

As shown in the dialogue state transitions below, the value of these validity variables will also be changed by the dialogue acts.

---

[2] This can be improved by encoding the indices of $x_{i,j,k}$ and $y_{i,j,l}$ with $logN + logN + logK + logL$ boolean variables, and maintain the information using a relation to map these indices to the values they correspond to.

Using the mappings of states and actions, we can compute a set of initial dialogue states — those that exist before taking into account the effects of any communication — from the fragments of world policy that individual agents possess:

$$ComputeDialState(WorldSA) =$$

$$\exists_{\boldsymbol{x}\in\mathcal{P}_{|W}} \left[WorldSA \wedge \bigwedge_i^N [\beta(s_{i|w}, s_{i,d}) \wedge \beta(a_{i|w}, s_{i|D}) \wedge \nu_0(s_{i|D})] \right],$$

We can also compute a mapping, denoted by $DJMAP$, between the dialogue states and the corresponding fragments of world policy:

$$ComputeDJMAP(DialS, NewWorldSA) =$$
$$\left[DialS \wedge NewWorldSA \wedge \bigwedge_i^N [\beta(s_{i|w}, s_{i,d}) \wedge \beta(a_{i|w}, s_{i|D})] \right]$$

and conversely we can compute a joint external world state and its policy action out of a dialogue state using the $DJMAP$ mapping:

$$ComputeJointSA(s_{i|D}) = \exists_{\boldsymbol{x}\in\mathcal{P}_{|D}\cup\bigcup_j \mathcal{P}_{j\neq i|W}} \left[s_{i|D} \wedge DJMAP \right]$$

The set of dialogue state transitions associated with $\mathcal{A}_{i|D}$ is:

$$\mathcal{R}_{i|D} = \{ \langle x_{i,i,k} = v \wedge cx_{i,j,k} = 0, tell(i, j, x_k, v),$$
$$x_{j,i,k} = v \wedge cx_{i,j,k} = 1 \wedge vx_{i,j,k} = 1 \rangle,$$
$$\langle y_{i,i,l} = v \wedge cy_{i,j,l} = 0, tell(i, j, y_l, v),$$
$$y_{j,i,k} = v \wedge cy_{i,j,k} = 1 \wedge vy_{i,j,k} = 1 \rangle \}$$

For now, we assume that the execution of communication actions will be much faster than that of actions in the external world — for example assuming that communication is carried out on a high speed network while external actions are carried out under the usual limitations of the physical world. This assumptions enables us to be sure that agents can always carry out the necessary communication before performing the external world actions that required the communication. This assumption can be relaxed, however, by adding variables that capture temporal information. This consideration is a topic for our future research.

By adding communication conditions to the nondeterministic planning algorithms proposed in [8], we obtain the communication-aware policy planning algorithm of Algorithm 3. In the algorithm, I will be set to the initial states which the team of agents will start with, and G will be set to the goal states which the team is intended to end up with, and $ComputePreImage$ can be either $ComputeWeakPreImage$ or $ComputeStrongPreImage$ defined in Figure 1 in Section 2, corresponding to the weak and strong solution concepts respectively. Strong acyclic solutions can be similarly constructed following the approaches used in [8] but omitted here for lack of space.

As for dialogue policy synthesis, the set of initial dialogue states can be computed using $ComputeDialState$ from the set of the new world policy segments, $NewSA$, and

---

Algorithm 2. Dialogue goal computation

1: **function** $ComputeDialGoal(NewWorldSA)$ {
    (1) $NewWorldSA$: A new external policy segment,
    (2) $IJMAP$: The global variable holding the dialogue states to world joint states mapping
    }
2:   Set $ComputeNextImage$ to use R_D
3:   $NewDialS \leftarrow ComputeDialState(NewWorldSA)$
4: **repeat**
5:     $DialS \leftarrow NewDialS$
6:     $NewDialS \leftarrow ComputeNextImage(DialS)$
7:     $DJMAP \leftarrow ComputeDJMAP(NewDialS, NewWorldSA)$
8: **until** $DialS = NewDialS \vee GoodExe(DJMAP)$
9: **return** $NewDialS$
10: **end function**

---

the set of dialogue goal states can be computed using the function $ComputeDialGoal$ are defined in Algorithm 2 where the function good for execution is defined as:

$$GoodExec(DJMAP) = [IJMAP \wedge IJMAP[\boldsymbol{x}, \boldsymbol{y}/\boldsymbol{x}', \boldsymbol{y}'] \wedge$$
$$\bigwedge_i^N \left[(\neg \bigwedge_{x_i \in \mathcal{P}_{|W}} (x_i \leftrightarrow x_i')) \wedge (\bigwedge_{y_i \in \mathcal{P}_{|D}} (y_i \leftrightarrow y_i')) \right]]$$
$$\leftrightarrow FALSE$$

which means that the $DJMAP$ has evolved into a mapping table in which different joint world policy items won't be mapped into one dialogue state. The $DJMAP$ table with this $GoodExec$ property can be used by every agent with $ComputeJointSA$ to obtain an unique external state-action pair. However, $ComputeDialGoal$ may return a goal dialogue state without satisfying the $GoodExec$ property. This means that the external policy is non-deterministic, and needs an external decision maker to choose an action.

Theorem 1 (Correctness). *If Algorithm 3 returns a policy π, then π is a weak or a strong solution to achieve the goals G from initial states I. If the algorithm returns $FAIL$, then there is no weak or strong solution.*

Proof. The algorithm does a backward breadth first search from the goal states with $ComputePreImage$ being set to a weak pre-image or a strong pre-image function. There is an additional step of computing dialogue policy to combine information from different agents to determine the current state and an additional action decision so that every agent can determine the next action uniquely. The correctness of the policy computation can be found in work on non-deterministic planning [8]. If the procedure failed, either there is no weak or strong solution to the joint transition model or the dialogue policy synthesis failed. The dialogue policy synthesis is guaranteed to succeed, because in worst case the joint state and additional decision of joint action is fully communicated, and the application of $PruneStates$ in Algorithm 3 and the way in which the dialogue states and $DJMAP$ are constructed in Algorithm 2 guarantees that no two dialogue states will be the same in the dialogue policy, so we avoid conflicting dialogue

Algorithm 3. World policy generation

```
 1: function ComputeWorldPolicy(I, G, ComputePreImage) {
    (1) I: Initial states,
    (2) G: Goal states,
    (3) ComputePreImage : A pre-image function }
 2: DJMAP ← ∅
 3: OldSA ← Fail
 4: SA ← ∅
 5: SA_D ← ∅
 6: while OldSA ≠ SA ∧ I ⊄ (G ∪ StatesOf(SA)) do
 7:     PreImage ← ComputePreImage(G ∪ StatesOf(SA))
 8:     NewSA ← PruneStates(PreImage, G ∪ StatesOf(SA))
 9:     if ∃i|joint(GetAction(proj_i(NewSA)))| > 1 then
10:         I_D ← ComputeDialState(NewSA)
11:         G_D ← ComputeDialGoal(NewSA)
12:         NewSA_D ← ComputePolicy(I_D, G_D, R_D, ComputePreImage)
13:         if NewSA_D = ∅ then
14:             return Fail
15:         end if
16:         SA_D ← SA_D ∪ NewSA_D
17:     end if
18:     OldSA ← SA ∪ NewSA
19: end while
20: if I ⊆ (G ∪ StatesOf(SA)) then
21:     return ⟨SA, SA_D⟩
22: else
23:     return Fail
24: end if
25: end function
```

action prescriptions. Therefore if the procedure to construct a solution fails, it is because there is no weak or strong solution.

7   An Example

Consider the following example, based on the example in [6]. Two agents, one representing an NGO (N) and one representing a peace keeping force (F), are working in a conflict zone. The agents (and the organizations they represent) work independently and have different agendas. N is based at A in Figure 2. F is based at point H. N's goal is to reach D to help the villagers there. F's goal is keeping the peace in general in the area, but it also has to protect N while N is carrying out its work. At any time, with some probability, some disruption may flare up at W. If this happens, only F has the surveillance data to know this is happening, and F must go to W to suppress the disturbance. The routes between different points are shown as arcs in Figure 2. N cannot traverse the routes $(J, W), (W, C), (W, B)$, when there is a disturbance at W, and it is only able to traverse (C, D) and (B, D) without harm when it is accompanied by F.

Algorithm 4. General policy generation

1: **function** $ComputePolicy(I, G, ComputePreImage)$ { (1) I: Initial states,
   (2) G: Goal states,
   (3) $ComputePreImage$: A pre-image function }
2: $OldSA \leftarrow Fail$
3: $SA \leftarrow \emptyset$
4: **while** $OldSA \neq SA \wedge I \nsubseteq (G \cup StatesOf(SA))$ **do**
5:      $PreImage \leftarrow ComputePreImage(G \cup StatesOf(SA))$
6:      $SA \leftarrow PruneStates(PreImage, G \cup StatesOf(SA))$
7:      $OldSA \leftarrow SA \cup SA$
8: **end while**
9: **if** $I \subseteq (G \cup StatesOf(SA))$ **then**
10:     **return** SA
11: **else**
12:     **return** Fail
13: **end if**
14: **end function**

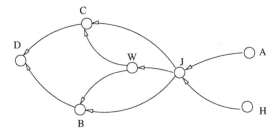

Fig. 2. An NGO team task

N can traverse the rest of the routes independently and F can traverse any route. The goal of the agents is to have N reach D and to have F put down the conflict in W if it happens.

We can formalize this as $\mathcal{P}_{S_N} = \{l_{N,L}\} \cup \{health\}$, $\mathcal{P}_{S_F} = \{l_{F,L}\} \cup \{war\}$, $\mathcal{P}_{A_N} = \{stay_N, move(N, L', L'')\}$, and $\mathcal{P}_{A_F} = \{move(F, L_1, L_2)$ where $L, L', L'' \in \{A, H, J, W, B, C, D\}$, $conflict$ means that there is a disturbance at point W, and $health$ means that N is not harmed.

Initially, $I = l_{N,A} \wedge l_{F,H} \wedge health \wedge (conflict \vee \neg conflict)$. The goal $G = l_{N,D} \wedge \neg conflict \wedge health$. The joint transition model $\mathcal{R}$ for the scenarios is as follows

$$\mathcal{R}_{move} = \langle l_{F,x} \wedge l_{N,y}, move(F, x, x') \wedge move(N, y, y'), l'_{F,x'} \wedge l'_{N,y'} \rangle$$
$$\mathcal{R}_{stay} = \langle TRUE, stay_N, TRUE \rangle \}$$
$$\mathcal{R}_{health} = \langle TRUE, \neg[move(F, B, D)] \wedge move(N, B, D), \neg health \rangle,$$
$$\langle TRUE, \neg[move(F, C, D)] \wedge move(N, C, D), \neg health \rangle,$$

We have additional conditions β_w and $\beta_{agent,route}$:

$$\beta_w = l_{F,W} \rightarrow \neg conflict$$

$$\beta_{F,route} = \bigwedge_{(x,x') \in Route} [l_{F,x} \wedge l'_{F,x'}]$$

$$\beta_{N,route} = \bigwedge_{(x,x') \in Route \setminus \{(J,W),(W,C),(W,B)\}} [l_{N,x} \wedge l'_{N,x'}]$$

where $Route$ is the directed graph of the routes showed in Figure 2. Overall,

$$\mathcal{R} = \mathcal{R}_{action} \wedge \mathcal{R}_{stay} \wedge \mathcal{R}_{health} \wedge \beta_w \wedge \beta_{F,route} \wedge \beta_{N,route}.$$

Algorithm 3 will generate the necessary individual world and dialogue policies. It works backwards from the set G of goal states. G only specifies F's location and the system (1) only allows N to travel to the destination D only if it is accompanied by F, and (2) includes no route from D back to W. This indicates that, at the end of the plan, F must also be in D. Therefore from the desired goal states, the backward chaining search will trace back to the state where either both F and N are in C or both are in B. Rolling back from these two joint states, if there is conflict in W, F must come from W where it can resolve the conflict; otherwise, F can come from either W or J. As for N, no matter whether it is in C or B, it must come from J. Therefore if there is no conflict at W, the algorithm will force F come directly from J (because $PruneStates$ will prune the longer paths). However, when F and N are in both at J (with a conflict at W), the algorithm will produce two valid joint actions: either both going to C or both going to B. Here let's assume one of them, for example F, seeks an external decision to decide the next step, say the result is going to B, then it must communicate the decision with N, so that they can both go to B to guarantee a chance of success. If there is conflict in W, F will go to W to resolve it, while N will reach B. As N and F don't know each other's positions, although they have a valid joint plan, they must communicate with each other so that N knows it will need to stay in B and wait for F to come, and F will know it will need to go to B instead of C. The same kind of communication about positions will be needed for all other locations except A and B where they again can decide by themselves to go to J without needing to communicate with each other.

8   The BDD Implementation

In the above, we have showed the natural connections between set operations on state transitions and their implicit representation using QBF formulae. We are working on an implementation that, like others in the non-deterministic planning world is based on a data structure called a Binary Decision Diagram (BDD) [3] which represents QBF formulae and makes it possible to perform efficient operations over them. A BDD is a rooted directed acyclic graph used to encode the set of truth assignments of a QBF. BDDs guarantee that the basic boolean operations on QBFs can be computed in quadratic time [3,12] as summarized in in Table 5. Other techniques to improve the efficiency are also available [7]. The intuition behind this efficiency is that BDD representation is a form of minimal description of the information encoded — the BDD for

Table 5. The mapping between QBF operators and BDD operators. ξ, ξ_1, ξ_2 are formulae in QBF; $G(\xi), G(\xi_1), G(\xi_2)$ are BDD representations for these formulae; $\| \cdot \|$ is the number of nodes used in the BDDs.

QBF/Set operator	BDD operator	Complexity
$\neg \xi$	$\neg G(\xi)$	$O(\|\xi\|)$
$\exists x_i(\xi)$	$G(\xi_{x_i=0}) \vee G(\xi_{x_i=1})$	$O(\|\xi\|^2)$
$\forall x_i(\xi)$	$G(\xi_{x_i=0}) \wedge G(\xi_{x_i=1})$	$O(\|\xi\|^2)$
$\xi_1 \wedge \xi_2$	$G(\xi_1) \wedge G(\xi_2)$	$O(\|\xi_1\| \cdot \|\xi_2\|)$
$\xi_1 \vee \xi_2$	$G(\xi_1) \vee G(\xi_2)$	$O(\|\xi_1\| \cdot \|\xi_2\|)$
$\xi_1 \rightarrow \xi_2$	$G(\xi_1) \rightarrow G(\xi_2)$	$O(\|\xi_1\| \cdot \|\xi_2\|)$
$|X| = 1$	$Sat\text{-}one(G(\xi(X)))$	$O(|x|)$

a QBF is actually the minimum automaton that accepts the corresponding set of truth assignments with respect to a specific variable ordering [5], and this minimality can be preserved across the basic boolean operations. In this way, the time and space complexity for searching the state space can be reduced exponentially due to the compactness of BDD compared to explicit search techniques. When searching the state space for a fixed point, a key step is to compute the image of a set of states according to the transition relation. During the process, the BDD encoding of the transition relation and the intermediate states may grow very large. Many approaches have been successfully applied to overcome these problems, including early quantification [15], quantification scheduling [7], transition partitioning [4], frontier simplification [11], and state set A^* branching [16].

9   Conclusions

This paper has presented a model of individual and joint action, suitable for describing the behavior of a multiagent team, including communication actions. The model is symbolic, and capable of handling non-deterministic actions. In addition to the model, we have provided procedures for creating joint plans, plans that include the communication necessary for plan execution — that is the detection and communication of information relevant to the execution of the plan. We believe this is the first time that this kind of planning model, drawn from the literature of non-deterministic planning, has been combined with a communication model and then applied to multiagent teams.

As discussed by [21], teamwork requires requires the establishment of joint intentions and the determination of which goals to achieve, the creation of a plan, the sharing of knowledge about the environment in which the team is operating, and the ability to monitor plan execution. While we do not claim that what we have described in this paper is a comprehensive model of teamwork — it is much less powerful and comprehensive than Teamcore [22] or Retsina [20], for example — it marks a useful step towards our overall goal of constructing a model of argumentation-based dialogue that can support many of the important aspects of teamwork. In particular, it deals with planning, albeit in a centralized way, the sharing of information,and a limited form of plan monitoring.

One obvious area of future work is moving from a centralized planning process, which just hands every agent a policy that will help the team achieve its goals, to a decentralized process in which agents can engage in a discussion of the best plan. For that we plan to combine our prior work on argumentation-based planning [23], which assumes a simple, deterministic model of actions, with the work we have described here. Another area of future work, which addresses the main area in which our model falls short of a model of teamwork, is to consider the formation of joint intentions. Here there is a rich vein of work to draw on, for instance [9,14], and we will seek to incorporate this into our model.

Acknowledgments

Research was sponsored by the U.S. Army Research Laboratory and the U.K. Ministry of Defence and was accomplished under Agreement Number W911NF-06-3-0001. The views and conclusions contained in this document are those of the author(s) and should not be interpreted as representing the official policies, either expressed or implied, of the U.S. Army Research Laboratory, the U.S. Government, the U.K. Ministry of Defence or the U.K. Government. The U.S. and U.K. Governments are authorized to reproduce and distribute reprints for Government purposes notwithstanding any copyright notation hereon.

References

1. Boutilier, C., Dean, T., Hanks, S.: Decision-theoretic planning: Structural assumptions and computational leverage. Journal of Artificial Intelligence Research 11, 1–94 (1999)
2. Bratman, M.E., Israel, D.J., Pollack, M.E.: Plans and resource-bounded practical reasoning. Computational Intelligence 4 (1988)
3. Bryant, R.E.: Symbolic boolean manipulation with ordered binary-decision diagrams. ACM Comput. Surv. 24(3), 293–318 (1992)
4. Burch, J.R., Clarke, E.M., Long, D.E.: Symbolic model checking with partitioned transition relations. In: International Conference on Very Large Scale Integration, pp. 49–58. North-Holland, Amsterdam (1991)
5. Burch, J.R., Clarke, E.M., Long, D.E., Mcmillan, K.L., Dill, D.L.: Symbolic model checking for sequential circuit verification. IEEE Transactions on Computer-Aided Design of Integrated Circuits and Systems 13, 401–424 (1994)
6. Burnett, C., Masato, D., McCallum, M., Norman, T.J., Giampapa, J., Kollingbaum, M.J., Sycara, K.: Agent support for mission planning under policy constraints. In: Proceedings of the Second Annual Conference of the ITA. Imperial College, London (2008)
7. Chauhan, P., Clarke, E.M., Jha, S., Kukula, J., Shiple, T., Veith, H., Wang, D.: Non-linear quantification scheduling in image computation. In: ICCAD 2001: Proceedings of the 2001 IEEE/ACM international conference on Computer-aided design, Piscataway, NJ, USA, pp. 293–298. IEEE Press, Los Alamitos (2001)
8. Cimatti, A., Pistore, M., Roveri, M., Traverso, P.: Weak, strong, and strong cyclic planning via symbolic model checking. Artificial Intelligence 147(1-2), 35–84 (2003)
9. Cohen, P., Levesque, H.: Intention is choice with commitment. Artficial Intelligence 42, 213–261 (1990)
10. Cohen, P., Levesque, H.: Teamwork. Nous 25(4) (1991)

11. Coudert, O., Berthet, C., Madre, J.C.: Verification of synchronous sequential machines based on symbolic execution. In: Automatic Verification Methods for Finite State Systems, pp. 365–373 (1989)
12. Coudert, O., Madre, J.C.: The implicit set paradigm: a new approach to finite state system verification. Formal Methods in System Design 6(2), 133–145 (1995)
13. Genesereth, M.R., Ginsberg, M.L., Rosenschein, J.S.: Cooperation without communication. In: Proceedings of the Fifth National Conference on Artificial Intelligence, Philadelphia, PA (1986)
14. Grosz, B., Kraus, S.: The evolution of sharedplans. In: Rao, A., Wooldridge, M. (eds.) Foundations and Theories of Rational Agency. Kluwer, Dordrecht (2003)
15. Hojati, R., Krishnan, S.C., Brayton, R.K.: Early quantification and partitioned transition relations. In: ICCD 1996: Proceedings of the 1996 International Conference on Computer Design, VLSI in Computers and Processors, Washington, DC, USA, pp. 12–19. IEEE Computer Society, Los Alamitos (1996)
16. Jensen, R.M., Veloso, M.M., Bryant, R.E.: State-set branching: Leveraging bdds for heuristic search. Artificial Intelligence 172(2-3), 103–139 (2008)
17. Parsons, S., McBurney, P.: Argumentation-based dialogues for agent coordination. Group Decision and Negotiation 12(5) (2003)
18. Parsons, S., Poltrock, S., Bowyer, H., Tang, Y.: Analysis of a recorded team coordination dialogue. In: Proceedings of the Second Annual Conference of the ITA. Imperial College, London (2008)
19. Sierra, C., Jennings, N.R., Noriega, P., Parsons, S.: A framework for argumentation-based negotiations. In: Rao, A., Singh, M.P., Wooldridge, M.J. (eds.) ATAL 1997. LNCS, vol. 1365, pp. 177–192. Springer, Heidelberg (1998)
20. Sycara, K., Paolucci, M., Giampapa, J., van Velsen, M.: The RETSINA multiagent infrastructure. Journal of Autonomous Agents and Multiagent Systems 7(1) (2003)
21. Sycara, K., Sukthankar, G.: Literature review of teamwork. Technical Report CMU-RI-TR-06-50, Carnegie Mellon University (November 2006)
22. Tambe, M.: Towards flexible teamwork. Journal of Artificial Intelligence Research 7 (1997)
23. Tang, Y., Parsons, S.: Argumentation-based dialogues for deliberation. In: Proceedings of the Fourth International Joint Conference on Autonomous Agents and Multiagent Systems, pp. 552–559. ACM Press, New York (2005)

Practical Reasoning Using Values*

Giving Meaning to Values

T.L. van der Weide, F. Dignum, J.-J.Ch. Meyer,
H. Prakken, and G.A.W. Vreeswijk

University of Utrecht
{tweide,dignum,jj,henry,gv}@cs.uu.nl

Abstract. Each person holds numerous values that represent what is believed to be important. As a result, our values influence our behavior and influence practical reasoning. Various argumentation approaches use values to justify actions, but assume knowledge about whether state transitions promote or demote values. However, this knowledge is typically disputable, since people give different meanings to the same value. This paper proposes an argumentation mechanism to argue about the meaning of an value and thus about whether state transitions promote or demote values. After giving an overview of how values are defined in social psychology, this paper defines values as preference orders and introduces several argument schemes to reason about preferences. These schemes are used to give meaning to values and to determine whether values are promoted or demoted. Furthermore, value systems are used for practical reasoning and allow resolving conflicts when pursuing your values. An example is given of how the new argument schemes can be used to do practical reasoning using values.

1 Introduction

People evaluate and select behavior that maximizes harmony with their values [1,2]. When arguing about what to do, values are used to motivate actions. Recent research [3,4,5] investigates the role of values in argumentation. However, the concept of values is considered to be ambiguous [6,7]. For example, some consider values as goals [2], others as attitudes [8]. One of the aims of this paper is to define the concept of values clearly and to show how it relates to goals as used in the agent literature.

Existing approaches [3,4] assume a function that determines what values are promoted and demoted given a state transition. For example, dropping a friend off at the airport promotes friendship. Whether a value is promoted depends on the meaning that is given to a value. However, what meaning should be given to a value is often disputable [9] and is subject to argumentation.

---

* The research reported here is part of the Interactive Collaborative Information Systems (ICIS) project, supported by the Dutch Ministry of Economic Affairs, grant nr: BSIK03024.

P. McBurney et al. (Eds.): ArgMAS 2009, LNAI 6057, pp. 79–93, 2010.

This papers proposes several argumentation schemes to argue about the meaning to be given to values. Our running example in this paper is a dialogue where values play a significant role. In this dialogue, the values *health* and *fun* play a role. This dialogue is used to illustrate that argumentation concerning values is needed.

Example 1. Consider the following dialogue between A and B:

A1: You should exercise twice a week because it improves your health.
B2: Why is it good for my health?
A3: Because exercise improves your stamina.
B4: But then I might as well go to work by bike.
A5: No, exercising is better for your health.
B6: But exercise is boring.
A7: What is more important: your health or having fun?
B8: I find my health is more important. I guess I should exercise.

In moves A1-A3, we can see a discussion about whether exercise promotes the value of health, which allows B to propose to bike to work in B4. If more aspects of being healthy are considered, the meaning given to the value of being healthy becomes more concise. This allows comparing states from the perspective of a value as seen in move A5. Finally, B6 shows that one cannot always promote all values and priorities between values can be used to solve such conflicts in B8.

This paper is structured as follows. In Section 2, we will illustrate the concept of values by giving definitions of values from social psychology and arguing how values relate to goals as used in the BDI literature. In Section 3, the concepts of perspective and influence between perspectives are introduced. Perspectives are aspects over which an agent may have preferences. Perspectives and influence between perspectives are used to define values. Furthermore, we show how these definitions relate to existing work. Section 5 applies the introduced argument schemes on the running example and we will end the paper with conclusions and future work in Section 6.

2   What Are Values?

The concept of value is considered ambiguous and efforts have been made to clearly define it [6,7]. However, there is a consensus on five common features of values [10]: values are (a) concepts or beliefs, (b) about desirable end states or behaviors, (c) that transcend specific situations, (d) guide selection or evaluation of behavior and events, and (e) are ordered by relative importance. These features have been incorporated by the Schwartz Value Theory (SVT) [2], which is based on [1]. We will use the SVT because it is seen as the state-of-the-art value theory [6].

Values are defined as *desirable trans-situational goals, varying in importance, that serve as guiding principles in the life of a person or other social entity* [2]. This definition will be the basis for our formalization. In the remainder of this section, we will summarize the SVT and compare it to the concept of goals as used in the BDI literature [13,14]. In section 3, we will define values formally.

2.1   Schwartz Value Theory

In [2], ten motivationally distinct broad and basic values are derived from three universal requirements of the human condition: needs of individuals as biological organisms, requisites of coordinated social interaction, and survival and welfare needs of groups. These ten basic values, also called value types, are intended to include all the core values recognized in cultures around the world and are the following: self-direction, stimulation, hedonism, achievement, power, security, conformity, tradition, benevolence, and universalism. Basic values are associated with specific values when promoting the specific value, promotes the central goal of the basic value. For example, the basic value *power* is defined as *social status and prestige, control or dominance over people and resources* and expresses social superiority, esteem, and avoiding or overcoming the threat of uncertainties by controlling relationships and resources. Specific values associated with the *power* basic value are social power, authority, and wealth.

The Schwartz Values Theory explicates dynamic conflict and harmony relations between the ten value types. For example, pursuing the value of being successful (achievement type) typically conflicts with the value of enhancing the welfare of others (universalism type), and pursuing the value of novelty (stimulation type) and change typically conflicts with values of tradition. In contrast, pursuing tradition values is congruent with pursuit of conformity values. Evidence for this theoretical structure has been found in samples from 67 nations [11].

2.2   Interpretation of Schwartz Value Theory

Schwartz defines values as guiding principles. We interpret a guiding principle as a goal that may or may not be achievable, does not change over time, and can be promoted to different degrees. A value is a construct that evaluates states and consequently can be used to evaluate state transitions. Following [3,12], we say that the transition from state s to state t promotes a value when that value is satisfied to a higher degree in t than in s. For example, the value *world peace* is not achievable, but we can say that in one state there is more world peace than in another state. When actions are seen as state transitions, you can evaluate actions by the degree in which your values are promoted. Furthermore, values are relatively stable over time. When someone tries to promote his/her values maximally or in other words, someone acts in order to achieve a state that is evaluated highest from his/her values, we say that his/her values serve as guiding principles.

We interpret a value being *trans-situational* as that a value is not limited in the situations to which they can be applied. Whether you can determine if a state transition promotes a value, does not depend on time, place, or objects. For example, the goal to bring your car to the garage tomorrow is not a value because it specifies a time, (tomorrow) a place (the garage), and an object (your car).

Each person holds numerous values. However, in the pursuit of all values conflicts can arise. We interpret values varying in importance as how people deal with situations of conflicting values. For example, when a person finds honesty more important than success and has to choose between lying to be successful or being honest and not successful, then this person will choose to be honest. A value system helps one to choose between alternatives, resolve conflicts, and make decisions [1].

Schwartz's definition does not state whether the values someone holds have to be consistent. We argue that someone's values have to be consistent, since it seems unrealistic that one finds both v and $\neg v$ important, e.g., people do not value both being healthy and being unhealthy. However, it is possible that someone believes that pursuing a combination of values is impossible. For example, when you believe that success requires lying, you cannot pursue both honesty and success. In this case, promoting one value will typically demote the other.

2.3   Values and Goals

Schwartz defines values as desirable trans-situational goals, but how does Schwartz's use of the concept of goal relate to goals as used in the traditional agent literature? For easy reading, we will call the concept of goals as used in the traditional agent literature *BDI goals*.

In [13,14], artificial agents have desires and BDI goals, both represented as states of the world. The set of desires can be inconsistent, e.g. I desire to be on Hawaii and to be skiing, which is impossible because you cannot be at two places at the same time. The set of BDI goals that an agent adopts must be consistent and achievable, which means that that agent has plans that achieve those BDI goals.

BDI goals are not trans-situational, because when the time, place and objects are not specified, one cannot check whether it is achievable. People do not stop trying to promote their values, so in this respect, values are similar to maintenance goals. For example, if you value honesty, then you want to be honest at all times. In addition, values can be unachievable and vary in importance unlike BDI goals. Consequently, values as defined by Schwartz cannot be represented by goals as defined in the agent literature, since the nature of values is different from the nature of BDI goals.

3   Formalizing Value Systems

Perelman argues in [9] that when people disagree upon a decision, they discuss apropos the applicable rule, the ends to be considered, the meaning to be given to values, the interpretation and characterization of facts. In this section we propose an argumentation mechanism to argue about what meaning should be given to values.

People use their values to evaluate states. However, since values are typically abstract (e.g. fairness or happiness), giving meaning to a value involves interpreting how concrete states relate to abstract values. Concrete interpretations of values are often disputable. For example, although two persons both hold the value of fairness, they may disagree about what they think is fair. What meaning is given to values determines whether actions promote or demote values.

When values are given meaning, people can use their values to compare states by determining the degree to which states satisfy their values. For example, the state in which one does not exercise is less healthy than the state where on exercises once a week, which is unhealthier than the state of exercising twice a week. In [12], a transition from one state to another can either promote, demote or be neutral towards a value.

Following [3,8], we define our notions using states. We assume a set S of states and we will denote single states with s and t. We will also introduce a number of argument schemes and associate critical questions and their corresponding attacks. We will not include critical questions and attacks that are directed at the premises.

In Section 3.1, the notion of perspective is defined and in Section 3.2, we define the notion of influence to give meaning to perspectives. In section 3.3, we will define values and agents' preferences using these notions. We will conclude this section with a small discussion. In Section 4 we will define argument schemes for practical reasoning which builds upon the argument schemes introduced in this section.

3.1   Perspectives

We introduce the notion of *perspective* to denote an aspect of states. We will use perspectives to evaluate states. For example, healthiness, amount of exercise, and fun are aspects of states one can use to evaluate states. We see perspectives as orderings over states. For example, the perspective 'healthiness' orders states by how healthy they are. Since states may satisfy a perspective equally, e.g. two states are just as fun, perspectives are preorders. Furthermore, perspectives are partial preorders because we want to allow that states can be incomparable.

Definition 1 (Perspective). *A perspective p is a partial preorder over states, denoted with $\leq_p$. We will use p, q, r to denote perspectives. When $s \leq_p t$ (with s and t worlds), we say that t is at least as preferred as s from perspective p.*

We can now use perspectives to evaluate aspects of states. Namely, if $s \leq_p t$ is true, then we say that state t is weakly preferred to another state s from perspective p.

Equivalence between states is defined as $s \equiv_p t$ iff $s \leq_p t$ and $t \leq_p s$. When $s \equiv_p t$, we say that s and t are equally preferred from perspective p. The strict order is defined as $s <_p t$ iff $s \leq_p t$ and $\neg(s \equiv_p t)$. When $s <_p t$, we say that t is strictly preferred over s from perspective p.

Example 2. There are four perspectives in our running example 1: exercise (denoted e), health (denoted hl), stamina (denoted st), and fun (denoted f). Furthermore, let exercise twice a week be the state e2w, the current situation be state cur, and biking to work be state bike. Then move A1 claims cur $<_e$ e2w, move B4 claims cur $<_e$ bike, and move A5 claims bike $<_e$ e2w.

3.2   Influence

When we do not know which of two states is preferred from a perspective, then we can try to infer that information. In this way, we give meaning to the perspective. We argue that this is often done in arguments. For example, when discussing whether something is healthy, we use information like exercise has a positive influence on health or that success makes you happy.

To give meaning to a perspective, we introduce the notion of influence. When perspective p positively influences perspective q, then this means that when a state is better from p, then in general, it also is better from q. For example, in general, having success positively influences happiness and in general, being healthy positively influences happiness. In this example, success, health, and happiness are perspectives. Because we say that it is the case in general, we cannot deductively infer more happiness in situations with more success. For example, because that situation may be unhealthy.

Definition 2 (Influence). *We denote that perspective p positively influences perspective q with the notation $p \uparrow q$. Similarly, we denote that p negatively influences q with $p \downarrow q$. The argument scheme to reason with influence is in Table 1.*

Table 1. Argument Scheme to Propagate Influence: ArgInfl

Premise	p positively influences q	$p \uparrow q$
Premise	t is better than s from p	$s <_p t$
Conclusion	t is better than s from q	$s <_q t$

	Critical Question	Attack
Alternative	Is q influenced by other perspectives?	$r \uparrow q$ and $t <_r s$, so $t <_q s$

With the notions of perspective and influence, we can defeasibly infer preferences from a perspective, even when the preferences are specified incompletely. This corresponds to Searle's observation that preference orders are typically not given, but are the product of practical reasoning [15].

Example 3. When we know that state t is preferred to state s from perspective p, i.e. $s <_p t$, and that p positively influence perspective q, i.e. $p \uparrow q$, then we do not know whether t is preferred to s from q, i.e. $s <_q t$. However, we can construct an argument using argument scheme ArgInfl as follows:

$$\frac{s <_p t \quad p \uparrow q}{s <_q t} \text{ ArgInfl} \tag{1}$$

When we would also know that perspective r positively influences q, but that s is preferred to t from r, then in the same way, we can use ArgInfl to construct an argument that rebuts the previous one. When arguments conflict with each other, argumentation frameworks can be used to determine which argument defeats the other, for example because one argument is stronger or preferred.

Example 4. In our running example, move A1 states that exercise positively influences health, i.e. $e \uparrow h$ and that B would exercise more when exercising twice a week, i.e. $\text{cur} <_e \text{e2w}$. These two statements are used to conclude that exercising twice a week is better for B's health. Furthermore, move A3 states that exercise improves stamina, i.e. $e \uparrow st$, and that stamina improves health, i.e. $st \uparrow h$. This is used to explain why exercise improves health.

When influence is chained, e.g. $p \uparrow q$ and $q \uparrow r$, we can still infer preferences, namely that p positively influences r, i.e. $p \uparrow r$. This allows us to explain influence. For example, if someone does not understand why exercise positively influence health, we can explain that exercise positively influences stamina and that stamina positively influences health.

Definition 3 (Chained Influence). *The argument scheme that chains influence is in table 2, but because there are 4 possibilities, table 2 only shows the structure. The specific argument schemes are as follows:*

$$\frac{p \uparrow q \quad q \uparrow r}{p \uparrow r} \qquad \frac{p \downarrow q \quad q \downarrow r}{p \uparrow r} \qquad \frac{p \uparrow q \quad q \downarrow r}{p \downarrow r} \qquad \frac{p \downarrow q \quad q \uparrow r}{p \downarrow r} \qquad (2)$$

Table 2. Argument Scheme to Chain Influence: Chn

Premise	p has a positive/negative influence on q	$p \uparrow q$ or $p \downarrow q$
Premise	q has a positive/negative influence on r	$q \uparrow r$ or $q \downarrow r$
Conclusion	p has a positive/negative influence on r	$p \uparrow r$ or $p \downarrow r$
	Critical Question	Attack
Alternative	Does p influence other perspectives that influence r?	E.g. $p \uparrow q_2$ and $q_2 \downarrow r$, so $p \downarrow r$

We can see influence between perspectives as a directed graph, where the edges are labeled with whether the influence is positive or negative.

When a cycle only contains edges of positive influence, e.g. health positively influences happiness and happiness positively influences health, then we can chain the cycle's influences into a single influence, i.e. $p \uparrow p$. This is not contradictory. When a cycle contains an even amount of negative edges, then chaining will result in $p \uparrow p$.

A cycle consisting of an uneven amount of negative edges results in $p \downarrow p$ after chaining, which is inconsistent. For example, if happiness negatively influences happiness $(p \downarrow p)$, then from more happiness you can conclude less happiness. When someone uses such inconsistent information, then you can attack his argument by using this inconsistency.

3.3   Agent's Preferences and Values

Searle argues that typically preference orders are not given, but are the product of practical reasoning [15]. We agree and argue that values play an important role when reasoning about preferences. Before defining values, we define an agent's preferences over states as follows.

Definition 4 (Agent's Preferences). *The preferences over states of agent α are modelled as a perspective denoted with $<_\alpha$, i.e. a preorder over states.*

When $s <_\alpha t$, we say that agent α prefers state t to state s or that state t is preferred to s from α's perspective.

Agents use the values they hold to evaluate and compare states. We use the predicate values(α, v), with α an agent and v a perspective, to denote that agent α holds the value to improve with respect to perspective v. We see the values of an agent as fundamental, i.e. agents cannot justify their values. Agent α's values is a set of perspectives V_α such that each value positively influences α's preference and for each value v the predicate values(α, v) holds.

If an agent α values perspective p, then p positively influences α's preferences, i.e. $p \uparrow \alpha$. If a perspective p positively influences an agent's preferences, then the agent does not need to hold the value to improve upon p, since p may indirectly influence α's preferences through one of α's values. In this case, the perspective is a means to promote one of α's (fundamental) values.

Table 3 contains an argument scheme to conclude that a perspective positively influences an agent's preferences if that agent values that perspective.

Table 3. Argument Scheme Value: Val

Premise	Agent α values perspective v	values(α, v)
Conclusion	v positively influences α's preferences	$v \uparrow \alpha$

We can now define when a state transition promotes or demotes a value as follows.

Definition 5 (Promoting/Demoting Values). *We say that the state transition from s to t promotes value v when $s <_v t$ and demotes v when $t <_v s$.*

Agents can now use their values to reason about what state is preferred. Although values are typically not defined on every pair of states, we can now use other perspectives and their influence on values to determine what is preferred.

Example 5. In our running example, there are two values: health and fun. A argues that B should act such that B's health is improved. Consequently, health is used as a guiding principle. Similarly, B argues that exercise is no fun (or in other words, exercise negatively influences fun), and that therefore B should not exercise, making fun a guiding principle.

3.4   Value Systems

When an agent reasons about what state is preferred, it can be the case that a state transition promotes some values and demotes other values. In this case, there is a conflict and we need a way to deal with this conflict.

Value systems can be used to resolve conflicts. Rokeach describes the notion of *value system* as follows [1]:

> A value system is a learned organization of principles and rules to help one choose between alternatives, resolve conflicts, and make decisions.

Inspired by [4], we will define a value system as a preference order on sets of values. For example, someone may prefer promoting happiness to promoting health, and even prefers promoting happiness to promoting equality and health. With such a value system, we can resolve several kinds of conflicts. Since a state transition either promotes, demotes or is neutral to a value, we need to work with sets of promoted and demoted values instead of saying that the demoted is the complement of the promoted values. Before we define a value system, we first need to determine what values are promoted and demoted by a state transition.

Definition 6 (Promoted Values). *The function pro* $: S \times S \to 2^V$ *determines the values promoted by the transition from one state to the other. This function works as follows:* $pro(s,t) = \{v \in V_\alpha | s <_v t\}$. *When* $pro(s,t) = V$, *we say that the transition from s to t promotes values V.*

Using the pro function, we can determine the demoted values as follows.

Definition 7 (Demoted Values). *The function dem* $: S \times S \to 2^V$ *determines the values demoted by the transition from one state to the other. This function works as follows:* $dem(s,t) = pro(t,s) = \{v \in V_\alpha | t <_v s\}$. *When* $dem(s,t) = V$, *we say that the transition from s to t demotes values V.*

When a state transition neither promotes nor demotes a value, e.g. $v \notin (dem(s,t) \cup pro(s,t))$, we say that that state transition is neutral from that value. This approach is basically the same as the approach in [12], where the function δ maps a state transition and a value to either promote, demote or neutral.

Next, we define value systems, which can be used to resolve value conflicts, e.g. a transition promotes one value and demotes another.

Definition 8 (Value System). *A value system is a preorder on sets of values. Agent* α*'s value system is denoted with the operator* $\prec_\alpha$. *When* $W \prec_\alpha V$, *we say that agent* α *prefers promoting set of values V to promoting set of values W. The argument scheme associated with value systems is in table 4.*

Table 4. Argument Scheme Value System: VS

Premise	the transition from s to t promotes V	$pro(s,t) = V$
Premise	the transition from s to t demotes W	$dem(s,t) = W$
Premise	α prefers V to W	$W \prec_\alpha V$
Conclusion	α prefers t to s	$s <_\alpha t$

We assume that people always prefer to promote maximal sets (regarding set inclusion), so when $V \subset W$ and $V, W \in V_\alpha$, then $V \prec_\alpha W$.

Example 6. Agent α's values are $V_\alpha = \{v, w\}$. When α prefers promoting value w to promoting value v, α's value system contains $\{v\} \prec_\alpha \{w\}$. The argument scheme about value systems can then be applied as follows.

$$\frac{\mathrm{pro}(s,t) = \{v\} \quad \mathrm{dem}(s,t) = \{w\} \quad \{v\} \prec_\alpha \{w\}}{s <_\alpha t} \; \mathrm{VS} \qquad (3)$$

Example 7. In move A7 of our running example, player A asks B whether B prefers health or fun. B then states that $\{\mathrm{fun}\} \prec_\alpha \{h\}$. Consequently, B should prefer transitions that promote h and demotes fun to the transition the only promotes *fun*.

3.5   Discussion

In [9], Perelman distinguishes between abstract values, e.g. justice or truth, and concrete values, e.g. France or the Church. Concrete values are seen as being attached to living beings, specific groups, or particular objects, considered as a unique entity. Furthermore, concrete values are often used to justify abstract values and the other way around. For example, justice is important (abstract value), because you do not want people to be stealing (concrete value) and France (concrete value) is good because there is justice (abstract value). How Perelman's notions of abstract and concrete values relate to Schwartz's notions of value types and values needs further investigation. This paper uses Schwartz's notions.

Influence is now defined abstractly and ignores whether the influence is causal, a correlation, or a definition. For example, that physical health has a positive influence on health is because of the definition of *health*. On the other hand, that exercise has a positive influence on stamina is a causal relation. The difference is that one can explain causal relations, whereas one can only explain definitions by referring to a dictionary. Consequently, one could refine the argument schemes introduced in this section by distinguishing between kinds of influence. Different critical questions can be associated with causal influence and definitional influence.

We could see an agent's preferences, its values and the perspectives that influence its values as a directed graph with as top nodes an agent's preference, the layer below that agent's values, and below the perspectives and values that influence the agent's values. This directed graph could be seen as a value hierarchy.

For example, in figure 1 boxes denote perspectives, grey boxes denote perspectives that are values, an arrow from perspective p to perspective q denotes that p positively influences q, and dotted arrows denote negative influence. Here, agent a values health, fun, and conformity. Valuing conformity means that one finds it important to comply with standards, rules, or laws. Being self-disciplined and obedient positively influence conformity. In this example however, a also values self-discipline and obedience meaning that a sees them as guiding principles,

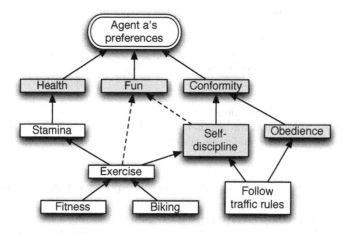

Fig. 1. Example Visualization of an Agent a's Values

which makes those perspectives desirable ends rather than means to an end. On the other hand, *exercise* is not a value, which means that a does not think exercise is important on its own, but only because it positively influences health. In other words, if a would be asked why exercise is important, a would say because it is good for a's health, whereas if a would be asked why health is important, a would perhaps say because it improves a quality of life.

We could have drawn an inference link between self-discipline and agent a's preferences, but this link is implicitly there through chaining.

4   Practical Reasoning with Values

Many factors like values, emotions, needs, attitudes, or habit can influence behavior significantly. In certain situations, values play a significant role when reasoning about what to do. To argue about such situations, argument schemes are needed that incorporate values into practical reasoning.

In [3], Atkinson incorporates values into practical reasoning by extending Walton's sufficient condition scheme [16] (*G is a goal for agent α, doing action A is sufficient for α to achieve G, therefore α ought to do action A*) as follows: *in the current circumstances, action A should be performed to bring about circumstances in which goal G is achieved, as this promotes value V.*

We alter Atkinson's scheme by replacing the values and goal premise by a more general premise about that the agent prefers one state to the other. An agent's values can be used to determine the agent's preferences between states. In table 5 we define an argument scheme to conclude that one should take an action.

Because we developed separate argument schemes in section 3 to conclude what is preferred, we can use this basic argument scheme and combine it with

Table 5. Argument Scheme Intention: Intend

Premise	The current state is s	$holds(s)$
Premise	Performing action a results in state t	$results(a, s, t)$
Premise	Agent α prefers t to s	$s <_\alpha t$
Conclusion	α should perform a	$shouldIntend(\alpha, a)$
	Critical Question	Attack
Alternative	Can α perform another action that results in a more preferable state?	$results(b, s, t_2)$ and $t <_\alpha t_2$

the other argument schemes to get the same expressive power as Atkinson's argument scheme.

For example, one could incorporate (BDI) goals by adding a scheme like: *Agent α has goal G, G is achieved in state s, G is not achieved in state t, therefore, α prefers s to t.* Furthermore, a scheme to generate goals can be added, for example: *Current state is s, agent α prefers state t to s, therefore, α should adopt the goal to achieve t.* This scheme can be extended to allow only realistic goals, i.e. goals for which one has a (realistic) plan, by adding the premise *α has a plan to achieve t.*

5   Running Example

In this section we will use example 1 from section 1 to show how to use the argument schemes as defined previously.

Player A starts the dialogue by suggesting B to exercise twice a week, since it will improve B's health. Implicitly, A is saying that exercising twice a week is better for B's health than what B is doing now and A is also assuming that B values health. Consequently, A gives the following argument (where cur is the current state, e2w is the state where B exercises twice a week, e is the exercise perspective, hl is the health perspective, and a is the action that B starts exercising twice a week):

$$\cfrac{holds(\mathtt{cur}) \quad results(a, \mathtt{cur}, \mathtt{e2w}) \quad \cfrac{\cfrac{\mathtt{cur} <_e \mathtt{e2w} \quad e \uparrow hl}{\mathtt{cur} <_{hl} \mathtt{e2w}}\ \text{Infl} \quad \cfrac{values(B, hl)}{hl \uparrow B}\ \text{Val}}{\mathtt{cur} <_B \mathtt{e2w}}\ \text{Infl}}{shouldIntend(B, a)}\ \text{Intend}$$

$$(4)$$

Next, B asks A for explanation for why exercise is good for B's health. In other words, B asks why the premise $e \uparrow hl$ is true. A answers B's question by claiming:

$$\frac{e \uparrow \mathtt{st} \quad s \uparrow hl}{e \uparrow hl}\ \text{Chn}$$

$$(5)$$

Now B understand and claims that he can also bike to work, called action b, which will also improve health:

$$\frac{holds(\texttt{cur}) \quad results(b, \texttt{cur}, \texttt{bike}) \quad \dfrac{\dfrac{\texttt{cur} <_e \texttt{bike} \quad e \uparrow hl}{\texttt{cur} <_{hl} \texttt{bike}} \text{ Infl} \quad \dfrac{\dfrac{\text{values}(B, hl)}{hl \uparrow B} \text{ Val}}{\texttt{cur} <_B \texttt{bike}} \text{ Infl}}{\texttt{cur} <_B \texttt{bike}} \text{ Intend}}{shouldIntend(B, b)}$$

$$(6)$$

However, A does not agree since biking to work is less healthy than exercising twice a week. A attacks B's use of the *Intend* argument scheme by giving an alternative action that is better:

$$\frac{results(b, \texttt{cur}, \texttt{e2w}) \quad \dfrac{\texttt{bike} <_{hl} \texttt{e2w} \quad \dfrac{\dfrac{\text{values}(B, hl)}{hl \uparrow B} \text{ Val}}{\text{Infl}}}{\texttt{bike} <_B \texttt{e2w}} \text{ Alternative}}{\neg\text{Intend}}$$

$$(7)$$

B does not respond to this claim and rebuts one of the premises of A's original claim by claiming that exercising is boring:

$$\frac{\texttt{e2w} <_{fun} \texttt{cur} \quad \dfrac{\dfrac{\text{values}(B, \text{fun})}{\text{fun} \uparrow B} \text{ Val}}{}}{\texttt{e2w} <_B \texttt{cur}} \text{ Infl}$$

$$(8)$$

We now have two arguments that rebut each other. Depending on B's value priorities, one argument will win. A responds by asking B whether he finds fun or health more important. B responds that health is more important than fun.

$$\frac{\text{pro}(\texttt{cur}, \texttt{e2w}) = \{hl\} \quad \text{dem}(\texttt{cur}, \texttt{e2w}) = \{\text{fun}\} \quad \{\text{fun}\} \prec_B \{hl\}}{\texttt{cur} <_B \texttt{e2w}} \text{ VS}$$

$$(9)$$

In the latter part of the dialogue, an argument is built to conclude that B should prefer exercising based on B's values. This argument takes into account B's value system and arguments concerning promotion and demotion of the values health and fun. However, this does not mean that B has to agree that he should exercise twice a week rather than biking to work, since it depends on how B accrues the arguments pro and con.

6   Conclusions

In this paper, we have introduced several argument schemes for practical reasoning and to reason about whether values are promoted. First, we have clarified the notion of values using social psychology literature. Next, we have introduced the notions of perspective and influence. Perspectives are defined as preorders on states. Values are then defined as perspectives that people use to evaluate and select actions. When it is not known what state is better from the perspective of a value, information about the influence between value perspectives and other perspectives is used to argue what state is better. Value systems are introduced to help resolve conflicts between values during the pursuit of values. Finally, we show how we can now do practical reasoning using this approach.

Our contribution in this paper allows arguments about what values mean, which is important according to Perelman [9]. Furthermore, our approach allows value preference orders to be incompletely specified, since we can reason about whether a state is better from the perspective of a value. This enables reasoning about preference orders, which is considered important by Searle [15].

6.1   Future Work

Our first step will be to fully formalize these argument schemes and to build an argumentation framework that allows accruing influence. Interesting extensions are to incorporate certainty of arguments, a distance measure between states from a perspective, e.g. s is much healthier than t, and the size of influence, e.g. exercising a bit more increases health significantly. Rather than having to completely specify a value system, we also think that using our perspective approach allows reasoning about value systems.

In [2], ten motivationally distinct value types are derived in order to be comprehensive of the core values recognized in cultures around the world. For each value type, several examples of values are given. We could formalize these ten value types by seeing them as values and we could start by using the example values as perspectives that positively influence the value types. Since these value types are shown to hold universally, having a model of these value types and the most common values, would give argumentation systems a useful general model to argue about values.

Furthermore, the Schwartz Values Theory explicates dynamic conflict and harmony relations between values. For example, pursuing the value of being successful typically conflicts with the value of enhancing the welfare of others and pursuing the value of novelty and change typically conflicts with values of tradition. In contrast, pursuing tradition values is congruent with pursuit of conformity values. Such relations between values could be represented as either positive or negative influence. However, in order to use this negative influence in argumentation, we need to explain why it is a negative influence. This may be case-dependent and thus requires a more thorough model.

References

1. Rokeach, M.: The nature of human values. Free Press, New York (1973)
2. Schwartz, S.: Universals in the content and structure of values: theoretical advances and empirical tests in 20 countries. Advances in experimental social psychology 25, 1–65 (1992)
3. Atkinson, K., Bench-Capon, T., McBurney, P.: Computational representation of practical argument. Synthese 152(2), 157–206 (2006)

4. Bench-Capon, T.: Persuasion in practical argument using value-based argumentation frameworks. Journal of Logic and Computation 13(3), 429–448 (2003)
5. Grasso, F., Cawsey, A., Jones, R.: Dialectical argumentation to solve conflicts in advice giving: A case study in the promotion of healthy nutrition. International Journal of Human-Computers Studies 53(6), 1077–1115 (2000)
6. Rohan, M.: A rose by any name? the values construct. Personality and Social Psychology Review 4(3), 255–277 (2000)
7. Castelfranchi, C., Miceli, M.: A cogntivie approach to values. Journal for the Theory of Social Behaviour 19(2), 170–193 (1989)
8. Atkinson, K., Bench-Capon, T.: Addressing moral problems through practical reasoning. Journal of Applied Logic 6(2), 135–151 (2008); Selected papers from the 8th International Workshop on Deontic Logic in Computer Science
9. Perelman, C., Olbrechts-Tyteca, L.: The New Rhetoric: A Treatise on Argumentation. University of Notre Dame Press (1969)
10. Schwartz, S., Bilsky, W.: Toward a universal psychological structure of human values. Journal of Personality and Social Psychology 53(3), 550–562 (1987)
11. Schwartz, S.: Robustness and fruitfulness of a theory of universals in individual values. Valores e trabalho (Values and work). Editora Universidade de Brasilia, Brasilia, pp. 56–95 (2005) (Téż manuskript, 2003b)
12. Atkinson, K., Bench-Capon, T.: Practical reasoning as presumptive argumentation using action based alternating transition systems. Artificial Intelligence 171(10-15), 855–874 (2007)
13. Cohen, P., Levesque, H.: Intention is choice with commitment. Artificial Intelligence 42(2-3), 213–261 (1990)
14. Rao, A.S., Georgeff, M.P.: Modeling rational agents within a bdi-architecture, pp. 473–484 (1991)
15. Searle, J.R.: Rationality in Action. Bradford Books (2001)
16. Walton, D.: Argumentation Schemes for Presumptive Reasoning. Lawrence Erlbaum Associates, Mahwah (1996)

Strategic Argumentation
in Rigorous Persuasion Dialogue

Joseph Devereux and Chris Reed

School of Computing, University of Dundee, Dundee, DD1 4HN, UK
{josephdevereux,chris}@computing.dundee.ac.uk

Abstract. Philosophical dialogue games have been used widely as models for protocols in multi-agent systems to improve flexibility, expressiveness, robustness and efficiency. However, many dialogue games are effectively based on propositional logic, which is not always sufficiently expressive for artificial reasoning. In particular they do not allow for a strong connection between computational models of dialogic argument and mature mathematical models of abstract argument structures, which support a range of sophisticated agent reasoning systems. In this paper we describe how an existing dialogue game — Walton & Krabbe's RPD_0 — may be adapted by using Dung Argumentation Frameworks in place of propositional logic. We call this new dialogue game RPD_{GD}, and describe some of its advantages over RPD_0, chiefly (i) that it allows the proponent to win by exploiting not just defects in the opponent's reasoning or inconsistency in its knowledge base, but also the incompleteness of its knowledge; and (ii) that it thus provides wider scope for strategic sophistication in multi-agent dialogue. We make two linked observations relating to strategy in RPD_{GD} dialogues — first, that there are minimal sets of beliefs that one agent must hold, in order to know (assuming the correctness of those beliefs) whether it can successfully persuade another; and second, that the would-be persuader may regulate its utterances, in order to avoid acquiring at least some of the information which is outside these minimal amounts and thus irrelevant. We consider these observations using the concepts *Minimum Sufficient Contextual Knowledge (MSCK)* and *fortification* respectively. We demonstrate that in even very simple situations a strategy informed by these concepts can mean the difference between winning and losing a given encounter.

1 Introduction

Dialogue games have been attracting more and more interest in multi-agent systems during recent years [1], as the philosophical questions which motivated their development overlap broadly with practical questions which arise in inter-agent communication. Dialogue games are concerned generally with enforcing standards of dialogic argumentation, and are typically defined by unambiguous rules to which a player's adherence is externally verifiable. The standards in some cases refer merely to logical coherence, but there are also games with

P. McBurney et al. (Eds.): ArgMAS 2009, LNAI 6057, pp. 94–113, 2010.

more restrictive standards, designed to exclude dialogic behaviour that is generally unhelpful (but not necessarily illogical), or tailored to a particular sort of goal-directed dialogue (such as persuasion dialogue). Thus dialogue games are a promising approach to the regulation of interactive behaviour, either in general or in narrower goal-oriented contexts.

Here we adapt Walton & Krabbe's RPD_0 [2] to define the game RPD_{GD}. Whereas RPD_0 is based on propositional logic, RPD_{GD} is based on Dung Argumentation Frameworks ($DAFs$) [3], and one of our main concerns is to show how $DAFs$ allow much wider scope for strategic sophistication relative to propositional logic. We regard a *strategy* as a player's approach to making decisions required for gameplay. *Strategic sophistication* exists (variously) in all strategies except the simple strategy, whereby all decisions are made by random choice.

We proceed (i) to summarise RPD_0; (ii) to describe RPD_{GD} and its advantages over RPD_0 in general; (iii) to demonstrate in particular the greater scope offered by RPD_{GD} for strategic sophistication, (iv) to compare related work; and (v) to emphasise some general conclusions.

2 RPD_0

RPD_0 is a protocol for *Rigorous Persuasion Dialogue*, intended to capture dialogues in which relevance is enforced by close restrictions on roles, commitment-withdrawal and choice of moves. Such dialogues involve a *proponent* and an *opponent* (of a proposal), and their rigour consists mainly in restrictions imposed on the opponent, whose role is purely responsive. The opponent has simply to challenge or to concede the proponent's assertions, incurring irrevocable commitments as it does so. The proponent, while also restricted in its moves, always has the initiative, and rigorous persuasion dialogue is essentially a matter of the proponent extracting commitments from the opponent. The opponent's commitments are very important, because the opponent may lose not only by conceding the proposal, but also by lapsing into inconsistency — by challenging (or conceding the complement of) a proposition to which it is already committed. Because RPD_0 is based on propositional logic, inconsistency implies everything, including the proposal.

The opponent is committed to whatever it concedes, and may also incur commitment through its challenges. If the opponent challenges only part of the proposal, the proponent may ascertain exactly where disagreement lies, and perhaps thereby induce a concession. Alternatively the proponent may question the opponent on its commitments, and thereby induce challenges or concessions. Otherwise the proponent may expand the dialogue's scope, by quizzing the opponent on altogether new theses. Such *free questions* must be accompanied by assertions of the corresponding theses, and thus the opponent must reply by either conceding or challenging the theses. Only a limited number of free questions may be asked.

The limitation of free questions encourages strategic sophistication, because when the quota is exhausted, the proponent has only the opponent's commitments and challenges to work with, and thus scope for further dialogue is constrained. Beyond this, however, RPD_0 offers very little scope for strategic sophistication, because it is founded on propositional logic. Thus for each of the proponent's assertions, the opponent may determine how the assertion relates to its beliefs, and thereby avoid challenging the assertion (if it is implied) or conceding it (if it is inconsistent). Such consistency-enforcement is uncommon in the human dialogues for which RPD_0 was designed, but could be the norm in a computational society. Furthermore, even if the opponent could not perfectly manage its knowledge base (KB), the proponent's scope for strategic sophistication would not be very much greater. The proponent might then follow strategies to *quicken* the process of either (i) finding existing inconsistency in the opponent's KB or (ii) 'tricking' the opponent into inconsistency by exploiting its defective reasoning. However, without limitation on the number of free questions, such strategies would affect merely the timing of the result. Though this could, in realistic implementations, alone justify the development of strategic reasoning; we are here interested in a broader strategic purview.

3 RPD_{GD}

One way of amending RPD_0 to enhance the scope for strategic sophistication is to replace the underlying logic with a nonmonotonic formalism. RPD_{GD} shows how this could be done, as its underlying logic is provided by Dung Argumentation Frameworks (*DAF*s) interpreted according to the grounded semantics [3]. Dung's is one of the best-known argument-based nonmonotonic formalisms, while the grounded semantics is one of the simplest of its semantics.

A *DAF* is a pair $\langle AR, attacks \rangle$, where AR is a set of abstract *arguments*, and *attacks* is a binary relation on AR defining attacks between arguments. Arguments may thus form chains linked by the attacks relation, and for any such chain $a_n \rightharpoonup a_{n-1} \rightharpoonup \ldots \rightharpoonup a_0$, odd-numbered and even-numbered arguments *indirectly attack* and *indirectly defend* a_0 respectively.

*DAF*s may be used as simple KBs for agents, and the grounded semantics is a simple means of interpreting such KBs to identify beliefs. The grounded semantics identifies a subset of a *DAF*'s arguments as its *grounded extension*. The grounded extension is defined by a recursive function, whereby the *DAF* is searched repeatedly for arguments whose attackers are all attacked by arguments found in previous searches. Thus first all unattacked arguments are found; then all arguments defended against all attackers by those unattacked arguments; and so on until the search which finds no new arguments. Thus every *DAF* has one and no more than one grounded extension, and an agent's beliefs may be defined unambiguously as the grounded extension of its KB.

RPD_{GD} aims to remain as close as possible to the specification of RPD_0 whilst making full use of the underlying *DAF*-based logic. The main differences are necessary to accommodate the different logic, or have been included to take advantage of obvious new possibilities which it offers. The most important differences involve negation, implication and questions. Negation is excluded as useless, as the arguments of a DAF are abstract entities, defined wholly by the attacks relation. Implication does not exist in DAFs either, but we identify the *indirect defence* relation as a useful, partial equivalent — with the difference that indirect defence can be interpreted as a type of weak, defeasible, contextual implication, in contrast to the guaranteed universal implication of propositional logic. Questions are more diverse in RPD_{GD}, as the protocol includes the new *inquiry* locution-type, with which the proponent may simply inquire about the opponent's KB, without either referring to the opponent's commitments or simultaneously asserting the content of the question (cf. *bound* and *free* questions in RPD_0). In RPD_0 such inquiries would be less useful, because (as will be shown) information acquired thereby could not help the proponent, unless the opponent's reasoning was defective.

Let $\mathcal{L}$ be a simple DAF-language corresponding to the propositional-logical-language used in RPD_0. An atomic sentence in $\mathcal{L}$ is an argument. Conjunctions $(S \wedge S')$ and (inclusive) disjunctions $(S \vee S')$ of sentences are also sentences. Corresponding to the implication-sentences in RPD_0 are the defence-implication sentences of the form $m \Rightarrow n$, where '$\Rightarrow$' indicates 'indirectly defends' and m and n are arguments. Finally there are the attack sentences of the form $m \rightarrow n$, where '$\rightarrow$' indicates 'attacks' and m and n are arguments as before.

RPD_{GD} may now be specified after the model of RPD_0 (cf. [2, pp158-161]). Italic capital letters represent ground formulas of $\mathcal{L}$, and italic lower-case letters represent arguments, except where otherwise stated.

Locution Rules

1. Permitted Locutions are of the following types:
   (a) *Statement*: $A!$ (A is either a ground formula of $\mathcal{L}$ or $\emptyset$. The proponent only *asserts* statements (makes *assertions*), while the opponent only *concedes* statements (makes *concessions*). The $\emptyset$-statement expresses ignorance or disbelief and may be used only by the opponent. A concession is made in response to the proponent, but the conceded sentence need not have been asserted by the proponent.)
   (b) *Challenge*: $(A \vee B)??$ (A challenge to a disjunction.)
   (c) *Challenge*: $A??$ (A is a ground formula which is either atomic, or of the form $m \rightarrow n$, or of the form $m \Rightarrow n$.)
   (d) *Challenge*: $(A \wedge B)??A?$ (A challenge to one half of a conjunction.)
   (e) *Challenge*: $(A \wedge B)??B?$ (A challenge to the other half of a conjunction.)
   (f) *Questions — Bound Questions*:
       Bound questions are bound in the sense that they refer to commitments of the opponent.
       i. $(A \vee B)?$ (A question referring to a disjunction.)
       ii. $(A \wedge B)?A?$ (A question referring to one half of a conjunction.)
       iii. $(A \wedge B)?B?$ (A question referring to the other half of a conjunction.)
       iv. $(m \Rightarrow n)?m!$ (A question referring to a defence-implication and accompanied by an assertion, the assertion being intended to elicit a concession — see Table 2.)

(g) *Questions — Free Questions*: $A?, A!$ (A question accompanied by an assertion; the opponent must either challenge or concede the assertion.)

(h) *Questions — Inquiries — $A???$* (An unaccompanied question. A may be a ground or non-ground formula in $\mathcal{L}$.)

(i) *Final Remarks*
  i. *I give up!*
  ii. *You said so yourself!*
  iii. *Your position is absurd!*

2. Each move is the utterance of a single locution.

Commitment Rules

1. The opponent has a commitment store—henceforth C_O — which is a (perhaps empty) set of ground formulas of $\mathcal{L}$. Whenever the opponent concedes a formula, that formula is added to C_O.

2. Each bound question refers to an element of C_O.

3. If the opponent expresses ignorance ($\emptyset$) in response to an inquiry of the form $inquire(X \rightharpoonup m)$, where X is a variable, m is added to C_O. Similarly, if the opponent expresses ignorance in response to an inquiry of the form $inquire(A_0 \lor \ldots \lor A_n)$, where each A_i is of the form $X \rightharpoonup m$ as before, each m is added to C_O.

4. If the opponent becomes committed to m and $m \rightharpoonup n$, having previously become committed to n, n is removed from C_O.

Structural Rules

1. The first move is a challenge of the proponent's proposal.

2. The proponent and the opponent move alternately.

3. In each of its moves, the proponent must either (i) defend a challenged assertion legally by the rules for challenge and defence (see Table 1); or (ii) question a member of C_O legally by the rules for question and answer (see Table 2); or (iii) ask a free question; or (iv) make an inquiry; or (v) make a final remark.

4. The proponent may not ask a question (free or bound) accompanied by an assertion, if it has already asked that question or uttered the assertion separately, unless C_O has expanded in the meantime. Nor may it repeat an unaccompanied assertion or inquiry,unless C_O has expanded in the meantime. Moreover the proponent may not ask any question or inquiry, such that the content of any of its permitted answers (permitted by the rules for question and answer) is in C_O.

5. The proponent may make the final remark *You said so yourself!'*, if and only if the opponent has either (i) responded to a bound question of the form $(m \Rightarrow n)?m!$ and such that m is in C_O, by conceding $o \land (o \rightharpoonup m)$; or (ii) challenged A, where A is in C_O.

6. The proponent may make the final remark *Your position is absurd!'*, if and only if the opponent has responded to a bound question of the form $(m \Rightarrow n)?m!$, by conceding $(o \land (o \rightharpoonup m))$ or $(o \land (o \rightharpoonup n))$, such that C_O contains p and $p \rightharpoonup o$.

Table 1. Rules for challenge and defence

Form of Sentence challenged	Form of Challenge	Permitted Defence(s)
$A \vee B$	$(A \vee B)??$	$A! \mid B!$
$A \wedge B$	$(A \wedge B)??A?$	$A!$
$A \wedge B$	$(A \wedge B)??B?$	$B!$
A	$A??$	—

Table 2. Rules for question and answer

Elem. of C_O questioned	Form of Question	Permitted Answer(s)
$A \vee B$	$(A \vee B)?$	$A! \mid B!$
$A \wedge B$	$(A \wedge B)?A?$	$A!$
$A \wedge B$	$(A \wedge B)?B?$	$B!$
$(m \Rightarrow n)$	$(m \Rightarrow n)?m!$	$n! \mid o \rightharpoonup m! \mid o \rightharpoonup n!$
—	$A?,A!$	$A! \mid A??$
—	$A???$ (A is ground)	$\emptyset! \mid A!$
—	$A???$ (A is non-ground)	$\emptyset! \mid A_i! \mid (A_0 \wedge \ldots \wedge A_n)!$ (each A_i is a ground instance of A)

7. Unless it is '*I give up!*', each of the opponent's moves must refer to the proponent's preceding move. If the proponent's preceding move was an (unaccompanied) assertion, the opponent must challenge the assertion. If it was a bound question, free question or inquiry, the opponent must answer the question/inquiry legally by the rules for question and answer (see Table 2).
8. Either player may utter '*I give up!*' as its move in any of its turns.

Win-and-Loss Rules

1. The player which utters '*I give up!*' loses the dialogue, and the other player wins.
2. The proponent wins if it utters (legally by the structural rules) either '*You said so yourself!*' or '*Your position is absurd!*'.
3. The opponent loses if it concedes the proponent's thesis.

3.1 Gameplay in RPD$_{\text{GD}}$

Fundamental differences between RPD$_{\text{GD}}$ and RPD$_0$ with respect to gameplay correspond to differences between the underlying logics —

1. *DAF*s do not have *PL*'s *PL*-implication; hence not all of the commitment-inducing mechanisms of RPD$_0$ are in RPD$_{\text{GD}}$.
2. *DAF*s' weak, defensive implication is not in *PL*; correspondingly, RPD$_{\text{GD}}$'s weak commitment-inducing mechanism (see locution rule 1.f.iv) has no exact equivalent in RPD$_0$.

3. *DAF*s' non-monotonicity vs. *PL*'s monotonicity; correspondingly, RPD$_{\text{GD}}$ has an *inquiry* locution-type (which allows the proponent to avoid blundering), whereas no such locution-type exists in RPD$_0$, and would not be similarly useful if it did.

RPD$_{\text{GD}}$ differs from RPD$_0$ also in allowing the proponent unlimited free questions, but this is not essential. Limiting free questions would create extra scope for strategic sophistication, just as it does in RPD$_0$. We allow unlimited free questions to highlight the extra possibilities for strategic sophistication created by the use of *DAF*s instead of *PL*. RPD$_{\text{GD}}$ is consequently very asymmetric — not only does the proponent always have the initiative, but it is impossible for the proponent to blunder in such a way as to ensure that it loses when it should have won — when the proposal is in the grounded extension of the union of the players' KBs.

Besides the particular differences 1–3 between gameplay under the two protocols, there are also two broader differences. The first is that, if the opponent is honest and open-minded, dialogues under RPD$_{\text{GD}}$ are less likely to fall into irresolvable disagreement. If an agent has a propositional-logical KB, consistency-maintenance would demand that the agent rejects an assertion which is inconsistent with any of its beliefs, regardless of supporting arguments. Whereas a KB expressed by a *DAF* is much more open, because an argument might move in and out of acceptability as the KB expands. With an honest and open-minded opponent, a dialogue under RPD$_{\text{GD}}$ would fall into irresolvable disagreement only when the proponent had uttered every argument in its KB attacking the opponent's position, and heard for every such argument a counter-argument independent of the argument(s) attacked.

The other broad difference between gameplay under the two protocols is that RPD$_{\text{GD}}$ offers a greater variety of strategies to the proponent. Under RPD$_0$ the proponent might induce the opponent to expand its KB, and would never risk anything (except wasting free questions) in doing so. Whereas under RPD$_{\text{GD}}$ such expansion may be riskier, as the proponent may thereby destroy some or all of its opportunities for victory. Such risks would exist where the proponent had only incomplete knowledge of the opponent's KB, and the opponent could construct new ways of defending its position with arguments and attacks asserted by the proponent. The point is important, because in RPD$_{\text{GD}}$ expanding the opponent's KB might be a way (indeed the *only* way, with a rational and perfectly-reasoning opponent) for the proponent to win.

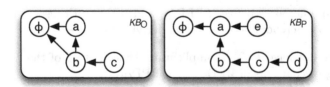

Fig. 1. The KBs of a game in which the proponent blunders

Table 3. The moves of a game in which the proponent blunders

Move	Opponent	Proponent
1	$challenge(\phi)??$	—
2	—	$question(b \wedge (b \rightharpoonup a))?, \; assert(b \wedge (b \rightharpoonup a))!$
3	$concede(b \wedge (b \rightharpoonup a))!$	—
4	—	$question(b \Rightarrow \phi)?, \; assert(b \Rightarrow \phi)!$
5	$concede(b \Rightarrow \phi)!$	—
6	—	$question(b \Rightarrow \phi)?b!$
7	$concede(c \rightharpoonup b)!$	—
8	—	$question(d \wedge (d \rightharpoonup c))?, \; assert(d \wedge (d \rightharpoonup c))!$
9	$concede(d \wedge (d \rightharpoonup c))!$	—
10	—	$question(b \Rightarrow \phi)?b!$
11	$concede(b \rightharpoonup \phi)!$	—
12	—	$I \; give \; up!$

Consider the example described by Fig. 1 and Table 3. The figure shows the players' initial KBs, and the table shows their moves in the subsequent dialogue. The proponent might have won by citing $(e \wedge (e \rightharpoonup a))$, but instead cited $(b \wedge (b \rightharpoonup a))$ and the subsequent 'chain' of arguments and attacks. Thereby it caused the opponent to believe b, which in its KB attacks ϕ. The proponent could not subsequently attack b, and in the end abandoned the dialogue, with good reason — in whatever way the proponent had continued the dialogue, the opponent could have open-mindedly and honestly avoided conceding ϕ.

Thus the example suggests that a proponent might do better by following a sophisticated strategy in giving its opponent new information, than by giving simply such information as seems most immediately useful. The example also shows how such a strategy might involve the use of *inquiry* locutions. If the proponent had inquired into what attacked and defended a in KB_O, it would have discovered that its case for a should not render b undefeated in KB_O.

That b's status can change from *defeated* to *undefeated* is possible only because the underlying logic is nonmonotonic. Thus corresponding status-changes are precluded in dialogues under RPD_0 (with its underlying PL), unless the opponent's reasoning is defective. Thus no correspondingly useful *inquiry* locution-type could be defined to extend RPD_0 — any instance of such a locution-type could not be useful, unless it was informed by insight into such defects or (less directly) it served to reveal such defects.

4   Strategy in RPD$_{\text{GD}}$

RPD$_{\text{GD}}$ provides scope for three sorts of strategic sophistication for the proponent. It may choose a move according to its perceived value in —

1. revealing inconsistency between the opponent's commitments and its beliefs;
2. creating such inconsistency by exploiting defects in the opponent's reasoning;
3. revealing blunders to be avoided in expanding the opponent's KB.

The strategic possibilities with respect to (1) and (2) correspond closely (but not exactly) to strategic possibilities offered by RPD_0, and will not be considered. We will concentrate instead on (3), presenting two concepts — *MSCK* and *fortification* — which are useful when considering how the proponent should formulate its strategy. Henceforth we will refer to a proponent P with proposal ϕ, KB_P ($= \langle AR_P, attacks_P \rangle$) and $beliefs_P$, and an opponent O with KB_O ($= \langle AR_O, attacks_O \rangle$) and $beliefs_O$.

4.1 Minimum Sufficient Contextual Knowledge

Let us consider what is most worth knowing about KB_O with respect to ϕ. Complete knowledge of $attacks_O$ includes complete knowledge of how ϕ is attacked and defended in KB_O. Thus it is sufficient to allow P to determine if and how it could devise a persuasive justification of ϕ. Everything in KB_O which remained hidden — those isolated arguments in KB_O, neither attackers nor attacked — would be irrelevant to P's task[1].

While complete knowledge of $attacks_O$ is thus sufficient, it is not necessary — for instance, an attack in KB_O by ϕ against a non-attacking argument absent from KB_P would be irrelevant. More generally, what is relevant and irrelevant about KB_O in a persuasion dialogue depends on (i) KB_O, (ii) KB_P, and (iii) ϕ. Let us specify the range of qualities of any *DAF*-based *KB*, to include every conceivably relevant attribute and to exclude every other attribute.

Specification 1. q *is a* quality *of a* DAF-*based KB* KB_X *iff (i) q includes no sentence which does not refer to the presence in or absence from* KB_X *of an argument/attack or set of arguments/attacks; and (ii) q includes at least one sentence.* KB_X^Q *denotes the set of all qualities of* KB_X.

Thus KB_O^Q collects sentences in different languages and of various reference: to each $a \in AR_O$ and each $att \in attacks_O$; to each $b \in beliefs_O$; to whether or not there exist arguments/attacks/beliefs fulfilling certain criteria in $KB_O/beliefs_O$; to which (if any) do so; and so on. It collects also all the converse qualities, expressing that $a' \notin AR_O$; that $att' \notin attacks_O$; and so on. It includes also sentences that do not refer *explicitly* to any argument or attack — for instance, if KB_O formed a weakly connected graph, KB_O^Q would include a sentence saying so. Such a sentence would not necessarily refer explicitly to any argument or attack, but it would at least refer implicitly to the presence of a set of attacks in KB_O such as to guarantee that the latter was weakly connected. On the other hand, KB_O^Q could not include, for instance, the sentence 'KB_O was last updated yesterday'. However, while such examples are easily found, we cannot yet enumerate the contents of KB_O^Q for any value which might be assigned to KB_O.

---

[1] If ϕ was itself one of these 'islands', it would be in O's beliefs. Thus, if P found that ϕ was not in the (weakly) connected parts of KB_O, it could safely conclude that O either believed or was unaware of ϕ and thus would not challenge it. There would therefore be no RPD_{GD} dialogue concerning ϕ between P and O.

Let us now specify *Minimum Sufficient Contextual Knowledge (MSCK)* as follows.

Specification 2. *Let* $S \subset KB_O^O$. S *is an instance of* MSCK *wrt* $\langle KB_P, KB_O, \phi \rangle$ *(more briefly, $_O^P MSCK_\phi$) iff*

1. *knowledge of S permits P to know if and how it can induce O to accept ϕ; and*
2. *there is no S' such that $S' \subset S$ and S' is an instance of $_O^P MSCK_\phi$.*

Let $_O^P \text{msck}_\phi^{All} = \{_O^P \text{msck}_\phi^0 \ldots _O^P \text{msck}_\phi^n\}$ be the set of all instances of $_O^P MSCK_\phi$.

We do not consider here how the proponent might acquire an instance of $_O^P MSCK_\phi$. This might (counter-intuitively) entail acquiring further knowledge of KB_O. However, the concept remains useful — *MSCK* is wholly separate from minimal knowledge gained in acquiring *MSCK*, and whether every instance of the former is also an instance of the latter (as would be ideal) depends on the information-gathering methods available to P.

We are here interested in *MSCK* itself and especially in ways of identifying intuitively more minimal instances of *MSCK*. Because the current definition of *MSCK* is not very sophisticated, one instance of *MSCK* might seem less minimal than another. Suppose, for instance —

$$KB_O = \langle \{a, b, \phi\}, \{a \rightharpoonup \phi\} \rangle$$
$$KB_P = \langle \{a, c, \phi\}, \{c \rightharpoonup a\} \rangle$$
$$S \quad = \{attacks_O = \{a \rightharpoonup \phi\}\}$$
$$S' \quad = \{(arguments_O = \{a, b, \phi\}),$$
$$(a \rightharpoonup \phi \in attacks_O), (b \rightharpoonup \phi \notin attacks_O), (\phi \rightharpoonup \phi \notin attacks_O)\}$$

S is an instance of $_O^P MSCK_\phi$. So too is S', even though the arguments and attacks to which S' explicitly refers strictly subsume those to which S explicitly refers. S refers also to a boundary of KB_O — that $attacks_O$ comprises just $a \rightharpoonup \phi$ — but S' refers also to a boundary — that $arguments_O$ comprises just a, b and ϕ. Thus S might be regarded as more minimal than S', by virtue of being more minimal in its *explicit* reference to the contents of KB_O and no less minimal in its reference to the boundaries of KB_O.

Let us henceforth consider only the first type of minimality — minimality with respect to contents-reference-explicitness. We specify this concept as follows —

Specification 3. *Let S be an instance of $_O^P MSCK_\phi$ and let E be the set of all arguments and attacks (whether in KB_O or not) to which S explicitly refers. S is minimal with respect to contents-reference-explicitness iff there exists no other instance S' of $_O^P MSCK_\phi$ such that $E' \subset E$, where E' is the set of all arguments and attacks (whether in KB_O or not) to which S' explicitly refers.*

We say that an argument or attack is *strictly relevant* to P's task iff it is in every instance of $_O^P MSCK_\phi$ which is minimal with respect to contents-reference-explicitness.

There is no obvious method for proving that an instance of $MSCK$ is also minimal with respect to contents-reference-explicitness. For instance, in the example above it seems likely that $a \rightharpoonup \phi$ is strictly relevant to P's task and thus that S is minimal with respect to contents-reference-explicitness, but without a proof we can claim only that S is closer to such minimality than S'. On the other hand, disproving minimality with respect to contents-reference-explicitness is more straightforward. In the example above S' is not minimal with respect to contents-reference-explicitness, because $E' \supset E$, where E' and E are the sets of arguments and attacks to which (respectively) S' and S explicitly refer.

In fact one does not need to consider S to guess that S' is not an instance of $_O^P MSCK_\phi$ which is minimal with respect to contents-reference-explicitness, because b — to which S' refers — is intuitively irrelevant to ϕ in KB_O. Thus no quality which explicitly refers to b can be in any instance of $_O^P MSCK_\phi$ which is minimal with respect to contents-reference-explicitness. This rule is specific to this particular instantiation of KB_P and KB_O, but it is merely a consequence of a more general rule. Multiple such rules might exist, defining multiple ranges of qualities which cannot be in any instance of $_O^P MSCK_\phi$ which is minimal with respect to contents-reference-explicitness.

More formally, we may envisage a series of sets $\langle _O^P irrelevant_\phi^0 \ldots _O^P irrelevant_\phi^n \rangle$, where each $_O^P irrelevant_\phi^i$ collects every member of KB_O^Q which fulfils criterion i and is thereby necessarily excluded from every instance of $_O^P MSCK_\phi$ which is minimal with respect to contents-reference-explicitness. Such irrelevance-criteria would not show P how to acquire such a minimal instance of $_O^P MSCK_\phi$, but they might allow P to save resources in information-gathering. For by referring to irrelevance-criteria, P might prevent itself from making inquiries which concerned irrelevant qualities of KB_O. Such inquiries would necessarily be either wholly redundant or replaceable with more specific inquiries.

By way of example we identify three irrelevance-criteria in Specification 4.

Specification 4. *Let* $KB_\cup$ *be the graph union of* KB_P *and* KB_O, *and let* $paths_\phi^{KB_\cup}$ *be the set of all acyclic paths in* $KB_\cup$ *which start in a leaf node and terminate in* ϕ. *Attacking and defending paths contain respectively odd and even numbers of attacks, and attacking and defending arguments occur alternately in each path. A path's elements are its arguments and attacks. Now —*

1. *Let* islands *be the set of arguments neither attacking nor attacked in* KB_O.

2. *Let* $paths_{silly}$ *be the set containing every path* $\in paths_\phi^{KB_\cup}$ *such that (2i) the final attack in* path *(i.e. the attack on* ϕ) *is not in* KB_O; *and (2ii) no argument (except* ϕ) *in* path *is in any other* path' $\in paths_\phi^{KB_\cup}$ *not fulfilling condition (2i).*

3. *Let* $paths_{safe}$ *be the set containing every path* $\in paths_\phi^{KB_\cup}$ *such that (3i)* path *defends* ϕ; *and (3ii) all elements of* path *are in* KB_O; *and (3iii) no argument in* path *is controversial wrt* ϕ *in* KB_O; *and (3iv) no argument (except* ϕ) *in* path *is in any other* path' $\in paths_\phi^{KB_\cup}$ *not fulfilling conditions (3i), (3ii) and (3iii).*

Thus for any path *multiple* others *may be considered when determining whether* path $\in$ paths$_{silly}$, *and if any* o $\in$ others *does not fulfil condition (2i), neither* path *nor any of* others *is in* paths$_{silly}$; *otherwise all are. And similarly for* paths$_{safe}$ *and conditions (3i), (3ii) and (3iii).*

In the artificial example of Figure 2 the vast majority of KB_O is covered by the three concepts. According to Proposition 1 below, an instance of $^{P}_{O}MSCK_\phi$ may refer explicitly to no arguments except o, p and ϕ.

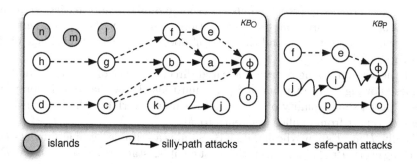

Fig. 2. Illustrating *islands, paths*$_{silly}$ and *paths*$_{safe}$

Proposition 1. *Let* qualities$_{islands}$, qualities$_{silly}$ *and* qualities$_{safe}$ *contain all qualities explicitly referring to any* i $\in$ islands *and any element of any path in* paths$_{silly}$ *and* paths$_{safe}$, *respectively. Let* q *be such that* q $\in$ (qualities$_{islands}$ $\cup$ qualities$_{silly}$ $\cup$ qualities$_{safe}$) *and such that* q *refers explicitly to some* i $\in$ islands *or some element* e *of some path in* paths$_{silly}$ *or* paths$_{safe}$ *such that* i $\neq \phi$ *and* e $\neq \phi$. q *is not in any instance of* $^{P}_{O}MSCK_\phi$ *which is minimal with respect to contents-reference-explicitness.*

Proof. Let KB_O^{sub} be a weakly connected subgraph of KB_O, possibly containing ϕ. P would need to consider KB_O^{sub} only if either (i) it contained an undefeated attacker of ϕ; or (ii) P could, by making a case for ϕ, inadvertently convert one of KB_O^{sub}'s arguments into an undefeated attacker of ϕ. Suppose (i) did not hold. (ii) would not hold either, if (a) there were no attacks in KB_O^{sub}. But even if there were attacks, there would be no danger if (b) KB_O^{sub} contained no argument attacking ϕ, and P could never rationally present a case which resulted in the connection of KB_O^{sub} to ϕ. And even if KB_O^{sub} did contain an argument attacking ϕ, there would be no danger if (c) every such argument was defeated in KB_O^{sub}, and P was unaware of every argument in KB_O^{sub}, except as it existed in KB_O^{sub}.

Now let q be as specified in Proposition 1. If $q \in$ qualities$_{islands}$, q must refer to a subgraph of KB_O fulfilling (a); if $q \in$ qualities$_{silly}$, q must refer to a subgraph of KB_O fulfilling (b); and if $q \in$ qualities$_{safe}$, q must refer to a subgraph of KB_O fulfilling (c).

We have just shown that there are areas of KB_O which are irrelevant to P's task, and that a definite subset of the members of our three categories of qualities refer to three such areas. Let us now, conversely, consider those areas of KB_O which are relevant to P's task. Let q' be a quality of KB_O whose sentences refer *only* to *islands* or elements of paths in $paths_{silly}$ and $paths_{safe}$. Let us now show that q' refers to none of those areas of KB_O which are relevant to P's task (except ϕ).

Any $_O^P msck_\phi^i$ must include knowledge of every undefeated direct attacker atr of ϕ in KB_O. Therefore for every atr, $_O^P msck_\phi^i$ might include $\{(atr \rightharpoonup \phi \in attacks_O), (atr \in beliefs_O)\}$ or some similarly informative set of qualities. It follows trivially from the specification of *islands*, $paths_{silly}$ and $paths_{safe}$, that q' cannot refer to atr, and thus that q' does not appear at this stage of the construction of $_O^P msck_\phi^i$.

Let the set containing every undefeated direct attacker of ϕ in KB_O be S_{atr}. Besides knowing every member of S_{atr}, P must also know that S_{atr} is complete. This is just a single quality of KB_O, and it cannot overlap with q', wrt explicit reference (apart from explicit reference to ϕ).

Finally, P must know whether its KB contains a suitable set of arguments Def attacking every $atr \in S_{atr}$. This is the most complex stage, because any $arg \in Def$ might itself be defeated in KB_O; and Def might reinstate a defeated direct attacker of ϕ in KB_O. This introduces a great many complications, but none of them can involve q', because every complication must be to do with a path to ϕ *jointly* constructable by P and O. q' cannot refer to any such path, because it refers only to *islands* or path(s) in $paths_{silly}$ or $paths_{safe}$. P could not rationally play any part in constructing any path in $paths_{silly}$; and could not possibly play any part in constructing any path using any element of any path in $paths_{safe}$, such that the constructed path was not itself already in $paths_{safe}$.

The concepts *islands*, $paths_{silly}$ and $paths_{safe}$ thus provide three criteria for determining whether a quality of KB_O is outside every instance of $_O^P MSCK_\phi$ which is minimal with respect to contents-reference-explicitness. How to determine all remaining such criteria, how to compare their relative usefulness, and how to use multiple (perhaps overlapping) criteria efficiently are questions for future work. It remains also to find a way of proving whether an instance of $MSCK$ is minimal with respect to contents-reference-explicitness.

We might also move beyond the *contents-reference-explicitness* criterion, to consider further minimality criteria. Ideally such work would result in a much more sophisticated definition for $MSCK$, with which P would be able to reason more efficiently in general about KB_O. Thus in sum, while the $MSCK$ of Specification 2 is an unsophisticated concept, there seems to be much room for refinement.

4.2 Fortification

Let us now consider practical consequences of different approaches to $MSCK$. We first define *fortification* as a simple mechanism around which P may build a general approach to argumentation, in which more or less attention may be paid to *MSCK*. We then show how an agent which uses fortification might benefit by paying careful attention to *MSCK*.

Consider the subset S of $attacks_O$ containing the attacks most obviously relevant to ϕ — for each $atk \in S$, $atk = (A \rightarrowtail \phi)$, where A is an undefeated argument in KB_O. Removing each $atk \in S$ from KB_O produces a DAF containing ϕ in its grounded extension. However, KB_O is a monotonic KB, and thus $beliefs_O$ can change only through the expansion of KB_O. Thus for every undefeated direct attacker a of ϕ in KB_O, P would need to know whether it could induce O to believe some b such that $b \rightarrowtail a$ held. To capture this idea, let us define the *fortification* function (FF) for DAFs and arguments as follows —

Definition 5. *Let $\mathcal{D}$ be a set of DAFs and $\mathcal{A}$ be a set of arguments.*

$$FF = (\mathcal{D} \times \mathcal{A}) \mapsto 2^{\mathcal{D}}$$

where, for every

$$DAF \ \ = \langle AR, attacks \rangle \ and$$
$$DAF_{ffd} = \langle AR_{ffd}, attacks_{ffd} \rangle \in FF(DAF, \phi) \ and$$
$$DAF_{ffg} = \langle AR_{ffg}, attacks_{ffg} \rangle = \langle (AR_{ffd} \setminus AR), (attacks_{ffd} \setminus attacks) \rangle,$$

1. $AR_{ffd} = AR \cup AR_{ffg}$ *and* $attacks_{ffd} = attacks \cup attacks_{ffg}$.
2. *For each* $(X \rightarrowtail Y) \in attacks_{ffg}$, Y *is a direct or indirect attacker of ϕ in* DAF.
3. *For each* $Arg \in AR_{ffg}$, *there exists some* $(X \rightarrowtail Y) \in attacks_{ffg}$ *such that* $Arg = X$ *or* $Arg = Y$.
4. *For each undefeated direct attacker* Z *of ϕ in* DAF, Z *is defeated in* DAF_{ffd}.

DAF_{ffd} *is a ϕ-fortified version of* DAF, *while* DAF_{ffg} *is a ϕ-fortifying framework for* DAF.

So DAF_{ffd} is DAF expanded to defeat all direct attackers of ϕ. Every element of DAF_{ffg} serves to defend ϕ, but some of the defence provided might be superfluous and thus DAF_{ffg} is not necessarily minimal. *FF* is thus intended to reflect a general, abstract way in which P might expand KB_O if it had complete knowledge of the undefeated direct and indirect attackers of ϕ in KB_O.

Suppose that P induced the expansion of KB_O into a ϕ-fortified version. Even so, O would not necessarily believe ϕ, as the examples in Figure 3 show. In DAF ϕ has one undefeated attacker — a — and both DAF' and DAF'' are sufficient to defeat a. But in so doing, DAF' converts b into an undefeated attacker of ϕ.

Let us now consider how ϕ could be excluded from the grounded extension of any $DAF_{\text{ffd}} = (DAF \cup DAF_{\text{ffg}})$. *Controversy* would necessarily be involved. An argument is *controversial* with respect to another if it both (directly or indirectly) attacks and indirectly defends that argument [3]. Because DAF_{ffg} defeats all undefeated direct attackers of ϕ in DAF, there would have to be controversy in either or both of (i) DAF and (ii) $(DAF \cup DAF_{\text{ffg}})$. However, as controversy need not significantly involve ϕ, controversy would not be a sufficient

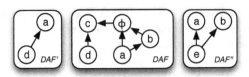

Fig. 3. Illustrating fortification — DAF' and DAF'' are both ϕ-fortifying frameworks for DAF, but while ϕ is acceptable in $DAF \cup DAF''$, it is not acceptable in $DAF \cup DAF'$

condition for ϕ's exclusion from the grounded extension of DAF_{ffd}. In effect $MSCK$ and fortification contribute to a notion of dialectical relevance in the sense of [4].

We finish by returning to the example of Figure 1 and Table 3, to show how P might have won if it had applied fortification with careful attention to $MSCK$. An alternative set of moves could be as shown in Table 4, where P follows the simple strategy of fortifying generously (to the fullest extent possible) for its proposal and anything which may serve in its defence, until either fortification is accomplished for all such arguments, or it finds something for which it cannot fortify.

Table 4. The moves of a game in which the proponent avoids blundering through careful use of fortification

Move	Opponent	Proponent
1	$challenge(\phi)??$	—
2	—	$inquire(X \rightharpoonup \phi)???$
3	$concede((a \rightharpoonup \phi) \wedge (b \rightharpoonup \phi))!$	—
4	—	$inquire((X \rightharpoonup e) \vee (Y \rightharpoonup c))???$
5	$concede(\emptyset)!$	—
6	—	$question(e \wedge (e \rightharpoonup a) \wedge c \wedge (c \rightharpoonup b))?,$ $assert(e \wedge (e \rightharpoonup a) \wedge c \wedge (c \rightharpoonup b))!$
7	$concede(e \wedge (e \rightharpoonup a) \wedge c \wedge (c \rightharpoonup b))!$	—
8	—	$question(e \Rightarrow \phi)?, assert(e \Rightarrow \phi)!$
9	$concede(e \Rightarrow \phi)!$	—
10	—	$question(e \Rightarrow \phi)?e!$
11	$I\ give\ up!$	—

Thus at Move 2 P prepares to fortify for ϕ by inquiring about direct attackers of ϕ. O mentions a and b (Move 3), thus informing P that fortification for ϕ must depend on fortification for direct attacker(s) of one or both of a and b. P knows of only one direct attacker for each — e and c respectively — and thus it prepares to fortify for e and c by inquiring about direct attackers of each (Move 4). O mentions none (Move 5), so P can expect that it will succeed — as in fact it does. P's strategy here is not perfect (fortifying very generously for ϕ, it unnecessarily argues against b), but it is good enough: it secures victory, unlike the careless, simple strategy illustrated earlier.

Let us finally consider $MSCK$ in this case. P's discoveries regarding KB_O may be expressed as the set of qualities S as follows —

$$S = \{ \ (\{X \mid X \rightharpoonup \phi \in attacks_O\} = \{a, b\}),$$
$$(\{Y \mid Y \rightharpoonup e \in attacks_O\} = \emptyset),$$
$$(\{Z \mid Z \rightharpoonup c \in attacks_O\} = \emptyset) \qquad \}$$

S is an instance of $^P_O MSCK_\phi$, but is not minimal with respect to contents-reference-explicitness, because it unnecessarily refers explicitly to b and c, neither of which are strictly relevant to its task. Two more promising candidates are S' and S'' as follows —

$$S' = \{ \ (\{W \mid (W \rightharpoonup \phi \in attacks_O),$$
$$(\{X \mid (X \rightharpoonup W \in attacks_O), (X \in beliefs_O)\} = \emptyset)\} = \{a\}),$$
$$(\phi \rightharpoonup \phi \notin attacks_O),$$
$$(\{Y \mid (a \rightharpoonup Y \in attacks_O), (a \neq \phi)\} = \emptyset),$$
$$(e \notin arguments_O) \qquad\qquad \}.$$

$$S' = \{ \ (\{W \mid (W \rightharpoonup \phi \in attacks_O),$$
$$(\{X \mid (X \rightharpoonup W \in attacks_O), (X \in beliefs_O)\} = \emptyset)\} = \{a\}),$$
$$(\phi \rightharpoonup \phi \notin attacks_O),$$
$$(\{Y \mid (a \rightharpoonup Y \in attacks_O), (a \neq \phi)\} = \emptyset),$$
$$(\{Z \mid (Z \rightharpoonup e \in attacks_O)\} = \emptyset) \qquad\qquad \}.$$

5 Related Work

RPD_0 has been little used in multi-agent systems, though its authors have otherwise been widely influential in the field[2]. It is used in [5], where the authors show how it could be used by agents which reason with multi-modal logics. However, the authors do not suggest any substantial modifications to the protocol and address only basic strategic considerations. Therefore in this section we focus on work on DAFs and strategy in computational dialogue games in general.

Amgoud & Maudet [6] consider strategy using a DAF-based framework which incorporates propositional logic and preference orderings over arguments, and a dialogue game based on Mackenzie's DC [7]. Among the strategic matters considered is choice of argumentative content, but as their choice-process involves only the choosing agent's KB — and not the other agent's — their work overlaps little with ours.

In later work with Hameurlain [8], Amgoud considers dialogue strategy differently, as a bipartite decision problem — for each move, an agent must decide (i) which type of locution to use, and (ii) what content to use in the locution. These decisions are influenced respectively by (i) strategic goals and strategic beliefs and (ii) functional goals and basic beliefs, where strategic elements are

---

[2] It is not clear why this should be, as some of RPD_0's main motivating problems — those of relevance and enforcing it in human dialogue — may arise in multi-agent dialogue too.

purely to do with dialogic practice, while functional/basic elements are to do with everything else. Thus which locution-type to use is a strategic matter, while what content to use is a functional/basic matter. They use a framework for argumentation-based decision-making under uncertainty to show how this decision problem may be tackled, which takes into account the weights of beliefs and the priorities of goals.

Amgoud & Hameurlain's approach is relevant to our work, as the strategic vs. functional/basic distinction might be useful for strategy in dialogue games, where moves are typically defined by locution-type and locution content. However, they do not go very far beyond the definition of the decision problem and the high-level reasoning framework — they do not, for instance, illustrate how an agent could take into account the dialogue-history at either the strategic or functional/basic levels. Thus their work is currently of relevance only as providing a wider context for the ideas in this paper. Kakas et al. [9] present an alternative framework, which might also accommodate our ideas, especially as it accounts for both protocol and strategy.

Oren et al. [10] have considered confidentiality as a strategic concern in argumentation. This is relevant to RPD_{GD} — for example, in the dialogue described in Table 4, the proponent reveals more of its KB than is necessary, and there might be contexts in which such superfluity would be unacceptable. An intuitive general approach would be to make fewer assertions and to ask more questions, though questions might reveal information too.

Black & Hunter [11] have considered strategy in enthymeme inquiry dialogue. Like ours, their protocol is defined as a dialogue game, and a player consults its strategy to select its next move from the range permitted by the protocol. However, in contrast to the adversarial, asymmetrical protocol presented here, their protocol is co-operative and symmetrical, the players aiming to jointly construct a jointly acceptable (and possibly enthymematic) argument for a given claim. The authors' treatment of strategy accordingly contrasts with the treatment of strategy given here. The authors define a single strategy to be used by both players, which necessarily leads to success, if success is possible — if an argument for a given claim is jointly constructable, the players will find that argument via a dialogue undertaken in accordance with the protocol and the strategy.

Bentahar et al. [12] present a model for adversarial persuasion dialogue in which both players may attempt to persuade the other, and in which the moves of each player are almost fully specified. Their protocol is novel in several respects, and like ours draws on dialogue games, being defined in terms of commitments, entry and exit conditions, and a dynamics determining the structure of dialogues. However, it differs from ours in leaving very little room for strategy. Agents have no choice regarding the locution-type used in their moves, except when required to decide whether to accept a commitment for which the other player has no justifying argument. On such occasions a player may *accept* or *refuse*, and chooses by consulting a complex trustworthiness model. It is on this aspect of strategy that the authors concentrate — no attention is paid, for instance, to how a player should choose which argument to use to attack the other player's previous commitment.

Dunne & McBurney [13] consider 'optimal utterances' in dialogue, but the dialogues they consider occur in fixed dialogue contexts, which are completely known to both players. Thus unlike in our scenario, each player has (in effect) complete knowledge of that part of the other's KB which overlaps with the dialogue context. Furthermore, the optimality they consider relates to dialogue length, rather than to whether one player persuades another.

We may finally compare our work with game theoretical approaches. Procaccia & Rosenschein [14], Riveret et al. [15] and Roth et al. [16] consider games with complete information, and thus their results are of limited relevance to this paper. However, Rahwan & Larson [17] use wholly ignorant agents in considering how their game-theoretical mechanism for DAF-based sceptical (grounded) argumentation may be strategy-proof. They prove that the the mechanism is strategy-proof only under the fairly restrictive condition that each player's set of arguments is free of direct/indirect conflict in the graph formed by the union of all players' DAFs — otherwise an agent might benefit from revealing only a subset of its arguments. This last point is reflected in the examples of Figure 1 and Tables 3 and 4 — the proponent fails when it is careless about revealing its DAF, and succeeds when it takes care.

The game theoretical approach has thus produced interesting results. Game theoretical approaches tend, however, to have a different focus — namely on designing protocols and mechanisms for communication, and determining whether or not these protocols are strategy-proof [17]. The approach rests on an assumption that the best way to tackle the challenges of rich communication is to design closed systems that require adherence to highly restrictive protocols which preclude strategy in communication. Our approach, however, in contrast, is to maintain the flexibility, expressiveness, and sophistication of protocols that are not strategy-proof, and then invest in the reasoning required to construct communicative strategies that can be robust and effective in such an open environment.

6   Conclusions and Future Work

The work described here forms a part of a programme of research into strategic argumentation. Though that programme is as yet young, the exploration of RPD$_{\mathrm{GD}}$ presented here supports two significant conclusions. First, abstract argumentation frameworks may be expected to allow greater scope for strategic sophistication in inter-agent dialogue games than is available in the original versions of those games founded upon propositional logics. While RPD$_0$ is a useful protocol for investigating some forms of "tightened up" human argumentation, the proponent's strategy is limited largely to ensuring that free questions are not wasted. In games of RPD$_{\mathrm{GD}}$, however, the proponent could blunder disastrously with any assertion, and thus strategy is far more prominent.

The second conclusion is that, while strategic reasoning is likely to be complex in the general case, it is possible to achieve significant strategic advances from even relatively simple foundational concepts such as *MSCK* and fortification. Fortification, in particular, is here under-developed, and exploring its role in more sophisticated strategies is an immediate avenue for further research.

The area of strategic agent argumentation is attracting rapidly increasing interest because of its centrality in building agents that can successfully compete in domains characterised by open, heterogeneous systems with complex market designs. This paper has shown how strategic techniques based on the intrinsic structure of argumentation frameworks can offer significant advantages in such challenging domains.

References

1. Prakken, H.: Formal systems for persuasion dialogue. The Knowledge Engineering Review 21, 163–188 (2006)
2. Walton, D.N., Krabbe, E.C.W.: Commitment in Dialogue. Basic Concepts of Interpersonal Reasoning. SUNY Press, Albany (1996)
3. Dung, P.M.: On the acceptability of arguments and its fundamental role in non-monotonic reasoning, logic programming and n-person games. Artificial Intelligence 77(2), 321–358 (1995)
4. Walton, D.: Dialectical Relevance in Persuasion Dialogue. Informal Logic 19(2, 3), 119–143 (1999)
5. Dignum, F., Dunin-Keplicz, B., Verbrugge, R.: Creating collective intention through dialogue. Logic Journal of IGPL 9(2), 289–304 (2001)
6. Amgoud, L., Maudet, N.: Strategical considerations for argumentative agents (preliminary report). In: Proceedings of the 9th International Workshop on Non-Monotonic Reasoning (NMR), pp. 409–417 (2002)
7. Mackenzie, J.D.: Question-begging in non-cumulative systems. Journal of Philosophical Logic 8, 117–133 (1979)
8. Amgoud, L., Hameurlain, N.: An Argumentation-Based Approach for Dialog Move Selection. In: Maudet, N., Parsons, S., Rahwan, I. (eds.) ArgMAS 2006. LNCS (LNAI), vol. 4766, pp. 128–141. Springer, Heidelberg (2007)
9. Kakas, A., Maudet, N., Moraitis, P.: Modular representation of agent interaction rules through argumentation. Journal of Autonomous Agents and Multiagent Systems 11(2), 189–206 (2005)
10. Oren, N., Norman, T., Preece, A.: Loose lips sink ships: a heuristic for argumentation. In: Proceedings of the Third International Workshop on Argumentation in Multi-Agent Systems (ArgMAS 2006), pp. 121–134 (2006)
11. Black, E., Hunter, A.: Using Enthymemes in an Inquiry Dialogue System. In: Proceedings of AAMAS 2008, pp. 437–444 (2008)
12. Bentahar, J., Moulin, B., Chaib-draa, B.: Specifying and implementing a persuasion dialogue game using commitments and arguments. In: Rahwan, I., Moraïtis, P., Reed, C. (eds.) ArgMAS 2004. LNCS (LNAI), vol. 3366, pp. 130–148. Springer, Heidelberg (2005)
13. Dunne, P., McBurney, P.: Concepts of optimal utterance in dialogue: selection and complexity. In: Dignum, F.P.M. (ed.) ACL 2003. LNCS (LNAI), vol. 2922, pp. 310–328. Springer, Heidelberg (2004)
14. Procaccia, A., Rosenschein, J.: Extensive-form argumentation games. In: Proceedings of the Third European Workshop on Multi-Agent Systems (EUMAS 2005), Brussels, Belgium, pp. 312–322 (2005)

15. Riveret, R., Prakken, H., Rotolo, A., Sartor, G.: Heuristics in argumentation: a game-theoretical investigation. In: Computational Models of Argument. Proceedings of COMMA 2008 (2008)
16. Roth, B., Riveret, R., Rotolo, A., Governatori, G.: Strategic argumentation: a game theoretical investigation. In: Proceedings of the 11th International Conference on Artificial intelligence and law, pp. 81–90. ACM Press, New York (2007)
17. Rahwan, I., Larson, K.: Mechanism design for abstract argumentation. In: Proceedings of AAMAS 2008, pp. 1031–1038 (2008)

Assumption-Based Argumentation for the Minimal Concession Strategy*

Maxime Morge and Paolo Mancarella

Dipartimento di Informatica, Università di Pisa
Largo Pontecorvo, 3 I-56127 Pisa, Italy
{morge,paolo}di.unipi.it
http://maxime.morge.org
http://www.di.unipi.it/~paolo

Abstract. Several recent works in the area of Artificial Intelligence focus on computational models of argumentation-based negotiation. However, even if computational models of arguments are used to encompass the reasoning of interacting agents, this logical approach does not come with an effective strategy for agents engaged in negotiations. In this paper we propose a realisation of the Minimal Concession (MC) strategy which has been theoretically validated. The main contribution of this paper is the integration of this intelligent strategy in a practical application by means of assumption-based argumentation. We claim here that the outcome of negotiations, which are guaranteed to terminate, is an optimal agreement (when possible) if the agents adopt the MC strategy.

1 Introduction

Negotiations occur in electronic procurement, commerce, health and government, amongst individuals, companies and organisations. In negotiations, the aim for all parties is to "make a deal" while bargaining over their interests, typically seeking to maximise their "good" (welfare), and prepared to concede some aspects, while insisting on others. Negotiations are time consuming, emotionally demanding and emotions may affect the quality of the outcomes of negotiations. These issues can be addressed by delegating (at least partially) negotiations to a multiagent system responsible for (or helping with) reaching agreements (semi-)automatically [1]. Within this approach, software agents are associated with stakeholders in negotiations. As pointed out by [2] (resp. [3]), there is a need for a solid theoretical foundation for negotiation (resp. argumentation-based negotiation) that covers algorithms and protocols, while determining which strategies are most effective under what circumstances.

Several recent works in the area of Artificial Intelligence focus on computational models of argumentation-based negotiation [4,5,6,7]. In these works, argumentation serves as a unifying medium to provide a model for agent-based

---

* This work is supported by the Sixth Framework IST programme of the EC, under the 035200 ARGUGRID project.

P. McBurney et al. (Eds.): ArgMAS 2009, LNAI 6057, pp. 114–133, 2010.

negotiation systems, in that it can support: the reasoning and decision-making process of agents [4], the inter-agent negotiation process to reach an agreement [5], the definition of contracts emerging from the negotiation [6,7,8] and, finally, the resolution of disputes and disagreements with respect to agreed contracts [9]. However, even if computational models of arguments are used to encompass the reasoning of interacting agents, few works are concerned by the strategy of agents engaged in negotiations and its properties. A first attempt in this direction is the Minimal Concession (MC) strategy proposed by [7]. However, the latter does not show how to fill the gap between the argumentation-based decision-making mechanism and its realisation for computing this negotiation strategy. Moreover, some assumptions are too strong with respect to our real-world scenario, e.g. the fact the agents know the preferences and the reservation values of the other agents. In this paper we propose a realisation of the MC strategy which has been practically validated. Actually, our strategy has been tested within industrial scenarios [10,11] from which we extract an intuitive and illustrative example. Moreover, we show here that negotiations are guaranteed to terminate. The negotiation outcome emerges from the interleaved decision-making processes of agents specified by the MC strategy. We claim that this outcome is an optimal agreement when it is possible. Argumentation logic is used to support the intelligent strategy of negotiating agents, to guide and empower negotiation amongst agents and to allow them to reach agreements. With the support of assumptions-based argumentation, agents select the "optimal" utterances to fulfil the preferences/constraints of users and the requirements imposed by the other agents. The main contribution of this paper is the integration of our intelligent strategy in a practical application by means of assumptions-based argumentation.

The paper is organised as follows. Section 2 introduces the basic notions of assumption-based argumentation in the background of our work. Section 3 introduces the walk-through example. Section 3 outlines the dialogue-game protocol we use. Section 5 defines our framework for decision making. Section 6 presents our realisation of the MC strategy. Section 7 highlights some properties of our protocol and our strategy. Section 8 briefly describes the deployment of the multiagent system responsible for the negotiation. Section 9 discusses some related works. Section 10 concludes with some directions for future work.

2   Assumption-Based Argumentation

Assumption-based argumentation [12] (ABA) is a general-purpose computational framework which allows to reason with incomplete information, whereby certain literals are assumptions, meaning that they can be assumed to hold as long as there is no evidence to the contrary. Moreover, ABA concretise Dung's abstract argumentation [13] (AA). Actually, all the semantics used in AA, which capture various degrees of collective justifications for a set of arguments, can be applied to ABA.

An ABA framework considers a deductive system augmented by a non-empty set of assumptions and a (total) mapping from assumptions to their contraries. In order to perform decision making, we consider here the generalisation of the original assumption-based argumentation framework and its computational mechanism, whereby multiple contraries are allowed [14].

Definition 1 (ABA). *An **assumption-based argumentation framework** is a tuple $ABF = \langle \mathcal{L}, \mathcal{R}, \mathcal{A}sm, \mathcal{C}on \rangle$ where:*

- *$(\mathcal{L}, \mathcal{R})$ is a deductive system where*
  - *$\mathcal{L}$ is a formal language consisting of countably many sentences,*
  - *$\mathcal{R}$ is a countable set of inference rules of the form $r: \alpha \leftarrow \alpha_1, \ldots, \alpha_n$ $(n \geq 0)$ where $\alpha \in \mathcal{L}$ is called the **head** of the rule, and the conjunction $\alpha_1, \ldots, \alpha_n$ is called the **body** of the rule, with $n \geq 0$ and $\alpha_i \in \mathcal{L}$ for each $i \in [1, n]$;*
- *$\mathcal{A}sm \subseteq \mathcal{L}$ is a non-empty set of **assumptions**. If $x \in \mathcal{A}sm$, then there is no inference rule in $\mathcal{R}$ such that x is the head of this rule;*
- *$\mathcal{C}on: \mathcal{A}sm \rightarrow 2^{\mathcal{L}}$ is a (total) mapping from assumptions into set of sentences in $\mathcal{L}$, i.e. their **contraries**.*

In the remainder of the paper, we restrict ourselves to finite deduction systems, i.e. with finite languages and finite set of rules. For simplicity, we also restrict ourselves to flat frameworks [12], in which assumptions do not occur as conclusions of inference rules.

We adopt here the tree-like structure for arguments proposed in [15] and we adapt it for ABA.

Definition 2 (Argument). *Let $ABF = \langle \mathcal{L}, \mathcal{R}, \mathcal{A}sm, \mathcal{C}on \rangle$ be an ABA framework. An **argument** $\bar{a}$ deducing the **conclusion** $c \in \mathcal{L}$ (denoted **conc**$(\bar{a})$) supported by a set of **assumptions** A in $\mathcal{A}sm$ (denoted **asm**$(\bar{a})$) is a tree where the root is c and each node is a sentence of $\mathcal{L}$. For each node :*

- *if the node is a leaf, then it is either an assumption in A or $\top^1$;*
- *if the node is not a leaf and it is $\alpha \in \mathcal{L}$, then there is an inference rule $\alpha \leftarrow \alpha_1, \ldots, \alpha_n$ in $\mathcal{R}$ and,*
  - *either $n = 0$ and $\top$ is its only child,*
  - *or $n > 0$ and the node has n children, $\alpha_1, \ldots, \alpha_n$.*

*We write $\bar{a} : A \vdash \alpha$ to denote an argument $\bar{a}$ such that **conc**$(\bar{a}) = \alpha$ and **asm**$(\bar{a}) = A$. The set of arguments built upon ABF is denoted by $\mathcal{A}(ABF)$.*

Our definition corresponds to the definition of tight argument in [16]. Arguments can be built by reasoning backwards as in the dialectical proof procedure proposed in [16] and extended in [14]. It is worth noticing that all the rules and assumptions of our arguments are useful to deduce their conclusion even if we do not explicitly enforce the minimality of the premises as in [17]. Moreover, we do not enforce the

---

[1] $\top$ denotes the unconditionally true statement.

consistency of the premises but this property will arise in the arguments computed by the dialectical proof procedure due to the attack relation.

In an assumption-based argumentation framework, the attack relation amongst arguments comes from the contraries which capture the notion of conflicts.

Definition 3 (Attack relation). *An argument $\bar{a}: A \vdash \alpha$ **attacks** an argument $\bar{b}: B \vdash \beta$ iff there is an assumption $x \in B$ such that $\alpha \in \mathcal{C}on(x)$. Similarly, we say that the set $\bar{S}$ of arguments attacks $\bar{b}$ when there is an argument $\bar{a} \in \bar{S}$ such that $\bar{a}$ **attacks** $\bar{b}$.*

According to the two previous definitions, ABA is clearly a concrete instantiation of AA where arguments are deductions and the attack relation comes from the contrary relation. Therefore, we can adopt Dung's calculus of opposition [13].

Definition 4 (Semantics). *Let $AF = \langle \mathcal{A}(ABF), \text{attacks} \rangle$ be our argumentation framework built upon the ABA framework $ABF = \langle \mathcal{L}, \mathcal{R}, \mathcal{A}sm, \mathcal{C}on \rangle$. A set of arguments $\bar{S} \subseteq \mathcal{A}(ABF)$ is:*

- * **conflict-free** iff $\forall \bar{a}, \bar{b} \in \bar{S}$ it is not the case that $\bar{a}$ attacks $\bar{b}$;*
- * **admissible** iff $\bar{S}$ is conflict-free and $\bar{S}$ attacks every argument $\bar{a}$ such that $\bar{a}$ attacks some arguments in $\bar{S}$.*

For simplicity, we restrict ourselves to admissible semantics.

3   Walk-Through Example

We consider e-procurement scenarios where buyers seek to purchase earth observation services from sellers [10]. Each agent represents a user, i.e. a service requester or a service provider. The negotiation of the fittest image is a complex task due to the number of possible choices, their characteristics and the preferences of the users. It makes this usecase interesting enough for the evaluation of our strategy [11]. For simplicity, we abstract away from the real world data of these features and we present here an intuitive scenario illustrating our strategy.

In our scenario, we consider a **buyer** that seeks to purchase a service $s(x)$ from a **seller**. The latter is responsible for the four following concrete instances of services: $s(a)$, $s(b)$, $s(c)$ and $s(d)$. These four concrete services reflect the combinations of their features (cf Fig. 1). For instance, the price of $s(a)$ is high (`Price(a,high)`), its resolution is low (`Resolution(a,low)`) and its delivery time

Table 1. Negotiation dialogue

Move	Speaker	Locution	Offer
mv_0	seller	assert	$s(a)$
mv_1	buyer	reply	$s(d)$
mv_2	seller	concede	$s(b)$
mv_3	buyer	concede	$s(c)$
mv_4	seller	accept	$s(c)$

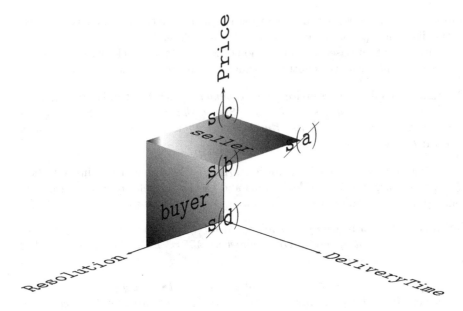

Fig. 1. Acceptability space of participants and proposals after the move mv₃

is high (`DeliveryTime(a, high)`). According to the preferences and the constraints of the user represented by the **buyer**: the cost must be low (`cheap`); the resolution of the service must be high (`good`); and the delivery time must be low (`fast`). Additionally, the **buyer** is not empowered to concede about the delivery time but it can concede indifferently about the resolution or the cost. According to the preferences and constraints of the user represented by the **seller**: the cost of the service must be high; the resolution of the service must be low; and the delivery time must be high (`slow`). The **seller** is not empowered to concede about the cost but it can concede indifferently about the resolution and the delivery time. The agents attempt to come to an agreement on the contract for the provision of a service $s(x)$. Taking into account some goals, preferences and constraints, the **buyer** (resp. the **seller**) needs to interactively solve a decision-making problem where the decision amounts to a service it can buy (resp. provide). Moreover, some decisions amount to the moves they can utter during the negotiation.

We consider the negotiation performed through the moves in Tab. 1. A move at time t: has an identifier, mv$_t$; it is uttered by a speaker, and the speech act is composed of a locution and a content, which consists of an offer. With the first moves, the **seller** and the **buyer** start with the proposals which are "optimal" for themselves, which are $s(a)$ and $s(d)$ respectively. In the third step of the negotiation, the **seller** can concede minimally either with $s(b)$ or with $s(c)$. Arbitrarily, it suggests $s(b)$ rather than $s(c)$, and so implicitly it rejects $s(d)$. The **buyer** rejects $s(b)$ since its delivery time is high, and so the **buyer** concedes minimally with $s(c)$. Finally, the **seller** accepts $s(c)$.

The evaluation of the services during the negotiation are represented at the three axis of the three dimension plot represented in Fig. 1. The acceptability space of the two participants is represented by shaded areas and depends on the delivery time (x-axis), on the resolution (y-axis) and the price (z-axis). As said previously, the four points of intersection reflect the combinations of their values. The services $s(a)$, $s(b)$ and $s(c)$ respect the constraints of the seller. According to the latter, $s(a)$ is preferred to $s(b)$ and $s(c)$, which are equally preferred. The services $s(d)$ and $s(c)$ respect the constraints of the buyer. According to the latter, $s(d)$ is preferred to $s(c)$.

4 Bilateral Bargaining Protocol

A negotiation is a social interaction amongst self-interested parties intended to resolve a dispute by verbal means and to produce an agreement upon a course of action. For instance, the aim for all parties is to "make a deal" while bargaining over their interests, typically seeking to maximise their individual welfare, and prepared to concede some aspects while insisting on others. In this section, we briefly present our game-based social model to handle the collaborative operations of agents. In particular, we present a dialogue-game protocol for bilateral bargaining.

According to the game metaphor for social interactions, agents are players which utter moves according to social rules.

Definition 5 (Dialogue-game). *Let us consider $\mathcal{L}$ a common object language and $\mathcal{ACL}$ a common agent communication language. A **dialogue-game** is a tuple $DG = \langle P, \Omega_M, H, T, proto, Z \rangle$ where:*

- *P is a set of agents called players;*
- *$\Omega_M \subseteq \mathcal{ACL}$ is a set of well-formed moves;*
- *H is a set of histories, the sequences of well-formed moves s.t. the speaker of a move is determined at each stage by the turn-taking function T and the moves agree with the protocol proto;*
- *$T: H \to P$ is the turn-taking function;*
- *proto: $H \to 2^{\Omega_M}$ is the function determining the legal moves which are allowed to expand an history;*
- *Z is the set of dialogues, i.e. the terminal histories.*

DG allows social interaction between agents. During a dialogue-game, players utter moves. Each dialogue is a maximally long sequence of moves. Let us now specify informally the elements of DG for bilateral bargainings.

In bilateral bargainings, there are two players, the initiator init and the responder resp, which utter moves each in turn. In our scenario, the initiator is the buyer and the responder is the seller. The **syntax** of moves is in conformance with a common **agent communication language**, $\mathcal{ACL}$. A move at time t: has an identifier, mv_t; is uttered by a speaker ($sp_t \in P$) and the speech act is composed of a locution loc_t and a content $content_t$. The possible locutions are: assert, reply, standstill, concede, accept and reject. The content consists of a sentence in the common object language, $\mathcal{L}$.

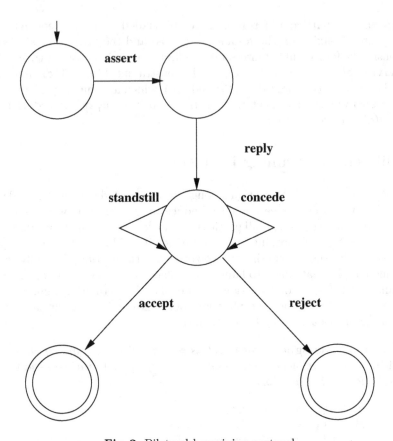

Fig. 2. Bilateral bargaining protocol

Given an history, the players share a **dialogue state**, depending on their previous moves. Considering the step $t \in \mathbb{N}$, the dialogue state is a tuple $\mathtt{DS}_t = \langle \mathtt{lloc}_t, \mathtt{loffer}_t(\mathtt{init}), \mathtt{loffer}_t(\mathtt{resp}), \mathtt{nbss}_t \rangle$ where:

- $\mathtt{lloc}_t$ is the last locution which has been uttered, possibly **none**;
- $\mathtt{loffer}_t(\mathtt{init})$ (resp. $\mathtt{loffer}_t(\mathtt{resp})$) represents the last offer of the initiator (resp. responder), i.e. the content of its last move;
- $\mathtt{nbss}_t$ is the number of consecutive **standstill** in the last moves.

Fig. 2 represents our dialogue-game protocol with the help of a deterministic finite-state automaton. A dialogue begins with a first offer when a player (the initiator or the responder) makes an **assert**. The legal responding speech act is **reply**. After that, the legal responding moves are standstills, concessions, acceptations and rejections. The legal responding moves to a concession/standstill are the same. An history is final and: i) the dialogue is a failure if it is closed by a **reject**; ii) the dialogue is a success if it is closed by an **accept**. The strategy interfaces with the dialogue-game protocol through the condition mechanism of utterances for a move. For example, at a certain point in the dialogue the agent is able to send `standstill` or `concede`. The choice of which locution and which content to send depends on the agent's strategy.

5   Decision Making

Taking into account the goals and preferences of the user, an agent needs to solve a decision-making problem where the decision amounts to an alternatives it can select. This agent uses argumentation in order to assess the suitability of alternatives and to identify "optimal" services. It argues internally to link the alternatives, their features and the benefits that these features guarantee under possibly incomplete knowledge. This section presents our framework to perform decision making, illustrated by our scenario.

Definition 6 (Decision framework). *A **decision framework** is a tuple* $DF = \langle \mathcal{L}, \mathcal{G}, \mathcal{D}, \mathcal{B}, \mathcal{R}, \mathcal{A}sm, \mathcal{C}on, \mathcal{P} \rangle$ *such that:*

- $\langle \mathcal{L}, \mathcal{R}, \mathcal{A}sm, \mathcal{C}on \rangle$ *is an ABA framework as defined in Def. 1 and* $\mathcal{L} = \mathcal{G} \cup \mathcal{D} \cup \mathcal{B}$ *where,*
  - $\mathcal{G}$ *is a set of literals in* $\mathcal{L}$ *called **goals**,*
  - $\mathcal{D}$ *is a set of assumptions in* $\mathcal{A}sm$ *called **decisions**,*
  - $\mathcal{B}$ *is a set of literals in* $\mathcal{L}$ *called **beliefs**;*
- $\mathcal{P} \subseteq \mathcal{G} \times \mathcal{G}$ *is a strict partial order over* $\mathcal{G}$, *called the **preference** relation.*

In the object language $\mathcal{L}$, we distinguish three disjoint components: a set of **goals** representing the objectives the agent wants to be fulfilled (e.g. `cheap`, `good` or `fast`); a set of **decisions** representing the possible services (e.g. `s(d)` or `s(c)`); a set of **beliefs**, representing the characteristics of the services (e.g. `Price(c, high)` or `Resolution(c, low)`). Decisions are **assumptions**. The multiple **contraries** capture the mutual exclusion of alternatives. For instance, we have $\mathcal{C}on(\mathbf{s(d)}) = \{\mathbf{s(a)}, \mathbf{s(b)}, \mathbf{s(c)}\}$.

The inference rules of the players are depicted in Tab. 2. All variables occurring in an inference rule are implicitly universally quantified over the whole rule. A rule with variables is a scheme standing for all its ground instances. The players are aware of the characteristics of the available services and the benefits that these features guarantee.

Table 2. The inference rules of the players

`expensive` ← `s(x), Price(x, high)`	`Price(b, high)` ←
`cheap` ← `s(x), Price(x, low)`	`Resolution(b, high)` ←
`good` ← `s(x), Resolution(x, high)`	`DeliveryTime(b, high)` ←
`bad` ← `s(x), Resolution(x, low)`	`Price(c, high)` ←
`fast` ← `s(x), DeliveryTime(x, low)`	`Resolution(c, low)` ←
`slow` ← `s(x), DeliveryTime(x, high)`	`DeliveryTime(c, low)` ←
`Price(a, high)` ←	`Price(d, low)` ←
`Resolution(a, low)` ←	`Resolution(d, low)` ←
`DeliveryTime(a, high)` ←	`DeliveryTime(d, low)` ←

We consider the **preference** relation $\mathcal{P}$ over the goals in $\mathcal{G}$, which is transitive, irreflexive and asymmetric. $g_1\mathcal{P}g_2$ can be read "g_1 is preferred to g_2". From the buyer's viewpoint, fast$\mathcal{P}$cheap, fast$\mathcal{P}$good, it is not the case that cheap$\mathcal{P}$good and it is not the case that good$\mathcal{P}$cheap. From the seller's viewpoint, expensive$\mathcal{P}$slow, expensive$\mathcal{P}$bad, it is not the case that bad$\mathcal{P}$slow and it is not the case that slow$\mathcal{P}$bad.

Formally, given an argument $\bar{a}$, let

$$\mathbf{dec}(\bar{a}) = \mathbf{asm}(\bar{a}) \cap \mathcal{D}$$

be the set of decisions supported by the argument $\bar{a}$.

Decisions are suggested to reach a goal if they are supported by arguments.

Definition 7 (Decisions). *Let $DF = \langle \mathcal{L}, \mathcal{G}, \mathcal{D}, \mathcal{B}, \mathcal{R}, \mathcal{A}sm, \mathcal{C}on, \mathcal{P} \rangle$ be a decision framework, $g \in \mathcal{G}$ be a goal and $D \subseteq \mathcal{D}$ be a set of decisions.*

- *The decisions D **argue for** g iff there exists an argument $\bar{a}$ such that $\mathbf{conc}(\bar{a}) = g$ and $\mathbf{dec}(\bar{a}) = D$.*
- *The decisions D **credulously argue for** g iff there exists an argument $\bar{a}$ in an admissible set of arguments such that $\mathbf{conc}(\bar{a}) = g$ and $\mathbf{dec}(\bar{a}) = D$.*
- *The decisions D **skeptically argue for** g iff for all admissible set of arguments $\bar{S}$ such that for some arguments $\bar{a}$ in $\bar{S}$ $\mathbf{conc}(\bar{a}) = g$, then $\mathbf{dec}(\bar{a}) = D$.*

We denote $val(D)$, $val_c(D)$ and $val_s(D)$ the set of goals in $\mathcal{G}$ for which the set of decisions D argues, credulously argues and skeptically argues, respectively.

Due to the uncertainties, some decisions satisfy goals for sure if they skeptically argue for them, or some decisions can possibly satisfy goals if they credulously argue for them. While the first case is required for convincing a risk-averse agent, the second case is enough to convince a risk-taking agent. We focus here on risk-taking agents.

Since agents can consider multiple objectives which may not be fulfilled all together by a set of non-conflicting decisions, high-ranked goals must be preferred to low-ranked goals.

Definition 8 (Preferences). *Let $DF = \langle \mathcal{L}, \mathcal{G}, \mathcal{D}, \mathcal{B}, \mathcal{R}, \mathcal{A}sm, \mathcal{C}on, \mathcal{P} \rangle$ be a decision framework. We consider G, G' two set of goals in $\mathcal{G}$ and D, D' two set of decisions in $\mathcal{D}$. G is **preferred** to G' (denoted $G\mathcal{P}G'$) iff*

1. *$G \supseteq G'$, and*
2. *$\forall g \in G \setminus G'$ there is no $g' \in G'$ such that $g'\mathcal{P}g$.*

*D is **preferred** to D' (denoted $D\mathcal{P}D'$) iff $val_c(D)\mathcal{P}val_c(D')$.*

The reservation value (denoted RV) is the minimal set of goals which needs to be reached by a set of decisions to be acceptable. Formally, given a reservation value RV, let
$$\mathbf{ad} = \{D(x) \mid \exists D \in \mathcal{D} \text{ such that } D(x) \in D \text{ and it is not the case that } RV\mathcal{P}val_c(D)\}$$
be the decisions which can be accepted by the agent.

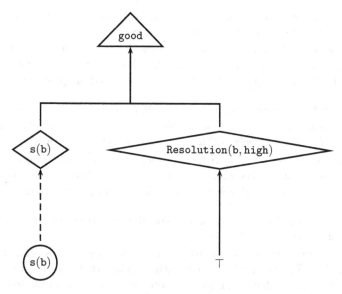

Fig. 3. Arguments concluding **good**

In our example, the argument $\bar{b}$ supports the service $s(b)$ due to its resolution. This argument is depicted in Fig. 3. While te resolution of **b** is a fact, the decision is an assumption. Some of the arguments are: $\bar{c}$ supporting the service $s(c)$ due to its delivery time; $\bar{d}_1$ supporting the service $s(d)$ due to its price and $\bar{d}_2$ supporting the service $s(d)$ due to its delivery time. The set of decisions $\{s(d)\}$ (resp. $\{s(b)\}$) is the only one which skeptically argues for **cheap** (resp. **good**) while both $\{s(c)\}$ and $\{s(d)\}$ credulously argue for **fast**. Since the **buyer** is not empowered to concede about the delivery time but it can concede about the other goals, its reservation value is $\{\text{fast}\}$. Therefore, both $\{s(c)\}$ and $\{s(d)\}$ are acceptable for the **buyer**. Since $\{s(d)\}$ credulously argue for **good** and this is not the case for $\{s(c)\}$, the **buyer** prefers $\{s(d)\}$ rather than $\{s(c)\}$. Since the **seller** is not empowered to concede about the cost but it can concede about the other goals, its reservation value is $\{\text{expensive}\}$. Therefore, $\{s(a)\}$, $\{s(b)\}$ and $\{s(c)\}$ are acceptable for the **seller**. Since $\{s(a)\}$ credulously argue for **slow** and **bad** while this is not the case for $\{s(b)\}$ and $\{s(c)\}$, the **seller** prefers $\{s(a)\}$ rather than $\{s(b)\}$ or $\{s(c)\}$ which are equally preferred.

6   Minimal Concession Strategy

Taking into account the preferences/goals of the user and the dialogue state, an agent needs to solve some decision-making problems where the decision amounts to a move it can utter. This agent uses argumentation in order to assess the suitability of moves and identify "optimal" moves. It argues internally to link the current dialogue state, the legal moves (their speech acts and their contents) and the resulting dialogue states of these moves under possibly incomplete knowledge.

This section presents how our argumentation approach realizes the Minimal Concession (MC) strategy, illustrated by our scenario.

A dialogue strategy is a plan that specifies the moves chosen by a player to achieve a particular goal. As defined in the classical game theory, this is the strategy of a player in a particular extensive game, a dialogue-game.

Definition 9 (Strategy). *Let* $DG = \langle P, \Omega_M, H, T, \texttt{proto}, Z \rangle$ *be a dialogue-game. A* **strategy** *of the player* $p \in P$ *is a function that assigns a move* $s_p(h)$ *to each nonterminal history* $h \in H \setminus Z$ *for which* $T(h) = p$. *For each strategy profile* $S = (s_p)_{p \in P}$, *we define the* **outcome** $O(S)$ *of* S *to be: either the content of the last move if the terminal history (that results when each player* $p \in P$ *follows the precepts of* s_p*) is successful, or nothing (denoted* θ*) if the terminal history is a failure.*

We consider here the MC strategy which specifies the move chosen by the player for every history when it is his turn to move.

In order to perform the MC strategy, an agent adopts a decision framework $DF = \langle \mathcal{L}, \mathcal{G}, \mathcal{D}, \mathcal{B}, \mathcal{R}, Asm, Con, \mathcal{P} \rangle$. The latter, as illustrated in the previous section, allows to perform decision making where the decision amounts to the service it can agree on. This DF must be extended to perform the MC strategy. For this purpose, we incorporate in the object language $\mathcal{L}$:

- the goal `respond` (resp. `optimal`) in $\mathcal{G}$ representing the objective of the agent which consists of responding (resp. uttering the "optimal" move);
- the decisions in $\mathcal{D}$ representing the possible locutions (e.g. `loc(standstill)` or `loc(concede)`). Obviously, the multiple contraries capture the mutual exclusion of the corresponding alternatives
  (e.g. $\{\texttt{loc(concede)}, \texttt{loc(accept)}, \texttt{loc(reject)}\} = Con(\texttt{loc(standstill)}))$;
- a set of beliefs in $\mathcal{B}$, related to the dialogue state,
  - the last locution of the interlocutor (e.g. `lloc(concede)`),
  - the last offers of the players (e.g. `loffer(seller, b)` or `loffer(buyer, d)`),
  - the previous offers of the players (e.g. `poffer(seller, a)`),
  - the offers which have been already (and implicitly) rejected by the interlocutor (e.g. `rejected(d)`);

Table 3. The additional inference rules of the **buyer** related to the dialogue state after the move $\texttt{mv}_2$

$$\texttt{lloc(concede)} \leftarrow \qquad\qquad (1)$$

$$\texttt{nbss(0)} \leftarrow \qquad\qquad (2)$$

$$\texttt{poffer(seller, a)} \leftarrow \qquad\qquad (3)$$

$$\texttt{loffer}(p, x) \leftarrow \texttt{poffer}(p, x) \qquad\qquad (4)$$

$$\texttt{loffer(seller, b)} \leftarrow \qquad\qquad (5)$$

$$\texttt{loffer(buyer, d)} \leftarrow \qquad\qquad (6)$$

$$\texttt{rejected}(x) \leftarrow \texttt{poffer(buyer}, x) \qquad\qquad (7)$$

— a set of assumptions in $\mathcal{A}sm$ representing that some alternatives have not been yet rejected (e.g. notrejected(c)), that some alternatives have not been proposed in the last move (e.g. notloffer(seller, c)) and that a number of standstills has not been reached (e.g. notnbss(3)).

The **preference** relation $\mathcal{P}$ on the goals in $\mathcal{G}$ is extended in order to take into account the new goals respond and optimal. Actually, these goals are incomparable with the other ones (e.g. cheap, good, fast). By adopting the MC strategy, the agent tries to utter the "optimal" utterances, optimal. If the agent cannot reach this goal, then the agents responds with a legal move, optimal$\mathcal{P}$respond

Table 4. The additional inference rules of the players related to the negotiation strategy

$$\text{optimal} \leftarrow \text{loc(assert)}, \text{lloc(none)} \tag{8}$$

$$\text{optimal} \leftarrow \text{loc(reply)}, \text{lloc(assert)} \tag{9}$$

$$\text{optimal} \leftarrow \text{loc(concede)}, \text{s}(x),$$
$$\text{lloc(reply)}, \text{notrejected}(x), \text{notloffer(seller}, x) \tag{10}$$

$$\text{respond} \leftarrow \text{loc(standstill)}, \text{s}(x),$$
$$\text{lloc(reply)}, \text{loffer(buyer}, x) \tag{11}$$

$$\text{optimal} \leftarrow \text{loc(concede)}, \text{s}(x),$$
$$\text{lloc(concede)}, \text{notrejected}(x), \text{notloffer(seller}, x) \tag{12}$$

$$\text{respond} \leftarrow \text{loc(standstill)}, \text{s}(x)$$
$$\text{lloc(concede)}, \text{loffer(buyer}, x) \tag{13}$$

$$\text{optimal} \leftarrow \text{loc(standstill)},$$
$$\text{lloc(standstill)}, \text{notnbss}(3) \tag{14}$$

$$\text{optimal} \leftarrow \text{loc(concede)}, \text{s}(x),$$
$$\text{lloc(standstill)}, \text{notrejected}(x),$$
$$\text{notloffer(seller}, x), \text{nbss}(3) \tag{15}$$

$$\text{respond} \leftarrow \text{loc(reject)}, \text{s}(x),$$
$$\text{lloc(standstill)}, \text{loffer(seller}, x),$$
$$\text{nbss}(3) \tag{16}$$

$$\text{optimal} \leftarrow \text{loc(accept)}, \text{s}(x),$$
$$\text{lloc(reply)},$$
$$\text{loffer(seller}, x) \tag{17}$$

$$\text{optimal} \leftarrow \text{loc(accept)}, \text{s}(x),$$
$$\text{lloc(concede)}, \text{notrejected}(x),$$
$$\text{loffer(seller}, x) \tag{18}$$

$$\text{optimal} \leftarrow \text{loc(accept)}, \text{s}(x),$$
$$\text{lloc(standstill)}, \text{notrejected}(x),$$
$$\text{loffer(seller}, x), \text{nbss}(3) \tag{19}$$

and respond $\in$ RV. Since this decision framework (in particular the rules) depends on the dialogue state of the history h, we denote it by
$DF_h = \langle \mathcal{L}, \mathcal{G}, \mathcal{D}, \mathcal{B}, \mathcal{R}_h, Asm, Con, \mathcal{P} \rangle$.

Some inference rules of the buyer are depicted in Tab. 2. While the additional rules related to the dialogue state after the move mv_2 are depicted in Tab. 3, the additional rules related to the negotiation strategy are depicted in Tab. 4. Let us consider these latter rules (8-19). While one of the players starts by asserting a first proposal (8), the other agent replies with a counter-proposal (9). An agent must adopt one of these attitudes: i) either it **stands still**, i.e. it repeats its previous proposal; ii) or it **concedes**, i.e. it withdraws to put forward one of its previous proposal and it considers another one. In order to articulate these attitudes, the MC strategy consists of adhering the reciprocity principle during the negotiation. If the interlocutor stands still, then the agent will stand still (14). Whenever the interlocutor has made a concession, it will reciprocate by conceding as well (12). If the agent is not able to concede (e.g. there is no other services which satisfy its constraints), the agent will standstill (13). It is worth noticing that the third step in the negotiation has a special status, in that the player has to concede (10). If the agent is not able to concede (e.g. there is no other service which satisfies its constraints), the agent will standstill (11). If an acceptable offer has been put forward by the interlocutor, the player accepts it (17-19). When the player can no more concede, it stops the negotiation (16). It is worth noticing that contrary to [7], our strategy does not stop the negotiation after 3 consecutive standstills but the strategy allows to concede after them (15). As we will see in the next section, this will allow a negotiation to succeed even if, contrary to [7], an agent does not know the preferences and the reservation value of the other agent.

Differently from [7], we do not assume that the agents know the preferences of their interlocutors. Therefore, we say that a decision is a **minimal** concession for a speaker since there is no other decisons which are preferred.

Definition 10 (Minimal concession). *Let $DF = \langle \mathcal{L}, \mathcal{G}, \mathcal{D}, \mathcal{B}, \mathcal{R}, Asm, Con, \mathcal{P} \rangle$ be a decision framework as defined in Section 5. The decision $dec \in \mathcal{D}$ is a **concession** wrt $dec' \in \mathcal{D}$ iff there exists a set of decisions D such that $dec \in D$ and for all $D' \subseteq D$ with $dec' \in D'$, it is not the case that $D\mathcal{P}D'$. The decision dec is a **minimal concession** wrt dec' iff it is a concession wrt dec' and there is no $dec'' \in \mathcal{D}$ such that*

- *dec'' is a concession wrt dec', and*
- *there is $D'' \subseteq D$ with $dec'' \in D''$ with $D''\mathcal{P}D$.*

The minimal concessions are computed by our decision framework. Concerning the negotiation, we say that an offer is a minimal concession for a speaker since there is no other offer which has not been already (and implicitly) rejected by the interlocutor and which is preferred by the speaker. The minimal concessions are computed by the decision framework proposed in this section. In our example, $s(c)$ is a minimal concession wrt $s(d)$. Actually, the buyer concedes the service $s(c)$ after the move mv_2 since $s(d)$ has been rejected.

7 Properties

The negotiation protocol, as well as the MC strategy, has useful properties. The negotiations always terminate. Moreover, if both players adopt the MC strategy, the negotiation is successful, when it is possible. Finally, the outcome is optimal.

Due to the finiteness assumption of the language, and hence the finiteness of possible decisions, the set of histories is also finite. Hence it is immediate that the negotiations always terminate.

Theorem 1 (Terminaison). *The dialogues are finite.*

Due to the finiteness assumption and the definition of the MC strategy over the potential agreements, it is not difficult to see that such negotiations are successful, if a potential agreement exists.

Theorem 2 (Success). *If both players adopt a MC strategy and a potential agreement exists, then the dialogue is a success.*

Differently from [7], a player will concede at a certain point even if its interlocutor stands still since it can no more concede. Therefore, the negotiation between two players adopting the MC strategy go throw the whole sets of acceptable services. In our example, $s(c)$, which fulfills the constraints of both of the participants, is the outcome of the successful dialogue.

Differently from [7], our realisation of the MC strategy allows to reach an agreement even if the agents do not know the preferences and the reservation value of the other agents. However, this realisation of the MC strategy is not in a pure symmetric Nash equilibrium.

The final agreement of the negotiation is said to be a Pareto optimal if it is not possible to strictly improve the individual welfare of an agent without making the other worse off. This is the case of our realisation of the MC strategy in a bilateral bargaining.

Claim 1 (Social welfare). *If both players adopt a MC strategy and a potential agreement exists, then the outcome of the dialogue is Pareto optimal.*

The outcome is Pareto optimal since the concessions are minimal.

8 Deployment

In this paper we have proposed a realisation of the MC strategy which has been practically validated. Actually, our strategy has been tested within industrial scenarios [10] from which we have extracted an intuitive and illustrative example.

We demonstrate in [11] the use of a fully decentralised multi-agent system supporting agent-automated service discovery, agent-automated service selection, and agent-automated negotiation of Service Level Agreements (SLAs) for the selected services. The system integrates

- GOLEM[2] (Generalized OntoLogical Environments for Multi-agent systems), an agent environment middleware [18]
- MARGO[3] (A Multiattribute ARGumentation frame- work for Opinion explanation), an argumentation-based mechanism for decision-making [19]. MARGO is written in Prolog and it is distributed under the GNU GPL. MARGO is built on top of CaSAPI[4] [14] (Credulous and Sceptical Argumentation: Prolog Implementation), a general-purpose tool for (several types of) assumption-based argumentation which is also written in Prolog
- PLATON[5] (Peer-to-Peer Load Adjusting Tree Over- lay Networks), a Peer-to-Peer platform supporting multi-attribute and range queries [20]

This system is used for service composition and orchestration within the ARGU-GRID[6] project. As discussed in [21], the PlATEM system (GOLEM + MARGO + PLATON) is interfaced with a semantic composition environment, allowing users to interact with their agents, and the GRIA grid middleware for the actual deployment of services.

Our system uses the MARGO tool for multi-attribute qualitative decision-making to support the decision on suitable services. Moreover, the MC strategy has been implemented by means of MARGO.

9   Related Works

Rahwan et al. [22] propose an analysis grid of strategies for agents engaged in negotiations. According to this grid, the factors which influence our strategy are: the goals (an optimal outcome here), the domain (represented in terms of multi-attribute choice here), the negotiation protocol, the abilities of agents (buy/sell services here), the values (promoted by the reciprocity principle here). While the strategy of our agents is directly influenced by the behaviour of its interlocutor, it is not clear how to situate this factor in the analysis grid of [22].

Few concrete strategies of agents engaged in negotiations have been proposed. For instance, Sierra et al. [23] propose different strategies based on arguments such as threats, rewards or appeals (e.g. to authority). More works are concerned by dialogues with theoretical issues rather than practical issues. In particular, some works aim at formalizing and implementing communication strategies for argumentative agents, specifying how an agent selects a move according to the dialogue state and the arguments it has. For instance, Amgoud and Parsons [24] define different attitudes: an agent can be agreeable/disagreeable, open-minded/argumentative or an elephant's child, depending on the the legal moves and their rational conditions of utterance. Differently from [24], our strategy takes into account also the overt behaviour of the interlocutor, since

---

[2] http://www.golem.cs.rhul.ac.uk
[3] http://margo.sourceforge.net
[4] http://casapi.sourceforge.net
[5] http://platonp2p.sourceforge.net
[6] http://www.argugrid.eu

this strategy is based on the reciprocity principle. More attitudes have been proposed in [25] (credulous, skeptical, cautious) based on the various degrees of justification captured by these different semantics of abstract argumentation. In this paper, we claim that, in negotiations, the different semantics allow us to distinguish risk-taking agents and risk-averse agents. In [24,25], some properties of these strategies have been studied, such as the existence/determinism of the responds of these strategies, as well as the impact of these attitudes on the result, and the termination and the complexity of the dialogue. In this paper, we have similar results expected for the complexity. The main difference between the work in [24,25] and our work is the type of dialogues which are considered. While [25] focus on theoretical dialogues, i.e. with discursive purposes, only concerned by beliefs, we are interested on bilateral bargaining dialogues between parties which aim at reaching a practical agreement, i.e a course of action.

Alternatively, Kakas et al. [26,27] consider the argumentation-based mechanism for decision-making [28] implemented in GORGIAS [29] to perform the communication strategy of agents which depends on the agent knowledge, roles, context and possibly on dynamic preferences. The work of Kakas, Maudet and Moraitis is guided by the requirements for communication strategies of an expressive and declarative language which is directly implementable. The Agent Argumentation Architecture model we have proposed in [30,31] shares with [32] (a) the vision of argumentative deliberation for internal agent modules and (b) the assumption that an agent can prioritize its needs. However, this paper focus on a simple strategy and the study of its properties in game-theoretical terms.

Adopting a game-theory perspective as well, Riveret et al. [33] model an argumentation dialogue [34] as an extensive game with perfect and complete information. While they focus on argumentation games in adjudication debates, we have considered here negotiation games where arguments are not push forward, but instead they are used to evaluate proposals. Moreover, they abstract away for the underlying logical language, whereas we concretise the structure of arguments. Rahwan and Larson [35] consider abstract argumentation as a game-theoretic mechanism design problem. In this perspective, Rahwan and Larson [36] analyse and design intuitive rational criteria for self-interested agents involved in adjudication games. These rational criteria extend the attitudes based on the different semantics of abstract argumentation (credulous, skeptical, cautious). An agent may aim at maximising (resp. minimising) the number of its own arguments which will be accepted (resp. rejected or considered as undecided) by a judge. An aggressive agent aims at maximising the number of arguments from other agents which will be rejected by a judge. Differently from [36], we have defined the underlying logical language, and so the agents' preferences are on the goals. Therefore, our agents try to maximise the number of goals which will be promoted by their agreements, and high-ranked goals are preferred to low-ranked goals.

10   Conclusions

In this paper we have presented a realisation of the minimal concession strategy which applies argumentation for generating and evaluating proposals during negotiations. According to this strategy, agents start the negotiation with their best proposals. During the negotiation, an agent may concede or stand still. It concedes minimally if the other agent has conceded in the previous step, or after the optimal offers for the participants have been put forward. It stands still if the other agent has stood still in the previous step. A concession is minimal for a speaker since there is no other alternative which has not been already (and implicitly) rejected by the interlocutor, and which is preferred by the speaker. Our realisation of the minimal concession strategy has useful properties: it guarantees that the outcome of the negotiation, which is guaranteed to terminate, is optimal when it is possible, even if the agents ignore the preferences and the reservation values of the other agents.

Our negotiation model only allows the exchange of proposals and counterproposals. Our plan for future work is to extend it and to extend the current strategy for exchanging, generating and evaluating arguments during negotiations. The extra information carried out by these arguments will allow agents to influence each other, and so it may allow to decrease the number messages required to reach an agreement. Our negotiation model can only handle negotiation about fixed item/service. In future works, we want to apply our argumentation-based mechanism for integrative negotiations rather than distributive negotiations. Contrary to distributive negotiations, all aspects are considered in [8] for a solution that maximizes the social welfare, such as new services to accommodate each other's needs for a better deal. We aim at adopting this negotiation model and extend the strategy to generate and evaluate additional sub-items.

Acknowledgements

We would like to thank the anonymous reviewers for their detailed comments on this paper. The authors thank Phan Minh Dung for many useful discussions on the topic of this work.

References

1. Jennings, N.R., Faratin, P., Lomuscio, A.R., Parsons, S., Sierra, C., Wooldridge, M.: Automated negotiation: prospects, methods and challenges. International Journal of Group Decision and Negotiation 10(2), 199–215 (2001)
2. Luck, M., McBurney, P.: Computing as interaction: agent and agreement technologies. In: Marik, V. (ed.) Proc. of the 2008 IEEE International Conference on Distributed Human-Machine Systems, Athens, Greece (March 2008)
3. Rahwan, I., Ramchurn, S.D., Jennings, N.R., McBurney, P., Parsons, S., Sonenberg, L.: Argumentation-based negotiation. The Knowledge Engineering Review 18(4), 343–375 (2003)

4. Kakas, A., Moraitis, P.: Adaptive agent negotiation via argumentation. In: Proc. 5th International Joint Conference on Autonomous Agents and Multi-Agent Systems (AAMAS), Hakodate, Japan, May 2006, pp. 384–391 (2006)
5. Amgoud, L., Dimopoulos, Y., Moraitis, P.: A unified and general framework for argumentation-based negotiation. In: Proc. 6th International Joint Conference on Autonomous Agents and Multi-Agent Systems (AAMAS), Honolulu, Hawaii, pp. 963–970 (2007)
6. Dimopoulos, Y., Moraitis, P., Amgoud, L.: Characterizing the outcomes of argumentation-based integrative negotiation. In: Proc. of IEEE/WIC/ACM International Conference on Intelligent Agent Technology (IAT), Sydney, Australia (2008)
7. Dung, P.M., Thang, P.M., Toni, F.: Towards argumentation-based contract negotiation. In: Proc. of the 2nd Second International Conference on Computational Models of Argument. IOS Press, Amsterdam (2008)
8. Dung, P.M., Thang, P.M., Hung, N.D.: Argument-based decision making and negotiation in e-business: Contracting a land lease for a computer assembly plant. In: Fisher, M., Sadri, F., Thielscher, M. (eds.) Computational Logic in Multi-Agent Systems. LNCS, vol. 5405, pp. 154–172. Springer, Heidelberg (2009)
9. Dung, P.M., Thang, P.M.: Modular argumentation for modelling legal doctrines in common law of contract. In: Proc. of The Twenty-First Annual Conference Legal Knowledge and Information Systems (JURIX). Frontiers in Artificial Intelligence and Applications, vol. 189, pp. 108–117 (2008)
10. Stournaras, T. (ed.): Concrete scenarios identification & simple use cases. Deliverable document D1.1 ARGUGRID (2007)
11. Bromuri, S., Urovi, V., Morge, M., Toni, F., Stathis, K.: A multi-agent system for service discovery, selection and negotiation. In: Proc. of the 8th International Joint Conference on Autonomous Agents and Multiagent Systems, AAMAS (2009) (Demonstration)
12. Bondarenko, A., Toni, F., Kowalski, R.: An assumption-based framework for non-monotonic reasoning. In: Nerode, A., Pereira, L. (eds.) Proc. of the 2nd International Workshop on Logic Programming and Non-Monotonic Reasoning (LPNMR). MIT Press, Cambridge (1993)
13. Dung, P.M.: On the acceptability of arguments and its fundamental role in non-monotonic reasoning, logic programming and n-person games. Artif. Intell. 77(2), 321–357 (1995)
14. Gartner, D., Toni, F.: CaSAPI: a system for credulous and sceptical argumentation. In: Simari, G., Torroni, P. (eds.) Proc. of the Workshop on Argumentation for Non-monotonic Reasoning (ArgNMR), pp. 80–95 (2007)
15. Vreeswijk, G.: Abstract argumentation systems. Artificial Intelligence 90(1-2), 225–279 (1997)
16. Dung, P.M., Kowalski, R.A., Toni, F.: Dialectic proof procedures for assumption-based, admissible argumentation. Artificial Intelligence 170(2), 114–159 (2006)
17. Amgoud, L., Cayrol, C.: On the acceptability of arguments in preference-based argumentation. In: Proc. of the 14th Conference on Uncertainty in Artificial Intelligence (UAI), Madison, Wisconsin, USA, pp. 1–7. Morgan Kaufmann, San Francisco (1998)
18. Bromuri, S., Stathis, K.: Situating cognitive agents in GOLEM. In: Weyns, D., Brueckner, S.A., Demazeau, Y. (eds.) EEMMAS 2007. LNCS (LNAI), vol. 5049, pp. 115–134. Springer, Heidelberg (2008)

19. Morge, M., Mancarella, P.: The hedgehog and the fox. An argumentation-based decision support system. In: Rahwan, I., Parsons, S., Reed, C. (eds.) ArgMAS 2007. LNCS (LNAI), vol. 4946, pp. 114–131. Springer, Heidelberg (2008)

20. Lymberopoulos, L., Bromuri, S., Stathis, K., Kafetzoglou, S., Grammatiko, M.: Towards a p2p discovery framework for an argumentative agent technology assisted grid. In: Proc. of the CoreGRID Workshop on Grid Programming Model, Grid and P2P systems Arhcitectures, Grid Systems, Tools, and Environments, Crete, Greece (June 2007)

21. Toni, F., Grammatikou, M., Kafetzoglou, S., Lymberopoulos, L., Papavassileiou, S., Gaertner, D., Morge, M., Bromuri, S., McGinnis, J., Stathis, K., Curcin, V., Ghanem, M., Guo, L.: The argugrid platform: An overview. In: Altmann, J., Neumann, D., Fahringer, T. (eds.) GECON 2008. LNCS, vol. 5206, pp. 217–225. Springer, Heidelberg (2008)

22. Rahwan, I., McBurney, P., Sonenberg, L.: Towards a theory of negotiation strategy (a preliminary report). In: Proc. of the AAMAS Workshop on Game Theoretic and Decision Theoretic Agents (GTDT), Melbourne, Australia, pp. 1–8 (2003)

23. Sierra, C., Jennings, N.R., Noriega, P., Parsons, S.: A framework for argumentation-based negotiation. In: Rao, A., Singh, M.P., Wooldridge, M.J. (eds.) ATAL 1997. LNCS, vol. 1365, pp. 177–192. Springer, Heidelberg (1998)

24. Amgoud, L., Parsons, S.: Agent dialogues with conflicting preferences. In: Meyer, J.-J.C., Tambe, M. (eds.) ATAL 2001. LNCS (LNAI), vol. 2333, pp. 190–205. Springer, Heidelberg (2002)

25. Parsons, S., Wooldridge, M., Amgoud, L.: Properties and complexity of some formal inter-agent dialogues. Journal of Logic and Computation 13(3), 347–376 (2003)

26. Kakas, A.C., Maudet, N., Moraitis, P.: Flexible agent dialogue strategies and societal communication protocols. In: Proc. of the 3rd International Joint Conference on Autonomous Agents and Multi-Agent Systems (AAMAS), pp. 1434–1435 (2004)

27. Kakas, A.C., Maudet, N., Moraitis, P.: Layered strategies and protocols for argumentation-based agent interaction. In: Rahwan, I., Moraïtis, P., Reed, C. (eds.) ArgMAS 2004. LNCS (LNAI), vol. 3366, pp. 64–77. Springer, Heidelberg (2005)

28. Kakas, A., Moraitis, P.: Argumentative-based decision-making for autonomous agents. In: Proc. of the 2nd International Joint Conference on Autonomous Agents and Multi-Agent Systems (AAMAS), pp. 883–890. ACM Press, New York (2003)

29. Demetriou, N., Kakas, A.C.: Argumentation with abduction. In: Proc. of the 4th Panhellenic Symposium on Logic (2003)

30. Morge, M., Stathis, K.: The agent argumentation architecture revisited. In: Proc. of the Sixth European Workshop on Multi-Agent Systems (EUMAS 2008), Bath, UK, pp. 1–15 (2007)

31. Morge, M., Stathis, K., Vercouter, L.: Arguing over motivations within the v3a-architecture for self-adaptation. In: Proc. of the 1st International Conference on Agents and Artificial Intelligence (ICAART), Porto, Portugal, pp. 1–6 (2009)

32. Kakas, A., Moraitis, P.: Argumentative-based decision-making for autonomous agents. In: Proc. of the 2nd International Joint Conference on Autonomous Agents and Multi-Agent Systems (AAMAS), pp. 883–890. ACM Press, New York (2003)

33. Riveret, R., Prakken, H., Rotolo, A., Sartor, G.: Heuristics in argumentation: A game theory investigation. In: Besnard, P., Doutre, S., Hunter, A. (eds.) Proc. of the 2nd International Conference on Computational Models of Argument (COMMA). Frontiers in Artificial Intelligence and Applications, vol. 172, pp. 324–335. IOS Press, Amsterdam (2008)

34. Prakken, H.: Coherence and flexibility in dialogue games for argumentation. Journal of Logic and Compuation 15(6), 1009–1040 (2005)
35. Rahwan, I., Larson, K.: Mechanism design for abstract argumentation. In: Proc. of the 7th International Conference on Autonomous Agents and Multiagent Systems (AAMAS), Estoril, Portugal, pp. 1031–1038 (2008)
36. Rahwan, I., Larson, K.: Pareto optimality in abstract argumentation. In: Proc. of the 23rd Conference on Artificial Intelligence (AAAI), California, USA, pp. 150–156. AAAI Press, Menlo Park (2008)

Subjective Effectiveness in Agent-to-Human Negotiation: A Frame x Personality Account

Yinping Yang[1], Ya Hui Michelle See[1,2], Andrew Ortony[1,3], and Jacinth Jia Xin Tan[2]

[1] Computational Cognition for Social Systems, Institute of High Performance Computing, Agency for Science, Technology, and Research (A*STAR), Singapore
[2] National University of Singapore, Singapore
[3] Northwestern University, Evanston, Illinois, USA
yangyp@ihpc.a-star.edu.sg, psysyhm@nus.edu.sg,
ortony@northwestern.edu, u0501364@nus.edu.sg

Abstract. This paper presents an empirical examination on the role of framing as a persuasion technique in agent-to-human negotiations. The primary hypothesis was that when a software agent frames the same offer in different ways it will have different consequences for a human counterpart's perceptions of the negotiation process and outcomes. A secondary hypothesis was that the subjective effectiveness of different frames will be influenced by the personality of the human counterpart. An experiment to test these hypotheses was conducted using a simulated software seller agent and a human buyer counterpart in a 4-issue negotiation task. The results demonstrated the influence of framing on human counterparts' judgments of subjective effectiveness–an influence that was moderated by the personality variable Need for Cognition. The findings illustrate the strategic impact of framing and personality on satisfaction in negotiation, suggesting that these variables should be taken into account in designing negotiating agents.

Keywords: frame, negotiation, satisfaction, personality, Need for Cognition, persuasion, agent-to-human negotiation, automated negotiation, experiment.

1 Introduction

Recently, spurred no doubt by the rapid growth of the electronic marketplace, there has been increasing interest in applying AI techniques to the design of autonomous agents that serve as surrogates for human decision-makers. Previous research in the agent-based negotiation community has explored persuasion techniques for argumentation-based protocols in which agents accompanied their offers with their underlying reasons in agent-to-agent negotiation settings [1, 2]. However, relatively little is known about the dynamics of argumentation and persuasion in agent-to-human negotiation contexts [3].

In an open, e-market environment, a software agent acting on behalf of its principal might have to negotiate with another software agent, or with a human agent. In the latter case, wherein a software agent negotiates with a human agent, it might be helpful for the software agent to be equipped not only with sophisticated intelligence, but

P. McBurney et al. (Eds.): ArgMAS 2009, LNAI 6057, pp. 134–149, 2010.

also with the kind of artful skills that enable strategically advantageous interactions [3, 4]. Thus *agent-to-human negotiation* creates a new and interesting area for research–one which bridges the gap between how negotiation is performed in human and in artificial worlds.

An important aspect of negotiation dynamics that social scientists who study cognitive processes, decision making, persuasion, and communication have studied is *framing*–a persuasion technique widely used in human-to-human communication. In decision theory terms, a *frame* refers to a "decision-maker's conception of the acts, outcomes, and contingencies associated with a particular choice" [5] (p. 453). The (software) agent-to-human negotiation context allows the examination of framing not only in terms of its economic, utility-based, effects but also in terms of its subjective consequences for human negotiation counterparts, and it is this aspect of framing that is the primary focus of this paper. Simply put, we explore the impact of different message frames on *subjective effectiveness*, defined as the extent to which an individual perceives positive psychological experiences in a negotiation situation [6].

Recent social psychological research suggests that there are four underlying dimensions in terms of which the subjective outcomes of a negotiation can be characterized: Feelings about the self, Feelings about the instrumental outcome, Feelings about the process, and Feelings about the relationship [7]. Such psychological perceptions are associated with long-term consequences such as willingness to interact with the same counterpart in future [6, 7]. Prior research has established that when the same information (logically speaking) is presented using different frames, the emotions people experience depend on whether they tend to focus on their aspirations or their obligations (i.e., on their regulatory focus) as they pursue their goals [8]. This raises the possibility that the differential impact of gain and loss frames might extend to different people's psychological perceptions in different ways. Another respect in which individuals might differ in how they respond to different message frames relates to their *motivation to process the information*. In the present study, when manipulating message frames, the economic utility of the offer is kept constant, so the messages do not differ in their substantive content. Differences in people's motivation to process information is captured by the Need for Cognition personality variable, the measurement scale for which assesses the tendency to engage in and enjoy effortful cognitive activity, or thinking [9]. In summary, we address the following two questions:

1. When a negotiating agent presents an offer to its human counterpart, how do different message frames (of the same offer) affect the counterpart's subjective evaluations of the negotiation process and outcome?

2. Do aspects of the human counterpart's personality moderate any such effects?

2 Message Frames

Among various types of message frames examined in the persuasion literature (e.g., image-focused versus quality-focused frames [10], affective versus cognitive frames [11]), one of the most extensively studied framing strategies are gain and loss frames [12]. Gain frames focus on the benefits of taking action whereas loss frames focus on the costs of failing to take action, both relative to the same desired state of affairs (e.g., [13]). For example, relative to the desired state of good cardiac health, a typical gain frame focuses on the potential beneficial outcome of having a healthy heart resulting from action: "If you follow this diet, you will have a healthy heart". In contrast, a typical loss frame focuses on the potential costly outcome of getting heart disease resulting from inaction: "If you don't follow this diet, you will get heart disease". Note that in these examples, the gain and loss frames are isomorphic with engaging and not engaging in action. The frames focus only on the presence of a gain or a loss–action for the gain, inaction for the loss.

However, it is also possible to consider frames that focus on the *absence of gains* (i.e., non-gains) and the *absence of losses* (i.e., non-losses). Continuing with the example of good cardiac health, a non-gain frame would be "If you don't follow this diet, you will not have a healthy heart," while the corresponding non-loss frame would be "If you follow this diet, you will not get heart disease." Table 1 illustrates the possible frames that can occur when the absence/presence dimension is crossed with the gain/loss dimension.

Table 1. Example of gain/loss frames crossed with presence/absence

	Presence	Absence
Gain	**Gain** If you follow this diet, you *will have a healthy heart.*	**Non-gain** If you don't follow this diet, you *will not have a healthy heart.*
Loss	**Loss** If you don't follow this diet, you *will get heart disease.*	**Non-Loss** If you follow this diet, you *will not get heart disease.*

Framing has been studied extensively with respect to how it affects people's behavior and their perceptions, especially their perceptions of risk. For example, an important finding resulting from Prospect Theory [14] indicates that people are more risk-averse when a decision problem is framed as a possible gain, and more risk-tolerant when it is framed as a possible loss. In general, many studies suggest that people tend to respond differently when presented with the possibility of gaining something as opposed to not losing something, or losing as opposed to not gaining something (e.g., [15]). Compared to conditions when outcomes are framed as losses or non-gains, negotiators tend to make fewer concessions and reach fewer agreements when outcomes are framed as gains or non-losses [16]. However, a recent meta-analysis [12] of 165 cases involving a total of more than 50,000 participants revealed that overall, loss frames were no more persuasive than gain frames.

Our work differs from existing research in two important respects. First, in the meta-analysis [12], gain frames and non-loss frames were classified together as gain frames, and loss and non-gain frames were classified together as loss frames. It is possible that these conflations (necessitated by the studies included in the analysis) mask differences that might have been found had gain and non-loss frames, and loss and non-gain frames been separated. In the present work, we considered both the *absence-presence* distinction and the *gain-loss* distinction. Second, disagreements about the effectiveness of frames basically revolve around the question of whether frames affect behavioral compliance or attitudes toward the recommended behavior.

However, our interest is in the *subjective effectiveness* of framing in negotiation, so our focus is on participants' perceptions toward the negotiation settlement, the counterpart, and the self.

An important subjective outcome of a negotiation is the negotiator's judgment about the faithfulness, friendliness, and flexibility of the other [6, 7]. When we apply the four distinctive frames in negotiation context, the gain and non-loss frames can be thought of as corresponding to a "promise" message whereas the loss and non-gain frames communicate a kind of "threat". Threats and promises are conditional commitments by the sender to do desirable or undesirable things for the message recipient as a function of the recipient's response [17-19]. In our context, when the final offer is presented as "if you don't accept my offer, I won't give you the free service-upgrade" (non-gain) or "if you don't accept my offer, I'll charge you for the service-upgrade" (loss), the offer has the form of a threat. This contrasts with offers in the form of promises, as in "if you accept my offer, I will give you a free service-upgrade" (gain) and "if you accept my offer, I won't charge you a free service-upgrade" (non-loss). It is easy to imagine that threats would elicit in the message receiver negative perceptions (e.g., of aggressiveness) of the message sender [20]. Research has suggested that threats that are more compellent [21], or that are associated with greater clarity [22, 23], or that can be presented in early-explicit or late-implicit manners [24] tend to be perceived more aggressive than otherwise. Therefore, when negotiators feel threatened, they are more likely to develop an aggressive/negative impression of the message sender, whereas they are more likely to experience more positive feelings towards the counterpart when the message is framed as a promise.

The various considerations discussed above, lead to the following two hypotheses:

Hypothesis 1. Negotiators are more likely to feel *satisfied with respect to their counterparts* when they accept offers with "promise" frames (gain/non-loss frames), than when they accept offers with "threat" frames (loss/non-gain frames).

In addition to considering how a negotiator feels about the other party, he or she is also likely to have feelings about the settlement per se. In fact, *satisfaction with the settlement* is the subjective outcome most usually evaluated in computer-supported negotiation experiments (e.g., [25-29]). *Satisfaction with the settlement* relates primarily to the subjective belief that a negotiator has achieved a fair, desirable, and/or efficient solution. We know from previous studies [e.g., 30, 31] that negotiators are more willing to make concessions when presented with a gain frame than with a loss frame. It is reasonable to suppose that the way in which a concession is made will influence other subjective perceptions such as feelings about the settlement and about oneself. That is, the subjective sense that one conceded voluntarily as opposed to having been pressured to concede might lead to a greater sense of satisfaction with the settlement, even though the objective outcomes don't differ–hence, the second hypothesis.

Hypothesis 2. Negotiators are more likely to feel *satisfied with respect to their settlements* when they accept offers with "promise" frames (gain/non-loss frames), than when they accept offers with "threat" frames (loss/non-gain frames).

3 The Moderating Role of Personality

The subjective effectiveness of a negotiation framed with gain, non-loss, non-gain, and loss frames is likely to be complicated by aspects of the recipient's cognitive-processing patterns. One interesting example of such processing patterns or styles is illustrated by recent research suggesting that processing *negation,* which involves higher order rule-based processes, is more cognitively demanding than processing material that does not involve negation [32]. Since offers presented with non-gain or non-loss frames involve negation, they require more cognitive effort to process than offers presented with gain or loss frames. This gives rise to (at least) two interesting possibilities. First, people might be insensitive to non-gain and non-loss frames. Therefore, the subjective effectiveness of a non-gain frame would be lower than that of a gain frame (but still higher than that of a loss frame), whereas the subjective effectiveness of a non-loss frame would actually be higher than that of a loss frame (but still lower than that of a gain frame). Another possibility is that people might be put off by the cognitive demands of non-gain or non-loss frames such that the subjective effectiveness of a non-gain frame would not only be lower than a gain frame but also a loss frame, with the same pattern observed for a non-loss frame. Therefore, the effect of framing on the subjective evaluations of a negotiation might well be moderated by the personality of the offer recipient, a possibility that we explore in terms of *Need for Cognition.*

The *Need for Cognition* (NC) personality variable characterizes an individual's chronic tendency to take on and enjoy effortful cognitive activities. People who are high in NC typically show an orientation toward mental challenges [33]. For instance, a high NC individual is more likely to have a positive attitude toward tasks that involve reasoning or problem solving, and which require considerable use of cognitive resources. Conversely, individuals who are low in NC are more dependent on heuristics (i.e., cognitive "short cuts"), external source (e.g., experts), or other processes which serve to simplify or reduce information processing. Such individuals prefer tasks that are relatively simple and which take less toll on their cognitive resources [14]. The role of NC in social psychological processes has been examined extensively in the psychology literature, with studies typically assessing NC using Cacioppo and Petty's *Need for Cognition Scale* [9]. This measure has demonstrated good reliability and the ability to predict a variety of outcomes in combination with other factors, and has revealed reliable differences not only in self-reported motivation but also in actual processing behavior [34].

In persuasion research, NC has been found to interact with the argument quality of persuasive messages to predict attitude change. In general, individuals high in NC distinguish strong and weak arguments to a greater extent than do those low in NC (e.g., [35-37]). On the other hand, individuals with low NC have also been found to differentiate source factors such as source attractiveness and perceived honesty more than those with high NC [36, 38]. Persistence of attitudes over time has also been found for those high but not low in NC [36, 39]. In the negotiation context, where information takes the form of negotiators' offers, we expect differences in negotiators' NC to result in different perceptions of the bargaining situation, and consequently, their attitude towards the process and outcome of the negotiation.

Individuals high in NC have a natural inclination to process information to a greater extent, therefore they are likely to experience more positivity when accepting an offer presented with a relatively complex frame compared to individuals low in NC. As mentioned above, processing negation, as is required for non-gain or non-loss frames requires more cognitive resources [32], so it might be that individuals high in NC are more satisfied (or less dissatisfied) with the negotiation process and outcome when presented with non-loss/non-gain offers because such offers appear more mentally challenging to process. More importantly, high NC individuals would have a more positive experience when processing the seemingly complex offer, and consequently, attribute the positive experience to perceptions of how well they carried themselves during the negotiation. Conversely, gain/loss frames appear simple since they take the affirmed form, which does not require additional cognitive effort to process. As such, those low in NC might have a more pleasant (or less unpleasant) experience processing the simple-to-digest gain/loss frames, and consequently develop more positive self-perceptions.

Hypothesis 3. High-NC negotiators are more likely to feel *satisfied with themselves* when they accept an offer with absence frames (non-gain/non-loss frames) as compared to presence frames (gain/loss frames), whereas low-NC negotiators are more like to feel *satisfied with themselves* when they accept an offer with presence frames (gain/loss frames) as opposed to absence frames (non-gain/non-loss frames).

4 Experiment

4.1 The Design

A 2x2 between-subject factorial experiment was designed to test our hypotheses. The negotiation context was created through an experimental procedure in which participants were assigned the role of a buyer who had to undertake an on-line four-issue negotiation to purchase laptop computers. The four issues were unit price, quantity, service level, and delivery terms. Although participants were not explicitly told, in fact that the seller was represented by a software agent[1] embedded in the website. Participants were randomly assigned to different treatment conditions. Figure 1 presents the experimental design.

In order to fill all the cells in the design (as shown in Figure 1), ninety-six undergraduate students were recruited from a large university. The data of participants who did not accept the seller's final offer (see Table 2) were discarded. As a means of encouraging participants to negotiate realistically for a "good deal," participants were told that not only would they receive $10 cash after the experiment, but that they would get an additional $10 if they were to achieve a utility score in the top 30%. In fact, all participants ended up with the same offer from the seller agent, and all were given an additional $10 after all of the experimental sessions were concluded.

---

[1] The software agent system was designed and developed for a research program that explores the influence of factors that play an important role in agent-to-human negotiations [1, 40].

Presence-Absence Frame

		Presence	Absence
	Gain	**gain** 13 participants	**non-gain** 13 participants
Gain-Loss Frame	Loss	**loss** 13 participants	**non-loss** 13 participants

Fig. 1. The Experimental Design. Each treatment cell included data from *13 participants* who accepted the seller agents' final offer in one of the *four framing conditions* (*gain, non-gain, loss, and non-loss*).

4.2 Negotiation Task

The task was adapted from a validated negotiation scenario based on real-world manufacturing contract negotiations originally developed by Jones [41] and used in various computer-based negotiation experiments (e.g., [25, 27, 28, 40]). Participants (buyers) were provided with a private utility table from which they could compute the utility of an offer by summing the utilities of each of the four issues in the offer. The structure of the task created 728 discrete alternatives to the negotiation agreement with utilities ranging from 0 to 100. In order to create a realistic "bottom line" condition, both buyers and the seller were given the same bargaining power, namely, BATNA (Best Alternative to a Negotiated Agreement) [42, 43] values that represented 44 utility points. Participants were told that they should obtain an agreement with as high a utility as possible, but because a reserve agreement already existed, there was no point in reaching an agreement with a utility below 45.

4.3 Independent Variable and Controlled Variables

There were two levels each of the two independent variables, corresponding to the four frames used by the selling agent to present the final offer–an offer which participants could either accept or reject. The objective effectiveness (utility) of the final offer was the same in all conditions and was designed to be sufficiently appealing that most participants could be expected to accept it.

Table 2 below illustrates how the four frames were presented in the final round of agent offers as they correspond to the gain/loss x absence/presence manipulation.

The negotiation rules were controlled by using the same one-way protocol for all conditions. The rule simply stated that the negotiation proceeds in rounds, at each round the seller will send an offer for the buyer to either accept or reject. The negotiation is completed when the buyer accepts one offer (agreement is achieved) or the buyer rejects the seller's final offer. The same negotiation task was used in all conditions. The negotiation website interface was the same for all participants across all conditions, and the experiment was administered to all participants by the same experimenter using the same standardized instruction script for all sessions.

Table 2. Negotiation rounds. Frame manipulation only for final offer (Round 4)

	Seller's offer and accompanying message	Utility (from utility table)
Round 1	Chris says: 　　Hello! My name is Chris. I am a sales manager at LaptopOnDemand. Thank you for your interest in our products. For laptop sales, we typically require a minimum purchase of 100 units and we can only ship in units of 20, with an average of 2 weeks for delivery. Sometimes, we are able to give a discounted price and a service upgrade. 　　The following offer package comes with "Silver" service level. I can give you $2250/unit and deliver in 3 weeks, provided that you will take 160 units	Unit Price: $2250/unit (13) Quantity: 160 units (8) Service Level: Silver (15) Delivery: 3 weeks (5) Total utility: (41)
Round 2	Chris says: 　　Okay. I can give you a discount if you order more units. If you can take 200 units, I can give you them for $2150/unit and delivery in 3 weeks. That would be with the "Silver" service level. What do you say?	Unit Price: $2150/unit (27) Quantity: 200 units (3) Service Level: Silver (15) Delivery: 3 weeks (5) Total utility: (50)
Round 3	Chris says: 　　Hmmm. Well if you take 200 units and are OK with having them shipped a week later, i.e., 4 weeks delivery, I can give you an even better discount: $2050/unit. The service level is the "Silver" one. How does that sound?	Unit Price: $2050/unit (39) Quantity: 200 units (3) Service Level: Silver (15) Delivery: 4 weeks (0) Total utility: (57)
Round 4	Chris says: 　　Okay. How about this? 200 units at $2050/unit, and 4 weeks delivery. 　　This is the best I can do. However, since it's a large order, I might be able to manage a service upgrade, That's a $2000 per annum value. 　　<frames inserted here> What do you say? 　　<frame a – **gain**> OK, so if you accept my offer this time, I'll give you the free service-upgrade to "Gold". 　　<frame b – **non-loss** > OK, so if you accept my offer this time, I won't charge you for the service-upgrade to "Gold". 　　<frame c – **non-gain** > OK, but if you don't accept my offer this time, I won't give you the free service-upgrade to "Gold". 　　<frame d – **loss** > OK, but if you don't accept my offer this time, I'll charge you for the service-upgrade to "Gold".	Unit Price: $2050/unit (39) Quantity: 200 units (3) Service Level: Gold (29) Delivery: 4 weeks (0) Total utility: (71)

4.4 The Dependent Variables and Moderating Variable

The subjective negotiation outcomes were evaluated using a post-negotiation questionnaire. Items were adapted from earlier negotiation experiments (e.g., [26, 27, 29, 44]) and the 16-item Subjective Value Inventory (SVI) that assesses subjective effectiveness [7]. The scales of this inventory are established and have shown good psychometric properties. The items for the key dependent variables are presented in Appendix A. The moderating variable, *Need for Cognition*, was assessed using the standard NC scale [9] (see Appendix B for sample items). This instrument was administered after participants completed the post-negotiation questionnaire.

4.5 Procedure

The experiment followed a standard three-stage procedure. In the *pre-negotiation phase*, participants were assigned the role of a purchasing manager for a bogus buyer organization known as Tan Brothers Electronics Inc. They were given an information sheet describing the task and providing background information on the company, the terms of negotiation, and a utility table summarizing the range of possible utilities that could be obtained. Participants were not explicitly told the utilities associated with each term, but could identify and add the utilities themselves by referring to the utility table. The higher the utility score obtained, the higher the overall profitability of the negotiated agreement. Participants were reminded that utility scores in the top 30% would be eligible for a cash bonus. They then completed a pre-negotiation questionnaire to ensure that they properly understood the task.

In the *negotiation phase, pa*rticipants first entered a unique Buyer ID that was later used to retrieve their responses to offers from the server log. They then began their negotiation with the counterpart. There was no time limit for the negotiation. In each negotiation, participants (buyers) encountered up to four negotiation rounds. The first three rounds were identical across all conditions. The utility scores associated with them were constructed in such a way as to render offer acceptance unlikely. In the last round, all participants received offers with the same utility score–a score well above their (predefined) bottom lines (see Table 2 above).

In the *post-negotiation phase,* after the settlement, participants were asked to complete the post-negotiation questionnaire as well as the personality assessment items. Participants were then debriefed, given $10 for their participation, and asked to keep their experience in the study confidential. The $10 cash bonus awards (in fact for all participants) were announced (and in most cases, collected) four weeks later.

5 Data Analysis and Results

Before addressing the main hypothesis, we assessed the reliability of the subjective negotiation outcome measures. Results showed acceptable values with a Cronbach's alpha greater than 0.7 on all three dimensions–satisfaction with settlement, self, and counterpart (see Appendix A). In addition, because we measured NC after the framing manipulation, we had to confirm that NC scores were indeed a stable personality difference and thus, not influenced by framing. Indeed, Need for Cognition scores did not differ as a function of frame conditions, $F (3, 48) = .82, p = .49$.

Three separate regression analyses were conducted with gain-loss frame, absence-presence frame and NC as predictors, and the subjective effectiveness measure of interest as the criterion variable in each analysis. In the first step, gain-loss frame, absence-presence frame, and centered NC scores were entered into the model. Following which, the interaction terms (i.e., gain-loss x absence-presence, NC x gain-loss, NC x absence-presence) were entered in the second step.

The analyses revealed *only* a 3-way interaction between NC, absence-presence frame, and gain-loss frame in *satisfaction with the counterpart*, $B = -.03$, $t(44) = -1.80$, $p = .09$. The interaction was decomposed by performing separate regression analyses for gain vs. loss frame, in terms of participants with low NC vs. high NC. The participants were categorized into those with NC scores one standard deviation below and one standard deviation above the mean respectively. Results showed that the 3-way interaction tended to be driven by low NCs experiencing less satisfaction with the counterpart after they accepted the non-gain frame as opposed to the other frames, $B = .78$, $t(48) = 2.04$, $p = .05$. For the high NCs, there were no significant differences in their satisfaction with counterpart in terms of efficiency among the four frames.

A similar pattern of result was also found for *satisfaction with the settlement*, i.e. a 3-way interaction between NC, absence-presence frame, and gain-loss frame, $B = -.04$, $t(44) = -2.44$, $p < .05$. When the interaction was decomposed in the same manner, results indicated that the interaction again was mainly driven by low NCs experiencing less satisfaction with the settlement after they accepted the non-gain frame as opposed to the other frames, $B = .82$, $t(48) = 2.29$, $p < .05$. There were also no significant differences in the satisfaction with the settlement for the high NCs across all frames.

The regression analysis revealed *only* a significant 2-way interaction between NC and absence-presence frame in *satisfaction with the self*, $B = -.03$, $t(49) = -2.55$, $p < .05$. The interaction was decomposed by performing separate regression analyses for participants with high NC versus those with low NC, again categorized by those with NC scores one standard deviation above and below the mean respectively. Results showed that among those high in NC, feelings about the self were more positive for those who accepted offers framed as *absences* (i.e. non-gain/non-loss) than for those who accepted offers framed as the *presence* of a gain or loss (i.e. gain/loss), $B = -.34$, $t(49) = -2.05$, $p < .05$. The reverse was found for participants low in NC, who tended to show more positive feelings about the self when they accepted the offer framed as the *presence* of a gain or loss (i.e. gain/loss) than when they accepted the offer framed as the *absence* of a gain or loss (i.e. non-gain/non-loss), $B = .29$, $t(49) = 1.71$, $p = .09$.

6 Discussion and Implications

6.1 Discussion

Our findings of no main effect indicate that there is no difference between offers framed as "promise" (gain/non-loss) versus those framed as "threat" (loss/non-gain) frames in any of the three dimensions of the subjective negotiation outcomes. Thus the prediction that promise (gain/non-loss) as opposed to threat (loss/non-gain) frames result in greater satisfaction with the counterpart (Hypothesis 1) and greater satisfaction with the settlement (Hypothesis 2) were not supported. Whether this prediction could be confirmed with a more sensitive design remains to be seen. However, interestingly, we observed a 3-way interaction among gain-loss, absence-presence frame, and NC on *satisfaction with the counterpart* and *satisfaction with the negotiation settlement*. That is, while high-NC negotiators were not affected by promise vs. threat, low-NC people tended to have less positive feelings about both the settlement and their counterpart (the seller agent) only after they accepted an offer presented in a *non-gain* frame. This suggests that the negative subjective consequence of issuing loss/non-gain frames was further coupled with the NC dimension. This may be due to the tendency that low-NC people feel less pleasant when they process the absence frame (i.e., non-gain). Therefore, between the two threat messages (loss and non-gain), the non-gain condition resulted in less positive subjective experience for the low-NC participants. Future research is needed to confirm this assertion.

Whereas Hypotheses 1 and 2 were not supported, there was support for Hypothesis 3 as evidenced by the absence/presence frame x NC interaction relative to *satisfaction with the self*. That is, participants high in NC were more satisfied with themselves after they accepted a non-gain/non-loss offer than a gain/loss offer, while those low in NC showed the opposite pattern. This result parallels the recent finding that perceived message complexity can impact processing of information among individuals who differ in NC. In particular, those high in NC reported greater motivational arousal and were more likely to use their background knowledge to process information, when they perceived a message as complex than when they perceived the same message to be simple. In contrast, individuals low in NC reported greater arousal and used their background knowledge (which was manipulated to be at the same level as the high NC individuals) they perceived the same message as simple rather than when they perceived the message as complex [34].

6.2 Implications

The results of this work lend credence to the idea that framing and individual differences are worth taking into account in the design of intelligent negotiation agents. Our results show that negotiators had different preferences towards the same offer presented in different frames, depending on their level of NC. Negotiators high in NC felt better about themselves after accepting offers presented with complex non-gain/non-loss frames, whereas simple gain/loss frames elicited greater positive feelings about the self only for negotiators low in NC–a frame matching effect.

In the simplest manner, one plausible application of this finding in the context of agent-to-human negotiation would be to determine the human negotiators' level of NC prior to the negotiation by including the Need for Cognition Scale as a questionnaire that negotiators would complete as part of the procedure to create a user profile. Alternatively, designers could look into programming seller agents that could detect the human counterpart's NC by exploiting various behavioral manifestation of NC. For example, since high NC is associated with deeper information processing than low NC, the time taken for high NC negotiators to process an offer might be longer than for those low in NC. As such, real time measures such as the time taken for mouse movement during the online negotiation might be used to estimate of depth of processing, and thus the negotiator's level of NC. Agents might also attempt to assess NC by monitoring pre-negotiation behaviors such as the type of information (simple vs. complex) the human counterparts tend to select in pre-negotiation internet surfing. Once the information regarding negotiators' level of NC is obtained, frame matching can be applied by providing negotiators with offers framed in the way that matches their NC.

The advantage of using behavioral manifestations of NC is that they are more readily observable in an online setting, where agent-to-human negotiation typically takes place. The disadvantage, of course, is that they raise all kinds of difficult-to-resolve privacy and ethical questions.

7 Conclusion

In this paper we introduced a frame x personality perspective on agent-to-human negotiation. We demonstrated that unlike the traditional use of gain/loss framing in persuasion, which considers only the presence of gains and losses, the inclusion of the absence/presence dimension provides another important distinction in terms of the negation of gains and losses, that is, non-gains and non-losses. In particular, we established that in the context of individual differences in *Need for Cognition*, the traditional simple gain/loss frames fit the preferences of negotiators low in NC, whereas the more complex non-gain/non-loss frames fit the preferences of those who are high in NC. This interaction between the absence/presence dimension and need for cognition was found to impact negotiators' feelings about themselves, which is an important subjective negotiation outcome that can influence future negotiation choices.

Acknowledgments. We are most grateful to Daniel O'Keefe and Gregory Kersten for their very helpful comments at various stages of this work.

References

1. Kraus, S.K., Sycara, K., Evenchik, A.: Reaching Agreements through Argumentation: A Logical Model and Implementation. Artificial Intelligence 104, 1–69 (1998)
2. Parsons, S., Sierra, C., Jennings, N.R.: Agents that Reason and Negotiate by Arguing. Journal of Logic and Computation 8, 261–292 (1998)
3. Huang, S., Lin, F., Yuan, Y.: Understanding Agent-based On-line Persuasion and Bargaining Strategies: An Empirical Study. International Journal of Electronic Commerce 11, 85–115 (2006)

 4. Yang, Y., Singhal, S.: Designing an Intelligent Agent that Negotiates Tactfully with Human Counterparts: A Conceptual Analysis and Modeling Framework. In: Proceedings of the 42nd Hawaii International Conferences on System Sciences (HICSS42), pp. 1–10. IEEE Publication, Big Island (2009)
 5. Tversky, A., Kahneman, D.: The Framing of Decisions and the Psychology of Choice. Science 211, 453–458 (1981)
 6. Thompson, L.: Negotiation Behavior and Outcomes: Empirical Evidence and Theoretical Issues. Psychological Bulletin 108, 515–532 (1990)
 7. Curhan, J.R., Elfenbein, H.A., Xu, H.: What Do people Value When They Negotiate? Mapping the Domain of Subjective Value in Negotiation. Journal of Personality and Social Psychology 3, 493–512 (2006)
 8. Idson, L.C., Liberman, N., Higgins, E.: Distinguishing Gains from Nonlosses and Losses from Nongains: A Regulatory Focus Perspective on Hedonic Intensity. Journal of Experimental Psychology 36, 252–274 (2000)
 9. Cacioppo, J.T., Petty, R.E., Kao, C.F.: The Efficient Assessment of Need for Cognition. Journal of Personality Assessment 48, 306–307 (1984)
10. Snyder, M., DeBono, K.G.: Appeals to Image and Claims About Quality: Understanding the Psychology of Advertising. Journal of Personality and Social Psychology 49, 586–597 (1985)
11. See, Y.H.M., Petty, R.E., Fabrigar, L.R.: Affective and Cognitive Meta-bases of Attitudes: Unique Effects on Information Interest and Persuasion. Journal of Personality and Social Psychology 94, 938–955 (2008)
12. O'Keefe, D.J., Jensen, J.D.: The Advantages of Compliance or the Disadvantages of Noncompliance? A Meta-analytic Review of the Relative Persuasive Effectiveness of Gain-framed and Loss-framed Messages. Communication Yearbook 30, 1–43 (2006)
13. Rothman, A.J., Salovey, P.: Shaping Perceptions to Motivate Healthy Behavior: The Role of Message Framing. Psychological Bulletin 121, 3–19 (1997)
14. Kahneman, D., Tversky, A.: Prospect Theory: An Analysis of Decisions Under Risk. Econometrica 47, 263–291 (1979)
15. Neale, M.A., Bazerman, M.H.: The Effects of Framing and Negotiator Overconfidence on Bargaining Behaviors and Outcomes. Academy of Management Journal 28, 34–49 (1985)
16. Bazerman, M.H., Neale, M.A.: Negotiating rationally. Free Press, New York (1992)
17. Schelling, T.C.: The Strategy of Conflict: Prospectus for a Reorientation of Game Theory. Journal of Conflict Resolution 2, 203–204 (1958)
18. Schelling, T.C.: The Strategy of Conflict. Harvard University Press, Cambridge (1960)
19. Tedeschi, J.T.: Threats and Promises. In: Swingle, P.G. (ed.) The Structure of Conflict, pp. 155–191. Academic Press, New York (1970)
20. Rubin, J.Z., Brown, B.R.: The Social Psychology of Bargaining and Negotiation. Academic Press, New York (1975)
21. Schlenker, B.R., Bonoma, T., Tedeschi, J.T., Pivnick, W.P.: Compliance to Threats as a Function of the Wording of the Threat and the Exploitativeness of the Threatener. Sociometry 33, 394–408 (1970)
22. Geiwitz, P.J.: The Effects of Threats on Prisoner's Dilemma. Behavioral Science 12, 232–233 (1967)
23. Rubin, J.Z., Lewicki, R.J.: A Three-factor Experimental Analysis of Promises and Threats. Journal of Applied Social Psychology 3, 240–257 (1973)

24. Sinaceur, M., Neale, M.A.: Not All Threats are Created Equal: How Implicitness and Timing Affect the Effectiveness of Threats in Negotiations. Group Decision and Negotiation 14, 63–85 (2005)
25. Delaney, M.M., Foroughi, A., Perkins, W.C.: An Empirical Study of the Efficacy of a Computerized Negotiation Support System (NSS). Decision Support Systems 20, 185–197 (1997)
26. Eliashberg, J., Gauvin, S., Lilien, G.L., Rangaswamy, A.: An Experimental Study of Alternative Preparation Aids for International Negotiations. Group Decision and Negotiation 1, 243–267 (1992)
27. Foroughi, A., Perkins, W.C., Jelassi, M.T.: An Empirical Study of an Interactive, Session-oriented Computerized Negotiation Support System. Group Decision and Negotiation 6, 485–512 (1995)
28. Lim, J., Yang, Y.P.: Enhancing Negotiators' Performance with Computer Support for Pre-Negotiation Preparation and Negotiation: An Experimental Investigation in an East Asian Context. Journal of Global Information Management 15, 18–42 (2007)
29. Rangaswamy, A., Shell, G.R.: Using Computers to Realize Joint Gains in Negotiations: Towards an Electronic Bargaining Table. Management Science 43, 1147–1163 (1997)
30. de Dreu, C., Carnevale, P., Emans, B., van de Vliert, E.: Effects of Gain-loss Frames in Negotiation: Loss Aversion, Mismatching, and Frame Adoption. Organizational Behavior and Human Decision Processes 60, 90–107 (1994)
31. Carnevale, P.J., Pruitt, D.G.: Negotiation and Mediation. Annual Review of Psychology 43, 531–582 (1992)
32. Deutsch, R., Gawronski, B., Strack, F.: At the Boundaries of Automaticity: Negation as Reflective Operation. Journal of Personality and Social Psychology 3, 385–405 (2006)
33. Cacioppo, J.T., Petty, R.E., Feinstein, J.A., Jarvis, W.B.G.: Dispositional Differences in Cognitive Motivation: The Life and Times of Individuals Varying in Need for Cognition. Psychological Bulletin 119, 197–253 (1996)
34. See, Y.H.M., Petty, R.E., Evans, L.M.: The Impact of perceived Message Complexity and Need for Cognition on Information Processing and Attitudes. Journal of Research in Personality 43, 880–889 (2009)
35. Cacioppo, J.T., Petty, R.E., Kao, C.F., Rodriguez, R.: Central and Peripheral Routes to Persuasion: An Individual Difference Perspective. Journal of Personality and Social Psychology 51, 1032–1043 (1986)
36. Haugtvedt, C.P., Petty, R.E., Cacioppo, J.T.: Need for Cognition and Advertising: Understanding the Role of Personality Variables in Consumer Behavior. Journal of Consumer Behavior 1, 239–260 (1992)
37. Inman, J.J., McAlister, L., Hoyer, W.D.: Promotion Signal: Proxy for a Price Cut? Journal of Consumer Research 17, 74–81 (1990)
38. Priester, J., Petty, R.E.: Source Attributions and Persuasion: Perceived Honesty as a Determinant of Message Scrutiny. Personality and Social Psychology Bulletin 21, 637–654 (1995)
39. Verplanken, B.: Persuasive Communication of Risk information: A Test of Cue versus Message Processing Effects in a Field Experiment. Personality and Social Psychology Bulletin 17, 188–193 (1991)
40. Yang, Y., Singhal, S., Xu, Y.: Offer with Choices and Accept with Delay: A Win-Win Strategy Model for Agent-Based Automated Negotiation. In: Proceedings of the 30th International Conference in Information Systems (ICIS 2009), Phoenix, Arizona, United States (2009)

41. Jones, B.H.: Analytical Mediation: An Empirical Examination of the Effects of Computer Support for Different Levels of Conflict in Two-Party Negotiation. Ph.D. dissertation, Indiana University Graduate School of Business, Bloomington, Indiana (1988)
42. Raiffa, H.: The Art and Science of Negotiations. Belknap/Harvard University Press, Cambridge (1982)
43. Fisher, R., Ury, W.: Getting to Yes. Houghton Mifflin, Boston (1981)
44. Oliver, R.L., Balakrishnan, P.V., Barry, B.: Outcome Satisfaction in Negotiation: A Test of Expectancy Disconfirmation. Organizational Behavior and Human Decision Processes 60, 252–275 (1994)

Appendix A: Sample Items of the Post-Negotiation Questionnaire (Adapted from [7, 26, 27, 29, 44])

Dependent Variables and Measurement items	Response options
Satisfaction with the settlement	
1. How satisfied are you with the outcome—i.e., the extent to which you expect the terms of your agreement (or lack of agreement) to benefit you?	1 = Not at all, 4 = Moderately, and 7 = Perfectly
2. How satisfied are you with the number of utility points you earned?	1 = Extremely dissatisfied , 4 = Indifferent, and 7 = Extremely satisfied
3. What do you think of the agreement?	1 = Much worse than I had hoped for, 4 = As expected , and 7 = Much better than I had hoped for
Satisfaction with the self	
1. Did you "lose face" (i.e., damage your sense of pride) in the negotiation? (Reverse coded)	1 = Not at all, 4 = Moderately, and 7 = A great deal; N.A.
2. Did this negotiation make you feel more or less competent as a negotiator?	1 = It made me feel less competent, 4 = It did not make me feel more or less competent, and 7 = It made me feel more competent;
3. Did you behave according to your own principles and values?	1 = Not at all, 4 = Moderately, and 7 = Perfectly; N.A.
4. Did this negotiation positively or negatively impact your self-image or your impression of yourself?	1 = It negatively impacted my self-image, 4 = It did not positively or negatively impact my self-image, and 7 = It positively impacted my self-image; N.A.
Satisfaction with the counterpart	
1. Do you feel the seller listened to your concerns?	1 = Not at all, 4 = Moderately, and 7 = Perfectly; N.A.
2. How satisfied are you with the ease (or difficulty) of reaching an agreement?	1 = Not at all satisfied, 4 = Moderately satisfied, and 7 = Perfectly satisfied
3. To what extent do you think the seller cared about your feelings?	1 = Not at all, 4 = Moderately, and 7 = Very much
4. To what extent do you think the seller cared about your interests and concerns?	1 = Not at all, 4 = Moderately, and 7 = Very much

Appendix B: Sample Items of the Need for Cognition Scale [9]

Statements	Response options
I prefer complex to simple problems.	1 = Extremely uncharacteristic, 3 = Uncertain, 5 = Extremely characteristic
I would rather do something that requires little thought than something that is sure to challenge my abilities.	1 = Extremely uncharacteristic, 3 = Uncertain, 5 = Extremely characteristic
I find satisfaction in deliberating hard for long hours.	1 = Extremely uncharacteristic, 3 = Uncertain, 5 = Extremely characteristic
I really enjoy a task that involves coming up with new solutions to problems.	1 = Extremely uncharacteristic, 3 = Uncertain, 5 = Extremely characteristic
Learning new ways to think doesn't excite me much.	1 = Extremely uncharacteristic, 3 = Uncertain, 5 = Extremely characteristic
It's enough for me that something gets the job done; I don't care how or why it works.	1 = Extremely uncharacteristic, 3 = Uncertain, 5 = Extremely characteristic

Dynamics in Argumentation with Single Extensions: Attack Refinement and the Grounded Extension (Extended Version)*

Guido Boella[1], Souhila Kaci[2], and Leendert van der Torre[3]

[1] Department of Computer Science, University of Torino, Italy
guido@di.unito.it
[2] Université Lille-Nord de France, Artois
CRIL, CNRS UMR 8188 - IUT de Lens
F-62307, France
kaci@cril.fr
[3] Computer Science and Communication
University of Luxembourg, Luxembourg
leon.vandertorre@uni.lu

Abstract. In this paper we consider the dynamics of abstract argumentation in Baroni and Giacomin's framework for the evaluation of extension based argumentation semantics. Following Baroni and Giacomin, we do not consider individual approaches, but we define general properties or postulates that individual approaches may satisfy. In particular, we define refinement properties for the attack relation in the framework. We illustrate the properties on the grounded extension. In this paper we consider only properties for the single extension case, and leave the multiple extension case to further research.

1 Introduction

Argumentation is a suitable framework for modeling interaction among agents. Dung introduced a framework for abstract argumentation with various kinds of so-called semantics. Baroni and Giacomin introduced a more general framework to study general principles of sets of semantics [1]. This is a very promising approach, since due to the increase of different semantics we need abstract principles to study the proposals, compare them, and select them for applications. So far Dung's argumentation framework has been mainly considered as static, in the sense that the argumentation framework is fixed. The dynamics of argumentation framework has attracted a recent interest where the problem of revising an argumentation framework has been addressed [6,8]. In this paper, we address complementary problems and study how the semantics of an argumentation framework remain unchanged when we change the set of the attack relations between them. More precisely, we address the following questions:

1. Which principles for refining (i.e., adding) attack relation?
2. Which of them are satisfied by grounded semantics?

---

* This is an extended version of [4].

P. McBurney et al. (Eds.): ArgMAS 2009, LNAI 6057, pp. 150–159, 2010.

We use the general framework of Baroni and Giacomin for arbitrary argumentation semantics, but we consider only semantics that give precisely one extension, like the grounded extension or the skeptical preferred semantics. We use Caminada's distinction between accepted, rejected and undecided arguments [5]. We find some results for the most popular semantics used in argumentation namely the grounded extension.

In this paper we consider only principles for the single extension case, and leave the multiple extension case to further research. Moreover, we consider only refinements which add only one attack relation.

The layout of this paper is as follows. In Section 2 we give necessary recall of Dung's argumentation framework, the framework of Baroni and Giacomin, Caminada labeling, and we introduce the notion of abstraction. In Section 3 we consider the refinement of attack relations. Lastly we conclude with related works and further research.

2   Formal Framework for Refinement Principles

2.1   Dung's Argumentation Framework

Argumentation is a reasoning model based on constructing arguments, determining potential conflicts between arguments and determining acceptable arguments. Dung's framework [7] is based on a binary *attack* relation. In Dung's framework, an argument is an abstract entity whose role is determined only by its relation to other arguments. Its structure and its origin are not known. We restrict ourselves to *finite* argumentation frameworks, i.e., in which the set of arguments is *finite*.

Definition 1 (Argumentation framework). *An argumentation framework is a tuple* $\langle \mathcal{B}, \rightarrow \rangle$ *where* $\mathcal{B}$ *is a finite set (of arguments) and* $\rightarrow$ *is a binary (attack) relation defined on* $\mathcal{B} \times \mathcal{B}$.

The output of $\langle \mathcal{B}, \rightarrow \rangle$ is derived from the set of selected acceptable arguments, called extensions, with respect to some acceptability semantics. We need the following definitions before we recall the most widely used acceptability semantics of arguments given in the literature.

Definition 2. *Let* $\langle \mathcal{B}, \rightarrow \rangle$ *be an argumentation framework. Let* $\mathcal{S} \subseteq \mathcal{B}$.

- $\mathcal{S}$ *defends* a *if* $\forall b \in \mathcal{B}$ *such that* $b \rightarrow a$, $\exists c \in \mathcal{S}$ *such that* $c \rightarrow b$.
- $\mathcal{S} \subseteq \mathcal{B}$ *is conflict-free if and only if there are no* $a, b \in \mathcal{S}$ *such that* $a \rightarrow b$.

The following definition summarizes the well-known acceptability semantics.

Definition 3 (Acceptability semantics). *Let* $AF = \langle \mathcal{B}, \rightarrow \rangle$ *be an argumentation framework. Let* $\mathcal{S} \subseteq \mathcal{B}$.

- $\mathcal{S}$ *is an* admissible *extension if and only if it is conflict-free and defends all its elements.*
- $\mathcal{S}$ *is a* complete extension *if and only if it is conflict-free and* $\mathcal{S} = \{a \mid \mathcal{S} \text{ defends } a\}$.
- $\mathcal{S}$ *is a* grounded extension *of* AF *if and only if* $\mathcal{S}$ *is the smallest (for set inclusion) complete extension of* AF.

- *S is a preferred extension of AF if and only if S is maximal (for set inclusion) among admissible extensions of AF.*
- *S is the skeptical preferred extension of AF if and only if S is the intersection of all preferred extensions of AF.*
- *S is a stable extension of AF if and only if S is conflict-free and attacks all arguments of $\mathcal{B} \setminus S$.*

Which semantics is most appropriate in which circumstances depends on the application domain of the argumentation theory. The grounded extension is the most basic one, in the sense that its conclusions are not controversial, each argumentation framework has a grounded extension (it may be the empty set), and this extension is unique. Grounded extension therefore plays an important role in the remainder of this paper. Preferred semantics is more credulous than the grounded extension. There always exists at least one preferred extension but it does not have to be unique. Stable extensions have an intuitive appeal, but its drawbacks are that extensions do not have to be unique and do not have to exist. Stable extensions are used, for example, in answer set programming, where it makes sense that some programs do not have a solution.

2.2 Baroni and Giacomin's Framework

In this paper we use the recently introduced formal framework for argumentation of Baroni and Giacomin [1]. It is more general than other frameworks, such as the one introduced by Dung, because they developed it for the evaluation of extension-based argumentation semantics. Examples of principles which can be expressed in their framework are given below.

Baroni and Giacomin assume that the set $\mathcal{B}$ represents the set of arguments produced by a reasoner at a given instant of time, and they therefore assume that $\mathcal{B}$ is finite, independently of the fact that the underlying mechanism of argument generation admits the existence of infinite sets of arguments. Like in Dung's original framework, they consider argumentation framework as a pair $\langle \mathcal{B}, \rightarrow \rangle$ where $\mathcal{B}$ is a set and $\rightarrow \subseteq (\mathcal{B} \times \mathcal{B})$ is a binary relation on $\mathcal{B}$, called attack relation. In the following it will be useful to explicitly refer to the set of all arguments which can be generated, which we call $\mathcal{N}$ for the universe of arguments.

The generalization of Baroni and Giacomin is based on a function $\mathcal{E}$ that maps argumentation frameworks $\langle \mathcal{B}, \rightarrow \rangle$ to its set of extensions, i.e., to a set of sets of arguments. However, this function is not formally defined. To be precise, they say: "An extension-based argumentation semantics is defined by specifying the criteria for deriving, for a generic argumentation framework, a set of extensions, where each extension represents a set of arguments considered to be acceptable together. Given a generic argumentation semantics $\mathcal{S}$, the set of extensions prescribed by $\mathcal{S}$ for a given argumentation framework AF is denoted as $\mathcal{E}_{\mathcal{S}}(AF)$". The following definition captures the above informal meaning of the function $\mathcal{E}$. Since Baroni and Giacomin do not give a name to the function $\mathcal{E}$, and it maps argumentation frameworks to the set of accepted arguments, we call $\mathcal{E}$ the *acceptance function*.

Definition 4. *Let $\mathcal{N}$ be the universe of arguments. A multiple extensions acceptance function $\mathcal{E} : \mathcal{N} \times 2^{\mathcal{N} \times \mathcal{N}} \to 2^{2^{\mathcal{N}}}$ is*

1. *a partial function which is defined for each argumentation framework $\langle \mathcal{B}, \rightarrow \rangle$ with finite $\mathcal{B} \subseteq \mathcal{N}$ and $\rightarrow \subseteq \mathcal{B} \times \mathcal{B}$, and*
2. *which maps an argumentation framework $\langle \mathcal{B}, \rightarrow \rangle$ to sets of subsets of $\mathcal{B}$: $\mathcal{E}(\langle \mathcal{B}, \rightarrow \rangle) \subseteq 2^{\mathcal{B}}$.*

The generality of the framework of Baroni and Giacomin follows from the fact that they have to define various principles which are built-in in Dung's framework. For example, Baroni and Giacomin identify the following two fundamental principles underlying the definition of extension-based semantics in Dung's framework, the *language independent* principle and the *conflict free* principle. See [1] for a discussion on these principles.

Definition 5 (Language independence). *Two argumentation frameworks $\mathcal{AF}_1 = \langle \mathcal{B}_1, \rightarrow_1 \rangle$ and $\mathcal{AF}_2 = \langle \mathcal{B}_2, \rightarrow_2 \rangle$ are isomorphic if and only if there is a bijective mapping $m : \mathcal{B}_1 \rightarrow \mathcal{B}_2$, such that $(\alpha, \beta) \in \rightarrow_1$ if and only if $(m(\alpha), m(\beta)) \in \rightarrow_2$. This is denoted as $\mathcal{AF}_1 \doteq_m \mathcal{AF}_2$.*

A semantics $\mathcal{S}$ satisfies the language independence principle *if and only if $\forall AF_1 = \langle \mathcal{B}_1, \rightarrow_1 \rangle$, $\forall AF_2 = \langle \mathcal{B}_2, \rightarrow_2 \rangle$ such that $AF_1 \doteq_m AF_2$ then $\mathcal{E}_\mathcal{S}(AF_2) = \{M(E) \mid E \in \mathcal{E}_\mathcal{S}(AF_1)\}$, where $M(E) = \{\beta \in \mathcal{B}_2 \mid \exists \alpha \in E, \beta = m(\alpha)\}$.*

Definition 6 (Conflict free). *Given an argumentation framework $AF = \langle \mathcal{B}, \rightarrow \rangle$, a set $S \subseteq \mathcal{B}$ is conflict free, denoted as $cf(S)$, iff $\nexists a, b \in S$ such that $a \rightarrow b$. A semantics $\mathcal{S}$ satisfies the conflict free principle if and only if $\forall AF, \forall E \in \mathcal{E}_\mathcal{S}(AF)$, E is conflict free.*

2.3   The Single Extension Case

In this paper we consider only the case in which the semantics of an argumentation framework contains precisely one extension. Examples are the grounded and the skeptical preferred extension.

Definition 7. *Let $\mathcal{N}$ be the universe of arguments. A single extension acceptance function $\mathcal{A} : \mathcal{N} \times 2^{\mathcal{N} \times \mathcal{N}} \rightarrow 2^{\mathcal{N}}$ is*

1. *a total function which is defined for each argumentation framework $\langle \mathcal{B}, \rightarrow \rangle$ with finite $\mathcal{B} \subseteq \mathcal{N}$ and $\rightarrow \subseteq \mathcal{B} \times \mathcal{B}$, and*
2. *which maps an argumentation framework $\langle \mathcal{B}, \rightarrow \rangle$ to subset of $\mathcal{B}$: $\mathcal{A}(\langle \mathcal{B}, \rightarrow \rangle) \subseteq \mathcal{B}$.*

Principles of Baroni and Giacomin defined for multiple acceptance functions such as directionality and conflict free are defined also for the single extension case, because the set of all single extension acceptance functions is a subset of the set of all multiple extensions acceptance functions. For example, a semantics $\mathcal{S}$ satisfies the conflict free principle when the unique extension is conflict free: $\forall AF, A_\mathcal{S}(AF)$ is conflict free.

The following gives a formal definition of the grounded extension.

Definition 8 (Grounded extension). *Let S be a conflict-free set of arguments and let $\mathcal{F} : 2^{\mathcal{B}} \rightarrow 2^{\mathcal{B}}$ be a function such that $\mathcal{F}(S) = \{a | S \text{ defends } a\}$. The grounded extension of an argumentation framework $AF = \langle \mathcal{B}, \rightarrow \rangle$ is:*

$$\mathcal{GE}(AF) = \bigcup \mathcal{F}_{i \geq 0}(\emptyset) = C_{AF} \cup [\bigcup \mathcal{F}_{i \geq 1}(C_{AF})],$$

C_{AF} *is the set of all non-attacked arguments.*

2.4   Refinement

We now define refinement relations between argumentation frameworks.

Definition 9 (Refinement). *Let* $\langle \mathcal{B}, \mathcal{R} \rangle$ *and* $\langle \mathcal{B}', \mathcal{S} \rangle$ *be two argumentation frameworks.*

- $\langle \mathcal{B}, \mathcal{R} \rangle$ *is an argument refinement from* $\langle \mathcal{B}', \mathcal{S} \rangle$ *iff* $\mathcal{B}' \subseteq \mathcal{B}$ *and* $\forall a, b \in \mathcal{B}'$, $a\mathcal{R}b$ *only if* $a\mathcal{S}b$.
- $\langle \mathcal{B}, \mathcal{R} \rangle$ *is an attack refinement from* $\langle \mathcal{B}', \mathcal{S} \rangle$ *iff* $\mathcal{B} = \mathcal{B}'$ *and* $\mathcal{S} \subseteq \mathcal{R}$.
- $\langle \mathcal{B}, \mathcal{R} \rangle$ *is an argument-attack refinement from* $\langle \mathcal{B}', \mathcal{S} \rangle$ *iff* $\mathcal{B}' \subseteq \mathcal{B}$ *and* $\mathcal{S} \subseteq \mathcal{R}$.

2.5   Caminada Labeling

In the definition of principles in the following section, it is useful to distinguish between two kinds of arguments which are not accepted, which we call rejected and undecided. This distinction is inspired by the labeling of argumentation frameworks introduced by Caminada [5], who shows that it is useful in the construction of extensions to partition arguments into three sets which are in the extension, out of the extension or still undecided. In particular, he proves that each complete extension corresponds to a labeling where an argument is in when all its attackers are out, and an argument is out when at least one of its attackers is in. We use this to distinguish rejected from undecided arguments, and we say that an argument is rejected (out) if it is attacked by an argument that is accepted (in). In other words, we only use the principle that an argument is out when one of its attackers is in.

Definition 10 (Rejected and undecided arguments). *Let* $\mathcal{A}(AF)$ *be the extension of an argumentation framework* $AF = \langle \mathcal{B}, \rightarrow \rangle$, *then* $\mathcal{B}$ *is partitioned into* $\mathcal{A}(AF)$, $\mathcal{R}(AF)$ *and* $\mathcal{U}(AF)$, *where:*

- $\mathcal{A}(AF)$ *is the set of accepted arguments, i.e., the extension,*
- $\mathcal{R}(AF) = \{a \in \mathcal{B} \mid \exists b \in \mathcal{A}(AF) : b \rightarrow a\}$ *is the set of rejected arguments, and*
- $\mathcal{U}(AF) = \mathcal{B} \setminus (\mathcal{A}(AF) \cup \mathcal{R}(AF))$ *is the set of undecided arguments.*

3   Attack Refinement Principles

We consider the situation where the set of arguments remains the same but the attack relation may grow (refinement). In particular, we consider principles where we add a single attack relation $a \rightarrow b$ to an argumentation framework. We distinguish whether arguments a and b are accepted, rejected or undecided.

Principle 1 (Attack refinement). *An acceptance function* $\mathcal{A}$ *satisfies the* $\mathcal{X}\mathcal{Y}$ *attack refinement principle, where* $\mathcal{X}, \mathcal{Y} \in \{\mathcal{A}, \mathcal{R}, \mathcal{U}\}$, *if for all argumentation frameworks* $AF = \langle \mathcal{B}, \rightarrow \rangle$, $\forall a \in \mathcal{X}(AF) \forall b \in \mathcal{Y}(AF)$: $\mathcal{A}(\langle \mathcal{B}, \rightarrow \cup \{a \rightarrow b\} \rangle) = \mathcal{A}(AF)$.

The following proposition states that the grounded extension satisfies five of the nine $\mathcal{A}\mathcal{A}, \mathcal{A}\mathcal{R}, \mathcal{A}\mathcal{U}, \mathcal{R}\mathcal{A}, \mathcal{R}\mathcal{R}, \mathcal{R}\mathcal{U}, \mathcal{U}\mathcal{A}, \mathcal{U}\mathcal{R}$ and $\mathcal{U}\mathcal{U}$ attack refinement principles.

Proposition 1. *The grounded extension satisfies the $\mathcal{AR}$, $\mathcal{RR}$, $\mathcal{UR}$, $\mathcal{RU}$ and $\mathcal{UU}$ attack refinement principles. It does not satisfy $\mathcal{AA}$, $\mathcal{AU}$, $\mathcal{RA}$ and $\mathcal{UA}$. Intuitively the satisfied principles reflect the following ideas:*

$\mathcal{AR}$, $\mathcal{RR}$, $\mathcal{UR}$: *the attacks on a rejected argument do not influence the extension. This principle holds for any attacker argument.*

$\mathcal{RU}$, $\mathcal{UU}$: *the attacks on an undecided argument do not influence the extension when the attacker is not accepted.*

Unsatisfied principles reflect the following ideas:

$\mathcal{AA}$: *extensions have to be conflict free.*

$\mathcal{UA}$: *in the grounded extension there is no undecided argument attacking an accepted argument.*

$\mathcal{AU}$: *an argument is rejected as soon as it is attacked by an accepted argument.*

$\mathcal{RA}$: *an attack from a rejected argument a to an accepted argument b influences the grounded extension when a is rejected only because of b.*

Proof. (sketch) Satisfied principles can be proven by induction. Take an argumentation framework and the refined one, and show that in each step of the construction of the grounded extension, the two remain the same. Counterexamples for $\mathcal{AA}$, $\mathcal{UA}$, $\mathcal{AU}$ and $\mathcal{RA}$ attack refinement are given below.

$\mathcal{AA}$: consider an argumentation framework composed of two arguments a and b such that none of them attacks the other. So both arguments are accepted and belong to the grounded extension. Let us now add an attack from a to b. Then b becomes rejected and the grounded extension contains a only.

$\mathcal{UA}$: consider an argumentation framework composed of three arguments a, b and c such that b and c attack each other. So both b and c are undecided and the grounded extension is composed of a only. Let us now add an attack from b to a. Then a becomes undecided and the grounded extension is empty.

$\mathcal{RA}$: consider an argumentation framework composed of two arguments a and b such that a attacks b. So b is rejected and the grounded extension is composed of a only. Let us now add an attack from b to a. Then a becomes undecided and the grounded extension is empty.

$\mathcal{AU}$: consider an argumentation framework composed of three arguments a, b and c such that b and c attack each other. Both b and c are undecided and the grounded extension is composed of a only. Let us now add an attack from from a to b. Then b becomes rejected and c is defended by a. The grounded extension is then composed of a and c.

The following example illustrates Proposition 1.

Example 1. See the two argumentation frameworks in Figure 1. On the left hand side, argument b and d are accepted using the grounded semantics, because there is no argument attacking them, and consequently argument a and c are rejected. Moreover, argument e and f are undecided since they are attacking each other. Finally, g is undecided too, since it is attacked by an undecided argument.

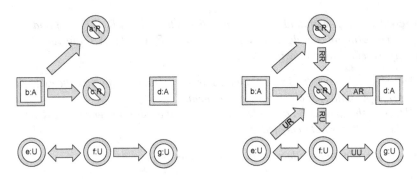

Fig. 1. The attack refinements of Example 1

On the right hand side, we have added an attack from argument a to argument c (a $\mathcal{RR}$ refinement), an attack from argument d to argument c (an $\mathcal{AR}$ refinement), an attack from argument e to argument c (an $\mathcal{UR}$ refinement), an attack from argument c to argument f (a $\mathcal{RU}$ refinement), and an attack from argument g to argument f (an $\mathcal{UU}$ refinement).

Again, we have that argument b and d are accepted, because there is no argument attacking them, and consequently argument a and c are rejected. Moreover, argument e and f are undecided since they are attacking each other. Finally, g is undecided too, since it is attack by an undecided argument. It follows also from Proposition 1 that the grounded extensions of the two argumentation frameworks are the same.

In the argumentation framework on the left hand side, we cannot add an attack from argument a to argument b (a $\mathcal{RA}$ refinement), because then argument a would no longer be accepted. Moreover, we cannot add an attack from argument b to argument d (an $\mathcal{AA}$ refinement), because then argument d would no longer be accepted. We cannot add an attack from argument g to argument d (an $\mathcal{UA}$ refinement), because then argument d would no longer be accepted. Finally, we cannot add an attack from argument b to argument e (an $\mathcal{AU}$ refinement), because then argument e would be rejected, and consequently argument f would be accepted.

$\mathcal{RA}$ attack refinement suggests that we can add an attack from a rejected argument a to an accepted argument b without changing the grounded extension if a is not rejected because of a. Formally, we have the following principle:

Principle 2 (Acyclic attack refinement). *An acceptance function $\mathcal{A}$ satisfies the acyclic $\mathcal{XY}$ attack refinement principle, where $\mathcal{X}, \mathcal{Y} \in \{\mathcal{A}, \mathcal{R}, \mathcal{U}\}$, if for all argumentation frameworks $AF = \langle \mathcal{B}, \rightarrow \rangle$, $\forall a \in \mathcal{X}(AF) \forall b \in \mathcal{Y}(AF)$: if there is no odd length sequence of attacks from b to a then $\mathcal{A}(\langle \mathcal{B}, \rightarrow \cup \{a \rightarrow b\} \rangle) = \mathcal{A}(AF)$.*

Proposition 2. *The grounded extension satisfies the acyclic $\mathcal{RA}$ attack refinement principle.*

The following two examples illustrate Proposition 2.

Example 2. Consider an argumentation framework composed of three arguments a, b and c such that c attacks a. The grounded extension is composed of b and c. Let us add an attack from a to b. The grounded extension remains unchanged since b is defended by c.

Now consider another argumentation framework composed of four arguments a, b, c and d such that b attacks d, d attacks a and c attacks a. The grounded extension is composed of b and c. Let us now add an attack from a to b. The grounded extension remains unchanged since b is defended by c.

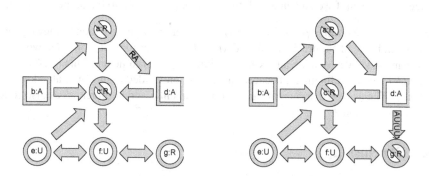

Fig. 2. The attack refinements of Example 3 and 5

Example 3 (Continued from Example 1). Consider the argumentation framework on the left hand side of Figure 2, which is derived from the argumentation framework at the right hand side of Figure 1 by adding an attack from argument a to argument d. This is an acyclic $\mathcal{RA}$ attack refinement, because there is no sequence of attacks from argument d to argument a. The accepted arguments are again argument a and argument d, as also follows form Proposition 2.

The case of $\mathcal{AU}$ attack refinement is more complicated since an attack from an accepted argument to an undecided argument changes the status of the latter to rejected. The following principle says that there are other undecided arguments that ensure that the extension does not change.

Principle 3 (Conditional attack refinement). *An acceptance function $\mathcal{A}$ satisfies the conditional $\mathcal{XY}(\mathcal{ZT})$ attack refinement principle, where $\mathcal{X}, \mathcal{Y}, \mathcal{Z}, \mathcal{T} \in \{\mathcal{A}, \mathcal{R}, \mathcal{U}\}$, if for all argumentation frameworks $AF = \langle \mathcal{B}, \rightarrow \rangle$, $\forall a \in \mathcal{X}(AF) \forall b \in \mathcal{Y}(AF)$: if $\forall c \in \mathcal{Z}(AF)$ with $b \rightarrow c$, $\exists d \neq b \in \mathcal{T}(AF)$ with $d \rightarrow c$, then $\mathcal{A}(\langle \mathcal{B}, \rightarrow \cup \{a \rightarrow b\} \rangle) = \mathcal{A}(AF)$.*

Proposition 3. *The grounded extension satisfies the conditional $\mathcal{AU}(\mathcal{UU})$ attack refinement principle.*

The following two examples illustrate Proposition 3.

Example 4. Consider an argumentation framework composed of five arguments a, b, c, d and e such that b and c attack each other, d and e attack each other and d attacks c. The arguments b, c, d and e are undecided so the grounded extension is composed of a only. Let us now add an attack from a to b. Then b becomes rejected however c is not accepted since it remains undecided because of the attack from an undecided argument d. Indeed the grounded extension remains unchanged.

Lastly if we add an attack from an undecided argument to an accepted argument, then it is very hard to identify an intuitive property. For example, let us consider an argumentation framework with three arguments a, b and c such that if a attacks c and vice versa. Then if we add an attack from a to b, then b will no longer be accepted.

Example 5 (Continued from Example 3). Consider the argumentation framework on the right hand side of Figure 2, which is derived from the argumentation framework at the left hand side by adding an attack from argument d to argument g. This is a conditional $\mathcal{AU}(\mathcal{UU})$ attack refinement, because there is an undecided argument e attacking argument f. The accepted arguments are again argument a and argument d, as also follows from Proposition 2.

4   Conclusion

4.1   Related Works

Besides the work of Baroni and Giacomin on principles for the evaluation of argumentation semantics, there is various work on dialogue and a few very recent approaches on the dynamics of argumentation. Cayrol et al. [6] define a typology of argument refinement (called revision in their paper). Then they define principles and conditions so that each type of refinement becomes a revision (called classical revision in their paper), i.e., the new argument is accepted. However they do not define general principles like we do. Rotstein et al. [8] introduce the notion of dynamics into the concept of abstract argumentation frameworks, by considering arguments built from evidence and claims. They do not consider abstract arguments and general principles like we do in this paper. Barringer et al. [2] consider internal dynamics by extending Dung's theory in various ways, but without considering general principles.

4.2   Summary and Further Research

In many situations, components o argumentation frameworks (arguments and attack relations) may change. In this paper, we study general principles when the grounded extension does not change when we add an attack relation. Most of them are unconditional and are satisfied by the grounded extension while some principles require additional conditions to be satisfied. The most interesting principles are listed in Table 1.

Argument refinement can be defined incrementally as the addition of an unconnected argument, and afterwards adding attack relations. Here we can distinguish again three cases, whether the added argument is accepted, rejected or undecided.

Attack and argument abstraction (i.e., removal) can be defined as the duals of attack refinement. However, which of the abstraction principles are satisfied by the grounded semantics, cannot be derived from the results in this paper. For example, the grounded semantics satisfies the $\mathcal{AA}, \mathcal{AU}, \mathcal{UA}, \mathcal{UR}, \mathcal{RA}, \mathcal{RU}$ and $\mathcal{RR}$ attack abstraction principles, leaving two interesting cases for further principles: the removal of an attack relation from an undecided argument to another undecided argument, i.e., $\mathcal{UU}$, and the removal

Table 1. Attack refinement: if $\forall AF = \langle \mathcal{B}, \rightarrow \rangle$ condition, then $\mathcal{A}(\langle \mathcal{B}, \rightarrow \cup \{a \rightarrow b\}\rangle) = \mathcal{A}(AF)$

Principle	Condition	Grounded extension
$\mathcal{AR}, \mathcal{RR}, \mathcal{UR}$	$b \in \mathcal{R}(AF)$	yes
$\mathcal{RU}, \mathcal{UU}$	$a \in \mathcal{R}(AF) \cup \mathcal{U}(AF), b \in \mathcal{U}(AF)$	yes
$\mathcal{AA}, \mathcal{UA}, \mathcal{RA}$	$b \in \mathcal{A}(AF)$	no
$\mathcal{AU}$	$a \in \mathcal{A}(AF), b \in \mathcal{U}(AF)$	no
Acyclic $\mathcal{RA}$	$a \in \mathcal{R}(AF), b \in \mathcal{A}(AF),$ no odd length sequence of attacks from b to a	yes
$\mathcal{AU}(\mathcal{UU})$	$a \in \mathcal{A}(AF), b \in \mathcal{U}(AF),$ $\forall c \in \mathcal{U}(AF)$ with $b \rightarrow c,$ $\exists d \neq b \in \mathcal{U}(AF)$ with $d \rightarrow c$	yes

of an attack relation from an argument that is accepted to an argument that is rejected, i.e., $\mathcal{AR}$. Thus, the interesting cases are different from the interesting cases for argument refinement. For a detailed analysis of these principles, we refer the reader to [3].

Besides the grounded semantics, other single extension semantics can be tested against our principles, such as the skeptical preferred semantics or the ideal semantics, and our principles can be generalized to the multiple extension case, for example for preferred or stable semantics.

References

1. Baroni, P., Giacomin, M.: On principle-based evaluation of extension-based argumentation semantics. Artificial Intelligence 171(10-15), 675–700 (2007)
2. Barringer, H., Gabbay, D.M., Woods, J.: Temporal dynamics of support and attack networks: From argumentation to zoology. In: Hutter, D., Stephan, W. (eds.) Mechanizing Mathematical Reasoning. LNCS (LNAI), vol. 2605, pp. 59–98. Springer, Heidelberg (2005)
3. Boella, G., Kaci, S., van der Torre, L.: Dynamics in argumentation with single extensions: Abstraction principles and the grounded extension. In: Sossai, C., Chemello, G. (eds.) ECSQARU 2009. LNCS, vol. 5590, pp. 107–118. Springer, Heidelberg (2009)
4. Boella, G., Kaci, S., van der Torre, L.: Dynamics in argumentation with single extensions: attack refinement and the grounded extension. In: 8th International Joint Conference on Autonomous Agents and Multiagent Systems (AAMAS 2009), pp. 1213–1214 (2009)
5. Caminada, M.: On the issue of reinstatement in argumentation. In: Fisher, M., van der Hoek, W., Konev, B., Lisitsa, A. (eds.) JELIA 2006. LNCS (LNAI), vol. 4160, pp. 111–123. Springer, Heidelberg (2006)
6. Cayrol, C., Dupin de Saint Cyr Bannay, F., Lagasquie-Schiex, M.C.: Revision of an argumentation system. In: 11th International Conference on Principles of Knowledge Representation and Reasoning (KR 2008), pp. 124–134 (2008)
7. Dung, P.M.: On the acceptability of arguments and its fundamental role in nonmonotonic reasoning, logic programming and n-person games. Artificial Intelligence 77(2), 321–357 (1995)
8. Rotstein, N.D., Moguillansky, M.O., Garcia, A.J., Simari, G.R.: An abstract argumentation framework for handling dynamics. In: Proceedings of the Argument, Dialogue and Decision Workshop in NMR 2008, Sydney, Australia, pp. 131–139 (2008)

Arguing Using Opponent Models

Nir Oren[1] and Timothy J. Norman[2]

[1] Dept. of Computer Science
King's College London
Strand, London
WC2R 2LS, United Kingdom
nir.oren@kcl.ac.uk
[2] Dept. of Computing Science
University of Aberdeen
Aberdeen
AB24 3UE
Scotland
t.j.norman@abdn.ac.uk

Abstract. While researchers have looked at many aspects of argumentation, an area often neglected is that of argumentation strategies. That is, given multiple possible arguments that an agent can put forth, which should be selected in what circumstances. In this paper we propose a heuristic that implements one such strategy. The heuristic is built around opponent modelling, and operates by selecting the line of argument that yields maximal utility, based on the opponent's expected response, as computed by the opponent model. An opponent model may be recursive, with the opponent modelling of the agent captured by the original agent's opponent model. Computing the utility for each possible line of argument is thus done using a variant of M* search, which in itself is an enhancement of min-max search. After describing the M* algorithm we show how it may be adapted to the argumentation domain, and then study what enhancements are possible for more specific types of dialogue. Finally, we discuss how this heuristic may be extended in future work, and its relevance to argumentation theory in general.

1 Introduction

Argumentation has emerged as a powerful reasoning mechanism in many domains. Applications tend to revolve around either the logical form of argument, identifying when an argument is, in some sense, acceptable. Some extension of Dung's seminal argument framework [8] is typically used in such applications, and domains have included negotiation [3] and normative conflict detection [12]. Another use of argumentation makes use of the dialogue level, and focuses on the interaction between different parties as the dialogue progresses. It is important to note that these two approaches are not mutually exclusive, but rather complementary. In describing argumentation systems, Prakken [18] identified four layers with which an argument framework must concern itself. These are the logical, dialectic, procedural, and heuristic layers. The first strand of research

P. McBurney et al. (Eds.): ArgMAS 2009, LNAI 6057, pp. 160–174, 2010.

primarily concerns itself with the logical and dialectic layers, while the second focuses on the procedural level. As Prakken notes, little work has dealt with the heuristic layer, which, among other things, deals with how agents should decide which argument to advance at different points in the dialogue.

In this paper, we focus on the heuristic layer, examining argument strategies. In other words, we attempt to determine what argument an agent should advance in order to achieve a certain goal. Previous work on the topic includes a utility based approach with one step lookahead [14], while another tack has focused on game theory and mechanism design [19,20] to ensure that dialogues are strategy free. Here, we look at how an agent may decide what utterance to advance by making use of opponent modelling. That is, given that agent α has a belief about agent β's knowledge and goals, we determine what argument the agent should advance to achieve its aims. Informally, we examine possible utterances from each position in the dialogue, creating a tree of possible dialogues. We then make use of techniques adapted from computer game playing, namely opponent model search and the M* algorithm [5], which is itself an extension of standard min-max search [22].

As an example of such a search, consider two agents (α and β) participating in a dialogue regarding whether to invade a small country. Agent α would like to persuade β that this is a prudent course of action. One possible line of argument is that the country has weapons of mass destruction, and that invading it will prevent the use of these weapons. If α knows that β cannot determine whether the country has such weapons, and that β may not ask α where it obtained its information from, then α will use this line of argument in the dialogue. However, if it knows that β knows that the country has no WMDs, it will not attempt to use this line of argument. Thus, α can make use of its model of β's knowledge in deciding what arguments to advance as part of a dialogue. The use of opponent modelling as an argument strategy has clear applications to many different scenarios, including persuasion type dialogues, and the domain of automated negotiation.

This paper's main contribution is a description of how a dialogue participant may decide what arguments to advance given that it has a model of the other dialogue party. We also show how the M* algorithm may be adapted for the argumentation domain, and provide some domain dependant enhancements to the search process, which results in a pruning of the dialogue tree.

After describing the M* algorithm in more detail in the next section, we show how M* can be adapted for the argumentation domain. Our initial effort, described in Section 3.1 deals with very general situations, and we show how our approach can be specialised for more specific types of dialogues and situations in Sections 3.2 and 3.3. Finally, we discuss a number of possible enhancements to our approach, and describe additional related work.

2   Background

In this section, we examine work in the field of opponent modelling. When participating in a competitive event in which strategy may affect the outcome, human players typically adjust their strategy in response to the opponent(s) they face.

On the other hand, artificial agents typically construct plans in which they assume that their opponent will play in the way most damaging to their goals, resulting in algorithms such as min-max search, and many of the results of game theory. Such approaches typically also assume that the opponent will use the same strategy as the player.

By making use of opponent modelling, it is possible to represent opponents with different goals and strategies to the agent doing the modelling. Such an approach raises a number of interesting possibilities. First, it allows for situations such as swindles and traps. The former occurs when a player may, due to an opponent's weakness, play a non-optimal move and still win, while the latter allows a player to play a weak move under the assumption that the opponent will view it as a strong move. Second, by explicitly modelling the opponent's goals, it is easier to deal with non-zero sum games. Other advantages gained by making use of strategies built around opponent modelling are described in [5].

The M* algorithm is similar to the min-max search algorithm, but makes use of an explicit opponent model to more accurately calculate the utility of a position. An opponent model (described as a player in [5]) is a pair $\langle f, O \rangle$ where f is an evaluation function, and O is an opponent model. The latter may also take on the special value of *NIL*, representing the case where no opponent model exists.

In this paper, we make use of a slightly modified form of this algorithm, but before describing this modified algorithm, we examine the original, which is shown in Algorithm 1.

Algorithm 1. $M^*(pos, depth, f_{pl}, oppModel)$

Require: A board position *pos*
Require: A search depth *depth*
Require: A position evaluation function f_{pl}
Require: An opponent model $oppModel = \{f_{pl}^o, oppModel^o\}$
1: **if** depth=0 **then**
2:    **return** $(NIL, f_{pl}(pos))$
3: **else**
4:    $maxUtil = -\infty$
5:    $PossibleMoves = MoveGen(pos)$
6:    **for all** $move \in PossibleMoves$ **do**
7:      **if** depth=1 **then**
8:        $playUtil = f_{pl}(move)$
9:      **else**
10:       $\langle oppMove, oppUtil \rangle = M^*(move, depth - 1, f_{pl}^o, oppModel^o)$
11:       $\langle playMove, playUtil \rangle = M^*(oppMove, depth - 2, \langle f_{pl}, oppModel \rangle)$
12:      **end if**
13:      **if** $playUtil > maxUtil$ **then**
14:        $maxUtil = playUtil$
15:        $maxMove = move$
16:      **end if**
17:    **end for**
18: **end if**
19: **return** $(maxMove, maxUtil)$

Informally, given a board position, a search depth, and an opponent model (consisting of the opponent's evaluation function and another opponent model), the algorithm returns the best move (and its value) by recursively computing what move the best move for the opponent would be for the given opponent model (line 11), based on what the opponent thinks the player's best move would be (line 10), and so on, until the maximal depth of search is reached. At this point, the utility of the current move can be computed (lines 2 and 8). The *MoveGen* function in line 5 is dependant on the rules of the game, and generates all possible moves from the current board position *pos*. It should be noted that it is easy to represent standard min-max search using the M* algorithm by using an opponent model of the form $(f, (-f, (f, \ldots)))$ to the depth of the search. It should also be noted that the algorithm assumes that the depth to which the opponent is modelled is greater than (or, more usually equal to) the depth to which the search takes place.

3   Approach

Argument strategies are employed by agents taking part in a dialogue. Arguments are thus added over time, and the goal of an agent's strategy involves deciding which utterance to make. For dialogue to take place, participants must agree on the rules governing the dialogue. These include not only the rules of the dialogue game itself [10], such as whether turn taking exists, what utterances may be made at which point, and the like, but also the rules governing the interactions between arguments; for example stating that *modus ponens* is valid.

3.1   Opponent Modelling for General Dialogues

We begin by assuming a very general type of dialogue game similar in spirit to the one proposed in [17]. This game is represented by agents advancing arguments. Arguments may take the form of more specific utterances such as "assert x", but such utterances are captured in abstract form, by being represented as arguments themselves. Thus, for example, an agent may make an argument a, and if another agent questions this argument (for example, by asking "why a?"), this could be viewed as an argument b which attacks a. A response could then be an argument c, attacking b, etc. We denote this set of abstract arguments *Args*.

A dialogue represents the utterances made by an agent. We define it very simply as follows:

Definition 1 (Dialogue). *A dialogue is an ordered set of arguments*

$$Dialogue = \{a, b, \ldots\}$$

such that Dialogue $\subseteq$ *Args.*

For convenience, and without loss of generality, we assume that only two dialogue participants exist, and that they take turns when making utterances. We do not therefore need to associate a dialogue participant with an utterance in our representation of a dialogue.

In order to abstract the rules governing a dialogue, we assume the existence of a generator function allowing us to compute the set of legal possible moves in a dialogue. This function is equivalent to the *MoveGen* function in Algorithm 1.

Definition 2 *(Move Generation). The function*

$$legalMoves : 2^{Dialogue} \rightarrow 2^{Args}$$

takes in a dialogue and returns the set of arguments that may be uttered by an agent at that point in the dialogue.

Note that only a single argument may be advanced by an agent during its turn (as this argument may actually encapsulate other arguments). Also, note that the legal moves function does not explicitly depend on the player making an utterance (though such information may be implicitly found by examining the dialogue's current length). The *legalMoves* function identifies *legal moves* rather than *possible moves* for a dialogue. That is, moves that are sanctioned by the rules of the game, rather than those moves that an agent may actually make based on factors such as its knowledge and goals.

At this point, we must define the structure of dialogue participants (also referred to as agents). An agent participating in a dialogue has a knowledge base identifying the arguments it is aware of, some goals it is trying to achieve, and an opponent model.

Definition 3 *(Agent). An agent is a tuple*

$$\langle KB, Goals, Opp \rangle$$

where $KB \subseteq Args$ is a knowledge base containing those arguments known by an agent, Goals is the agent's goal function, and is described in Definition 4, while Opp is an opponent model as detailed in Definition 5.

An agent participates in a dialogue to achieve certain goals. Different dialogues may meet these goals to a greater or lesser extent. An agent may thus assign a utility to a dialogue, and this is modelled by the *Goals* function. This utility may depend on many factors, including the arguments introduced within the dialogue, the agent introducing these arguments, the arguments deemed admissible by some argumentation semantics at some stage of the dialogue, and the like.

Definition 4 *(Goals). A Goals function takes in a dialogue, and returns its utility.*

$$Goals : 2^{Dialogue} \rightarrow \mathbb{R}$$

An opponent model is meant to represent an agent, and thus looks very similar to Definition 3. However, we must also handle the situation where an agent has no recursive model of its opponent. We start by representing this situation, and then recursively defining more complex, nested opponent models.

Definition 5. *(Opponent Model)*

An opponent model is incrementally defined as follows:

- $\langle KB, Goals, \emptyset \rangle$ *is an opponent model*
- $\langle KB, Goals, Opp \rangle$, *where Opp is an opponent model.*

Here, $KB \subseteq Args$ and $Goals : 2^{Dialogue} \to \mathbb{R}$ are a knowledge base and goal function respectively.

Given an agent with some knowledge base, goal function and opponent model, together with a *legalMoves* function representing the dialogue game's rules, an agent may decide what utterance to make (i.e. what argument to advance) by following the slightly modified version of M*, called M^*_{gd} shown in Algorithm 2.

Algorithm 2. $M^*_{gd}(dia, depth, agent, legalMoves)$

Require: A dialogue *dia*
Require: A search depth *depth*
Require: An agent *agent* $= \langle KB, Goals, oppModel \rangle$
Require: A move generation function *legalMoves*
 1: **if** depth=0 **then**
 2:    **return** $(NIL, Goals(dia))$
 3: **else**
 4:    $maxUtil = -\infty$
 5:    $PossibleMoves = legalMoves(dia) \cap KB$
 6:    **for all** $move \in PossibleMoves$ **do**
 7:       **if** depth=1 **then**
 8:         $playUtil = Goals(dia \cup \{move\})$
 9:       **else**
10:         $\langle oppMove, oppUtil \rangle = M^*_{gd}(dia \cup \{move\}, depth-1, oppModel, legalMoves)$

11:         $\langle playMove, playUtil \rangle = M^*_{gd}(dia \cup \{move, oppMove\}, depth - 2,$
                          $agent, legalMoves)$
12:       **end if**
13:       **if** $playUtil > maxUtil$ **then**
14:         $maxUtil = playUtil$
15:         $maxMove = move$
16:       **end if**
17:    **end for**
18: **end if**
19: **return** $(maxMove, maxUtil)$

Apart from the different specification of an agent, line 5 ensures that an agent not only uses moves generated by the *legalMoves* function, but filters these to ensure that it only uses moves that it believes are possible (according to its knowledge base). Also, note that on line 10, the opponent model is treated as an agent when passed as a parameter to the algorithm.

The M^*_{gd} algorithm is very general, in the sense that it does not make use of any of the properties of argument that would differentiate it from other types of search. In the remainder of this section, we take a closer look at the *legalMoves* and *Goals* functions, showing how they may be specialised to represent more specific dialogues, and how these specialisations may aid in pruning the possible dialogue tree.

3.2   Pruning by Legal Moves

One of the focuses of argumentation research examines how groups of arguments interact. Typically, this interaction is built around the notion of attack, and more controversially support, between arguments. The arguments advanced by (rational) agents in the course of a dialogue are aimed at achieving their goals, either by building up support for, or attacking other arguments [2].

Various semantics for argument frameworks have been proposed [8,13]. These semantics, when given a set of arguments and the interactions between them, identify which sets of arguments may be viewed as, in some sense, consistent with each other. In most cases, it makes little sense for an agent to introduce an argument which would not be deemed consistent, and so we begin by showing how this notion may be added to the agent's reasoning process.

Filtering the set of arguments that may be advanced is the task of the *legalMoves* function. We must, therefore, specialise this function as follows:

- Introduce the notion of an argument system; rather than having the arguments *Args* in isolation, we define an argument system consisting of *Args* and a set of relations between subsets (or elements) of *Args*. For example, a Dung-style argument system is a tuple $\langle Args, Attacks \rangle$ where $Attacks \subseteq Args \times Args$.
- Add a semantics under which the concept of "additional information" can be judged. In the case of a Dung-style argument system, these may be preferred, grounded, stable, or some other semantics.

Definition 6 *(The Legal Moves Function for Argument Systems).* *The legalMoves function for an argument system AS is a function*

$$legalMoves : AS \times Semantics \times Dialogue \to 2^{Args}$$

This function takes in an argument system AS, together with an associated semantics Semantics, and a dialogue, and returns a set of possible arguments.

For example, in a Dung-style argument system, the *legalMoves* function could be defined as follows[1]:

---

[1] Note that this definition means that only an argument relevant (in the sense of Definition 7) to some argument may be introduced in this dialogue game. However, a relevance-aware agent (Definition 8) considers arguments relevant to its goals, maintaining the distinction between legal moves and moves relevant to it. Note also that this *legalMoves* function allows an agent to introduce arguments that attack its own arguments, which may not be allowed in some dialogues.

$legalMoves(AS, DSemantics, Dialogue) =\{\textbf{pass}\}\cup$
$\{a|a \in Args$ and
$DSemantics(\langle Dialogue \cup \{a\}, Attacks\rangle)$
$\neq DSemantics(\langle Dialogue, Attacks\rangle)\}$

Where **pass** is a move meaning no utterance is made[2], $AS = \langle Args, Attacks\rangle$
and $DSemantics : 2^{AS} \rightarrow 2^{Args}$ captures the appropriate Dung-style preferred,
grounded or stable semantics.

This *legalMoves* function requires that a legal move be one that changes the
conclusions that can be drawn from the dialogue if it were to terminate at this
point. In other words, a legal move is one that changes the set of arguments that
are contained in the grounded, preferred or whatever extension that is required
by the semantics. As a consequence of this, the dialogue tree of moves excludes
those that do not alter the accepted set of arguments, and so this function
ensures that a dialogue will terminate (assuming a finite set of arguments).

It is important to note that the *legalMoves* function captures both the rules
of the dialogue game's locutions, and the contents of these locutions, mixing the
dialogue game's syntax with its semantics.

3.3 Filtering Using Relevance

Often, a dialogue participant's goals revolve around having the other parties
accept, or reject a single argument. In such a situation, arguments that are not
directly relevant to this single argument may be ignored when searching the
possible move tree. This notion is related, but different to the idea presented in
the previous section. The *legalMoves* function captures all legal moves according
to a dialogue. A relevant move is a legal move that also affects the agent's goals.
We define one argument as relevant to another if it can affect its status in some
way.

Definition 7 *(Relevance).* *Given*

- *Two arguments a, b*
- *The set of all arguments Args*
- *A semantics for argument, which is able to determine the status of an argument given a set of arguments using the function $Semantics(c, X)$ where $c \in Args$ and $X \subseteq Args$*

We say that a is relevant to b (in the context of some argument system) if $\exists X \subseteq Args$ such that $a \notin X$ and $Semantics(b, X) \neq Semantics(b, X \cup \{a\})$. We may write $relevant(a, b)$ to indicate that a is relevant to b.

*In dialogues where an agent may pass to end the game, a **pass** move is also considered relevant. In such games, $relevant(\textbf{pass}, A)$ for any $A \in Args$ also holds.*

---

[2] A dialogue game typically ends after all agents consecutively pass.

While the *legalMoves* function *may* make use of the underlying argument system's semantics, the determination of relevance of an argument *must* employ the system's semantics.

Within a Dung-style argument framework, an argument is relevant if there is a path within the argument graph between it and some other argument. This makes sense intuitively, as the argument has the potential to affect the other argument's status (by directly, or indirectly attacking, or reinstating it).

Support is another way of having one argument affect another. In many dialogue types, an argument's premises have to be introduced before the argument itself may be used. A number of semantics have been proposed to deal with support [13,1,9], and any are appropriate for the purposes of this algorithm[3].

As mentioned above, the notion of relevance requires that an agent be able to specifically identify its goals. We extend the notion of an agent to capture this as follows:

Definition 8 (Relevance-Aware Agent). *A relevance-aware agent is a tuple*

$$\langle KB, Goals, GoalArguments, Opp \rangle$$

where $KB \subseteq Args$, $Goals : 2^{Dialogue} \rightarrow \mathbb{R}$ *and Opp is an opponent model as in Definition 3, and* $GoalArguments \subseteq Args$.

As discussed below, a relevance-aware agent utilises Algorithm 3 to consider only arguments which are relevant to its *GoalArguments* in its search. If the *GoalArguments* set is small (in comparison to the arguments returned by the *legalMoves* function), this may lead to a considerable pruning of the search tree. If we assume a single argument within *GoalArguments*, then the notion of relevance presented here is equivalent to R1 relevance in the work of Parsons et al. [16].

As the number of *GoalArguments* increase, the usefulness of the relevance optimization decreases, as more arguments typically become relevant. In order for the relevance based approach to function, the *Goals* function must also be constrained.

Since the utility of a dialogue is only evaluated once the tree is expanded to the maximum search depth, we cannot simply alter the agent's *Goal* function to include the notion of relevance. Instead, an agent must filter the set of possible moves to be evaluated based on its goals. To do this, a relevance-aware agent invokes Algorithm 3 using

$$M^*_{rel}(dia, depth, \langle KB, Goals, Opp \rangle, GoalArguments, legalMoves)$$

---

[3] It should be noted that the dialogues resulting from a framework such as [13] are very different to those obtained from a Dung style framework. In the latter, the dialogue would begin with the goal arguments being introduced, and attacks on those arguments (and attacks on those attacks) introduced in subsequent moves. However, the former approach requires that all arguments be supported, meaning that the dialogue would progress by first introducing arguments as premises, and then build on these premises with additional arguments, until the goal arguments are introduced. Attacks on introduced arguments may still occur at any time.

Algorithm 3. $M_{rel}^*(dia, depth, agent, goalArguments, legalMoves)$

Require: A dialogue dia
Require: A search depth $depth$
Require: An agent $agent = \langle KB, Goals, oppModel \rangle$
Require: A set of arguments $goalArguments$
Require: A move generation function $legalMoves$
1: **if** $depth = 0$ **then**
2:     **return** $(NIL, Goals(dia))$
3: **else**
4:     $maxUtil = -\infty$
5:     $PossibleMoves = legalMoves(dia) \cap KB$
6:     **for all** $move \in PossibleMoves$ **do**
7:         **if** $\nexists a \in goalArguments$ such that $relevant(move, a)$ **then**
8:             $PossibleMoves = PossibleMoves \backslash move$
9:         **end if**
10:     **end for**
11:     **for all** $move \in PossibleMoves$ **do**
12:         **if** $depth = 1$ **then**
13:             $playUtil = Goals(dia \cup \{move\})$
14:         **else**
15:             $\langle oppMove, oppUtil \rangle = M_{rel}^*(dia \cup \{move\}, depth - 1,$
                                $oppModel, goalArguments, legalMoves)$
16:             $\langle playMove, playUtil \rangle = M_{rel}^*(dia \cup \{move, oppMove\}, depth - 2,$
                                $agent, goalArguments, legalMoves)$
17:         **end if**
18:         **if** $playUtil > maxUtil$ **then**
19:             $maxUtil = playUtil$
20:             $maxMove = move$
21:         **end if**
22:     **end for**
23: **end if**
24: **return** $(maxMove, maxUtil)$

Where $dia, depth$ and $legalMoves$ are dependent on the dialogue and the agent's capabilities.

It is clear that the relevant moves form a subset of the legal moves for a dialogue. Thus, for all $g \in GoalArguments$

$$\bigcup_g \{a | a \in Args \text{ and } relevant(a, g)\} \subseteq legalMoves(AS, Semantics, Dialogue)$$

If this subset relation is strict, the notion of relevance is useful in pruning the search tree. However, even in this case, we still filter by using the $legalMoves$ function (line 5) before filtering by relevance, as we assume that this operation is computationally cheaper than relevance filtering.

Lines 6–10 filter out irrelevant moves. It should be noted that the relevance-aware agent's $GoalArguments$ are used at all depths of this algorithm, as any move that does not affect these goals can be ignored by the agent. This follows from the idea that if the other party makes (what are considered) irrelevant arguments, these have no effects on the arguments introduced by the agent.

As a simple example, consider the relevance-aware agent

$$\langle \{a, c\}, \{a\}, \{a\}, \langle \{b\}, \{\neg a\}, \langle \{d\}, \{a\}, \{\} \rangle \rangle \rangle$$

Here, $\neg a$ represents a goal that a is not deemed acceptable according to the game's semantics. We may assume that only a single argument may be introduced by an agent during its turn (or that it may pass), and assume Dung-style argument system with grounded semantics.

$$AS = (\{a, b, c, d\}, \{(b, a), (d, b)\})$$

For simplicity, we represent goals as single arguments rather than dialogues; we assume that all dialogues containing the goal argument are worth 10 utility, less one utility for every argument the agent advances.

Then at the first level of argument, arguments a, c, and passing are all legal moves according to the agent's knowledge base and semantics. However, a and pass are the only relevant moves, and the agent must then determine what the opponent will play in response to a. According to its opponent model, the opponent could play b. However, argument c is not relevant, and the agent will thus not consider whether the opponent will play it or not. The algorithm shows that if the opponent plays b, it believes that the agent will play d (even though it does not actually know d). Since playing a move will cost the opponent utility, the agent believes that the opponent will pass.

If instead, the agent passes, it will gain no utility, while the opponent would also pass, and would gain 10 utility. Thus, the agent will utter a, and if its opponent model is accurate, will win the game when the opponent passes.

Given perfect information, the agent should not have won this game. Furthermore, the agent gains 10 utility, while the opponent gains 0 utility.

4   Discussion

This paper is built around the idea of an agent being able to assign utility to a dialogue. While the assignment of positive utility to a dialogue represents the agent meeting some of its goals, negative utility can arise from a number of dialogue-dependent situations. These obviously include the agent not meeting its goals, and, more interestingly, may occur when some other argument is introduced (c.f. [15]), or when the agent actually makes use of an argument (for example, as a premise to one of its own arguments). Work such as [14] examines some of these utility assignment approaches in more detail, but performs only one step lookahead when selecting an utterance.

As discussed in Section 2, it is possible to model a min-max opponent by making use of an opponent model of the form $(f, (-f, (f, \ldots)))$ to the depth of the search. Constructing a min-max opponent model for the argumentation domain requires incorporating a knowledge base into the opponent model. Two natural choices for an opponent's knowledge base arise. First, it could be identical to the original agent's knowledge base. Second, it could contain all arguments in the system. Since min-max is inherently pessimistic, the latter approach makes sense for the opponent's model, while the former knowledge base would represent the opponent's model of the agent. It has been shown that an agent making use of the M^* strategy will perform no worse than an agent utilising min-max search [5], and this result can be trivially mapped to our extensions of the strategy.

The worst case computational complexity of the M^* algorithm, and thus our heuristic is bounded by $(b + 1)^{d-1}$ where b represents the branching factor, and d the search depth. Clearly, computational techniques that prune the tree are important if the algorithm is to be used in real world situations. The techniques described in Section 3.2 and 3.3 reduce the branching factor, and perform pruning of the dialogue tree respectively. Furthermore, depending on the form of the utility function, an adaptation of $\alpha\beta$-pruning may be applied to M^*[5]. This adaptation is particularly applicable to persuasion dialogues, where an agent meeting its goals usually means that its opponent fails to meet their goals. Other techniques, such as transposition tables can also yield significant computational savings, even when the utility function is relatively complex.

Moore [11] suggested that any strategy for argument must meet three criteria, namely to maintain the focus of the dispute, build its point of view, or attack the opponent's one, and select an argument that fulfils the previous two objectives. The inclusion of relevance, and the filtering of the legal moves function allows an agent to include these criteria within its reasoning process. Clearly, any utterance made as a result of a reasoning process meeting Moore's criteria will itself meet the criteria.

Additional work dealing with argument strategy includes the work of Riveret [20,21], who, like us, builds a tree of dialogues, and computes game theoretic equilibria to determine which move an agent should make. However, he assumes that the agent's knowledge and goals are perfectly known, an assumption which does not hold in many situations. Riveret's work is more general than ours in one sense, namely in that the dialogues they investigate do not assume that agents make a single utterance during their turn, or indeed, take turns in an orderly manner. However, our approach can easily be extended to include this generalisation. Rahwan [19] has also examined the notion of strategy within argument, but focused on showing how dialogues may be designed so as to make them strategy-proof.

We have begun implementing and evaluating the performance of agents making use of opponent modelling as part of their argument strategy. Our initial results indicate that this approach outperforms techniques such as min-max search, but still need to investigate issues such as the effects of errors in the opponent model on the quality of the strategy, and the tradeoffs between search time and search quality when increasing the search depth.

It is clear that the introduction of an argument by an opponent may cause an update in our knowledge base or opponent model (for example, if an argument a supports an argument b, which in turn supports argument c and we believe that our opponent's goal is argument c, the introduction of a should cause us to believe that our opponent knows b). Our algorithms cater for such updates implicitly; the agent's opponent model at the appropriate depth of the expanded dialogue tree *should* include the fact that the opponent knows b. In the future, we intend to provide more constraints on the form of the agent and its opponent model, capturing notions such as knowledge/belief revision.

Another area of future work involves extending our algorithms to make use of probabilistic opponent modelling [7]. In this paper, we assumed that an agent had a single model of its opponent. However, probabilistic opponent modelling would allow an agent to reason with imperfect information about its opponent, a situation that commonly arises in real world situations. The addition of probabilistic opponent modelling opens up many exciting avenues for research. For example, an agent may have two strategies open to it; one that will yield it a high utility, but assumes that there is a high chance that its opponent does not know a key fact, and the other yielding less utility, but being much safer. In such a situation, the agent must take into account the *risk* of making certain utterances, and we intend to investigate how such considerations can form part of an agent's argument strategy.

Finally, we have assumed throughout the paper that an agent has some opponent model, with an arbitrary evaluation function and knowledge base. However, we have not examined how an agent may learn an opponent model during the course of a dialogue, or over repeated interactions with an opponent. Some work on this topic exists in the context of game playing [6], and we intend to apply it to the argumentation domain.

5   Conclusions

In this paper, we showed how an agent may decide on which utterances to advance in the course of an argument by making use of an opponent model. By making use of an opponent model, the agent can discover lines of argument that may take advantage of its opponent's beliefs and goals. Such lines of argument would not be discovered by a more naïve strategy, such as min-max, which would assume that the opponent's goals are diametrically opposed to its own.

We also showed how various aspects of the argumentation domain, namely the notion of relevance, and the interactions between arguments, may be used to reduce the computational complexity of searching for an argument while making use of opponent modelling.

To our knowledge, no work on argument strategies has yet utilised the notion of an opponent model to the same extent as we have. The introduction of opponent modelling opens up a number of avenues for future research, and also allows for the creation of new, and novel strategies for argument.

References

1. Amgoud, L., Cayrol, C., Lagasquie-Schiex, M.-C.: On the bipolarity in argumentation frameworks. In: Proceedings of the 10th International Workshop on Nonmonotonic Reasoning, pp. 1–9. Whistler, Canada (2004)
2. Amgoud, L., Maudet, N.: Strategical considerations for argumentative agents (preliminary report). In: Proceedings of the 9th International Workshop on Nonmonotonic Reasoning, pp. 399–407 (2002)
3. Amgoud, L., Prade, H.: Generation and evaluation of different types of arguments in negotiation. In: Proceedings of the 10th International Workshop on Nonmonotonic Reasoning (2004)
4. Besnard, P., Doutre, S., Hunter, A. (eds.): Computational Models of Argument: Proceedings of COMMA 2008. Frontiers in Artificial Intelligence and Applications, Toulouse, France, May 28-30, vol. 172. IOS Press, Amsterdam (2008)
5. Carmel, D., Markovitch, S.: Incorporating opponent models into adversary search. In: Proceedings of the Thirteenth National Conference on Artificial Intelligence, pp. 120–125. AAAI, Menlo Park (1996)
6. Carmel, D., Markovitch, S.: Model-based learning of interaction strategies in multi-agent systems. Journal of Experimental and Theoretical Artificial Intelligence 10(3), 309–332 (1998)
7. Donkers, H.H.L.M., Uiterwijk, J.W.H.M., van den Herik, H.J.: Probabilistic opponent-model search. Information Sciences 135(3-4), 123–149 (2001)
8. Dung, P.M.: On the acceptability of arguments and its fundamental role in nonmonotonic reasoning, logic programming and n-person games. Artificial Intelligence 77(2), 321–357 (1995)
9. Martínez, D.C., García, A.J., Simari, G.R.: Progressive defeat paths in abstract argumentation frameworks. In: Lamontagne, L., Marchand, M. (eds.) Canadian AI 2006. LNCS (LNAI), vol. 4013, pp. 242–253. Springer, Heidelberg (2006)
10. McBurney, P., Parsons, S.: Dialogue games in multi-agent systems. Informal Logic 22(3), 257–274 (2002)
11. Moore, D.: Dialogue game theory for intelligent tutoring systems. PhD thesis, Leeds Metropolitan University (1993)
12. Oren, N., Luck, M., Miles, S., Norman, T.J.: An argumentation inspired heuristic for resolving normative conflict. In: Proceedings of The Fifth Workshop on Coordination, Organizations, Institutions, and Norms in Agent Systems (COIN@AAMAS 2008), Estoril, Portugal, pp. 41–56 (2008)
13. Oren, N., Norman, T.J.: Semantics for evidence-based argumentation. In: Besnard, et al. (eds.) [4], pp. 276–284
14. Oren, N., Norman, T.J., Preece, A.: Arguing with confidential information. In: Proceedings of the 18th European Conference on Artificial Intelligence, Riva del Garda, Italy, August 2006, pp. 280–284 (2006)
15. Oren, N., Norman, T.J., Preece, A.: Loose lips sink ships: a heuristic for argumentation. In: Proceedings of the Third International Workshop on Argumentation in Multi-Agent Systems, Hakodate, Japan, May 2006, pp. 121–134 (2006)
16. Parsons, S., McBurney, P., Sklar, E., Wooldridge, M.: On the relevance of utterances in formal inter-agent dialogues. In: AAMAS 2007: Proceedings of the 6th international joint conference on Autonomous agents and multiagent systems, pp. 1–8. ACM, New York (2007)
17. Prakken, H.: Relating protocols for dynamic dispute with logics for defeasible argumentation. Synthese 127, 187–219 (2001)

18. Prakken, H., Sartor, G.: Computational Logic: Logic Programming and Beyond. In: Essays In Honour of Robert A. Kowalski, Part II. LNCS, vol. 2048, pp. 342–380. Springer, Heidelberg (2002)
19. Rahwan, I., Larson, K.: Mechanism design for abstract argumentation. In: Proceedings of AAMAS 2008 (2008)
20. Riveret, R., Prakken, H., Rotolo, A., Sartor, G.: Heuristics in argumentation: A game theory investigation. In: Besnard, et al. (eds.) [4], pp. 324–335
21. Riveret, R., Rotolo, N., Sartor, G., Prakken, H., Roth, B.: Success chances in argument games: a probabilistic approach to legal disputes. In: Proceedings of the 20th Anniversary International Conference on Legal Knowledge and Information Systems (Jurix 2007), Amsterdam, The Netherlands, pp. 99–108 (2007)
22. Shannon, C.E.: Programming a computer for playing chess. Philosophical Magazine 41, 256–275 (1950)

Realizing Argumentation in Multi-agent Systems Using Defeasible Logic Programming

Matthias Thimm

Information Engineering Group, Department for Computer Science,
Technische Universität Dortmund, Germany

Abstract. We describe a working multi-agent architecture based on *Defeasible Logic Programming* (DeLP) where agents are engaged in an argumentation to reach a common conclusion. Due to the distributed approach personalities and opinions of the individual agents give rise to arguments and counterarguments concerning a particular query. This distribution of information leads to more intuitive modeling of argumentation from the point of view of knowledge representation. We establish a sound theoretical framework of a specific type of argumentation in multi-agent systems and describe the computational issues involved in it. A formal comparison of the framework to DeLP is given and it is shown that the modeling specific scenarios of argumentation in the distributed setting bears a more rational representation. The framework described in this paper has been fully implemented and a short description of its features is given.

1 Introduction

Argumentation has become a very active field in computer science research [5]. It deals with representing and investigating relationships between arguments and can be seen as a special form of non-monotonic reasoning. By constructing arguments for specific claims and determining which arguments are acceptable in this set of arguments one can identify a set of claims that should be believed. Besides the point of determining the actual beliefs argumentation also gives reasons why to believe in a particular statement. Furthermore, argumentation is also a rational choice for representing dialogues between agents. Thus, there are mainly two issues computational models of argumentation are concerned with in the context of artificial intelligence, namely describing models of commonsense reasoning techniques within a single agent and formalizing meaningful communication between agents in a multi-agent system, e. g. negotiation and persuasion [12,4]. In this paper we take a hybrid approach by modeling a multi-agent system where the agents are capable of argumentation but use argumentation in order to reach a common conclusion that can be regarded as the whole system's opinion on the given topic. From an outside point of view, the system can be seen as a reasoning engine that determines if a given query can be validated. Internally, the system comprises of several agents which may have different beliefs and opinions. A special agent, the *moderator* or judge, takes queries from the

P. McBurney et al. (Eds.): ArgMAS 2009, LNAI 6057, pp. 175–194, 2010.

outside and controls the argumentation of the agents on the inside related to the given query. Each agent maintains his own personal view and additionally there is some global and certain knowledge available to all agents. Agents use their knowledge to construct arguments and counterarguments to arguments of other agents. The moderator overseers the argumentation and finally makes a decision on its outcome.

As the underlying logical foundation we use *Defeasible Logic Programming* (DeLP) [10] which is a form of defeasible argumentation [15]. DeLP is an approach to realise non-monotonic reasoning via dialectical argumentation by relating arguments and counterarguments for a given logical query. It employs logic programming as representation formalism and differentiates between strict and defeasible rules. Queries in the form of literals can be asked and arguments for and against literals are constructed using strict and defeasible rules. Counterarguments for arguments can be determined and a dialectical process that considers all arguments and counterarguments for the query is used in order to decide whether the query is believed by the agent or not.

This paper proposes and discusses an approach for a distributed system which provides the capability of argumentation using the notions of DeLP. In this system agents exchange arguments and counterarguments in order to answer queries given from outside the system. The framework establishes a border between its interior and exterior as from outside the system it is seen as a general reasoning engine. Internally this reasoning is accomplished by defeasible argumentation where every agent tries to support or defeat the given query by generating arguments for or against it and by generating counterarguments against other agents' arguments. In the end the most plausible argument prevails and its conclusion is the answer to the original query. We build on previous work [19,20] but give a much more detailed description of the computational issues in multi-agent argumentation and some description on an implementation.

The paper is organized as follows. In Section 2 we give a brief overview on defeasible logic programming adapted to our needs. In Section 3 we formalize the multi-agent setting and give detailed logical descriptions of the individual components and continue with computational techniques that implement this formalization. We give a brief overview on the implementation of the proposed system afterwards in Section 5. In Section 6 we review some related work and conclude with some final remarks.

2   Defeasible Logic Programming

The basic elements of *Defeasible Logic Programming* (DeLP) are facts and rules. Let $\mathcal{L}$ denote a set of ground literals, where a literal h is a ground atom A or a negated ground atom $\sim A$, where the symbol $\sim$ represents the strong negation. Overlining will be used to denote the complement of a literal with respect to strong negation, i.e., it is $\overline{p} = \sim p$ and $\overline{\sim p} = p$ for a ground atom p. A single literal $h \in \mathcal{L}$ is also called a *fact*.

The set of rules is divided into strict rules, i.e. rules encoding strict consequences, and defeasible rules which derive uncertain or defeasible conclusions. A *strict rule* is an ordered pair $h \leftarrow B$, where $h \in \mathcal{L}$ and $B \subseteq \mathcal{L}$. A *defeasible rule* is an ordered pair $h \prec B$, where $h \in \mathcal{L}$ and $B \subseteq \mathcal{L}$. A defeasible rule is used to describe tentative knowledge as in "birds fly". We use the functions $body/1$ and $head/1$ to refer to the head resp. body of a defeasible or strict rule. Strict and defeasible rules are ground. However, following the usual convention, some examples will use "schematic rules" with variables (denoted with an initial uppercase letter). Let DEF_X resp. STR_X be the set of all defeasible resp. strict rules, that can be constructed from literals in $X \subseteq \mathcal{L}$. We will omit the subscripts when referring to the whole set of literals $\mathcal{L}$, e.g. we write DEF for $\mathsf{DEF}_\mathcal{L}$.

Using facts, strict and defeasible rules, one is able to derive additional beliefs as in other rule-based systems. Let $X \subseteq \mathcal{L} \cup \mathsf{STR} \cup \mathsf{DEF}$ be a set of facts, strict rules, defeasible rules, and let furthermore $h \in \mathcal{L}$. A *(defeasible) derivation* of h from X, denoted $X \mid\!\sim h$, consists of a finite sequence $h_1, \ldots, h_n = h$ of literals $(h_i \in \mathcal{L})$ such that h_i is a fact $(h_i \in X)$ or there is a strict or defeasible rule in X with head h_i and body $b_1, \ldots, b_k$, where every b_l $(1 \leq l \leq k)$ is an element h_j with $j < i$. If the derivation of a literal h only uses facts and strict rules, the derivation is called a *strict* derivation. A set X is *contradictory*, denoted $X \mid\!\sim \perp$, iff there exist defeasible derivations for two complementary literals from X. Every agent in our framework maintains a *local belief base* that is comprised of defeasible rules and thus describes the agent's own (uncertain) knowledge. Furthermore the framework provides a *global belief base*, consisting of facts and strict rules, that describes common knowledge to all agents.

Definition 1 (Belief bases). *A* global belief base $\Pi \subseteq \mathcal{L} \cup \mathsf{STR}$ *is a non-contradictory set of strict rules and facts. A set of defeasible rules $\Delta \subseteq \mathsf{DEF}$ is called a* local belief base.

Observe, that we require the global belief base to be non-contradictory. This is justifiable as the information stored in the global belief base should be regarded as indisputable by the agents. Hence, the agents undertake their argumentation only based on their own local belief bases, which can be—in general—contradictory to each other.

Example 1. Let a global belief base Π and local belief bases Δ_1 and Δ_2 be given by

$$
\Pi = \left\{ \begin{array}{l} chicken(tina) \\ scared(tina) \\ penguin(tweety) \\ bird(X) \leftarrow chicken(X) \\ bird(X) \leftarrow penguin(X) \\ \sim\!flies(X) \leftarrow penguin(X) \end{array} \right\} ,
$$

$$
\Delta_1 = \left\{ \begin{array}{l} flies(X) \prec bird(X) \\ flies(X) \prec chicken(X), scared(X) \end{array} \right\} ,
$$

$$
\Delta_2 = \left\{ \begin{array}{l} \sim\!flies(X) \prec chicken(X) \\ nests\_in\_trees(X) \prec flies(X) \end{array} \right\} .
$$

The global belief base Π contains the facts, that Tina is a scared chicken and that Tweety is penguin. The strict rules state that all chickens and all penguins are birds, and penguins cannot fly. The defeasible rules of the local belief base Δ_1 express that birds and scared chickens normally fly. The defeasible rules of the local belief base Δ_2 express that chickens normally do not fly and something that flies normally nests in trees.

As a means to reveal different opinions about certain pieces of information, agents use their local belief bases to construct arguments.

Definition 2 (Argument, Subargument). *Let $h \in \mathcal{L}$ be a literal and let Π resp. Δ be a global resp. local belief base. $\langle \mathcal{A}, h \rangle$ is an argument for h, iff 1.) $\mathcal{A} \subseteq \Delta$, 2.) there exists a defeasible derivation of h from $\Pi \cup \mathcal{A}$, 3.) the set $\Pi \cup \mathcal{A}$ is non-contradictory, and 4.) $\mathcal{A}$ is minimal with respect to set inclusion. The literal h will be called conclusion and the set $\mathcal{A}$ will be called support of the argument $\langle \mathcal{A}, h \rangle$. An argument $\langle \mathcal{B}, q \rangle$ is a subargument of an argument $\langle \mathcal{A}, h \rangle$, iff $\mathcal{B} \subseteq \mathcal{A}$. Let $\mathsf{ARG}_{\Pi, \Delta}$ be the set of all arguments that can be built from Π and Δ.*

Two literals h and h_1 *disagree* regarding a global belief base Π, iff the set $\Pi \cup \{h, h_1\}$ is contradictory. Two complementary literals p and $\sim p$ disagree trivially, because for every Π the set $\Pi \cup \{p, \sim p\}$ is contradictory. But two literals which are not contradictory, can disagree as well. For $\Pi = \{(\sim h \leftarrow b), (h \leftarrow a)\}$ the literals a and b disagree, because $\Pi \cup \{a, b\}$ is contradictory. We call an argument $\langle \mathcal{A}_1, h_1 \rangle$ a *counterargument* to an argument $\langle \mathcal{A}_2, h_2 \rangle$ at a literal h, iff there is a subargument $\langle \mathcal{A}, h \rangle$ of $\langle \mathcal{A}_2, h_2 \rangle$ such that h and h_1 disagree. If $\langle \mathcal{A}_1, h_1 \rangle$ is a counterargument to $\langle \mathcal{A}_2, h_2 \rangle$ at a literal h, then the subargument $\langle \mathcal{A}, h \rangle$ of $\langle \mathcal{A}_2, h_2 \rangle$ is called the *disagreement subargument*.

In order to deal with counterarguments to other arguments, a central aspect of defeasible logic programming is a formal comparison criterion among arguments. A possible preference relation among arguments is *Generalized Specificity* [17]. According to this criterion an argument is preferred to another argument, iff the former one is more *specific* than the latter, i.e., (informally) iff the former one uses more facts or less rules. For example, $\langle \{c \prec a, b\}, c \rangle$ is more specific than $\langle \{\sim c \prec a\}, \sim c \rangle$. For a formal definition and desirable properties of preference criterions in general see [17,10]. For the rest of this paper we use $\succ$ to denote an arbitrary but fixed preference criterion among arguments. The preference criterion is needed to decide whether an argument defeats another or not, as disagreement does not imply preference.

Definition 3 (Defeater). *An argument $\langle \mathcal{A}_1, h_1 \rangle$ is a defeater of an argument $\langle \mathcal{A}_2, h_2 \rangle$, iff there is a subargument $\langle \mathcal{A}, h \rangle$ of $\langle \mathcal{A}_2, h_2 \rangle$ such that $\langle \mathcal{A}_1, h_1 \rangle$ is a counterargument of $\langle \mathcal{A}_2, h_2 \rangle$ at literal h and either $\langle \mathcal{A}_1, h_1 \rangle \succ \langle \mathcal{A}, h \rangle$ (proper defeat) or $\langle \mathcal{A}_1, h_1 \rangle \not\succ \langle \mathcal{A}, h \rangle$ and $\langle \mathcal{A}, h \rangle \not\succ \langle \mathcal{A}_1, h_1 \rangle$ (blocking defeat).*

When considering sequences of arguments, the definition of defeat is not sufficient to describe a conclusive argumentation line. Defeat only takes an argument and its counterargument into consideration, but disregards preceding arguments.

But we expect also properties like *non-circularity* or *concordance* from an argumentation sequence. See [10] for a more detailed motivation of acceptable argumentation lines.

Definition 4 (Acceptable Argumentation Line). *Let Π be a global belief base. Let $\Lambda = [\langle \mathcal{A}_1, h_1 \rangle, \ldots, \langle \mathcal{A}_m, h_m \rangle]$ be a sequence of some arguments. Λ is called an* acceptable argumentation line, *iff 1.) Λ is a finite sequence, 2.) every argument $\langle \mathcal{A}_i, h_i \rangle$ with $i > 1$ is a defeater of its predecessor $\langle \mathcal{A}_{i-1}, h_{i-1} \rangle$ and if $\langle \mathcal{A}_i, h_i \rangle$ is a blocking defeater of $\langle \mathcal{A}_{i-1}, h_{i-1} \rangle$ and $\langle \mathcal{A}_{i+1}, h_{i+1} \rangle$ exists, then $\langle \mathcal{A}_{i+1}, h_{i+1} \rangle$ is a proper defeater of $\langle \mathcal{A}_i, h_i \rangle$, 3.) $\Pi \cup \mathcal{A}_1 \cup \mathcal{A}_3 \cup \ldots$ is non-contradictory (concordance of supporting arguments), 4.) $\Pi \cup \mathcal{A}_2 \cup \mathcal{A}_4 \cup \ldots$ is non-contradictory (concordance of interfering arguments), and 5.)no argument $\langle \mathcal{A}_k, h_k \rangle$ is a subargument of an argument $\langle \mathcal{A}_i, h_i \rangle$ with $i < k$. Let* SEQ *denote the set of all sequences of arguments that can be built using rules from* DEF, STR *and facts from* $\mathcal{L}$.

We use the notation $\Lambda + \langle \mathcal{A}, h \rangle$ to denote the concatenation of argumentation lines and arguments.

In DeLP a literal h is *warranted*, if there is an argument $\langle \mathcal{A}, h \rangle$ which is non-defeated in the end. To decide whether $\langle \mathcal{A}, h \rangle$ is defeated or not, every acceptable argumentation line starting with $\langle \mathcal{A}, h \rangle$ has to be considered.

Definition 5 (Dialectical Tree). *Let Π be a global belief base and $\Delta_1, \ldots, \Delta_n$ be local belief bases. Let $\langle \mathcal{A}_0, h_0 \rangle$ be an argument. A dialectical tree for $\langle \mathcal{A}_0, h_0 \rangle$, denoted $\mathcal{T}_{\langle \mathcal{A}_0, h_0 \rangle}$, is defined as follows.*

1. *The root of $\mathcal{T}$ is $\langle \mathcal{A}_0, h_0 \rangle$.*
2. *Let $\langle \mathcal{A}_n, h_n \rangle$ be a node in $\mathcal{T}$ and let $\Lambda = [\langle \mathcal{A}_0, h_0 \rangle, \ldots, \langle \mathcal{A}_n, h_n \rangle]$ be the sequence of nodes from the root to $\langle \mathcal{A}_n, h_n \rangle$. Let $\langle \mathcal{B}_1, q_1 \rangle, \ldots, \langle \mathcal{B}_k, q_k \rangle$ be the defeaters of $\langle \mathcal{A}_n, h_n \rangle$. For every defeater $\langle \mathcal{B}_i, q_i \rangle$ with $1 \le i \le k$ such that the argumentation line $\Lambda' = [\langle \mathcal{A}_0, h_0 \rangle, \ldots, \langle \mathcal{A}_n, h_n \rangle, \langle \mathcal{B}_i, q_i \rangle]$ is acceptable, the node $\langle \mathcal{A}_n, h_n \rangle$ has a child $\langle \mathcal{B}_i, q_i \rangle$. If there is no such $\langle \mathcal{B}_i, q_i \rangle$, the node $\langle \mathcal{A}_n, h_n \rangle$ is a leaf.*

Let DIA *denote the set of all dialectical trees with arguments that can be built using rules from* DEF, STR *and facts from* $\mathcal{L}$.

In order to decide whether the argument at the root of a given dialectical tree is defeated or not, it is necessary to perform a *bottom-up*-analysis of the tree. Every leaf of the tree is marked "undefeated" and every inner node is marked "defeated", if it has at least one child node marked "undefeated". Otherwise it is marked "undefeated". Let $\mathcal{T}^*_{\langle \mathcal{A}, h \rangle}$ denote the marked dialectical tree of $\mathcal{T}_{\langle \mathcal{A}, h \rangle}$.

We call a literal h *warranted*, iff there is an argument $\langle \mathcal{A}, h \rangle$ for h such that the root of the marked dialectical tree $\mathcal{T}^*_{\langle \mathcal{A}, h \rangle}$ is marked "undefeated". Then $\langle \mathcal{A}, h \rangle$ is a *warrant* for h. Observe that, if a literal h is a fact or has a strict derivation from a global belief base Π alone, then h is also warranted as there are no counterarguments for $\langle \emptyset, h \rangle$. The answer of a DeLP interpreter to a literal h is YES iff h is warranted, NO iff $\overline{h}$ is warranted, and UNDECIDED iff neither h nor $\overline{h}$ are warranted. Notice, that it can not be the case that both h and $\overline{h}$ are warranted [21].

3   The Formal Agent Architecture

Our framework consists of several agents and a central moderator, which co-ordinates the argumentation process undertaken by the agents. An overview of this system is depicted in Figure 1. The moderator accepts a query, consisting of a single literal, and asks the agents to argue about its warrant status, i.e., whether the literal or its complement can be supported by an ultimately un-defeated argument. In a first round, every agent is asked by the moderator to deliver arguments directly supporting the query or its complement. For every argument, the moderator initializes a dialectical tree with this argument as its root. Then for any of these dialectical trees agents are asked to bring up coun-terarguments for current leaves, thus mutually building up the final tree. Agents use the global belief base of the system, which contains strict knowledge, and their own local belief bases consisting of defeasible knowledge to generate argu-ments. Eventually the system returns an answer to the questioner that describes the final status of the literal based on the agents' individual beliefs.

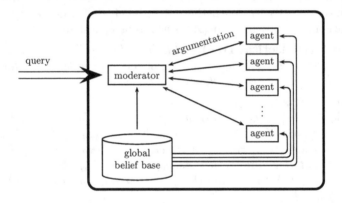

Fig. 1. An overview of the framework

We now describe the components of the distributed framework, namely the moderator and the agents, using a functional description of their intended be-haviour. As the framework is flexible, many different definitions of the functions to be presented can be thought of. But we restrain them on the notions of DeLP as described above, so we use the subscript "D" to denote the DeLP specific def-inition. Furthermore we give specific algorithms describing the behavior of the system in the next section. true When the moderator receives arguments from the agents, he builds up several dialectical trees and finally he has to evaluate them using the bottom-up evaluation method described above.

Definition 6 (Analysis function χ_D). *The* analysis function χ_D *is a function* $\chi_D : \mathsf{DIA} \to \{\mathsf{false}, \mathsf{true}\}$ *such that for every dialectical tree* $v \in \mathsf{DIA}$ *it holds* $\chi_D(v) = \mathsf{true}$ *iff the root argument of* v^* *is marked "undefeated".*

Furthermore the evaluation of dialectical trees makes only sense, if the tree was built up according to the definition of an acceptable argumentation line. Hence, the moderator and the agents as well, have to check whether new arguments are valid in the current argumentation line.

Definition 7 (Acceptance function $\eta_{D,\succ}$). *For a given preference relation $\succ$ among arguments, the* acceptance function $\eta_{D,\succ}$ *is a function $\eta_{D,\succ} : \mathsf{SEQ} \to \{\mathsf{false}, \mathsf{true}\}$ such that for every argument sequence $\Lambda \in \mathsf{SEQ}$ it holds $\eta_{D,\succ}(\Lambda) = \mathsf{true}$ iff Λ is acceptable according to Definition 4.*

It is possible to assume different acceptance functions for different agents according to different definitions of an acceptable argumentation line. But in our multi-agent system, we assume $\eta_{D,\succ}$ to be fixed and the same for the moderator and all agents by convention.

At the end of the argumentation process for a query h, the agents have produced a set of dialectical trees with root arguments for h or $\overline{h}$, respectively. As we have to distinguish several different cases, the moderator has to decide, whether the query h is warranted, the negation of h is warranted, or none of them are warranted in the framework. Let $\mathfrak{P}(S)$ denote the power set of a set S.

Definition 8 (Decision function μ_D). *The* decision function μ_D *is a function $\mu_D : \mathfrak{P}(\mathsf{DIA}) \to \{\mathsf{YES}, \mathsf{NO}, \mathsf{UNDECIDED}, \mathsf{UNKNOWN}\}$. Let $Q_{\dot{p}} \subseteq \mathsf{DIA}$ such that all root arguments of dialectical trees in $Q_{\dot{p}}$ are arguments for p or for $\overline{p}$, then μ_D is defined as*

1. *$\mu_D(Q_{\dot{p}}) = \mathsf{YES}$, if there is a dialectical tree $\upsilon \in Q_{\dot{p}}$ s.t. the root of υ is an argument for p and $\chi_D(\upsilon) = \mathsf{true}$.*
2. *$\mu_D(Q_{\dot{p}}) = \mathsf{NO}$, if there is a dialectical tree $\upsilon \in Q_{\dot{p}}$ s.t. the root of υ is an argument for $\overline{p}$ and $\chi_D(\upsilon) = \mathsf{true}$.*
3. *$\mu_D(Q_{\dot{p}}) = \mathsf{UNDECIDED}$, if $\chi_D(\upsilon) = \mathsf{false}$ for all $\upsilon \in Q_{\dot{p}}$.*
4. *$\mu_D(Q_{\dot{p}}) = \mathsf{UNKNOWN}$, if p is not in the language ($p \notin \mathcal{L}$).*

The function μ_D is well-defined, as it cannot be the case that both conditions 1. and 2. are simultaneously fulfilled, see for example [21].

The above functions are sufficient to define the moderator of the framework.

Definition 9 (Moderator). *For a given preference relation $\succ$ among arguments, the* moderator *is a tuple $(\mu_D, \chi_D, \eta_{D,\succ})$.*

An overview of the moderator is depicted in Figure 2. There, the analysis-module is responsible for the evaluation of the received arguments while the coordination-module is responsible for querying the agents for arguments in a systematic way. Furthermore, the moderator acts as an interface between the outside of the system and the system's interior by explicitly separating external (with the user) and internal communication (with the agents).

The agents of the framework provide two functionalities. First, they propose initial arguments for a given literal (or its negation) submitted by the moderator of the framework, which will be roots of the dialectical trees to be constructed. For a given query h it may be necessary to examine both, all dialectical trees

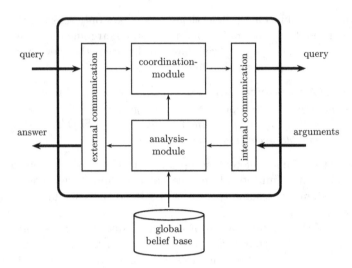

Fig. 2. The internal components of a moderator

with a root argument for h and all dialectical trees with a root argument for $\overline{h}$, as a query for h can only be answered with NO if there is a warrant for $\overline{h}$. Second, the agents propose counterarguments to arguments of other agents that are valid in the given argumentation line. We neglect the case that agents can give counterarguments to their own arguments here for simplicity. We achieve this by ensuring that each agent's local belief base is consistent with respect to the global belief base (see below). An agent is not obliged to return all his valid arguments for a given query or all his counterarguments for a given argument. Therefore, it is possible to model different kinds of argumentation strategies given different instantiations of the following argument functions.

Definition 10 (Root argument function). *Let Π be a global belief base and let Δ be a local belief base. A root argument function $\varphi_{\Pi,\Delta}$ is a function $\varphi_{\Pi,\Delta} : \mathcal{L} \to \mathfrak{P}(\mathrm{ARG}_{\Pi,\Delta})$ such that for every literal $h \in \mathcal{L}$ the set $\varphi_{\Pi,\Delta}(h)$ is a set of arguments for h or for $\overline{h}$ from Π and Δ.*

Definition 11 (Counterargument function). *Let Π be a global belief base and let Δ be a local belief base. A counterargument function $\psi_{\Pi,\Delta}$ is a function $\psi_{\Pi,\Delta} : \mathsf{SEQ} \to \mathfrak{P}(\mathrm{ARG}_{\Pi,\Delta})$ such that for every argumentation sequence $\Lambda \in \mathsf{SEQ}$ the set $\psi_{\Pi,\Delta}(\Lambda)$ is a set of attacks from Π and Δ on the last argument of Λ and for every $\langle \mathcal{B}, h \rangle \in \psi_{\Pi,\Delta}(\Lambda)$ it holds that $\eta_{\mathsf{D},\succ}(\Lambda + \langle \mathcal{B}, h \rangle) = \mathsf{true}$.*

Here we assume that the root argument and counterargument functions of all agents are the same and especially *complete*, i.e., they return all possible arguments for the given situation and do not omit one. As a consequence, we do not talk about *strategies* in this paper [16]. By carefully selecting the arguments, an agent brings forward during an argumentation, he may be able to change its outcome. Furthermore, the definition above also prohibits agents to come up with arguments that cannot be constructed from their own beliefs. This is necessary in order to prevent agents from making up new arguments or bring up arguments they cannot know of. Here, we assume that agents are completely honest about their arguments and always bring forward all arguments that are acceptable in the current context. Therefore, agents are assumed to be cooperative and that they are interested in the true outcome of the argumentation given the subjective beliefs at hand. Thus, given the above definitions an agent of the framework is defined as follows.

Definition 12 (Agent). *An agent is a tuple* $(\Delta, \varphi_{\Pi,\Delta}, \psi_{\Pi,\Delta})$ *with a local belief base* Δ, *a root argument function* $\varphi_{\Pi,\Delta}$ *and a counterargument function* $\psi_{\Pi,\Delta}$.

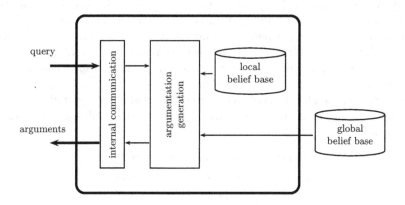

Fig. 3. An agent

An overview of an agent is depicted in Figure 3.

Finally, the definition of a distributed argumentation system can be given as follows.

Definition 13 (Distributed argumentation system). *A* distributed argumentation system T *is a tuple* $T = (M, \Pi, \{A_1, \ldots, A_n\})$ *with a moderator* M, *a global belief base* Π *and agents* $A_1, \ldots, A_n$.

For what is coming we assume that each agent's local belief base is consistent with Π, i.e., it is $\Pi \cup \Delta_i \not\vdash \bot$ for an agent A_i. By doing so, we forbid agents to counterargue their own arguments. Still, the union of the local belief bases of all agents and the global belief base may remain inconsistent, i.e. $\Pi \cup \Delta_1 \cup \ldots \cup \Delta_n \vdash \bot$ and thus gives rise to argumentation between the agents. We illustrate the above ideas with a simple example.

Example 2. Anna and Bob are planning for their holiday trip. They have already narrowed down the possible holiday destinations to *hawaii* and *switzerland*, but as they can only afford for one trip the two possibilities are mutually exclusive ($\sim goto(hawaii) \leftarrow goto(switzerland)$ and $\sim goto(switzerland) \leftarrow$

goto(hawaii)). Furthermore, common knowledge includes that switzerland is a good place for skiing (*skiing(switzerland)*) and hawaii has access to the ocean (*ocean(hawaii)*). But they had already learned that hawaii also has a dangerous sea life (*dangerousSealife(hawaii)*). Furthermore, if they decide to go to switzerland, they can go by train (*goByTrain(switzerland)*) but have to get a ski pass (*needSkiPass(switzerland)*).

In order to decide whether to go to hawaii or switzerland, the different opinions of the two persons lead to a different structure of there local belief bases. While Anna likes swimming in the ocean (*goto(X)* $\prec$ *swimming(X)* and *swimming(X)* $\prec$ *ocean(X)*), Bob prefers to ski (*goto(X)* $\prec$ *skiing(X)*). He thinks also that a cheap holiday should be preferred (*goto(X)* $\prec$ *cheap(X)*) and that going by train is a reasonable justification to consider a holiday cheap (*cheap(X)* $\prec$ *goByTrain(X)*). Anna insists on her to have the possibility to swim ($\sim$*goto(X)* $\prec$ $\sim$*swimming(X)* and $\sim$*swimming(X)* $\prec$ $\sim$*ocean(X)*) and thinks that the need of ski pass does not constitute a holiday trip to be cheap ($\sim$*cheap(X)* $\prec$ *needSkiPass(X)*). At last, Bob thinks that a dangerous sea life in the ocean should prevent anyone to swim ($\sim$*swimming(X)* $\prec$ *ocean(X)*, *dangerousSealife(X)*).

In summary, the global belief base Π and the local belief bases of Bob (Δ_{Bob}) and Anna (Δ_{Anna}) that constitute the above described multi-agent system are given as follows:

$$\Pi = \{ \sim goto(hawaii) \leftarrow goto(switzerland).$$
$$\sim goto(switzerland) \leftarrow goto(hawaii).$$
$$skiing(switzerland). \quad ocean(hawaii).$$
$$goByTrain(switzerland). \quad dangerousSealife(hawaii).$$
$$needSkiPass(switzerland). \}$$

$$\Delta_{Bob} = \{ goto(X) \prec skiing(X).$$
$$goto(X) \prec cheap(X).$$
$$cheap(X) \prec goByTrain(X).$$
$$\sim swimming(X) \prec ocean(X), dangerousSealife(X). \}$$

$$\Delta_{Anna} = \{ goto(X) \prec swimming(X).$$
$$swimming(X) \prec ocean(X).$$
$$\sim goto(X) \prec \sim swimming(X).$$
$$\sim swimming(X) \prec \sim ocean(X).$$
$$\sim cheap(X) \prec needSkiPass(X). \}$$

We will continue this scenario in Example 3.

Given a system T and a query h (a literal), the framework checks whether h is warranted as follows. First, the moderator of T asks all agents for initial arguments for h and for $\overline{h}$ and starts a dialectical tree with each of them as root arguments. Then for each of these arguments, the moderator asks every agent for counterarguments and incorporates them into the corresponding dialectical trees accordingly. This process is repeated for every new argument until no more arguments can be constructed. Eventually the moderator analyses the resulting dialectical trees and returns the appropriate answer to the questioner. A dialectical tree built via this process is called an *argumentation product*. The answer behaviour of T is determined by the decision function of its moderator and is formalized as follows.

Definition 14 (Argumentation product). *Let $h \in \mathcal{L}$ be a query and $T = (M, \Pi, \{A_1, \ldots, A_n\})$ a system with $M = (\mu_D, \chi_D, \eta_{D, \succ})$ and $A_i = (\Delta_i, \varphi_i, \psi_i)$ for $1 \le i \le n$. A dialectical tree $\upsilon \in$ DIA is called an* argumentation product *of T and h, iff the following conditions hold:*

1. *there exists a j with $1 \le j \le n$ such that the root of υ is an element of $\varphi_j(h)$, and*
2. *for every path $\Lambda = [\langle A_1, h_1 \rangle, \ldots, \langle A_n, h_n \rangle]$ in υ and the set K of child nodes of $\langle A_n, h_n \rangle$ it holds $K = \{\langle B, h' \rangle \mid \langle B, h' \rangle \in \psi_1(\Lambda) \cup \ldots \cup \psi_n(\Lambda)$ and $\eta_{D, \succ}(\Lambda + \langle B, h' \rangle) = \mathsf{true}\}$ (K is the set of all acceptable attacks on Λ).*

Example 3. We continue Example 2. Assume that *Generalized Specificity* is the chosen preference relation among arguments and let $goto(switzerland)$ be the query under consideration. Both agents, Anna and Bob, can put forward initial arguments for and against the query $goto(switzerland)$. For example, Bob has the argument $\langle \mathcal{A}, goto(switzerland) \rangle$ with

$$\mathcal{A} \quad = \quad \{ \quad goto(switzerland) \prec cheap(switzerland),$$
$$cheap(switzerland) \prec goByTrain(switzerland) \quad \}$$

which makes use of the fact $goByTrain(switzerland)$. When asked for counterarguments to $\langle \mathcal{A}, goto(switzerland) \rangle$ Anna responds by bringing up $\langle \mathcal{B}_1, \sim goto(switzerland) \rangle$ and $\langle \mathcal{B}_2, \sim cheap(switzerland) \rangle$ with

$$\mathcal{B}_1 \quad = \quad \{ \quad goto(hawaii) \prec swimming(hawaii),$$
$$swimming(hawaii) \prec ocean(hawaii) \quad \}$$

which makes use of the fact $ocean(hawaii)$ and the rule $\sim goto(switzerland) \leftarrow goto(hawaii)$ and

$$\mathcal{B}_2 \quad = \quad \{ \quad \sim cheap(switzerland) \prec needSkiPass(switzerland) \quad \}$$

which makes use of the fact $needSkiPass(switzerland)$. Observe that both arguments $\langle \mathcal{B}_1, \sim goto(switzerland) \rangle$ and $\langle \mathcal{B}_2, \sim cheap(switzerland) \rangle$ are blocking defeaters for $\langle \mathcal{A}, goto(switzerland) \rangle$. Hence, Bob can only bring forward the proper attack $\langle \mathcal{C}, \sim swimming(hawaii) \rangle$ with

$$\mathcal{C} = \{ \sim swimming(hawaii) \prec ocean(hawaii), dangerousSealife(hawaii) \}$$

to the argument $\langle \mathcal{B}_1, \sim goto(switzerland) \rangle$. All other possible counterarguments to $\langle \mathcal{B}_1, \sim goto(switzerland) \rangle$ or $\langle \mathcal{B}_2, \sim cheap(switzerland) \rangle$ would result in an unacceptable argumentation line. No other arguments can be brought forward by Anna and Bob and the resulting argumentation product is shown in Figure 4 (left). Analyzing the tree yields that the root argument $\langle \mathcal{A}, goto(switzerland) \rangle$ is defeated due to its undefeated defeater $\langle \mathcal{B}_2, \sim cheap(switzerland) \rangle$.

Bob can bring forward another argument $\langle \mathcal{D}, goto(switzerland) \rangle$ for the initial query $goto(switzerland)$ with

$$\mathcal{D} = \{ \ goto(switzerland) \prec skiing(switzerland) \}$$

that uses the fact $skiing(switzerland)$ and is brought forward by Bob. Anna can respond to $\langle \mathcal{D}, goto(switzerland) \rangle$ by stating again $\langle \mathcal{B}_1, \sim goto(switzerland) \rangle$. No other counterarguments can be brought forward by her. And again, Bob responds to the argument $\langle \mathcal{D}, goto(switzerland) \rangle$ by bringing up the proper attack $\langle \mathcal{C}, \sim swimming(hawaii) \rangle$ and thus completes the only argumentation line in the current dialectical tree, see Figure 4 (right). The analysis of the resulting argumentation product reveals $\langle \mathcal{D}, goto(switzerland) \rangle$ to be undefeated and thus the answer of the system to the query $goto(switzerland)$ is YES.

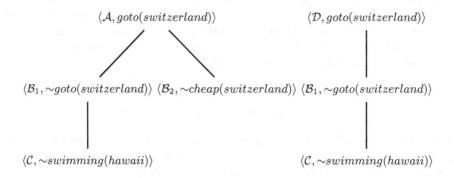

Fig. 4. Two argumentation products from Example 3

We complete this section by comparing the answer behaviors of our framework and DeLP. In contrast to our framework, DeLP represents its knowledge in a single *defeasible logic program* (de.l.p.) P which is a tuple $P = (\Pi, \Delta)$ with a set Π of strict rules and facts and a set Δ of defeasible rules. Therefore, any defeasible logic program can be represented using our framework by just modeling a single agent system and setting its global belief base to Π and the agent's local belief base to Δ. The other way round is not always possible as the following example shows.

Example 4. Let $T = (M, \Pi, \{A_1, A_2\})$ be distributed argumentation system and let Δ_1 and Δ_2 be the local belief bases of A_1 and A_2 with

$$\Delta_1 = \{(b \prec a), (b \prec a, c)\}$$
$$\Delta_2 = \{(\sim b \prec a), (c \prec d)\}$$

and let furthermore $\Pi = \{a, d\}$. Given the query b, T yields two argumentation products—that each consist of just a single argumentation line—$[\langle\{(b \prec a)\}, b\rangle,$ $\langle\{(\sim b \prec a)\}, \sim b\rangle]$ and $[\langle\{(\sim b \prec a)\}, \sim b\rangle, \langle\{(b \prec a)\}, b\rangle]$. As the roots of both argumentation products will be marked "defeated", the answer of T on b is UNDECIDED.

Simply joining the belief bases of the system yields a *de.l.p.* $P = (\Pi', \Delta')$ with $\Pi' = \{a, d\}$ and

$$\Delta = \{(b \prec a), (b \prec a, c), (\sim b \prec a), (c \prec d)\}$$

and results when queried with b among others the dialectical tree—that consists of just a single argumentation line as well— $[\langle\{(b \prec a)\}, b\rangle, \langle\{(\sim b \prec a)\}, \sim b\rangle, \langle\{(b \prec a, c), (c \prec d)\}, b\rangle]$. As there the root will be marked with "undefeated", the answer of P on b is YES.

The above example shows that there are instances of distributed argumentation frameworks that cannot be represented directly by a single defeasible logic program while maintaining its properties from the point of view of knowledge representation. The reason for the different answer behavior of T and P in Example 4 is the "misplaced" rule $c \prec d$, which can not be used for any argument on the query b by A_2. One might argue that the presence of this rule in the local belief base of A_2 makes no sense as he cannot make any use of it. This is true concerning the argumentative capabilities of the specific scenario described in Example 4. But usually, agents are situated in an evolving system and an agent's now unused knowledge might come in handy in a future scenario. Furthermore, the role of agents might differ and usually an agent might have other responsibilities than just participating in an argumentation. Thus, from the perspective of knowledge representation Example 4 should be interpreted as an advantage and not a drawback of the system. Yet another perspective arises when considering that the agents are cooperative and are trying to come up with all possible arguments including those that can only be constructed by sharing knowledge. One way of incorporating this is to give agents the ability to ask other agents for subarguments and ensuring truthfulness of all agents [8]. In another paper [19], we extended our framework in a more expressive way by allowing the agents to form *collaborations*. In a collaboration each agent is truthful to all other agents in the collaboration and knowledge can easily be transferred. This allows the agents in a collaboration to conjointly build arguments. When considering the whole set of agents as one collaboration we get the same answer behavior as with DeLP. More details on collaborations in distributed argumentation systems can be found in [19].

4   Realizing Argumentation

After the theoretical elaboration of our framework in the previous section, we are now going describe the behavior of the agents and the whole system in terms of algorithms that implement the abstract functions defined above.

The control of the argumentation process is mainly handled by the moderator of the system. Given a specific query to the system, the moderator starts by asking each agent for arguments for or against the query's literal. Afterwards, for each initial argument the moderator builds recursively a dialectical tree by asking all agents for counterarguments to the intermediate "leafs" of the trees. If no agent can give any more counterarguments, the process finishes and the moderator analyses the given trees and returns the appropriate answer to the caller.

What follows is a description of the individual algorithms used in this process by the agents themselves, in particular implementations of the root argument, counterargument, and acceptance functions.

4.1   Generating Root Arguments

The first step in distributed argumentation in our framework consists of the generation of root arguments, i. e. arguments that form the root of a dialectical tree and directly refer to the given query. Let Π be a global belief base and Δ the local belief base of the agent under consideration. In order to retrieve a well-defined answer to the query h, all dialectical trees for both literals h and $\overline{h}$ have to be determined, as the non-existence of undefeated arguments for h does not automatically result in the answer NO. To distinguish the cases NO and UNDECIDED, one must verify the existence or non-existence of undefeated arguments for $\overline{h}$. Hence, if h is a query, the moderator asks all agents for arguments for h and for $\overline{h}$. The general algorithm to determine the arguments for and against the query is depicted in Algorithm 1. The algorithm uses the algorithm Arguments which is described below.

In order to determine all arguments for a literal h, given a global belief base Π and the local belief base Δ, the algorithm Arguments has to compute all possible derivations of h from Π and Δ. If h is a fact in Π then h has the sole argument $\langle \emptyset, h \rangle$ [10]. Otherwise the algorithm Arguments uses backward-chaining to construct all possible arguments. The algorithm starts by searching for strict and defeasible rules with conclusion h. It then iteratively tries to find derivations of the body literals of the rules. The algorithm maintains a stack S that consists of tuples (R, L) with a set of rules R and a set of literals L. The element R contains the defeasible rules already added to this (partial) argument and L contains the literals that have not been derived yet. By constantly expanding these partial arguments with new rules from the agent's local belief

---

Algorithm 1. RootArguments

```
01 RootArguments(h,Δ,Π)
02     queryArguments = Arguments(h,Δ,Π);
03     nqueryArguments = Arguments(h̄,Δ,Π);
04     return queryArguments ∪ nqueryArguments;
```

---

base full arguments are being built in the component R. If L is empty the initial literal can be derived using the defeasible rules in R and the strict knowledge in Π. At the end of the algorithm non-minimal arguments are removed to meet the minimality condition of arguments. The complete algorithm can be seen in Algorithm 2.

Algorithm 2. Arguments

```
01  Arguments(conclusion, Δ, Π)
02      if conclusion is a fact in Π then
03          return {⟨∅, conclusion⟩}
04      S = ∅
05      arguments = ∅
06      for each rule r : conclusion ←-- b₁,...,bₙ ∈ Δ ∪ Π do
07          if r is a defeasible rule then
08              Push ({r}, {b₁,...,bₙ})  on S
09          else
10              Push ({}, {b₁,...,bₙ}) on S
11      while S not empty do
12          Pop (R, L) from S
13          if L is empty then
14              arguments = arguments ∪ {⟨ R, conclusion ⟩}
15          else
16              Pop l from L
17              if l is a fact in Π then
18                  Push (R, L) on S
19              else
20                  for each rule r : l ←-- b₁,...,bₙ ∈ Δ ∪ Π do
21                      if r is a defeasible rule then
22                          R' = R ∪ {r}
23                      L' = L
24                      for each b_i with 1 ≤ i ≤ n do
25                          if b_i is not the head of a rule in R' then
26                              L' = L' ∪ {bᵢ}
27                      Push (R', L') on S
28      for each a ∈ arguments do
29          if there exists a' ∈ arguments with a ≠ a'
30                          and a is a subargument of a'
31              arguments = arguments \ {a'}
32      return arguments
```

Observe that in line 25/26 only the literals b_i are added to the set L that are not already derivable from the available rules. Partial arguments that cannot be completed are automatically dropped by the algorithm as no extension of them is added again to the stack S.

Based on the algorithm RootArguments we are able to define the root argument function $\varphi_{\Pi,\Delta}$ for DeLP.

Definition 15 ($\varphi_{\Pi,\Delta}$). *Let Π be a global belief base, Δ be a local belief base, and h a literal. Then the function $\varphi_{\Pi,\Delta} : \mathcal{L} \to \mathfrak{P}(ARG_{\Pi,\Delta})$ is defined as*

$$\varphi_{\Pi,\Delta}(h) =_{def} \texttt{RootArguments}(h,\Delta,\Pi).$$

The algorithm `Arguments` is sound and complete in the following sense (The proof is omitted but can be found in [18]).

Proposition 1. *Let h be a literal, Δ a local belief base, and Π a global belief base. Then `Arguments`(h,Δ,Π) is a set of arguments for h. Furthermore, for every argument $\langle A, h \rangle$ with respect to Π and Δ it is $\langle A, h \rangle \in$ `Arguments`(h,Δ,Π).*

The soundness and completeness of the algorithm `RootArguments` follows directly.

4.2   Generating Counterarguments

Let $\Lambda = (\langle A_1, h_1 \rangle, \ldots, \langle A_n, h_n \rangle)$ be an argumentation line. Another important task of an agent is to propose counterarguments $\langle B, b \rangle$ for $\langle A_n, h_n \rangle$, such that $\Lambda' = \Lambda + \langle B, b \rangle$ is an acceptable argumentation line. To describe the generation of counterarguments in an algorithmic manner we need the notion of *potentially counterarguing literals*. Let again Δ be the local belief base of the agent under consideration.

Definition 16 (Potentially counterarguing literals). *Let Π be a global belief base, Δ a local belief base, and $\langle A, h \rangle$ an argument. Then the set of potentially counterarguing literals $pcl_{\Pi,\Delta}(\langle A, h \rangle)$ is defined by*

$$pcl_{\Pi,\Delta}(\langle A, h \rangle) = \{f \mid \Pi \cup A \cup \{f\} \vdash \bot\}.$$

Hence, for every conclusion h' of a counterargument $\langle B, h' \rangle$ with $B \subseteq \Delta$ to $\langle A, h \rangle$ it must hold $h' \in pcl_{\Pi,\Delta}(\langle A, h \rangle)$. Therefore it is sufficient to look only for potential counterarguments among the arguments with conclusion in $pcl_{\Pi,\Delta}(\langle A, h \rangle)$.

For an argument $\langle A, h \rangle$ the set $pcl_{\Pi,\Delta}(\langle A, h \rangle)$ can be characterized as follows. Let $A = \{h_1 \prec B_1, \ldots, h_m \prec B_m\}$, then all literals $\overline{h_1}, \ldots, \overline{h_m}$ are potentially counterarguing literals, as for every h_i ($1 \leq i \leq n$), $\langle A, h \rangle$ contains a subargument for h_i. Furthermore, due to the derivation of the literals $\{h_1, \ldots, h_n\}$ by $\langle A, h \rangle$ strict rules in Π might get "fired". Negations of the conclusions of these strict rules are also potentially counterarguing literals. Algorithm 3 describes

---

Algorithm 3. PCL
```
01  PCL(⟨A,h⟩,Δ,Π)
02      pcl₁ = {h̄ |  h ≺ B  ∈ A}
03      pcl₂ = {f̄ | Π ∪ Δ ∪ pcl₁ ⊢ f,  Π ∪ Δ ⊬ f}
04      return pcl₁ ∪ pcl₂
```

---

this computation. In order to validate the acceptability of potential counter-arguments within the given argumentation line, the algorithm `Acceptable` (see Algorithm 4) must be applied, which is a straightforward implementation of Definition 4. In the algorithm, $\succ$ is an arbitrary preference relation, e. g. *Generalized Specificity* [17].

Algorithm 4. `Acceptable`

```
01  Acceptable([⟨𝒜₁,h₁⟩,...,⟨𝒜ₙ,hₙ⟩],⟨ℬ,h⟩,Π)
02      let ⟨𝒜',h'⟩ be the disagreement sub-argument
03          of ⟨𝒜ₙ,hₙ⟩ relative to ⟨ℬ,h⟩
04      if ℬ ⊆ 𝒜ⱼ for one 1 ≤ j ≤ n then return false
05      if n is even then
06          if 𝒜₁ ∪ 𝒜₃...∪ 𝒜ₙ₋₁ ∪ ℬ ∪ Π |∼ ⊥ then return false
07      if n is odd then
08          if 𝒜₂ ∪ 𝒜₄...∪ 𝒜ₙ ∪ ℬ ∪ Π) |∼ ⊥ then return false
09      if ⟨𝒜',h'⟩ ≻ ⟨ℬ,h⟩ then return false
10      if n > 1 then
11          if ⟨𝒜ₙ,hₙ⟩ and ⟨𝒜ₙ₋₁,hₙ₋₁⟩ are incomparable with
12                      respect to ≻ then
13              if not ⟨ℬ,h⟩ ≻ ⟨𝒜',h'⟩ then return false
14      return true
```

Based on the algorithm `Acceptable` the acceptance function $\eta_{\mathsf{D},\succ}$ can be defined as follows.

Definition 17 ($\eta_{\mathsf{D},\succ}$). *Let Π be a global belief base, Δ be a local belief base, Λ be an argumentation line, and $\langle \mathcal{A}, h \rangle$ be an argument. The function $\eta_{\mathsf{D},\succ} : \Sigma(\Omega) \to \{\mathsf{false}, \mathsf{true}\}$ is defined as*

$$\eta_{\mathsf{D},\succ}(\Lambda + \langle \mathcal{A}, h \rangle) =_{def} \begin{cases} \mathsf{true} \ \ if \ Acceptable(\Lambda, \langle \mathcal{A}, h \rangle, \Pi) = true \\ \mathsf{false} \ \ otherwise \end{cases}.$$

Given a global belief base Π, a local belief base Δ and an argumentation line $\Lambda = [\langle \mathcal{A}_1, h_1 \rangle, \dots, \langle \mathcal{A}_n, h_n \rangle]$ the algorithm `Attacks` (see Algorithm 1.5) uses the algorithm `Arguments` to compute all arguments with conclusions in $pcl_{\Pi,\Delta}(\langle \mathcal{A}, h \rangle)$. All these arguments that are acceptable regarding Λ are added to the result set. Using algorithm `Attacks` the counterargument function $\psi_{\Pi,\Delta}$ can be defined as follows.

Definition 18 ($\psi_{\Pi,\Delta}$). *Let Π be a global belief base, Δ be a local belief base, and Λ be an argumentation line. The function $\psi_{\Pi,\Delta} : \Sigma \to \mathfrak{P}(\Omega)$ is defined as*

$$\psi_{\Pi,\Delta}(\Lambda) =_{def} Attacks(\Lambda, \Delta, \Pi).$$

The soundness and completeness of the algorithm `Attacks` follows directly from Proposition 1.

Algorithm 5. Attacks

```
01  Attacks((⟨A₁, s₁⟩, ..., ⟨Aₙ, sₙ⟩), Δ, Π)
02      pcl = PCL(⟨A_n, s_n⟩, Δ, Π)
03      result = ∅
04      for each d ∈ pcl do
05          arguments = Arguments(d, Δ, Π)
06          for each ⟨B, d⟩ ∈ arguments do
07              if Acceptable((⟨A₁, s₁⟩, ..., ⟨Aₙ, sₙ⟩), ⟨B, d⟩, Π) then
08                  result = result ∪ {⟨B, d⟩}
09      return result
```

---

5   Implementation

The system described in this paper has been fully implemented in Java and can be directly obtained from the author[1]. Besides the general argumentation capabilities described above, also the comparison relation *Generalized Specificity* [17] has been implemented. This has been done using its characterization by activation sets [17]. The framework also supports the representation of P-DeLP [2], which is an extension of DeLP using a possibilistic language. Within P-DeLP defeasible rules are annotated with reals that measure the certainty of the rules. The comparison relation for arguments in P-DeLP derives naturally from the annotated numbers by aggregating the annotations of all rules in an argument and using these as necessity measures. Therefore, the implemented framework features two powerful representation languages for defeasible argumentation and two comparison relations for arguments.

The framework allows the specification of local belief bases of an arbitrary number of agents and the specification of the global belief base within the chosen language. The user can query the system for the warrant status of literals and the result of the argumentation process is visualized as a set of dialectical trees.

The framework has been applied to a real world example involving two agents acting as accuser and defender in a legal case [18]. There, the specific setting of the multi-agent scenario in our framework has a real-world analogy (at least in german law, see [18]). Both, accuser and defender state arguments for and against a specific claim, for example the guilt or innocence of a given accused, but these arguments are evaluated by a neutral moderator, in this case the judge.

6   Related Work and Final Remarks

The research on argumentation in multi-agent systems is a very active field [12]. Current research includes besides others argumentation-based negotiation approaches [11], persuasion [4,13] and general dialogue formalizations [3,8]. All these approaches are related to the framework developed here regarding the aim

---

[1] matthias.thimm@tu-dortmund.de

of formalizing agent interaction in form of argumentation. But, to our knowledge, the framework of Black [8,7] is the only one which also uses defeasible logic programming as the underlying representation formalism to model distributed argumentation. There, Black develops formal protocols for both argument inquiry and warrant inquiry dialogues. Warrant inquiry dialogues are similar in concept as the approach pursued in this paper as a warrant inquiry dialogue formalizes the communication needed for building up a common dialectical tree for a given claim in a multi agent setting. Furthermore, argument inquiry dialogues are used to mutually construct arguments within a set of agents and thus is similar to the approach of introducing collaborations in our framework [19].

Also related to the work reported here is the framework of [1]. They use extended logic programs to model an agent's belief and define a notion of distributed argumentation using these extended logic programs. The framework uses the argumentation semantics from [14] and defines a notion of cooperation, that allows the agents to share their beliefs in order to construct new arguments. As this framework uses extended logic programs as the underlying representation formalism, it has a declarative semantics in contrast to the dialectical semantics of DeLP used here. Yet, in another work [19] we also extended the framework described here by introducing *collaborations* that allow the agents to share their beliefs and construct new arguments.

In this paper, we have developed a multi-agent architecture that uses argumentation in order to reach a common conclusion acceptable by all agents. The framework uses *Defeasible Logic Programming* as the underlying argumentation mechanism but distributes the beliefs among several agents. We have given a functional formalization of the system and described the computational issues involved in implementing it. The framework has successfully been implemented and applied to a real world example.

Ongoing research includes collaborations in the multi-agent setting [19], security issues in agent interactions [6] and a generalization of the framework to abstract argumentation systems. The complex dialectical semantics of DeLP does not offer a quite understandable anticipation of the interaction of arguments. Thus we aim at extending the described framework to abstract argumentation systems [9] in order to enrich it with a declarative semantics.

References

1. de Almeida, I.C., Alferes, J.J.: An argumentation-based negotiation for distributed extended logic programs. In: Proceedings of CLIMA VII, pp. 191–210 (2006)
2. Alsinet, T., Chesñevar, C.I., Godo, L., Simari, G.R.: A logic programming framework for possibilistic argumentation: Formalization and logical properties. Fuzzy Sets and Systems (2008)
3. Atkinson, K., Bench-Capon, T., McBurney, P.: A dialogue game protocol for multi-agent argument over proposals for action. Autonomous Agents and Multi-Agent Systems 11(2), 153–171 (2005)
4. Bench-Capon, T.J.M.: Persuasion in practical argument using value based argumentation frameworks. Journal of Logic and Computation 13(3), 429–448 (2003)

5. Bench-Capon, T.J.M., Dunne, P.E.: Argumentation in artificial intelligence. Artificial Intelligence 171, 619–641 (2007)
6. Biskup, J., Kern-Isberner, G., Thimm, M.: Towards enforcement of confidentiality in agent interactions. In: Proceedings of the 12th International Workshop on Non-Monotonic Reasoning, pp. 104–112 (2008)
7. Black, E.: A Generative Framework for Argumentation-Based Inquiry Dialogues. Ph.D. thesis, University College London (2007)
8. Black, E., Hunter, A.: An inquiry dialogue system. Autonomous Agents and Multi-Agent Systems 19(2), 173–209 (2009)
9. Dung, P.M.: On the acceptability of arguments and its fundamental role in non-monotonic reasoning, logic programming and n-person games. Artificial Intelligence 77(2), 321–358 (1995)
10. García, A., Simari, G.: Defeasible logic programming: An argumentative approach. Theory and Practice of Logic Programming 4(1-2), 95–138 (2004)
11. Karunatillake, N.C., Jennings, N.R., Rahwan, I., Norman, T.J.: Argument-based negotiation in a social context. In: Proceedings of the 4th international joint conference on Autonomous agents and multiagent systems, pp. 1331–1332. ACM, New York (2005)
12. Maudet, N., Parsons, S., Rahwan, I.: Argumentation in multi-agent systems: Context and recent developments. In: Third International Workshop on Argumentation in Multi-Agent Systems, pp. 1–16 (2007)
13. Perrussel, L., Doutre, S., Thévenin, J.M., McBurney, P.: A persuasion dialog for gaining access to information. In: Rahwan, I., Parsons, S., Reed, C. (eds.) ArgMAS 2007. LNCS (LNAI), vol. 4946, pp. 63–79. Springer, Heidelberg (2008)
14. Prakken, H.: Dialectical proof theory for defeasible argumentation with defeasible priorities (preliminary report). In: Model Age Workshop, pp. 202–215 (1997)
15. Prakken, H., Vreeswijk, G.: Logical systems for defeasible argumentation. In: Handbook of Philosophical Logic, vol. 4, pp. 219–318. Kluwer, Dordrecht (2002)
16. Roth, B., Riveret, R., Rotolo, A., Governatori, G.: Strategic Argumentation: A Game Theoretical Investigation. In: Proceedings of the 11th International Conference on Artificial Intelligence and Law, pp. 81–90. ACM Press, New York (2007)
17. Stolzenburg, F., García, A., Chesnevar, C.I., Simari, G.: Computing generalized specificity. Journal of Non-Classical Logics 13(1), 87–113 (2003)
18. Thimm, M.: Verteilte logikbasierte Argumentation: Konzeption, Implementierung und Anwendung im Rechtswesen. VDM Verlag Dr. Müller (2008)
19. Thimm, M., Garcia, A.J., Kern-Isberner, G., Simari, G.R.: Using collaborations for distributed argumentation with defeasible logic programming. In: Proceedings of the 12th International Workshop on Non-Monotonic Reasoning, pp. 179–188 (2008)
20. Thimm, M., Kern-Isberner, G.: A distributed argumentation framework using defeasible logic programming. In: Proceedings of the 2nd International Conference on Computational Models of Argument, pp. 381–392. IOS Press, Amsterdam (2008)
21. Thimm, M., Kern-Isberner, G.: On the relationship of defeasible argumentation and answer set programming. In: Proceedings of the 2nd International Conference on Computational Models of Argument, pp. 393–404. IOS Press, Amsterdam (2008)

Computing Abductive Argumentation
in Answer Set Programming

Toshiko Wakaki[1], Katsumi Nitta[2], and Hajime Sawamura[3]

[1] Shibaura Institute of Technology
307 Fukasaku, Minuma-ku, Saitama-City, Saitama, 337–8570 Japan
twakaki@sic.shibaura-it.ac.jp
[2] Tokyo Institute of Technology
4259 Nagatsuta, Midori-ku, Yokohama 226–8502, Japan
nitta@dis.titech.ac.jp
[3] Niigata University, 8050, 2-cho, Ikarashi, Niigata, 950-2181 Japan
sawamura@ie.niigata-u.ac.jp

Abstract. In our daily life, humans often argue with each other using *abductive knowledge* which includes not only facts known to be true but also hypotheses that may be expected to be true. This paper presents a novel approach to find out every *skeptical* (resp. *credulous*) explanation which is the set of hypotheses needed to *skeptically* (resp. *credulously*) justify the argument supporting a disputer's claim based on abductive knowledge base under the specified argumentation semantics. The main subject of this paper is the definition of the Abductive Argumentation Framework which is equivalent to the widely adopted Dung's framework except handling hypotheses, and from which skeptical (resp. credulous) explanations in argumentation can be defined. In general, there are multiple explanations under the specified argumentation semantics. Our approach is capable of finding out all of them by means of applying traditional abductive logic programming to our previous work of computing argumentation semantics in answer set programming (ASP). Thus this study eventually reveals the greatest advantage of applying ASP to the crucial decision problems in the research field of argumentation.

1 Introduction

Dung's frameworks for abstract argumentation [5] have gained wide acceptance and are the basis for the implementation of concrete formalisms in the research field of deductive argumentation. In fact, considerable efforts have been invested in proof procedures (e.g. [7,13]) to decide whether an argument supporting a given goal G is skeptically (resp. credulously) justified w.r.t. a set of arguments associated with agent's knowledge base (e.g. an extended logic program) along with the notion of attack under the particular argumentation semantics.

In our daily life, however, humans often argue with each other using abductive knowledge [19] which includes not only a set T of *facts* that are known to be true as usually used in deductive argumentation but also a set H of candidate *hypotheses* that may be expected to be true. In legal domain, for example, in the situation that

P. McBurney et al. (Eds.): ArgMAS 2009, LNAI 6057, pp. 195–215, 2010.

the claim G of a disputer's argument is not guaranteed to be justified with assuming no hypotheses, disputers often want to find out what subset of H so called *explanation* along with T enable them to justify the argument supporting their claim G, that is, leading them to win in the argumentation of the court. Let us illustrate our awareness of the issues on abductive argumentation with a motivational example.

Example 1. If parts required for the project arrive in time and money is paid for parts, then the project may be finished. Unless Jack does work, the project never be finished. If Mary works, Jack always works. If the project is executed in the national holidays, Jack does not work.

The knowledge given in the example is represented by the extended logic program P as follows.

$$P: \quad finish(project) \leftarrow arrive(parts),\ pay(money),\ not\ \neg finish(project),$$
$$\neg finish(project) \leftarrow not\ work(jack),$$
$$work(jack) \leftarrow work(mary),$$
$$\neg work(jack) \leftarrow holiday(project).$$

Obviously, there is only one justified argument associated with P whose claim is $\neg finish(project)$. We have, however, the following set H of candidate hypotheses which may be true in the near future:

$$H = \{arrive(parts),\ pay(money),\ work(mary),\ holiday(project)\},$$

and the project leader has the strong claim $finish(project)$, whereas his manager may not agree the claim since he worries about if Jack surely works at any time. Then in their meeting to discuss about how to proceed the project, the leader eagerly wants to find out the subset E of H *to skeptically justify* the argument whose conclusion is his claim $finish(project)$ under the argumentation semantics, e.g. preferred semantics, whereas his manager would like to find out the set $E' \subseteq H$ of hypotheses *not to credulously justify* the argument supporting his opponent's claim, $finish(project)$. Hence, if assuming $E_6 = \{arr(p),\ pay(m),\ w(ma)\} \subseteq H$ along with P, the argument

$$Ag_1 = [\ fin(pro) \leftarrow arr(p),\ pay(m),\ not\ \neg fin(pro);\ arr(p) \leftarrow;\ par(m) \leftarrow]\ ^{[1]}$$

which has the conclusion $fin(pro)$ is skeptically justified under preferred semantics, whereas Ag_1 is not credulously justified under the semantics even if assuming, for example, any E_1, E_2, E_3, E_5 as follows together with P:

$$E_1 = \emptyset, \quad E_2 = \{ho(pro)\}, \quad E_3 = \{w(ma)\}, \quad E_5 = \{w(ma),\ ho(pro)\}.\ ^{[2]}$$

Thus the proponent, the leader, wants to find out the set E_6 of hypotheses called *skeptical* explanation, whereas his opponent, the manager, needs some E_i ($i = 1, 2, 3, 5$) called *credulous anti-explanation* for the argument Ag_1 whose conclusion is the proponent's claim, $finish(project)$.

---

[1] Here $finish(project)$, $arrive(parts)$, $pay(money)$, $work(jack)$, $work(mary)$, $holiday(project)$ are abbreviated as $fin(pro), arr(p), pay(m), w(j), w(ma), ho(pro)$.

[2] Each E_i is named corresponding to explanations in Fig. 1 shown in section 3.2.

The aim of this paper is to explore an approach to compute skeptical explanations as well as credulous anti-explanations of the argument supporting a given claim automatically. To the best of our knowledge, however, there are few studies to find such explanations. Thus this paper presents a novel approach to find every *skeptical* explanation (resp. *credulous* anti-explanation) which is the set of hypotheses needed to *skeptically* justify (resp. not to *credulously* justify) the argument supporting a disputer's claim based on abductive knowledge base under the specified argumentation semantics. The main subject of this paper is the definition of the Abductive Argumentation Framework which is equivalent to the widely adopted Dung's framework except handling hypotheses, and from which skeptical explanations (resp. *credulous* anti-explanations) in argumentation can be defined. In general, there are multiple explanations under the specified argumentation semantics. Our approach is capable of finding out all of them by means of applying traditional abductive logic programming to our previous work of computing argumentation semantics in answer set programming (ASP). Thus this study reveals the greatest advantage of applying ASP to the crucial problems in the research field of argumentation.

This paper is organized as follows. In Section 2, we provide preliminaries. In Section 3, we present our abductive logic programs and theorems which enable to compute skeptical explanations (resp. *credulous* anti-explanations) automatically by applying traditional abductive logic programming. Finally, we conclude by discussing some related works in Section 5.

2 Preliminaries

We briefly review the basic notions used throughout this paper.

2.1 Abductive Logic Programming Based on Answer Set Semantics

The logic programs we consider in this paper are extended logic programs (ELPs), which have two kinds of negation, i.e. classical negation ($\neg$) along with negation as failure (*not*) defined as follows.

Definition 1. *An extended logic program (ELP) is a set of rules of the form:*

$$L \leftarrow L_1, \ldots, L_m, not L_{m+1}, \ldots, not L_n, \qquad (1)$$

or of the form:

$$\leftarrow L_1, \ldots, L_m, not L_{m+1}, \ldots, not L_n, \qquad (2)$$

where L and L_i's are literals, i.e. either atoms or atoms preceded by the classical negation sign $\neg$ and $n \geq m \geq 0$. The symbol " not" denotes negation as failure. We call a literal preceded by "not" a NAF-literal. For a rule r of the form (1), we call L the head of the rule, head(r), and $\{L_1, \ldots, L_m, not L_{m+1}, \ldots, not L_n\}$ the body of the rule, body(r). Especially, body(r)$^+$ and body(r)$^-$ denote $\{L_1, \ldots, L_m\}$ and $\{L_{m+1}, \ldots, L_n\}$ respectively. We often write $L \leftarrow body(r)^+, not \ body(r)^-$ instead of (1) by using sets, body(r)$^+$ and body(r)$^-$. Each rule of the form (2) is called an integrity constraint. For a rule with an empty body, we may write

L instead of $L \leftarrow$. As usual, a rule with variables stands for the set of its ground instances.

The semantics of ELPs is given by the *answer sets semantics* [10,9]. Let P be an ELP and Lit_P be the set of ground literals in the language of P. Then an answer set S of P is the subset of Lit_P whose detailed definition is omitted due to space limitation. An answer set is *consistent* if it is not Lit_P. A program P is *consistent* if it has a consistent answer set; otherwise, P is *inconsistent*. We write $P \models L$ if a literal L is included in every answer set of P.

An abductive program and explanations w.r.t.a given observation are defined according to [17] as follows.

Definition 2. (Abductive Programs)
An abductive program is a pair $\langle T, H \rangle$ where

- *H is a set of ground literals of the language of T and is called set of hypotheses or abducibles,*
- *T is an extended logic program called the facts. The head of each rule from T are not in H.*

Definition 3. (Explanations for an Observation) [17]
Let $\langle T, H \rangle$ be an abductive program and G a ground literal representing a positive observation. E is a skeptical (resp. credulous) explanation of G w.r.t. $\langle T, H \rangle$ iff

1 $T \cup E \models G$ (resp. G is true in some answer set of $T \cup E$)
2 $T \cup E$ is consistent, and $E \subseteq H$.

On the other hand, given a literal G representing a negative observation, E is a credulous (resp. skeptical) anti-explanation of G w.r.t. $\langle T, H \rangle$ iff

1 $T \cup E \not\models G$ (resp. G is true in no answer set of $T \cup E$)
2 $T \cup E$ is consistent, and $E \subseteq H$.

Definition 4.
Let $\langle T, H \rangle$ be an abductive program and E be a subset of H. We say that $\langle T, H \rangle$ is consistent if there is an answer set of $T \cup E$ for some E.

The following proposition is useful to compute explanations as well as anti-explanations in ASP.

Proposition 1.
[19] Let $\langle T, H \rangle$ be a consistent abductive program and G be a positive (resp. negative) observation. We define $\Gamma(H)$ as a set of rules as follows:

$$\Gamma(H) \overset{def}{=} \{ h' \leftarrow not\ h,\ h \leftarrow not\ h' \mid h \in H \}$$

where h' is a newly introduced ground literal corresponding to each ground literal $h \in H$. Then E is a credulous explanation (resp. anti-explanation) of G w.r.t. $\langle T, H \rangle$ if and only if there is an answer set S for $T \cup \Gamma(H) \cup \{ \leftarrow not\ G \}$ (resp. $T \cup \Gamma(H) \cup \{ G' \leftarrow not\ G \} \cup \{ \leftarrow not\ G' \}$) such that $E = S \cap H$, where G' is a newly introduced ground literal.

2.2 Concrete/Abstract Argumentation Frameworks and Acceptability Semantics

Concrete argumentation formalisms for ELP [14,18] are defined as follows.

Definition 5 (Arguments). *Let P be an extended logic program whose rules have the form (1). An argument associated with P is a finite sequence $A = [r_1, \ldots, r_n]$ of ground instances of rules $r_i \in P$ such that for every $1 \leq i \leq n$, for every literal L_j in the body of r_i there is a $k > i$ such that $head(r_k) = L_j$.*
The head of a rule in A, i.e. $head(r_i)$ is called a conclusion of A, whereas a NAF-literal not L in the body of a rule of A is called an assumption of A. We write $assm(A)$ for the set of assumptions and $conc(A)$ for the set of conclusions of an argument A. Especially we call the head of the first rule r_1 the claim of an argument A as written $claim(A)$.
A subargument of A is a subsequence of A which is an argument. An argument A with a conclusion L is a minimal argument for L if there is no subargument of A with conclusion L. An argument A is minimal if it is minimal for its claim, i.e. $claim(A)$. Given an extended logic program P, the set of minimal arguments associated with P is denoted by $Args_P$.

As usual, the notions of attack such as "rebut", "undercut", "attack", "defeat" abbreviated to r, u, a, d are defined as a binary relation over $Args_P$ as follows.

Definition 6 (Rebut, Undercut, Attack, Defeat). *For two arguments, A_1 and A_2, the notions of attack such as rebut, undercut, attack, defeat (r, u, a, d for short) are defined as follows:*

- *A_1 rebuts A_2, i.e. $(A_1, A_2) \in$ r if there exists a literal L such that $L \in conc(A_1)$ and $\neg L \in conc(A_2)$;*
- *A_1 undercuts A_2, i.e. $(A_1, A_2) \in$ u if there exists a literal L such that $L \in conc(A_1)$ and not $L \in assm(A_2)$;*
- *A_1 attacks A_2, i.e. $(A_1, A_2) \in$ a if A_1 rebuts or undercuts A_2;*
- *A_1 defeats A_2, i.e. $(A_1, A_2) \in$ d if A_1 undercuts A_2, or A_1 rebuts A_2 and A_2 does not undercut A_1.*

Prakken *et al.* proposed an argumentation semantics for an ELP, which is defined as the set of justified arguments [14,18], whereas Dung presented an abstract argumentation framework and acceptability semantics [5] defined as follows.

Definition 7 (Argumentation Frameworks). *An argumentation framework is a pair (Ar, def) where Ar is a set of arguments and def is a binary relation over Ar, i.e. def $\subseteq$ Ar $\times$ Ar. $(a, b) \in$ def, or equivalently a def b, means that a attacks b. A set S of arguments attacks an argument a if a is attacked by an argument of S.*

Definition 8 (Acceptable / Conflict-free). *A set $S \subseteq$ Ar is conflict-free iff there are no arguments a and b in S such that a attacks b. An argument $a \in$ Ar is acceptable w.r.t. a set $S \subseteq$ Ar iff for any $b \in$ Ar such that $(b, a) \in$ def, there exists $c \in S$ such that $(c, b) \in$ def.*

Definition 9. (Acceptability Semantics)
Let Args $\subseteq$ Ar be a conflict-free set of arguments and $F : 2^{Ar} \to 2^{Ar}$ be a function with $F(Args) = \{a \mid a$ is acceptable w.r.t. Args\}.

Acceptability Semantics is defined as follows. Args is admissible iff Args $\subseteq$ F(Args). Args is a complete extension iff Args = F(Args). Args is a grounded extension iff Args is a minimal (w.r.t. set-inclusion) complete extension. Args is a preferred extension iff Args is a maximal (w.r.t. set-inclusion) complete extension. Args is a stable extension iff Args is a preferred extension that attacks every argument in Ar \ Args.

Definition 10. (Credulous Justification vs. Skeptical Justification)
Let (Ar, def) be an argumentation framework and Sname be one of complete, stable, preferred, grounded *and* semistable. *Then for an argument $a \in Ar$,*

- *a is credulously justified (w.r.t. (Ar, def)) under Sname semantics iff a is contained in at least one Sname extension of (Ar, def);*
- *a is skeptically justified (w.r.t. (Ar, def)) under Sname semantics iff a is contained in every Sname extension of (Ar, def).*

Caminada showed that Dung's acceptability semantics along with semi-stable semantics proposed by him [4] can be computed through his reinstatement labellings [3] as follows.

Definition 11. *Let (Ar, def) be a Dung-style argumentation framework. An AF-labelling is a (total) function $\mathcal{L} : Ar \to \{$in, out, undec\}. We define* in$(\mathcal{L})$ *as $\{ a \in Ar \mid \mathcal{L}(a) = $in\},* out$(\mathcal{L})$ *as $\{ a \in Ar \mid \mathcal{L}(a) = $out\} and* undec$(\mathcal{L})$ *as $\{ a \in Ar \mid \mathcal{L}(a) = $undec\}.*

Definition 12 (Reinstatement Labellings). *Let $\mathcal{L}$ be an AF-labelling. We say that $\mathcal{L}$ is a reinstatement labelling iff it satisfies the following conditions:*

- *$\forall a \in Ar : (\mathcal{L}(a) = $out $\equiv \exists b \in Ar : (b$ def $a \wedge \mathcal{L}(b) = in))$ and*
- *$\forall a \in Ar : (\mathcal{L}(a) = $in $\equiv \forall b \in Ar : (b$ def $a \supset \mathcal{L}(b) = out))$.*

Results 1 (Caminada, 2006) [3]

- The following concepts are equivalent: (a) complete extensions; (b) reinstatement labellings.
- The following concepts are equivalent: (a) grounded extensions; (b) reinstatement labellings with minimal **in**; (c) reinstatement labellings with minimal **out**; (d) reinstatement labellings with maximal **undec**.
- The following concepts are equivalent: (a) preferred extensions; (b) reinstatement labellings with maximal **in**; (c) reinstatement labellings with maximal **out**.
- The following concepts are equivalent: (a) stable extensions; (b) reinstatement labellings with empty **undec**.
- The following concepts are equivalent: (a) semi-stable extensions; (b) reinstatement labellings with minimal **undec**.

With respect to decision problems about extension membership of an argument, there are *skeptical* (resp. *credulous*) approaches under particular argument-based semantics, which are defined in terms of reinstatement labellings as follows.

Definition 13. (Skeptical / Credulous Query-Answering) *[3,13]*
Given an argumentation framework (Ar, def) and an argument $a \in Ar$, the following holds for each argument-based semantics:

- *a is skeptically (resp. credulously) justified iff it is labelled* in *in every (resp. at least one) reasonable position (=reinstatement labelling).*
- *a is skeptically (resp. credulously) overruled iff it is labelled* out *in every (resp. at least one) reasonable position.*
- *Otherwise, a is skeptically (resp. credulously) defensible.*

We have presented a method for computing Dung's standard argumentation semantics in ASP setting based on Caminada's reinstatement labellings [20].

3   Computing Abductive Argumentation in ASP

In this section, it is shown that given abductive knowledge expressed by $\langle P, H \rangle$, every subset of hypotheses $E \subseteq H$ to skeptically justify (resp. not to credulously justify) the argument supporting a disputer's claim G can be found as the skeptical explanation (resp. credulous anti-explanation) of the proposed abductive program $\langle T, H \rangle$, where T is the extended logic program constructed by extending our previous work computing argumentation semantics in ASP.

In the following, firstly we introduce additional definitions for deductive argumentation for notational convenience, secondly present our formalization for abductive argumentation, and finally address how to compute abductive argumentation in ASP.

3.1   Deductive Argumentation

Definition 14. (Concrete vs Abstract Argumentation Frameworks)
Let P be an ELP, $Args_P$ be the set of minimal arguments associated with P and $attacks_P$ be the binary relation over $Args_P$ defined according to some notion of attack (e.g. r, u, a, d*). Then we call $AF_P \overset{def}{=} (Args_P, attacks_P)$ the "concrete argumentation framework" associated with P.*

Now, let us name each argument from $Args_P$. Let Ar be a set of names of arguments in $Args_P$ such that $|Ar| = |Args_P|$. Then each concrete argument $A \in Args_P$ is named $a \in Ar$ such that $a = name(A)$ where name is a bijection function name : $Args_P \to Ar$. In addition, let def be defined as a binary relation over Ar such that $(a, b) \in def$ iff $(A, B) \in attacks_P$ for a pair of arguments, $A, B \in Args_P$ whose names are $a = name(A)$ and $b = name(B)$ respectively.

Then we call $AF \overset{def}{=} (Ar, def)$ constructed from $AF_P \overset{def}{=} (Args_P, attacks_P)$ the "abstract argumentation framework" corresponding to its concrete one.

Although Dung's argumentation semantics is defined for abstract argumentation frameworks, it is also given for concrete argumentation frameworks as follows.

Proposition 2. (Deductive Argumentation). *Let $(Args_P, attack_P)$ be the concrete argumentation framework associated with ELP P, (Ar, def) be its abstract one, and Sname be the name of the particular argumentation semantics such as* complete, stable, preferred *and* grounded. *For an argument $A \in Args_P$ whose name is $a \in Ar$ (i.e. $a = name(A)$),*

- *A is credulously justified w.r.t. $(Args_P, attack_P)$ under Sname semantics iff a is credulously justified w.r.t. (Ar, def) under Sname semantics iff a is contained in at least one Sname extension of (Ar, def);*
- *A is skeptically justified w.r.t. $(Args_P, attack_P)$ under Sname semantics iff a is skeptically justified w.r.t. (Ar, def) under Sname semantics iff a is contained in every Sname extension of (Ar, def).*

3.2   Abductive Argumentation Frameworks

As mentioned in the introduction, we suppose that arguing agent has the abductive knowledge base expressed by an abductive program $\langle P, H \rangle$ as follows.

Definition 15. (Abductive Programs in Argumentation)
An agent has an abductive program $\langle P, H \rangle$, where

- *P is an extended logic program called the facts. The head of each rule from P is not in H,*
- *H is a set of ground literals of the language of P and is called hypotheses or abducibles.*

Here, without loss of generality, we suppose $body(r)^- \cap H = \emptyset$ for any rule $r \in P$ with respect to an abductive program $\langle P, H \rangle$. In other words, any hypothesis $h \in H$ may occur in $body(r)^+$ but not in $body(r)^-$. (See Appendix with respect to $\langle P, H \rangle$ such that $body(r)^- \cap H \neq \emptyset$ for some rule $r \in P$.)

Definition 16. (Abductive Arguments)
For an abductive program $\langle P, H \rangle$, $Args_{P \cup H}$ denotes the set of minimal arguments associated with $P \cup H$. We call an argument $Ag \in Args_{P \cup H}$ an "abductive argument associated with $\langle P, H \rangle$".

For an abductive argument Ag associated with $\langle P, H \rangle$,

- *$hyp(Ag)$ is defined as the subset of H such that $hyp(Ag) = conc(Ag) \cap H$. We call $hyp(Ag)$ "the set of hypotheses for an abductive argument Ag".*
- *If $claim(Ag) \notin H$, Ag is called a **goal** argument; otherwise a **hypothetical argument**.*

Definition 17. (Active Arguments)
*For an abductive program $\langle P, H \rangle$, let Ag be an abductive argument associated with $\langle P, H \rangle$. If $hyp(Ag) \subseteq E$ for $E \subseteq H$, Ag is called **active** w.r.t. E; otherwise **inactive** w.r.t. E.*

Example 2. For the abductive program $\langle P, H \rangle$ given in Example 1, $Args_{P \cup H}$ consists of four goal arguments as follows:

$Ag_1 = [fin(pro) \leftarrow arr(p), \, pay(m), \, not \, \neg fin(pro); \, arr(p); \, pay(m)]$
$Ag_2 = [\neg fin(pro) \leftarrow not \, w(j)]$
$Ag_3 = [w(j) \leftarrow w(ma); \, w(ma)]$
$Ag_4 = [\neg w(j) \leftarrow ho(pro); \, ho(pro)]$

and four hypothetical arguments belonging to $Args_H$ as follows:

$Ag_5 = [arr(p) \leftarrow], \; Ag_6 = [pay(m) \leftarrow], \; Ag_7 = [w(ma) \leftarrow], \; Ag_8 = [ho(pro) \leftarrow].$

For example, for $E_4 = \{arr(p), \, pay(m)\}$, Ag_1, Ag_2 are active w.r.t. E_4 since $hyp(Ag_1) = \{arr(p), \, pay(m)\} = E_4$ and $hyp(Ag_2) = \emptyset \subseteq E_4$, whereas Ag_3, Ag_4 are inactive since $hyp(Ag_3) = \{w(ma)\} \not\subseteq E_4$ and $hyp(Ag_4) = \{ho(pro)\} \not\subseteq E_4$.

Definition 18. (Abductive Argumentation Frameworks)

Let $\langle P, H \rangle$ be an abductive program. For $E \subseteq H$, let $Args_{P \cup E}$ be a set of minimal arguments associated with $P \cup E$ and $attack_{P \cup E}$ be a binary relation over $Args_{P \cup E}$ built according to some notion of attack such as r, u, a, d. Then $AF_{P \cup E} \overset{def}{=} (Args_{P \cup E}, attack_{P \cup E})$ is called an argumentation framework for $E \subseteq H$ associated with an abductive program $\langle P, H \rangle$. Note that $Args_{P \cup E} \subseteq Args_{P \cup H}$ and $attack_{P \cup E} \subseteq attack_{P \cup H}$. Let $Hyp(Args_{P \cup E})$ be a set of hypotheses occurring in goal arguments belonging to $Args_{P \cup E} \setminus Args_E$ as follows:

$$Hyp(Args_{P \cup E}) = \bigcup_{Ag \in Args_{P \cup E} \setminus Args_E} hyp(Ag)$$

- *$(Args_{P \cup E}, attack_{P \cup E})$ is called **redundant** w.r.t. E if $Hyp(Args_{P \cup E}) \subset E$; otherwise, (i.e. if $Hyp(Args_{P \cup E}) = E$) **non-redundant** w.r.t. E.*
- *We say such E for a non-redundant $AF_{P \cup E} = (Args_{P \cup E}, attack_{P \cup E})$ is nonredundant. Non-redundant $AF_{P \cup E}$ is called an **abductive argumentation framework** (or AAF, for short) for $E \subseteq H$ associated with $\langle P, H \rangle$ [3].*

Note that any argument $Arg \in Args_{P \cup H}$ which is inactive w.r.t. E does not belong to an abductive argumentation framework $AF_{P \cup E}$ for $E \subseteq H$.

Example 3. Consider the abductive program $\langle P, H \rangle$ given in Example 1. For $E = \{pay(m), \, w(ma)\}$, $Args_{P \cup E}$ is $\{Ag_2, Ag_3\} \cup Args_E$ where $Args_E = \{Ag_5, Ag_7\}$. If we use **attack**, the argumentation framework $AF_{P \cup E}$ for E is as follows.

$$AF_{P \cup E} = (\{Ag_2, Ag_3, Ag_5, Ag_7\}, \{(Ag_3, Ag_2)\}).$$

Since $Hyp(Args_{P \cup E}) = hyp(Ag_2) \cup hyp(Ag_3) = \{w(ma)\} \subset E$, $AF_{P \cup E}$ is redundant w.r.t. E. On the other hand, for $E' = \{w(ma)\}$, the argumentation framework $AF_{P \cup E'}$ for E' is as follows:

$$AF_{P \cup E'} = (\{Ag_2, Ag_3, Ag_7\}, \{(Ag_3, Ag_2)\}),$$

---

[3] Active arguments as well as non-redundancy w.r.t. E are also addressed in [16].

which is not redundant w.r.t. E' since $Hyp(Args_{P \cup E'}) = hyp(Ag_2) \cup hyp(Ag_3) = \{w(ma)\} = E'$. Hence, $AF_{P \cup E'}$ is the abductive argumentation framework associated with $\langle P, H \rangle$ though $AF_{P \cup E}$ is not. With respect to this $\langle P, H \rangle$, there exist (*non-redundant*) abductive argumentation frameworks for eight $E \subseteq H$. Fig. 1 shows all of them along with the respective reinstatement labellings (i.e. complete extensions) though hypothetical arguments are not depicted in each argumentation framework. Since $AF_{P \cup E}$ is redundant w.r.t. any E s.t. $E = E_i \cup \{arr(p)\}$, $E = E_i \cup \{pay(m)\}$ ($i = 1, 2, 3, 5$), such cases are not shown in the figure.

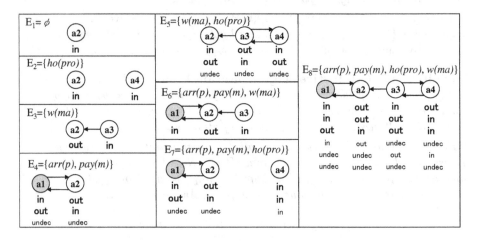

Fig. 1. Abductive argumentation frameworks for eight $E \subseteq H$

Explanations and anti-explanations of a goal argument are defined as follows.

Definition 19. (Explanations/Anti-explanations of a Goal Argument)
Let $\langle P, H \rangle$ be an abductive program, $(Args_{P \cup E}, attack_{P \cup E})$ be an abductive argumentation framework for $E \subseteq H$ associated with $\langle P, H \rangle$ and Sname be any Dung's argumentation semantics. We say that, for a ground literal $G \notin H$,

- *E is a **skeptical (resp. credulous) explanation** of an argument $Ag \in Args_{P \cup E}$ whose claim is G under Sname semantics if an argument Ag such that $claim(Ag) = G$ is skeptically (resp. credulously) justified w.r.t. $(Args_{P \cup E}, attack_{P \cup E})$ under Sname semantics, and*
- *E is a **credulous (resp. skeptical) anti-explanation** of an argument $Ag \in Args_{P \cup E}$ whose claim is G under Sname semantics if an argument Ag such that $claim(Ag) = G$ is not credulously (resp. skeptically) justified w.r.t. $(Args_{P \cup E}, attack_{P \cup E})$ under Sname semantics.*

Example 4. Let us consider Example 2, where we use `attack` as the notion of attack. In Fig.1, reinstatement labellings written in bold face express preferred extensions. Thus w.r.t. the argument A_1 whose claim is $finish(project)$, E_6 is the skeptical explanation and E_4, E_6, E_7, E_8 are the credulous explanations under preferred semantics. On the other hand, E_1, E_2, E_3, E_5 are its credulous anti-explanations, and any E_i $(1 \leq i \leq 8)$ except E_6 is the skeptical anti-explanation.

3.3 Computing Abductive Argumentation in ASP

In this subsection, we show that explanations / anti-explanations of a goal argument under the particular semantics can be computed by applying traditional abductive logic programming to the abductive program $\langle T, H \rangle$ translated from a given abductive knowledge base $\langle P, H \rangle$, where T is an extended logic program constructed by extending our previous work of computing argumentation semantics in answer set programming (ASP) [20].

ELP T translated from $\langle P, H \rangle$ consists of three ELPs, that is, Π, Γ and Ξ, where $\Pi \cup E$ for any $E \subseteq H$ is a **guess program** whose answer set embeds Caminada's reinstatement labelling $\mathcal{L}$, i.e. a complete extension $\mathcal{E}$ of an abstract argumentation framework (Ar, def) w.r.t. E corresponding to the concrete one $AF_{P \cup E} = (Args_{P \cup E}, attack_{P \cup E})$ whose $Args_{P \cup E}$ inevitably includes a goal argument, whereas $\Gamma \cup \Xi$ abbreviated as Π_{check} is a **check program** to check not only if $AF_{P \cup E}$ is an abductive argumentation framework but also whether the candidate $\mathcal{E}$ is an extension of the specified semantics. First of all, we show ELP Π as follows.

Definition 20. *Let $\langle P, H \rangle$ be an abductive program given as an agent's knowledge base, and $AF_{P \cup H}$ be an argumentation framework $(Args_{P \cup H}, attack_{P \cup H})$ associated with $P \cup H$. Then ELP Π w.r.t. $AF_{P \cup H}$ is defined as $\Pi_{AF} \cup \Pi_{Lab}$, where Π_{AF} is the set of domain-independent rules as follows:*

1. *for any argument $A \in Args_{P \cup H}$ such that $a = name(A)$ and $hyp(A) \subseteq H$,*
   $$ag(a) \leftarrow hyp(A),$$
2. *for any $(A, B) \in attack_{P \cup H}$ such that $a = name(A)$ and $b = name(B)$,*
   $$def(a, b) \leftarrow ag(a), ag(b),$$
3. *for any goal argument $C \in Args_{P \cup H} \setminus Args_H$ whose name is $c = name(C)$,*
   $$goal(c) \leftarrow,$$

Π_{Lab} is the set of domain-independent rules as follows:

4. $in(X) \leftarrow ag(X), not\ ng(X),$
   $ng(X) \leftarrow ag(X), ag(Y), in(Y), def(Y, X),$
   $ng(X) \leftarrow ag(X), ag(Y), undec(Y), def(Y, X),$
5. $out(X) \leftarrow ag(X), ag(Y), in(Y), def(Y, X),$
6. $undec(X) \leftarrow ag(X), not\ in(X), not\ out(X),$
7. $ok \leftarrow ag(X), goal(X),$
   $\leftarrow not\ ok.$

where X, Y are individual variables, and ag, def, $goal$, in, out, $undec$, ng are predicate symbols. $ag(a)$ means that a is an argument, and $def(a, b)$ expresses $(a, b) \in def$ for a binary relation def.

Rule no.1 along with $E \subseteq H$ means that, if $hyp(A) \subseteq E$, the argument A becomes active, and hence $ag(a)$ is true, i.e. $a \in Ar$ for $a = name(A)$. Rule no.2 means that, if arguments $A, B \in Args_{P \cup H}$ whose names are a, b respectively are active w.r.t. $E \subseteq H$, then $(a, b) \in def$ for a pair $(A, B) \in attack_{P \cup H}$. For an argument $a \in Ar$, $in(a)$ (resp. $out(a)$, $undec(a)$) means that a is labelled in (resp. out, undec). Rules no.4 $\sim$ no.6 faithfully express the reinstatement labellings given in Definition 12 by means of ASP [20]. Rules no.3 and no.7 are additionally provided in order to exclude the useless argumentation frameworks having no goal arguments.

Hereafter, let $\mathcal{B}_{\Pi \cup H}$ denote the Herbrand base of $\Pi \cup H$. We define the set $Lit_{\Pi \cup H}$ as follows.

$$Lit_{\Pi \cup H} = \mathcal{B}_{\Pi \cup H} \cup \{L \mid L \text{ is } \neg A \text{ for } A \in \mathcal{B}_{\Pi \cup H}\}$$

Moreover, for an answer set S and a set X, we write $S|_X \overset{def}{=} S \cap X$ which we call X-projection of S. The set $\mathcal{I}$ is defined w.r.t. $\langle P, H \rangle$ as follows,

$$\mathcal{I} \overset{def}{=} \{in(a) \mid a \in Ar\},$$

where $Ar \overset{def}{=} \{a \mid a = name(A) \text{ for } A \in Args_{P \cup H}\}$.

Based on Caminada's Results 1, the soundness and completeness Theorems similar to Theorem 1 in [20] immediately holds w.r.t. Π as follows.

Lemma 1. (Soundness and Completeness Theorems)
Let $\langle P, H \rangle$ be an abductive program. Then there is a complete extension $\mathcal{E}$ such that $\mathcal{E} = \{a \mid in(a) \in S|_{\mathcal{I}}\}$ for (Ar, def) w.r.t. $E \subseteq H$ corresponding to the concrete argumentation framework $(Args_{P \cup E}, attack_{P \cup E})$ such that $Args_{P \cup E} \setminus Args_E \neq \emptyset$ if S is an answer set of $\Pi \cup E$. Conversely, there is the answer set S of $\Pi \cup E$ such that $S|_{\mathcal{I}} = \{in(a) \mid a \in \mathcal{E}\}$ if $\mathcal{E}$ is a complete extension for (Ar, def) w.r.t. $E \subseteq H$ corresponding to the concrete argumentation framework $(Args_{P \cup E}, attack_{P \cup E})$ such that $Args_{P \cup E} \setminus Args_E \neq \emptyset$.

Example 5. Consider the abductive program $\langle P, H \rangle$ given in Example 1. $Args_{P \cup H}$ is shown in Example 2. If we use **attack**, the binary relation $attack_{P \cup H}$ over $Args_{P \cup H}$ is obtained as follows:

$$\{(Ag_1, Ag_2), (Ag_2, Ag_1), (Ag_3, Ag_2), (Ag_3, Ag_4), (Ag_4, Ag_3)\}$$

Now in order to construct Π w.r.t. this $(Args_{P \cup H}, attack_{P \cup H})$, let each argument Ag_i shown in Example 2 be named a_i $(1 \leq i \leq 8)$ respectively. Since Ag_j $(1 \leq j \leq 4)$ are goal arguments and $hyp(Ag_1) = \{arr(p), pay(m)\}$, $hyp(Ag_2) = \emptyset$, $hyp(Ag_3) = \{w(ma)\}$, $hyp(Ag_4) = \{ho(pro)\}$ and so on, we have Π_{AF} as follows:

$\Pi_{AF} = \{ag(a1) \leftarrow arr(p), pay(m), \quad ag(a2) \leftarrow, \quad ag(a3) \leftarrow w(ma),$
$\quad ag(a4) \leftarrow ho(pro), \quad ag(a5) \leftarrow arr(p), \quad ag(a6) \leftarrow pay(m).$
$\quad ag(a7) \leftarrow w(ma), \quad ag(a8) \leftarrow ho(pro), \quad def(a1, a2) \leftarrow ag(a1), ag(a2),$
$\quad def(a2, a1) \leftarrow ag(a2), ag(a1), \quad def(a3, a2) \leftarrow ag(a3), ag(a2),$
$\quad def(a3, a4) \leftarrow ag(a3), ag(a4), \quad def(a4, a3) \leftarrow ag(a4), ag(a3),$
$\quad goal(a1) \leftarrow, \quad goal(a2) \leftarrow, \quad goal(a3) \leftarrow, \quad goal(a4) \leftarrow\}$

For $E_4 = \{arr(p),\ pay(m)\} \subseteq H$, for example, $\Pi \cup E_4$ (i.e. $\Pi_{AF} \cup \Pi_{Lab} \cup E_4$) has the following three answer sets S_1, S_2, S_3 expressing the respective reinstatement labellings of the argumentation framework for E_4 shown in Fig.1:

$$S_1 = \{in(a1), out(a2), in(a5), in(a6)\} \cup E_4 \cup \mathcal{M} \cup \{ng(a2)\},$$
$$S_2 = \{out(a1), in(a2), in(a5), in(a6)\} \cup E_4 \cup \mathcal{M} \cup \{ng(a1)\},$$
$$S_3 = \{undec(a1), undec(a2), in(a5), in(a6)\} \cup E_4 \cup \mathcal{M} \cup \{ng(a1), ng(a2)\},$$

where $\mathcal{M} = \{ag(a1), ag(a2), ag(a5), ag(a6), def(a1, a2), def(a2, a1), ok, goal(a1),$
$$goal(a2), goal(a3), goal(a4)\}.$$

According to Lemma 1, we can obtain three complete extensions $\{a1, a5, a6\}$, $\{a2, a5, a6\}$, $\{a5, a6\}$ from S_1, S_2, S_3 for the abstract argumentation framework w.r.t. $E_4 = \{arr(p),\ pay(m)\}$, where only $a1$ and $a2$ are goal arguments.

To obtain every explanation E in abductive argumentation, we should take into account every argumentation framework s.t. (Ar, def) w.r.t. any $E \in 2^H$, in other words, $\Pi \cup E$ w.r.t. any $E \in 2^H$. In order to establish this, Lemma 1 for $\Pi \cup E$ is extended into Theorem 1 for $\Pi \cup \Gamma(H)$ as follows where $\Gamma(H) \overset{def}{=} \{h' \leftarrow not\ h,\ h \leftarrow not\ h'|\ h \in H\ \}$ as mentioned in Proposition 1.

Theorem 1. (Soundness and Completeness Theorems)
Let $\langle P, H \rangle$ be an abductive program. Then there is the complete extension $\mathcal{E}$ such that $\mathcal{E} = \{\ a \mid in(a) \in S|_{\mathcal{I}}\}$ for $AF=(Ar,\ def)$ w.r.t. E corresponding to the concrete argumentation framework $(Args_{P \cup E}, attack_{P \cup E})$ such that $Args_{P \cup E} \setminus Args_E \neq \emptyset$ for $E = S|_H \in 2^H$ if S is an answer set of $\Pi \cup \Gamma(H)$. Conversely, there is the answer set S of $\Pi \cup \Gamma(H)$ such that $S|_{\mathcal{I}} = \{in(a) \mid a \in \mathcal{E}\}$ and $S|_H = E$ if $\mathcal{E}$ is a complete extension for $(Ar,\ def)$ w.r.t. E corresponding to the concrete argumentation framework $(Args_{P \cup E}, attack_{P \cup E})$ such that $Args_{P \cup E} \setminus Args_E \neq \emptyset$ for some $E \in 2^H$.

Now, we explain the translated logic program $\Pi \cup \Pi_{check}$ along with $\Gamma(H)$ for abduction, which integrates the guess program $\Pi \cup \Gamma(H)$ and the *check program* Π_{check} like our previous work [20]. Hereafter, let S and M denote answer sets of the guess program $\Pi \cup \Gamma(H)$, and $\Pi \cup \Gamma(H) \cup \Pi_{check}$ respectively.

Our idea is that, $\Pi \cup \Gamma(H) \cup \Pi_{check}$ generates an answer set M (if exists) which embeds some answer set S of the guess program $\Pi \cup \Gamma(H)$ s.t. $\mathcal{E} = \{a \mid in(a) \in S|_{\mathcal{I}} = M|_{\mathcal{I}}\}$ is a complete extension w.r.t. AF for $E = M|_H = S|_H \in 2^H$ (due to Theorem 1) unless the required conditions are violated for the candidate answer set S embedded in M (i.e. the candidate extension $\mathcal{E}$ w.r.t. AF for such E), that is tested by the check program Π_{check}. In our approach, Π_{check} tests not only if the concrete $AF_{P \cup E}=(Args_{P \cup E}, attack_{P \cup E})$ corresponding to AF w.r.t. $E = M|_H$ is non-redundant w.r.t. such E but also if the candidate $\mathcal{E}$ is the extension of the specified semantics.

In more precisely speaking, the first condition about non-redundancy w.r.t. E is equivalently expressed that there is no E' such that $E' \subset E$ with keeping $Args_{P \cup E} \setminus Args_E = Args_{P \cup E'} \setminus Args'_E$ for any $E' \subseteq H$. On the other hand, the second condition is given as maximal **in** (resp. minimal **in**, empty **undec**) according to Caminada's Result 1 so that the candidate $\mathcal{E}$ may be the preferred extension (resp. grounded, stable extension). That is, in other words, w.r.t. the candidate answer set S, $\mathbf{in}(\mathcal{L}) = \{a \mid in(a) \in S\}$ is a preferred extension (resp. grounded extension) if and only if there is no answer set S' of $\Pi \cup E$ for $E = S|_H$ expressing the reinstatement labelling $\mathcal{L}'$ such that $\mathbf{in}(\mathcal{L}') = \{a \mid in(a) \in S'\}$ satisfies $\mathbf{in}(\mathcal{L}) \subset \mathbf{in}(\mathcal{L}')$ (resp. $\mathbf{in}(\mathcal{L}') \subset \mathbf{in}(\mathcal{L})$), whereas $\mathbf{in}(\mathcal{L}) = \{a \mid in(a) \in S\}$ is a stable extension if and only if $\mathbf{undec}(\mathcal{L}) = \{a \mid undec(a) \in S\}$ is empty.

To construct such Π_{check}, we prepare some definitions as follows.

Definition 21. *Let AS be a set of answer sets of ELP $\Pi \cup \Gamma(H)$ s.t.*

$$\Gamma(H) \overset{def}{=} \{h' \leftarrow not\ h,\ h \leftarrow not\ h' \mid h \in H \}$$

where h' is a newly introduced ground literal corresponding to each ground literal $h \in H$ and ξ be the cardinality of AS, i.e. $|AS|$. Then there is a bijective function $\psi : AS \rightarrow \{1, 2, \dots, \xi\}$ such that for each $S \in AS$, there is an integer j ($1 \le j \le \xi$) such that $\psi(S) = j$, which we call such j a cardinal number of S.

In order to realize our idea mentioned above, we use the techniques of *meta-programming* as well as integrity constraints as used in our previous work [20].

First, we provide two sets, $\mathcal{C}$ and $\mathcal{C}_H$ which consist of newly introduced constants L_ts expressing atoms in $\mathcal{I} = \{in(a) \mid a = name(A)\ for\ A \in Args_{P \cup H}\}$ and constants δ_hs expressing literals in H respectively as follows.

$$\mathcal{C} \overset{def}{=} \{L_t \mid L_t \text{ is the individual constant expressing an atom } L \in \mathcal{I}\}$$
$$\mathcal{C}_H \overset{def}{=} \{\delta_h \mid \delta_h \text{ is the individual constant expressing a literal } h \in H\}$$

Moreover unary and binary predicate symbols, m_1 and m_2 are introduced, where m_1 expresses the information of the candidate answer set S to be tested, whereas m_2 expresses the information of any answer set S' of $\Pi \cup \Gamma(H)$ so that Π_{check} can check if the candidate S satisfies conditions addressed above.

Their meanings are given as follows. With respect to the constant $L_t \in \mathcal{C}$ denoting an atom $L \in \mathcal{I}$ and an answer set M of $\Pi \cup \Gamma(H) \cup \Pi_{check}$,

(a) $m_1(L_t) \in M$ means $L \in M|_{\mathcal{I}} = S|_{\mathcal{I}}$ for some answer set $S = M \cap Lit_{\Pi \cup H}$ of $\Pi \cup \Gamma(H)$. Such S expresses the candidate complete extension $\mathcal{E} = \{a \mid in(a) \in S|_{\mathcal{I}} = M|_{\mathcal{I}}\}$ to be tested.

(b) $m_2(L_t, j) \in M$ means $L \in S'|_{\mathcal{I}}$ for the answer set S' of $\Pi \cup \Gamma(H)$ such that $\psi(S') = j$ ($1 \le j \le \xi$).

Similar relationship between $\delta_h \in \mathcal{C}_H$ and $h \in H$ also holds. For example, let $ia \in \mathcal{C}$ and $\delta_h \in \mathcal{C}_H$ denote $in(a) \in \mathcal{I}$ and $h \in H$ respectively. Then it holds that, w.r.t. M, $S \subseteq M$ and any answer S' of $\Pi \cup \Gamma(H)$ s.t. $\psi(S') = j$ ($1 \le j \le \xi$) defined above,

$$m_1(ia) \in M \quad \text{iff} \quad in(a) \in S|_{\mathcal{I}}, \qquad m_2(ia, j) \in M \quad \text{iff} \quad in(a) \in S'|_{\mathcal{I}}$$
$$m_1(\delta_h) \in M \quad \text{iff} \quad h \in S|_H, \qquad m_2(\delta_h, j) \in M \quad \text{iff} \quad h \in S'|_H.$$

Second, integrity constraints are included in Π_{check} in order to test two conditions mentioned above.

Now, we are ready to show translated logic programs for abductive argumentation as follows.

Definition 22. *For an abductive program $\langle P, H \rangle$, let $(Args_{P \cup H}, attack_{P \cup H})$ be an concrete argumentation framework associated with $P \cup H$ constructed according to some notion of attack. Then the translated logic programs for complete, preferred, grounded and stable semantics are defined as ELPs as follows:*

$$tr[Args_{P \cup H}, attack_{P \cup H}; \texttt{complete}] \stackrel{def}{=} \Pi \cup \Gamma \cup \Xi,$$

$$tr[Args_{P \cup H}, attack_{P \cup H}; \texttt{stable}] \stackrel{def}{=} \Pi \cup \Gamma \cup \Xi \cup \{\leftarrow undec(X)\},$$

$$tr[Args_{P \cup H}, attack_{P \cup H}; \texttt{preferred}] \stackrel{def}{=} \Pi \cup \Gamma \cup \Xi_{pr},$$

$$tr[Args_{P \cup H}, attack_{P \cup H}; \texttt{grounded}] \stackrel{def}{=} \Pi \cup \Gamma \cup \Xi_{gr},$$

where Γ is the set of domain dependent rules as follows:

8. *for any $L \in \mathcal{I}$ and $h \in H$*
   $$m_1(L_t) \leftarrow L, \qquad m_1(\delta_h) \leftarrow h,$$
   where $L_t \in C$ and $\delta_h \in C_H$ are terms expressing the atom L and the literal h respectively.
9. *for any answer set S' of $\Pi \cup \Gamma(H)$ such that $\psi(S') = j$ $(1 \le j \le \xi)$,*
   $$m_2(\alpha, j) \leftarrow, \qquad m_2(L_t, j) \leftarrow, \qquad m_2(\delta_h, j) \leftarrow, \qquad cno(j) \leftarrow,$$
   where α is the name of a goal argument s.t. $ag(\alpha), goal(\alpha) \in S'$, and $L_t \in C$ and $\delta_h \in C_H$ denote the atom $L \in S'|_{\mathcal{I}}$ and the literal $h \in S'|_H$ respectively.
10. *for any $L_t \in C$ and any $\delta_h \in C_H$,*
    $$i(L_t) \leftarrow, \qquad ab(\delta_h) \leftarrow .$$

On the other hand, Ξ, Ξ_{pr}, Ξ_{gr} are sets of domain-independent rules such that Ξ has rules of no. 11, Ξ_{pr} has rules of no. 11, no,12 and no. 13 and Ξ_{gr} has rules of no. 11, no.12 and no. 14 as follows:

11. $m_1(X) \leftarrow goal(X), ag(X),$
    $f_1(Y) \leftarrow cno(Y), m_1(X), goal(X), not\ m_2(X, Y),$
    $f_2(Y) \leftarrow goal(X), m_2(X, Y), not\ m_1(X),$
    $f(Y) \leftarrow cno(Y), not\ f_1(Y), not\ f_2(Y),$
    $c_1(Y) \leftarrow f(Y), m_1(X), ab(X), not\ m_2(X, Y).$
    $d_1(Y) \leftarrow f(Y), m_2(X, Y), ab(X), not\ m_1(X).$
    $\leftarrow c_1(Y), not\ d_1(Y),$
12. $h_1(Y) \leftarrow cno(Y), m_1(X), ab(X), not\ m_2(X, Y),$
    $h_2(Y) \leftarrow ab(X), m_2(X, Y), not\ m_1(X),$
    $h(Y) \leftarrow cno(Y), not\ h_1(Y), not\ h_2(Y),$
    $c(Y) \leftarrow h(Y), m_1(X), i(X), not\ m_2(X, Y),$
    $d(Y) \leftarrow h(Y), m_2(X, Y), i(X), not\ m_1(X),$
13. $\leftarrow d(Y), not\ c(Y),$
14. $\leftarrow c(Y), not\ d(Y).$

where X, Y are individual variables, and i, ab, cno, f_1, f_2, f, h_1, h_2, h, c_1, d_1, c, d are predicate symbols.

Due to rules no.8, for the candidate answer set S of $\Pi \cup \Gamma(H)$, $S|_{\mathcal{I}}$ as well as $S|_H$ are embedded in M by means of m_1, $L_t \in \mathcal{C}$ and $\delta_h \in \mathcal{C}_H$. Due to rules no.9, for each answer set S' of $\Pi \cup \Gamma(H)$ s.t. $\psi(S') = j$ $(1 \leq j \leq \xi)$, the information of $S'|_{\mathcal{I}}$, $S'|_H$, j and $ag(\alpha) \in S'$ s.t. $goal(\alpha) \in S'$ are embedded in M by means of m_2. Rules no.10 means that, if $i(L_t)$ and δ_h are true, then the constants L_t and δ_h express some atom $L \in \mathcal{I}$ and some literal $h \in H$ respectively. Using information of Γ embedded in M, rules no.11 check if AF to which the candidate $\mathcal{E}$ belongs is non-redundant w.r.t. $E = M|_H$, and rules no.12 as well as no.13 (resp. no.14) check if the candidate complete extension $\mathcal{E} = \{a \mid in(a) \in M|_I\}$ is the extension of preferred (resp. grounded) semantics.

With respect to the translated logic programs, the following theorems hold:

Theorem 2. (Soundness and Completeness Theorems)
Let $\langle P, H \rangle$ be an abductive program and Sname be any name of Dung's argumentation semantics. Then there is the extension $\mathcal{E} = \{ a \mid in(a) \in M|_{\mathcal{I}} \}$ of Sname semantics w.r.t. the abductive argumentation framework for $E = M|_H$ associated with $\langle P, H \rangle$ if M is an answer set of $tr[Args_{P \cup H}, attack_{P \cup H}; Sname] \cup \Gamma(H)$. Conversely, there is the answer set M of $tr[Args_{P \cup H}, attack_{P \cup H}; Sname] \cup \Gamma(H)$ such that $M|_{\mathcal{I}} = \{in(a) \mid a \in \mathcal{E}\}$ and $M|_H = E$ if $\mathcal{E}$ is an extension of Sname semantics w.r.t. the abductive argumentation framework for some $E \subseteq H$ associated with $\langle P, H \rangle$.

Proof: This is proved by slightly extending the proof of soundness and completeness theorems given in [20].

Theorem 3. *Let Sname be any name of Dung's argumentation semantics. Given a ground literal $G \notin H$ and an abductive program $\langle P, H \rangle$, E is skeptical (resp. credulous) explanation such that an argument $Ag \in Args_{P \cup E}$ having a claim G is skeptically (resp. credulously) justified under Sname semantics w.r.t. the abductive argumentation framework for $E \subseteq H$ associated with $\langle P, H \rangle$ if and only if E is the skeptical (resp. credulous) explanation of the positive observation $in(a)$ such that $a = name(Ag)$ and $G = claim(Ag)$ w.r.t. the consistent abductive program $\langle tr[Args_{P \cup H}, attack_{P \cup H}; Sname], H \rangle$.*

Proof: This is easily proved based on Theorem 2 and Proposition 1

Theorem 4. *Let Sname be any name of Dung's argumentation semantics. Given a ground literal $G \notin H$ and an abductive program $\langle P, H \rangle$, E is a credulous (resp. skeptical) anti-explanation such that an argument $Ag \in Args_{P \cup E}$ having a claim G is not credulously (resp. not skeptically) justified under Sname semantics w.r.t. the abductive argumentation framework for $E \subseteq H$ associated with $\langle P, H \rangle$ if and only if $E \subseteq H$ is the credulous (resp. skeptical) anti-explanation of the negative observation $in(a)$ such that $a = name(Ag)$ and $G = claim(Ag)$ w.r.t. the consistent abductive program $\langle tr[Args_{P \cup H}, attack_{P \cup H}; Sname], H \rangle$.*

Proof: This is easily proved based on Theorem 2 and Proposition 1.

Example 6. Consider the abductive program $\langle P, H \rangle$ in Example 1. The proponent's claim $finish(project)$ is given. Let us find the skeptical (resp. credulous) explanation E such that the argument whose claim is $finish(project)$ is skeptically (resp. credulously) justified under preferred semantics w.r.t. the abductive argumentation framework for $E \subseteq H$ associated with $\langle P, H \rangle$. Π is obtained in Example 5. Firstly we define $\mathcal{I}$ according to $Args_{P \cup H}$ shown in Example 2 as follows:

$$\mathcal{I} = \{in(aj) \mid aj = name(Ag_j) \text{ s.t. } Ag_j \in Args_{P \cup H} \ (1 \leq j \leq 8)\}.$$

To express each atom $in(aj)$ by the constant i_aj, we define the set $\mathcal{C}$ corresponding to $\mathcal{I}$ as follows: $\mathcal{C} = \{i\_a1, i\_a2, i\_a3, i\_a4, i\_a5, i\_a6, i\_a7, i\_a8\}$.

Similarly w.r.t. $H = \{arr(p), pay(m), w(ma), ho(pro)\}$, we define $\mathcal{C}_H$ as follows:

$$\mathcal{C}_H = \{a\_p, \ p\_m, \ w\_m, \ h\_p\}.$$

Now using these symbols, Γ has rules w.r.t. no.8 as follows.

$$m_1(i\_aj) \leftarrow in(aj), \ (1 \leq j \leq 8) \qquad m_1(a\_p) \leftarrow arr(p),$$
$$m_1(p\_m) \leftarrow pay(m), \qquad m_1(w\_m) \leftarrow w(ma), \qquad m_1(h\_p) \leftarrow ho(pro).$$

Next, it is obvious that there is an answer set S of $\Pi \cup \Gamma(H)$ such that $S \cap Lit_{\Pi \cup H} = U$ if and only if there is an answer set U of $\Pi \cup E$ for some $E \subseteq H$. Thus let us regard the answer set S_1 of $\Pi \cup E_4$ shown in Example 5 as the answer set S' of $\Pi \cup \Gamma(H)$ such that $\psi(S') = k$ for some integer k $(1 \leq k \leq \xi)$, where $\xi = |AS| = 31$ for the set AS of the answer sets of $\Pi \cup \Gamma(H)$. Then w.r.t. no.9, for such answer set S' of $\Pi \cup \Gamma(H)$ s.t. $\psi(S') = k$, Γ has rules as follows,

$$m_2(a1, k) \leftarrow, \qquad m_2(a2, k) \leftarrow,$$

since $ag(a1), goal(a1), ag(a2), goal(a2) \in S_1$, together with, $m_2(i\_a1, k) \leftarrow$, $m_2(i\_a5, k) \leftarrow$, $m_2(i\_a6, k) \leftarrow$, $m_2(a\_p, k) \leftarrow$, $m_2(p\_m, k) \leftarrow$, $cno(k) \leftarrow$, since $in(a1), in(a5), in(a6), arr(p), pay(m) \in S_1$. W.r.t. no.10, Γ has rules s.t. $i(i\_aj) \leftarrow$, $(1 \leq j \leq 8)$ $ab(a\_p) \leftarrow$, $ab(p\_m) \leftarrow$, $ab(w\_m) \leftarrow$, $ab(h\_p) \leftarrow$.
Note that, according to Theorem 2, the preferred (resp. complete) extension w.r.t. abductive argumentation frameworks for $E \subseteq H$ shown in Fig.1 is obtained as $\mathcal{E} = \{a \mid in(a) \in M|_{\mathcal{I}}\}$ from an answer set M of $\Pi \cup \Gamma \cup \Xi_{pr} \cup \Gamma(H)$ (resp. $\Pi \cup \Gamma \cup \Xi \cup \Gamma(H)$) s.t. $M|_H = E$. Now, $\Pi \cup \Gamma \cup \Xi_{pr} \cup \Gamma(H) \cup \{\leftarrow not \ in(a1)\}$ has five answer sets M_1, M_2, M_3, M_4, M_5 including $in(a1)$, which embed five preferred extensions including $a1$ for four abductive argumentation frameworks as depicted in Fig. 1 respectively. Thus, according to Theorem 3, each explanation E of the positive observation $in(a1)$ such that $a1 = name(Ag_1)$ and $claim(Ag_1) = fin(pro)$ w.r.t. the consistent abductive program $\langle \Pi \cup \Gamma \cup \Xi_{pr}, H \rangle$ is obtained as $M|_H$ from the respective answer set M as follows:

for M_1, $E_4 = M_1|_H = \{arr(p), \ pay(m)\}$,
for M_2, $E_6 = M_2|_H = \{arr(p), \ pay(m), \ w(ma)\}$,
for M_3, $E_7 = M_3|_H = \{arr(p), \ pay(m), \ ho(pro)\}$,
for M_4, $E_8 = M_4|_H = \{arr(p), \ pay(m), \ w(ma), \ ho(pro)\}$,
for M_5, $E_8 = M_5|_H = \{arr(p), \ pay(m), \ w(ma), \ ho(pro)\}$.

On the other hand, we can decide the credulous explanation E_6 is also the skeptical explanation since $\Pi \cup \Gamma \cup \Xi_{pr} \cup \Gamma(H) \cup \{t \leftarrow arr(p), pay(m), w(ma),$ $not\ ho(pro)\} \cup \{\leftarrow not\ t\} \cup \{\leftarrow in(a1)\}$ is inconsistent. Similarly, w.r.t. the credulous explanation E_4, we can decide it is not the skeptical explanation since $\Pi \cup \Gamma \cup \Xi_{pr} \cup \Gamma(H) \cup \{t \leftarrow arr(p), pay(m), not\ w(ma), not\ ho(pro)\} \cup \{\leftarrow not\ t\} \cup \{\leftarrow in(a1)\}$ is consistent.

4 Related Work

Rotstein *et al.* [16] proposed the *dynamic argumentation framework* (DAF) capable of dealing with dynamics through the consideration of a varying set of evidence. In some sense, their DAF is conceptually similar to our *abductive argumentation framework* (AAF) because the set of evidence representing the current state of the world defines the particular instance of the DAF, whereas the set of hypotheses defines the particular instance of the AAF in our approach, and both the DAF and the AAF are regarded as the extended ones of Dung's argumentation frameworks by introducing dynamics and abduction respectively. Such correspondence is not surprising. In fact, Sakama and Inoue showed in [17] that dynamics of knowledge base can be handled based on abduction.

With respect to applying ASP to the research field of argumentation, there are a few studies so far. To the best of our knowledge, Nieves *et al.* [12] are the first to apply ASP to compute preferred extension based on Besnard and Doutre's results [1]. On the other hand, quite recently we presented the method to compute argumentation semantics along with semi-stable semantics [4] in ASP based on Caminada's reinstatement labellings. Our approach presented in this paper indicates not only there is another important application of ASP to argumentation but also abductive argumentation is successfully established by extending our previous work to compute argumentation semantics in ASP [20].

Assumption-Based Argumentation (ABA) [2,6,11], [15, Chapter 10] can be interpreted as specific concrete interpretations of Dung's abstract argumentation frameworks and the abductive proof procedure (e.g. [11]) was developed to compute preferred extensions or acceptability semantics in the framework of ABA. However there are crucial differences between their works and ours though both make use of abduction. First, in the approach of ABA, there are no ideas about abductive argumentation (e.g. AAFs) but abduction is used to compute deductive argumentation such as preferred extensions and acceptability semantics by extending the SLDNF resolution, whereas in our approach, *abductive logic programming* based on answer set semantics [9,10,17] is applied to compute abductive argumentation such as skeptical explanations as well as credulous anti-explanations defined from AAF. Second, for the instance of ABA frameworks for logic programming, an argument defined by ABA has *assumptions* as its premises which are limited to the negation as failure literals (NAF-literals), whereas given an agent's abductive knowledge base $\langle P, H \rangle$, our approach deals with an abductive argument whose rules may have *hypotheses* from H in literals as well as NAF-literals of their body.

5   Conclusion

So far w.r.t. *deductive argumentation*, a significant amount of work has been done on proof procedures for Dung's various argumentation semantics as well as on concrete formalisms based on the Dung's theory. However, though *abductive argumentation* is crucially required for arguing multi-agents in various application domains as addressed in [13], there have been proposed few works w.r.t. abductive argumentation as far as we know. In this paper, we present a novel formalism of abductive argumentation to find hypotheses supporting a disputer's claim, which is established based on our previous work [20] to compute argumentation semantics in ASP.

The main contribution of this paper is as follows. First, we give the definition of abductive argumentation frameworks (AAFs) from which skeptical (resp. *credulous*) explanations to justify a goal argument supporting a given claim are defined. Second, we show that such skeptical (resp. *credulous*) explanations to justify the particular goal argument are obtained based on answer set semantics, or ASP by applying abductive logic programming to the extended logic program translated from the agent's abductive knowledge.

For notational simplicity, we do not address how to compute abductive argumentation under semi-stable semantics in this paper. However, explanations as well as anti-explanations defined from AAF under semi-stable semantics are also easily formalized and computed in the ASP setting in the similar way of those for other argumentation semantics by extending our previous work [20] which copes with semi-stable semantics.

We have already implemented the prototype system using the ASP solver, *dlv* [8] and JAVA language based on our method for abductive argumentation, whose execution results verify the correctness of our theorems.

Our future works are not only to analyze the computational complexity of the method presented in this paper but also to apply it to the practical multi-agent's negotiating system to assess our approach in ASP settings.

Acknowledgments. This research is partially supported by Grant-in-Aid for Scientific Research from JSPS, No. 20500141.

References

1. Besnard, P., Doutre, S.: Checking the acceptability of a set of arguments. In: Proc. of the 10th International Workshop on Non-Monotonic Reasoning, pp. 59–64 (2004)
2. Bondarenko, A., Dung, P.M., Kowalski, R.A., Toni, F.: An abstract, argumentation-theoretic approach to default reasoning. Artificial Intelligence 93(1), 63–101 (1997)
3. Caminada, M.: On the issue of reinstatement in argumentation. In: Fisher, M., van der Hoek, W., Konev, B., Lisitsa, A. (eds.) JELIA 2006. LNCS (LNAI), vol. 4160, pp. 111–123. Springer, Heidelberg (2006)
4. Caminada, M.: Semi-stable semantics. In: Proc. of the first International Conference on Computational Models of Argument (COMMA 2006), pp. 121–130 (2006)

5. Dung, P.M.: On the acceptability of arguments and its fundamental role in non-monotonic reasoning, logic programming, and n-person games. Artificial Intelligence 77, 321–357 (1995)
6. Dung, P.M.: An argumentation theoretic foundation of Logic Programming. The Journal of Logic Programming 22(2), 151–177 (1995); A shortened version appeared as Negations as hypothesis: An abductive foundation for logic programming. In: Proc. of ICLP 1991, pp. 3–17. MIT Press, Cambridge (1991)
7. Dung, P.M., Kowalski, R.A., Toni, F.: Dialectic proof procedures for assumption-based, admissible argumentation. Artificial Intelligence 170(2), 114–159 (2006)
8. Eiter, T., Leone, N., Mateis, C., Pfeifer, G., Scarcello, F.: A deductive system for nonmonotonic reasoning. In: Fuhrbach, U., Dix, J., Nerode, A. (eds.) LPNMR 1997. LNCS, vol. 1265, pp. 364–375. Springer, Heidelberg (1997), http://www.dbai.tuwien.ac.at/proj/dlv/
9. Gelfond, M., Lifschitz, V.: The stable model semantics for logic programming. In: Proceedings of the fifth International Conference and Symposium on Logic Programming (ICLP/SLP 1988), pp. 1070–1080. MIT Press, Cambridge (1988)
10. Gelfond, M., Lifschitz, V.: Classical negation in logic programs and disjunctive databases. New Generation Computing 9, 365–385 (1991)
11. Kakas, A.C., Kowalski, R.A., Toni, F.: Abductive Logic Programming. Journal of Logic and Computation 2(6), 719–770 (1992)
12. Nieves, J.C., Cortes, U., Osorio, M.: Preferred extensions as stable models. Theory and Practice of Logic Programming 8(4), 527–543 (2008)
13. Prakken, H., Vreeswijk, G.A.W.: Logics for defeasible argumentation. In: Gabbay, D.M., Guenthner, F. (eds.) Handbook of Philosophical Logic, 2nd edn., vol. 4, pp. 218–319. Kluwer, Dordecht (2001)
14. Prakken, H., Sartor, G.: Argument-Based Extended Logic Programming with Defeasible Priorities. Journal of Applied Non-Classical Logics 7(1), 25–75 (1997)
15. Rahwan, I., Simari, G.R. (eds.): Argumentation in Artificial Intelligence. Springer, Heidelberg (2009)
16. Rotstein, N.D., Moguillansky, M.O., Garcia, A.J., Simari, G.R.: An abstract argumentation framework for handling dynamics. In: Proceedings of 12th International Workshop on Non-Monotonic Reasoning (NMR 2008), pp. 131–139 (2008)
17. Sakama, C., Inoue, K.: An abductive framework for computing knowledge base updates. Theory and Practice of Logic Programming 3(6), 671–713 (2003)
18. Schweimeier, R., Schroeder, M.: A Parameterised Hierarchy of Argumentation Semantics for Extended Logic Programming and its Application to the Well-founded Semantics. In: Theory and Practice of Logic Programming, vol. 5(1, 2), pp. 207–242. Cambridge University Press, Cambridge (2005)
19. Wakaki, T., Satoh, K., Nitta, K., Sakurai, S.: Finding Priorities of Circumscription Policy as a Skeptical Explanation in Abduction. Journal of IEICE Transactions on Information and Systems E-81D(10), 1111–1119 (1998)
20. Wakaki, T., Nitta, K.: Computing argumentation semantics in answer set programming. In: New Frontiers in Artificial Intelligence. LNCS (LNAI), vol. 5547, pp. 254–269. Springer, Heidelberg (2009)

Appendix: Hypotheses Occurring in NAF-Literals of ELP

Suppose an abductive program $\langle P, H \rangle$ s.t. $body(r)^- \cap H \neq \emptyset$ for some rule $r \in P$ and a ground literal $G \notin H$ are given. The following theorem shows that under the particular argumentation semantics, skeptical and credulous explanations (resp. anti-explanations) of an argument having the claim G w.r.t. AAFs associated with $\langle P, H \rangle$ are equivalent to the respective ones w.r.t. AAFs associated with the reduced abductive program $\langle \Psi, H \rangle$ s.t. $body(r')^- \cap H = \emptyset$ for any rule $r' \in \Psi$ defined as follows.

Definition 23. *Let $\langle P, H \rangle$ be an abductive program s.t. $body(r)^- \cap H \neq \emptyset$ for some rule $r \in P$ and ℓ_h be the newly introduced literal with respect to each $h \in body(r)^- \cap H$. Then $\langle \Psi, H \rangle$ is defined as the abductive program reduced from $\langle P, H \rangle$ s.t. $body(r')^- \cap H = \emptyset$ for any rule $r' \in \Psi$ as follows. For a rule $r \in P$,*

1. *if $body(r)^- \cap H \neq \emptyset$, Ψ has the rule of the form such that "not h" occurred in the body of r is replaced with "not ℓ_h" along with the rules of the form "$\ell_h \leftarrow h$" w.r.t. any $h \in body(r)^- \cap H$,*
2. *otherwise, $r \in \Psi$.*

Theorem 5. *Let $\langle P, H \rangle$ be an abductive program and $\langle \Psi, H \rangle$ be its reduced one. For a ground literal $G \notin H$ occurring in P and $E \subseteq H$,*

• *E is a skeptical (resp. credulous) explanation of an argument $Ag \in Args_{P \cup E}$ whose claim is G under Sname semantics if and only if E is a skeptical (resp. credulous) explanation of an argument $Ag' \in Args_{\Psi \cup E}$ whose claim is G under Sname semantics.*
• *Similar results also hold w.r.t. a credulous (resp. skeptical) anti-explanation.*

Example 7. For the following abductive program $\langle P, H \rangle$ such that,

$$P = \{p \leftarrow q, \ a, \quad \neg p \leftarrow not \ \neg b, \quad q \leftarrow\} \qquad H = \{a, \neg b\}$$

its reduced abductive program $\langle \Psi, H \rangle$ is shown as follows,

$$\Psi = \{p \leftarrow q, \ a, \quad \neg p \leftarrow not \ \ell, \quad q \leftarrow, \quad \ell \leftarrow \neg b\} \qquad H = \{a, \neg b\}$$

where ℓ is a newly introduced literal corresponding to $\neg b$. For example, for $E = \{a, \neg b\}$, $Args_{P \cup E}$ is obtained as $\{Ag_1, Ag_2, Ag_3, Ag_4, Ag_5\}$, where

$$Ag_1 = [p \leftarrow q, a; \ q; \ a], Ag_2 = [\neg p \leftarrow not \neg b], Ag_3 = [q], Ag_4 = [a], Ag_5 = [\neg b],$$

and $Args_{\Psi \cup E}$ is obtained as $\{Ag_1, Ag_2', Ag_3, Ag_4, Ag_5, Ag_5'\}$, where

$$Ag_2' = [\neg p \leftarrow not \ \ell], \quad Ag_5' = [\ell \leftarrow \neg b; \neg b].$$

If we use `attack` as the notion of attack, the abductive argumentation frameworks associated with $P \cup E$ and $\Psi \cup E$ for $E = \{a, \neg b\}$ are obtained as follows:

$$AAF_{P \cup E} = (Args_{P \cup E}, \{(Ag_1, Ag_2), (Ag_2, Ag_1), (Ag_5, Ag_2)\}),$$
$$AAF_{\Psi \cup E} = (Args_{\Psi \cup E}, \{(Ag_1, Ag_2'), (Ag_2', Ag_1), (Ag_5', Ag_2')\}),$$

where $claim(Ag_1)=p$, $claim(Ag_2)=claim(Ag_2')=\neg p$, $claim(Ag_3)=q$ for $p, \neg p, q \notin H$. Then $E = \{a, \neg b\}$ is the skeptical explanation of Ag_1 whose claim is p w.r.t. $AAF_{P \cup E}$ under preferred (resp. grounded) semantics as is also w.r.t. $AAF_{\Psi \cup E}$.

Multi-Party Argument from Experience

Maya Wardeh, Trevor Bench-Capon, and Frans Coenen

Department of Computer Science, The University of Liverpool, Liverpool, UK

Abstract. A framework, PISA, for conducting dialogues to resolve disputes concerning the correct categorisation of particular cases, is described. Unlike previous systems to conduct such dialogues, which have typically involved only two agents, PISA allows any number of agents to take part, facilitating discussion of cases which permit many possible categorizations. A particular feature of the framework is that the agents argue directly from individual repositories of experiences rather than from a previously engineered knowledge base, as is the usual case, and so the knowledge engineering bottleneck is avoided. Argument from experience is enabled by real time data-mining conducted by individual agents to find reasons to support their viewpoints, and critique the arguments of other parties. Multiparty dialogues raise a number of significant issues, necessitating appropriate design choices. The paper describes how these issues were resolved and implemented in PISA, and illustrates the operation of PISA using an example based on a dataset relating to nursery provision. Finally some experiments comparing PISA with other classifiers are reported.

Keywords: Argumentation, Data mining, Dialogue Games.

1 Introduction

In [19] PADUA (Persuasive Argumentation Using Association Rules), a protocol to enable two agents to argue about the classification of a case was presented. The distinguishing feature of PADUA was that the arguments used by the agents were derived directly from a database of previous examples using data mining techniques, with each participant drawing on a separate database of examples. The authors termed this *arguing from experience*, to contrast this style of argument with the typical form of persuasion dialogues, in which each agent uses a separate knowledge base in which domain expertise is represented as a set of rules [14]. Strategies for PADUA dialogues were discussed in [17] and PADUA was evaluated on a substantial dataset relating to welfare benefits in [18]. In this paper PISA (Pooling Information from Several Agents) is present, which extends PADUA to allow any number of software agents to engage in the dialogue. This is particularly useful when the classification is not binary, since each possible classification can have its own champion.

To date research into persuasive argumentation dialogues have largely been confined to scenarios with two agents: very few examples of dialogue with several agents can be found in the literature. The main issues regarding multi-party

P. McBurney et al. (Eds.): ArgMAS 2009, LNAI 6057, pp. 216–235, 2010.

dialogues in general were identified in [8] and [16]. In this paper the authors address the issues identified in [8] and [16] and resolve them in ways appropriate to the style of dialogue supported by PISA.

The rest of this paper is organized as follows: in Section 2 details of the notion of multiparty argument from experience are considered. The PISA framework is introduced in Section 3 and solutions to issues raised in Section 2 presented. In Section 4 a series of experiments is described to explore the operation of PISA. Finally Section 5 concludes the paper.

2 Multi Party Argument from Experience

2.1 Arguing from Experience

The aim of PISA is to allow a number of agents, each with their own private database of examples, to debate (argue) the correct classification of a new case. The classification is not intended to be binary: the examples can be classified in one of a number of ways, and each possible classification will be championed by one of the parties to the dialogue. Because the agents will use their database of examples directly, rather than drawing on a set of rules engineered in some previous analysis stage, this is referred to as *arguing from experience*. PISA is based on previous work [19] which established a set of basic speech acts for argument from experience dialogues between two parties. These speech acts were inspired by work on case based reasoning in law, which forms arguments on the basis of precedent cases, especially the work carried out by Ashley [3] and Aleven [2]. A key difference, however, between arguing from experience and case based reasoning is that all of an individual agent's experiences (represented by a dataset of previous examples) are used collectively, rather than a single case being identified as a precedent. Unlike legal decisions authority comes from the frequency of occurrence in the set of examples rather than endorsement of a particular decision by an appropriate court.

When arguing from experience, rather than drawing rules from a knowledge base, the agents use data mining techniques to discover associations between features of the case under consideration and the appropriate classification according to their previous experience. This approach features several advantages:

1. Such arguments are often found in practice: many people do not develop a theory from their experience, but when confronted with a new problem recall past examples.
2. It avoids the knowledge engineering bottleneck that occurs when belief bases must be constructed.
3. There is no need to commit to a theory in advance of the discussion: the information can be deployed as best meets the need of the current situation.
4. It allows agents to share experiences that may differ: one agent may have encountered types of case that another has not. This is why it important that each agent uses its own database.

Using their distinct databases PISA agents produce reasons for and against classifications by mining Association Rules (ARs) from their datasets using Association Rule Mining (ARM) techniques [1], [6]. ARs [1] are probabilistic relationships expressed as rules of the form $X \rightarrow Y$ read as *if X is true then Y is likely to be true*, or *X is a reason to think Y is true* where X and Y are disjoint subsets of some global set of attributes. Likelihood is usually represented in terms of a *confidence value* expressed as a percentage. This is calculated as $support(XY) \times 100/support(X)$, where the support of an itemset I is the number of records in the data set in which the itemset I occurs. To limit the number of rules generated, only itemsets whose support is above a user specified *support threshold*, referred to as *frequent itemsets*, are used to generate ARs. To further limit the number of associations only those rules whose confidence exceeds a user specified confidence threshold are accepted.

In the context of this paper the antecedent of an AR represents a set of reasons for believing that a given example should be classified as expressed in the consequent. There are six speech acts (moves) used in PADUA, which can be seen as falling into three categories as follows:

1. **Propose Rule.** Move that allows generalizations of experience to be cited, by which a new rule with a confidence higher than a certain threshold is proposed.
2. **Attacking moves.** Moves that argue that the reasons given in a proposed rule are not decisive in this case. This can be achieved using one of three speech acts as follows:
   - **Distinguish.** When a player plays a distinguish move, it adds some new premise(s) to a previously proposed rule, so that the confidence of the new rule is lower than the confidence of the original rule.
   - **Counter Rule.** This is similar to the "propose rule" move, but is used to cite a generalization leading to a different classification.
   - **Unwanted Consequences.** Using this move a player suggests that certain consequences (conclusions) of the proposed rule do not match the case under consideration.
3. **Refining moves.** These moves enable a rule to be refined to meet objections. This can be achieved using one of two speech acts:
   - **Increase Confidence.** Here a player adds one or more premises to a rule that has been previously been proposed to increase the confidence of the rule.
   - **Withdraw unwanted consequences.** Here a player excludes the unwanted consequences of a rule that has been previously proposed, while maintaining a certain level of confidence.

For each of the above six moves a set of legal next moves (i.e. moves that can possibly follow each move) is defined. Table 1 summarizes the rules for "next moves", and indicates where a new set of reasons is introduced to the discussion.

While the above model can be applied to a number of application areas such as legal argumentation and other classification problems [18], where agents can

Table 1. Speech acts (moves) in PISA

Move	Label	Next Move	New Rule
1	Propose Rule	3,2,4	Yes
2	Distinguish	3,5,1	No
3	Unwanted Cons	6,1	No
4	Counter Rule	3,2,1	Yes
5	Increase Conf	3,2,4	Yes
6	Withdraw Unwanted	3,2,4	Yes

benefit from differences in experience to solve a case, PADUA is restricted to two players only. The work presented here significantly extends this model to provide an environment in which three or more participants can argue with the others using the set of speech acts listed above, drawing their arguments from individual databases. Since extension from the two player setting is not straightforward, before describing this multi-player framework in detail the main issues to be addressed in multiparty dialogues in general and multiparty argument from experience in particular, will be reviewed.

2.2 Issues in Multiparty Argument from Experience

The main concern facing multiparty argument from experience is how to allow for an indefinite number of agents to engage in the debate without jeopardizing the basic argument from experience protocol proposed in [19]. There are a number of issues of relevance in any multiparty dialogue. The following summary of these issues is based on the issues identified in [8] and [16]:

1. *System openness*: Multiparty argument from experience dialogues can either be closed or open. A closed dialogue starts with N players and continues with the same N players until the end; no new participants are allowed to join the dialogue once it has started, and players cannot leave the dialogue while it is in progress. Open dialogues are the opposite, players are free to join or leave at any time.

2. *Roles:* In two-party argument from experience there are only two roles, the proponent and the opponent, but in multiparty dialogues the situation is more complicated. There may be several proponents and several opponents of a thesis. Alternatively there may be several participants each with their own distinct options. Also, some parties within the dialogue can take a neutral point of view, or stand as mediator between the opposing parties. Also, linguistically speaking, in two player dialogues one (and only one) player

can speak per turn (the *speaker*) while the other listens (the *listener* or *hearer*). In multiparty dialogues there can be more than one listener per turn. Moreover, one can argue that there can be more than one speaker per turn, since in real life people may start talking at the same time, interrupt each other or compete with each other for attention (the loudest wins).

3. *Addressing*: Multiparty argument from experience should implement a clear addressing policy which can take one of two forms: either public broadcasting where all the players listen to what the speaker is saying, or targeted broadcasting of the speech act to some players (but not all of them).

4. *Turn taking*: The turn taking policies of two-party dialogues is straightforward, the listener becomes the speaker when the current speaker finishes. This is not the case in multiparty dialogues, and hence such a simple policy cannot be applied to multiparty argument. In persuasion dialogues the decision whether all players are given permission to talk when they want, or they have to wait for their designated turns, can greatly influence the final outcome of the dialogue.

5. *Termination*: In [19] the argument from experience dialogue terminated once one party could not argue any further (has nothing more to say). This simple rule is not sufficient for multiparty dialogues where the dialogue may be terminated either when all the other players are convinced or once the majority of them are. Another issue regarding termination is that sometimes players may fail to convince each other and could end up playing for ever, if there were no mechanism to end such dialogues. Finally in some scenarios the game may end without one single player dominating the others: in these cases there should also be a mechanism to determine the winner of the game or simply to allow ties to take place.

The above are issues that must be addressed in any system for multiparty dialogue. There are no right or wrong answers, the questions must be resolved appropriately for the particular context. The following section describes how these issues are resolved in the PISA system.

3   PISA

This section introduces the proposed model for multiparty argument from experience, PISA (Pooling Information from Several Agents), a protocol designed to enable multi-agent dialogues. The scenarios envisaged by the PISA model are those where there are several options for a particular point of view (a classification), and each one of these options is advocated by one or more software agents. Additionally in PISA there is one software agent, the chairperson, which does not advocate any position, but rather manages the dialogue and facilitates communication between the advocates.

This style of dialogue thus determines the *roles* of the players: a chairperson, and, for every option, at least one player acting as its advocate. If more than one player shares the same position, then these players join forces and form a group (see Sub-section 3.6). Each participant or group is in principle the defender of its own thesis, and an opponent of the rest of the players or groups; although PISA does allow players to temporarily defend another player's thesis where appropriate for strategic reasons.

PISA dialogues are *open* dialogues, in the sense that participants (other than the chair) may enter or leave when they wish. For *turn taking*, a structure with rounds is adopted, rather than a linear structure where agents are selected as the next speaker in turn. In each round, any agent who can make a move can do so: the chair then updates a central argument structure, and another round occurs. The central argument structure acts as a coordination artifact as proposed by Oliva et al [13]. In any round there are a number of *speakers* (players that participate in that round) and a number of *addressees* (the players whose positions are under attack). The remaining players (i.e. those who did not participate and were not attacked in the given round) need to be aware of the developments in the dialogue and are therefore assumed to be passive *listeners*.

There is no limitation on the number of groups (players) that can participate in any round; but, in order to simplify the game, each group (player) is limited to one move per round. This turn taking policy gives the participants a rich context to explore strategy issues in the best way possible. It also simplifies the game, allowing players to skip rounds, i.e. remain silent, if they think that making a move at this stage does not provide them with an advantage. Finally, this structure allows agents to play their attacks and counter attacks as soon as they wish and they do not have to wait for their turn to contribute.

The above is not perhaps the most usual structure for human meetings, but it can be found, for example, in some board games. It is suggested that this structure is particularly appropriate for the PISA context in order to achieve fairness, particularly since every advocate is playing for themselves, and has to regard every other advocate as an opponent (even though they may temporarily focus their efforts on a particular opponent, or effectively form temporary coalitions against a particular opponent). For *addressing*, every move after the first move attacks a move of some other agent and so, as noted above, that agent can be regarded as the "addressee" of that move, and the others as "listeners". The game will *terminate* when no agent makes a contribution for two rounds or after some limiting number of rounds have been played. Two silent rounds are necessary to ensure that the agents have really finished and not silent for tactical reasons. The termination of the game is thus guaranteed (see Sub-section 3.2 for further discussion). The model is essentially that of a facilitated discussion, with the chairperson acting as facilitator. In the following sub-sections the realization of this model is described in more detail.

3.1   Control Structure

The suggested control structure for PISA consists of a dialogue facilitator, the chairperson, who is responsible for monitoring and guiding an indefinite number of groups of players, where each group comprises all of the players who have joined the game and who share the same objective. The chairperson is also responsible for the central argument structure used to coordinate the dialogue: namely the argumentation tree (see Sub-section 3.3 for further detail).

When a new game commences the chairperson randomly orders the groups participating in the game, the first player proposes a new rule and the chairperson adds it to the argumentation tree. This is called the first argumentation round. In each of the subsequent rounds all the players who can and wish to attack any of the arguments played in the previous rounds are allowed to offer their arguments and the chairperson adds them to the argumentation tree. The suggested facilitated discussion protocol using the argumentation tree as a mediating artifact enjoys the following advantages:

- It increases the flexibility of the overall PISA system. By assigning the majority of protocol surveillance to the chairperson the system gains great flexibility. For example the system could be switched from closed to open (and vice versa) by applying a few limited changes to the chairperson behaviour, while the rest of the players remain unaffected.
- It is a very simple structure: there is no complicated turn taking procedure involving a choice of the next player, allowing the internal implementation of the player agents to be kept as simple as possible.
- It provides a fair dialogue environment: the organizational configuration of the dialogue is neutralized by restricting the control tasks to the chairperson who is not allowed to take sides in the dialogue. This means that no one player is privileged to speak while the others must remain silent.

One of the interesting questions, in the context of multiparty argumentation is whether participants are allowed to repeat any dialogue moves or not. In PISA two or more participants may consider playing the same move, or playing different moves, with the same content. This may happen when a number of participants coincidentally attack a particular previous move using the same attack and/or the same content, in the same round. A careful consideration of the different aspects of the generic protocol described in Sub-section 2.1, and its multiparty adaption, is essential to identifying situations where repeating arguments could be tolerated. Such consideration raises a number of questions:

- Q1: Could a participant play similar moves against the same opponent?
- Q2: Could a participant play similar moves against different opponents?
- Q3: Could different participants play similar moves against the same opponent?

Two moves (or attacks) are considered similar if have the same speech act (e.g. distinguish or counter rule) and similar content. The latter condition applies if the association rules of both moves are identical (same premises, consequents and confidence value), or if both moves have the same premises and consequents but different confidence values.

To answer the above questions, two guiding principles should be kept in mind. The first is that no participant is allowed to repeat the same move against the same opponent, if this move introduces a new rule (or in PISA terms) if it could be represented by a green node on the Argumentation Tree (Q1). The second principle is that the formation of endless loops in the dialogue must be avoided. Taking these two principles into consideration, a set of three rules could be applied (triggered) in situations of repetitions:

- One Participant cannot repeat the same attacking move (with the same AR) against different opponents (Q2) if:
  - This attack is either a distinguishing or unwanted consequences attack.
  - Or, if all of the other previously played moves using this attack are still green (undefeated) on the Argumentation Tree.
- Participants cannot attack their opponents using moves that have already been played against and defeated by these opponents (Q1).
- If two or more participants have coincidentally attacked the same opponent, in the same round, using the similar attacks (as identified above). Then if the confidence is equal in all of these attacks, then the participant under these attacks is required to defend its proposal against them once only (Q3). Otherwise the chairperson chooses the attack with the highest confidence (lowest confidence in case of distinguishing) and discards the rest.

3.2 Game Termination

The chairperson terminates a PISA game when two rounds have passed and the argument state has not changed. The reason for waiting two rounds is that sometimes some players may choose to skip some rounds for strategic reasons. Therefore, if a round is passed without any move being played, the chairperson has to warn all the players that if they have anything to say the next round is their last chance to do so if they wish to prevent the game from ending.

Termination, as described above, is called *legal termination*; however there are also cases in which the game should be exceptionally terminated (i.e. *exceptional termination*). In this case the chairperson has the authority to terminate the game if only one player remains active after all the other players have withdrawn (in which case the surviving player wins the game). Also, if the game has taken more than N rounds, the chairperson will end the game; the assumption is that if the parties can not agree in N rounds, where N is sufficiently large, then they will never agree. In this case no one wins the game. Some further discussion relating to termination, regarding how the winner is determined, is given in Sub-section 3.6.

3.3 Argumentation Tree

The notion of an *Argumentation Tree* is used to describe the central data structure representing the game's arguments, and the attack relations between those arguments. This tree acts as a mediating artifact for the dialogue as described in [13]. The tree structure used in PISA differs from other argumentation structures used in the literature as it consists of arguments played by several players. It uses four colours to mark the status of the arguments played so far, and two types of links: *explicit links* (edges) representing direct attacks, and *implicit links* representing indirect attacks. The issue of addressing is solved via the direct links: speech acts are addressed to the participants who played the argument attacked by those acts, except for the first move in the game which is addressed to all the other players. This type of addressing is a public broadcast as all the participants can "listen" to what "speakers" are saying by consulting the tree.

The PISA Argumentation Tree data structure consists of *Nodes*, *Links* and the *Green Confidence* value. Nodes represent the speech acts made in the game. Each node has a colour (green, blue, red or purple) representing the status of this node (and hence the argument represented by it) in the current round of the game. Nodes are either green or blue when introduced, depending on whether they propose a new rule or only attempt to undermine an existing one. Red nodes are those directly under attack and purple nodes are those indirectly under attack. Nodes change their colour as defined in Table 2. Links represent the explicit attack relationships between nodes. Finally the Green Confidence value is a global value associated with the tree and is the confidence value of the undefeated green node with the highest confidence.

Table 2. The Argumentation Tree Colours

Colour New Rule	Meaning	Changes To
Green	A (1, 4, 5 or 6) move node, undefeated in the given round.	(To red) If attacked by at least one undefeated node. (To purple) if indirectly attacked by an undefeated green node with higher confidence.
Red	The node is defeated in the given round.	(To green) if all attacks against the node are successfully defeated and the original node colour was green. (To blue) if all attacks against the node are successfully defeated and the original node colour was blue.
Blue	A (2 or 3) move node undefeated in the given round	(To red) If attacked by at least one undefeated node.
Purple	A (1, 4, 5 or 6) move node indirectly attacked by a higher confidence green node, played by a different player (group).	(To green) if all attacks against the node are successfully defeated, and if the move indirectly attacking this node was defeated. (To red) if successfully attacked by at least one undefeated node.

When a player plays some move (m), the move must satisfy a number of conditions in order to be added as a node to the argumentation tree, otherwise the move will be rejected. The conditions of acceptance are as follows:

- Move m is added to the tree only if it changes the colouring of the tree (consequently a player cannot add an argument that enhances its position in the game if such a move does not change the tree colouring).
- A player can put forward one move only per round (deciding which rule to play is a strategy issue).
- Moves (1, 4, 5, 6) implicitly attack all the other (1, 4, 5, 6) moves played by other players which have lower confidence.
- Moves (2, 6) affect only the nodes they directly attack.
- Moves (1, 4, 5, 6) explicitly attack the (2, 6) nodes they are associated with (if any).
- Participants should not play moves that weaken their position (i.e. a player should not put forward moves that change the colouring of the argumentation tree such that another player would take the lead). This condition holds when a player tries to attack blue nodes that were originally made to attack an argument proposed by other players.

3.4 Winner Announcement/Tie Break

Once a game has terminated, the chairperson consults the argumentation tree to determine the winner. The winner should satisfy one of the following conditions:

1. All the green nodes belong to the winner.
2. If there are no green nodes, and all the blue nodes were played by the same player, that player wins.

There are two cases where a game will end with no clear winner. The first is where there is more than one green node with the same confidence on the argumentation tree at the end of the game belonging to different participants and no green nodes with higher confidence. The second is where the game ends without any green nodes on the argumentation tree but with blue nodes belonging to more than one player.

The first case is considered to be a *strong tie* situation, as the players have actually proposed classifications within the game. One possible solution may be to start a new game between the tying parties only and see how this game ends. But there is nothing to guarantee that this game will not also end up in a tie. In this case the chairperson may be forced to announce a tie (after the second game or after a suitable number of games between the tying parties).

The second case is considered a *weak tie* situation, as the tied players did not actually have any proposed classifications at the end of the game, but has simply prevented anyone from establishing a satisfactory classification. In such cases starting a game between the tied players may be of benefit, but with the requirement that the players should propose as many reasons for their classification as they can.

3.5 Players' Strategies

In PISA, players' strategies can be a key factor in determining the winner of the dialogues, as the more sophisticated the strategy used the greater the agent's chances of winning against their opponents. PISA strategies are categorized according to the understanding of the status of the argumentation tree involved. The status of the argumentation tree is the state of the tree at the start of each round. Players can either take this status into consideration or not. Those who pay attention to this status can generally be considered "smarter" than those who do not, as they are more responsive to the changes in the game. PISA strategies fall into three main *strategy types* (types 1, 2 and 3) which are derived from the basic fact that players have the freedom to choose when and how frequently they are going to attack their opponents. Each is discussed below.

Type1: Attack whenever possible: Players attack whenever they can do so with a legal move. Players may adopt this strategy to enhance their chances of winning the game by being as aggressive as possible. This type of strategy is divided into three sub types:

1. Attack whenever possible by proposing new rules.
2. Attack whenever possible by undermining the opponent.
3. Tree dependent attack whenever possible: players using this strategy try to read the tree and anticipate the best possible attack. This strategy combines the previous two giving the players the freedom to use either of them depending on the position of other players in the game. For example if proposing a counter rule would not yield the best undefeated rule, the player will first attempt to reduce the confidence of the current best rule.

Type2: Attack only when needed: Players attack their opponent only when needed, typically when all their proposed rules so far have been successfully attacked by other players, or when their attempts to undermine all the other players have failed (because the other players successfully defended their positions). In other words the strategy is for the player to wait as long as its current proposal is secure (not under attacked). Also by waiting and monitoring other players' moves; players get a better chance to predict their opponents' moves and plan their actions accordingly. This type of strategy is also divided into three sub types:

1. Attack only when needed by proposing rules: players using this strategy will only attack when they no longer have any green nodes on the tree, by proposing a new rule (or any other equivalent move). If they have a green node these players will "wait and see".
2. Attack only when needed by undermining the opponent: These players do not move if they have a green node, or all the blue nodes belong to them.
3. Tree dependent attack only when needed: Players following this strategy try to use the tree to determine their best next move. This strategy combines the previous two giving the players the freedom to use either of them depending on the position of other players in the game.

Type3: Attack to prevent forecasted threat: Using this type of strategy a player may be able to anticipate the upcoming attacks against its proposals and therefore either change these proposals (i.e. the moves to be played) or attack the other players before they have the chance to attack its positions.

Where attack takes the form of proposing new rules the player is said to be in *build* mode, whereas if the attack uses undermining the player is said to be in *destroy* mode.

3.6 Groups

In PISA players advocating the same thesis are required to act as a *single group of players*. Every group is allowed one and only one argument per round. This restriction aims to simplify PISA dialogues. The PISA notion of groups prevents participants sharing the same objective from arguing without consulting each other and consequently causing contradictions amongst themselves or attacking each other. This may, however, lead to a situation in which the weaker parties (within the groups) are forced to withdraw from the game and the remaining stronger members no longer have sufficient shared experience to win. Two factors are essential to each group: the strategy factor and the experience factor. The strategy factor concerns the strategies of the individual players in the group. In some cases, all the members may have incorporated the same strategy, while in others each member applies its own strategy and thus a strategy ranking is required in order to determine who is going to be the group leader. The second factor relates to the experience of the group's members, measured in relation to the size of the dataset in which this experience is stored. Thus, an individual player with (say) 1200 records in its database is considered more experienced than one with only (say) 600 records.

Each group has a leader, the player applying the best strategy, where strategies are ranked according to their level of understanding of the argumentation tree, and the dialogue process. The leader guides the inter-group dialogue, and decides which one of the moves suggested by all the members is the best to be played next in the game, as follows:

- The leader's most essential task, as far as the group is concerned, is to select the best move at every round of the dialogue, from the selection of moves suggested by the group's members. The leader often chooses the moves following its own strategy. However this does not mean that the leader will select its own move all the time. Rather, the leader aims at selecting the best move from amongst the suggested moves. For instance, the move with the highest confidence. Here, the differences in the members' experiences will greatly influence the leader's decision: members with different experience will often promote different content for their chosen moves, even where all the members apply similar strategies.
- The leader can compel the more experienced members (if any) to act according to the leader's strategy. This happens on a round by round basis. If a more experienced member suggests one move, in a given round, and if the leader assumes that a similar move with a better confidence, or a move with a different speech act better matching the game context, could be produced

by this player, then the leader can ask this player to attempt generating another move using the leader's strategy. The leader then compares the new move (the one produced using its own strategy parameters) against the old one (the one the player has initially suggested) and chooses the best move. Consider, for example, the case where one of the experienced players has suggested a destroy move (following its own strategy) distinguishing some previously undefeated move in the dialogue. Then the leader will ask it to produce a build move. If this player replies with a build move with a high confidence (say higher than the moves suggested by the other members) then the leader will discard this player's initial move, otherwise it will discard the new move. Information about the members experience and strategy is available to its leader, through a simple dialogue, by which the leader request this information from the group's members. Additional conditions are applied to ensure that the leader uses the above authority only when needed; thus if the experienced members of the group apply weak strategies, and where other members have failed to produce adequate moves.

- The leader can redirect moves suggested by the other members against opponents other than the ones they have chosen. For instance, if one member suggests an *"increase confidence"* move against one opponent (say for strategic reasons), then the leader may change this move to a *"propose new rule"* and directs it against another opponent (say because this opponent threatens the group more than the one originally picked upon by the group member). Here as well, the leader is allowed to redirect the members' moves only when redirection is more rewarding according to the leader's strategy than the original move.

Thus, inter-group dialogue is a variation of targeted broadcasting, in which only group members can listen to what they are saying, while other players are completely unaware of these conversations. The leader can also redirect other members' moves against different opponents, or advise them to follow its own strategy, an act that makes the group benefit from both the smartness of the leader and the experience of other more straightforward players.

4 Example

PISA has been fully implemented in Java, and uses the TFPC tool described in [5] to mine its association rules (ARs). PISA has been applied to several datasets, including the welfare benefits application used to evaluate PISA [18] and a dataset drawn from an application to process applications for a nursery school in Ljubljana [12]. In this section the kinds of dialogues produced by PISA are illustrated, using the nursery dataset from the UCL data repository[1].

The Nursery data set was derived from a hierarchical decision model originally developed to rank applications for nursery schools. It was used during the 1980s when there was excessive enrolment to these schools in Ljubljana, Slovenia, where

---

[1] UCI machine learning repository: http://archive.ics.uci.edu/ml/datasets/Nursery

there were often two applications for every place. The final decision depended on eight factors forming three sub problems: the occupation of parents and the child's current nursery provision; the family structure and its financial standing; and the social and health picture of the family. The model was developed using the DECMAK expert system shell for decision making [4].

The original data set consisted of 12960 records (past cases) classified into five levels of priority: (i) not recommended, (ii) recommended, (iii) highly recommended, (iv) priority and (v) special priority. The distribution of the classes in terms of records was as follows: 4320, 2, 328, 4266 and 4044 (33.33%, 0.015%, 2.53%, 32.91% and 31.204%). Note that the "recommended" class has only two examples (insufficient to support the generation of arguments); thus, for the purpose of this experiment, the two records for the recommended class were removed from the data set, giving a four player game. Note also that the highly recommended classification is rare, and that it is this kind of rarely encountered case which is often misclassified. The dataset features 8 attributes other than the class attribute, which take the following values:[2]

- Parents occupation: usual, pretentious, of great pretension
- Childs nursery: proper, less proper, improper, critical, very critical
- Form of the family: complete, completed, incomplete, foster
- Number of children: 1,2,3, more than 3
- Housing conditions: convenient, less convenient, critical
- Financial standing of the family: convenient, inconvenient
- Social conditions: non-problematic, slightly problematic, problematic
- Health conditions: recommended, priority, not recommended

4.1 A PISA Debate

For the example PISA was operated with four agents, each representing one of the four "nursery" classifications (see above). The agents were labelled as follows: NR (not recommended), HR (highly recommended), PR (priority) and SP (special priority). An example case, which should be classified as highly recommended, was used since this is the rarest, and hence the classification most likely to be in dispute. Specifically the case has attributes: the parents have a usual occupation, has less than proper nursery, completed family, two children, convenient housing, inconvenient finance, non problematic social conditions and recommended health conditions recommended. For the test run the confidence level to 50% and the support level to 1%: both of these are deliberately low so as to get as detailed a dialogue as possible. These values are also well established as the default thresholds in the data mining community.

HR is invited to propose a rule and suggests the following association: *usual occupation, less than proper nursery, convenient housing and recommended health → highly recommended* with a confidence of 52.38%. This rule is attacked by the other three agents in round two:

---

[2] The terminology for the attributes is that of [12]: the translation is sometimes quaint.

NR: proposes a counter rule: usual occupation, complete family, 2 children, convenient housing and inconvenient finance → with confidence 55.55%.

PR: also proposes a counter rule: recommended health → priority with confidence 55.72%.

SP: distinguishes the original rule since where the family is complete the confidence of the proposed rule falls to only 20%.

Note that SP does not propose a rule of its own. Since the case falls into the narrow band of highly recommended, reasons for the classifications on either side might be expected, but not the very different special priority. None the less, SP can play a useful role in critiquing the arguments of the other players.

At this stage PR is ahead as it has the best unattacked rule. (The reader might find it helpful to refer to the completed argument tree shown in Figure 1 as the debate develops.) In round three all four players move:

HR: proposes a counter rule to attack the current best rule. In fact it has an excellent rule: usual parent, less than proper nursery, complete family, convenient housing and recommended health → highly recommended with confidence 85.71%.

NR: distinguishes PR's argument in the previous round by pointing out that usual occupation and recommended health only gives priority with a confidence of 18.64%.

PR: proposes a counter rule against NR's rule of round two: usual occupation and less than proper nursery and recommended health → priority with confidence 61.16%.

SP: also distinguishes PR's second round rule by pointing to the usual occupation, but from their database the modified rule has confidence of 19.94%.

Now HR is back in the lead. Note that in fact the proposed rule is the same as the rule as modified by SP in round 2. This difference in confidence is explained by the fact that SP may have very few highly recommended cases in its database. In round four SP has no move. The other two agents can, however, make moves:

NR: distinguishes PR's rule from round three, by pointing out that recommended health reduces the confidence of the priority classification to only 20%.

PR: proposes a counter rule against HR's rule of round three: less than proper nursery, completed form, inconvenient finance and recommended health → priority with confidence 86.95%.

Now PR is winning, but in round five this can be distinguished by NR, since the addition of non-problematic social problems reduces the confidence to just 20%. In round six PR proposes another rule: *usual occupation and less than proper nursery and recommended health → priority* with confidence 65.95%. This, however, can be distinguished by HR since adding non-problematic social behaviour again reduces the confidence to 20%. This reinstates the argument of HR made in round 3. No more arguments are possible at this stage, and so the final classification is *highly recommended*.

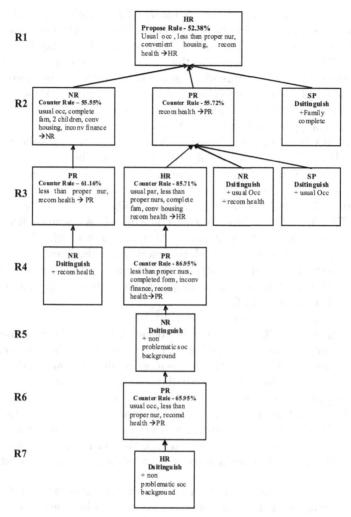

Fig. 1. Completed Argument Tree

4.2   Evaluation

To evaluate the effectiveness of PISA as a classifier, PISA was evaluated against a variety of standard classifiers using a number of datasets varying in size and structure. A series of cross-validation tests were performed. Here the results from the experiments with the nursery data used in the example debate are first presented.

Five other classifiers were used, operating on the union of the data sets:

- **TFPC:** TFPC, Total From Partial Classification [6], is a Classification Association Rule Mining (CARM) algorithm founded on the TFP (Total From Partial) Association Rule Mining (ARM) algorithm; which, in turn, is an extension of the Apriori-T (Apriori Total) ARM algorithm [1]. TFPC is designed to produce Classification Association Rules (CARs) whereas Apriori-T and TFP are designed to generate Association Rules (ARs). In its simplest form TFPC determines a classification according to given support and confidence thresholds. The nature of the selected thresholds is therefore the most significant influencing factors on classification accuracy. A more sophisticated version of TFPC uses a hill climbing technique to find a best accuracy given start support and confidence thresholds.

- **CBA:** CBA (Classification Based on Associations) is a Classification Association Rule Mining (CARM) algorithm developed by Bing Liu et al [10]. CBA operates using a two stage approach to generating a classifier:
  1. Generating a complete set of CARs.
  2. Prune the set of CARs to produce a classifier.
- **CMAR:** CMAR (Classification based on Multiple Association Rules) is another CARM algorithm developed by Wenmin Li et al [9]. CMAR also operates using a two stage approach to generating a classifier:
  1. Generating the complete set of CARs according to a user supplied support threshold to determine frequent (large) item sets, and confidence threshold to confirm CRs.
  2. Prune this set to produce a classifier.
- **Decision Trees:** Classification using decision trees was one of the earliest forms of data mining. Ross Quinlan's C4.5 is arguably the most referenced decision tree algorithm [15]. One of the most significant issues in decision tree generation is deciding on which attribute to split. Various algorithms have been proposed in the literature. Two are used here: Most frequently supported (or Random) Decision Trees (**RDT**) and Information Gain Decision Trees (**IGDT**). The first selects the first attribute in a list of attributes order according to its support frequency within the entire data set. Information gain [11] is one of the standard measures used in decision tree construction.

To evaluate PISA using the Nursery dataset the data was distributed amongst four groups, comprising of one player each (each advocating one of the four possible classifications discussed in the previous sub-section). 10 fold cross validation was then applied using 50% as the confidence level and 1% as the support threshold. PISA games were played among the four participants to classify 400 cases, 100 cases representing each of the four possible classifications. To evaluate the effect of groups, the nursery dataset was also sub-divided over four groups each of four players. The same 10 fold tests were then applied. The results of both tests are shown in Table 3.

As can be seen from these results, PISA performs consistently well - out performing the other association rule classifiers, and giving comparable results to the decision tree methods, which are particularly well suited to the nursery dataset. Interestingly PISA performs better using groups than individual players: it seems that the greater the number of separate databases the greater the number of arguments found, enabling a more thorough exploration of the problem.

Table 3. Cross Validation tests on Nursery Data

Test	4 players	4 groups	TFPC	CBA	CMAR	Rand	Igain
1	96.75	98.5	63.25	72	69.75	100	96.5
2	94	99.75	63	70	70.25	100	99
3	96.5	99	63.25	73.75	70.25	100	99
4	94.75	99.75	63	72.75	69.5	100	99
5	95.5	99	63.25	70.75	69.75	100	99
6	96	98.75	63	71.75	69.75	100	99
7	97.25	99.75	63.25	72.75	69.25	100	99
8	93.75	99.5	63.25	72.75	70.25	100	99
9	96	98	63.25	73.75	69.75	100	99
10	94	99	63	72.75	70	100	99
Summary	95.45	99.1	63.15	72.3	69.85	100	98.75

One motivation for using PISA as a classifier is that by allowing agents with different points of view to debate their reasons will produce classifications that are robust in the face of noisy datasets, where the previous examples include a significant number of misclassifications. This conjecture is particularly explored in the context of the welfare benefits data set [18], since decisions on such benefits typically exhibit high error rates, often as high as 30%. In [18] it was found that PADUA was indeed able to perform well in the face of extensive noise. Although there is not sufficient space to discuss the welfare benefits dataset in detail here, the main results will be reported. Cross validation tests were performed using a dataset of 3000 records, of which 600 (20%) were incorrectly classified. PISA was tested, with four players and with four groups each of four players, against the same five classifiers as the nursery data. The results are shown in Table 4.

Table 4. Cross Validation tests on Noisy Nursery Data

Test	4 players	4 groups	TFPC	CBA	CMAR	Rand	Igain
1	92.46	97.46	64.26	69.31	61.57	93.24	90.74
2	91.93	98.50	63.29	69.31	60.60	93.38	90.05
3	91.77	98.39	63.29	69.31	61.57	93.38	90.05
4	92.08	98.15	58.36	69.31	61.67	93.38	90.05
5	92.33	97.31	64.55	69.31	61.57	93.38	90.05
6	93.76	98.62	60.40	69.71	61.60	93.38	90.05
7	94.03	98.15	59.59	69.71	61.57	93.38	90.05
8	91.17	98.35	59.71	69.83	61.57	93.38	90.05
9	93.65	90.46	59.71	69.31	61.60	93.38	90.05
10	93.27	96.63	64.55	68.93	61.62	92.95	90.02
Summary	92.64	97.20	61.77	69.40	61.49	93.32	90.11

Notice from these results that the decision tree techniques, which were able to perform almost perfectly on clean data, exhibit a falling off of performance when a significant degree of noise is introduced. PISA also has some deterioration, but, especially when groups are used, this is relatively slight. Indeed, in these experiments, the PISA classifier with groups achieved the highest level of performance. These results are very encouraging, and the intention is to explore this point further in future experiments.

5   Concluding Remarks

In this paper the PISA argumentation from experience framework has been described. The mechanisms and strategies used to facilitate multi-party argumentation were considered, as well as the design and implementation of PISA. The operation of the system was illustrated using an example. Results, comparing PISA with conventional classifiers, were also reported. Consequently it is suggested that the PISA framework offers the following advantages:

- It allows argumentation between any number of players rather than the more usual two. This requires consideration and resolution of a range of issues associated with dialogues with more than two participants
- It operates without the need for a Knowledge Base but instead allows players to generate arguments using data mining techniques.
- The resulting decision making appears to be robust in the face of misclassifications in some of the data sets.
- The process leads to a reasoned consensus; which is not obtained through, for example, voting, increasing the acceptability of the outcome to all parties.

References

1. Agrawal, R., Imielinski, T., Swami, A.N.: Mining association rules between sets of items in large databases. In: Buneman, P., Jajodia, S. (eds.) SIGMOD Conference, pp. 207–216. ACM Press, New York (1993)
2. Aleven, V.: Teaching Case Based Argumentation Through an Example and Models. Phd thesis, University of Pittsburgh, Pittsburgh, PA, USA (1997)
3. Ashley, K.D.: Modeling Legal Argument. MIT Press, Cambridge (1990)
4. Bohanec, M., Rajkovic, V.: Expert system for decision making. Sistemica 1(1), 145–157 (1990)
5. Coenen, F.: The lucs-kdd tfpc classification association rule mining algorithm. Department of Computer Science, University of Liverpool (2004)
6. Coenen, F., Leng, P.H., Ahmed, S.: Data structure for association rule mining: T-trees and p-trees. IEEE Trans. Knowl. Data Eng. 16(6), 774–778 (2004)
7. Dignum, F. (ed.): ACL 2003. LNCS, vol. 2922. Springer, Heidelberg (2003)
8. Dignum, F., Vreeswijk, G.: Towards a testbed for multi-party dialogues. In: Dignum, F. (ed.) [7], pp. 212–230
9. Li, W., Han, J., Pei, J.: Cmar: Accurate and efficient classification based on multiple class-association rules. In: Cercone, N., Lin, T.Y., Wu, X. (eds.) ICDM, pp. 369–376. IEEE Computer Society, Los Alamitos (2001)
10. Liu, B., Hsu, W., Ma, Y.: Integrating classification and association rule mining. In: KDD, pp. 80–86 (1998)
11. Mitchell, T.: Machine Learning. McGraw-Hill, New York (1997)

12. Olave, M., Rajkovi, V., Bohanec, M.: An application for admission in public school systems. In: Expert Systems in Public Administration, pp. 145–160 (1989)
13. Oliva, E., Viroli, M., Omicini, A., McBurney, P.: Argumentation and artifact for dialogue support. In: ArgMAS, pp. 24–38 (2008)
14. Prakken, H.: Formal systems for persuasion dialogue. Knowledge Eng. Review 21(2), 163–188 (2006)
15. Quinlan, J.R.: C4.5: Programs for Machine Learning. Morgan Kaufmann Publishers, San Francisco (1998)
16. Traum, D.R.: Issues in multiparty dialogues. In: Dignum, F. (ed.) [7], pp. 201–211
17. Wardeh, M., Bench-Capon, T.J.M., Coenen, F.: Padua protocol: Strategies and tactics. In: Mellouli, K. (ed.) ECSQARU 2007. LNCS (LNAI), vol. 4724, pp. 465–476. Springer, Heidelberg (2007)
18. Wardeh, M., Bench-Capon, T.J.M., Coenen, F.: Argument based moderation of benefit assessment. In: JURIX, pp. 128–137. IOS Press, Amsterdam (2008)
19. Wardeh, M., Bench-Capon, T.J.M., Coenen, F.: Arguments from experience: The padua protocol. In: Besnard, P., Doutre, S., Hunter, A. (eds.) COMMA. Frontiers in Artificial Intelligence and Applications, vol. 172, pp. 405–416. IOS Press, Amsterdam (2008)

Using Ontology Modularization for Efficient Negotiation over Ontology Correspondences in MAS

Paul Doran[1], Valentina Tamma[1], Terry R. Payne[1], and Ignazio Palmisano[2]

[1] Department of Computer Science, University of Liverpool,
Liverpool L69 3BX, United Kingdom
{P.Doran,V.Tamma,T.R.Payne}@liverpool.ac.uk
[2] School of Computer Science, University of Manchester, UK
ignazio.palmisano@cs.manchester.ac.uk

Abstract. Efficient agent communication in open and dynamic environments relies on the agents ability to reach a mutual understanding over message exchanges. Such environments are characterized by the existence of heterogeneous agents that commit to different ontologies, with no prior assumptions regarding the use of shared vocabularies. Various approaches have therefore considered how mutually acceptable mappings may be determined dynamically between agents through negotiation. In particular, this paper focusses on the *meaning based negotiation* approach, proposed by Laera *et al* [1], that makes use of argumentation in order to select a set of mappings that is deemed acceptable by both agents. However, this process can be highly complex, reaching $\Pi_2^{(p)}$-complete. Whilst it is non-trivial to reduce this complexity, we have explored the use of ontology modularization as a means of reducing the space of possible concepts over which the agents have to negotiate. In this paper, we propose an approach that combines modularization with argumentation to generate focused domains of discourse to facilitate communication. We empirically demonstrate that we can not only reduce the number of alignments required to reach consensus by an average of 75%, but that in 41% of cases, we can identify those agents that would not be able to fully satisfy the request, without the need for negotiation.

1 Introduction

The ability to communicate, and hence collaborate, delegate tasks or answer queries is one of the key capabilities of an agent within a Multi-Agent System. This communication can only be facilitated if there is some shared understanding of the messages that the agents exchange. Whilst implicit assumptions regarding the terminology or vocabulary may be acceptable within small, closed environments (where all the agents are known at design time), it becomes imperative to specify explicit vocabularies or ontologies to support communication as environments open up, or the heterogeneity of large systems increases. The use of formally defined ontologies has increased significantly due to the combined emergence of optimized, description-logic reasoners, and standards for representing

P. McBurney et al. (Eds.): ArgMAS 2009, LNAI 6057, pp. 236–255, 2010.

ontologies [2]. Thus, agents can share the same representation language, utilize domain models that are semantically rich, and make inferences over queries in a decidable manner. However, this is predicated upon the notion of a single, shared ontology, or a set of *correspondences* or mappings[1] that map semantically related entities from one ontology to another.

The ability to dynamically reconcile heterogeneous ontologies within open environments (where no assumptions are made with respect to the ontologies used) is dependent on an agent's ability to agree on a set of acceptable correspondences between the elements in its ontology with those of another. Various approaches attempt to resolve ontological mismatches within open environments [3,1,4], including negotiation approaches that collaboratively search a space of correspondences to find a mutually acceptable set, and thus facilitate communication. This search can become prohibitively costly as the sizes of the ontologies grow, and thus a reduction of this search space is highly desirable. This can be particularly significant as ontologies may consist of several loosely connected or overlapping sub-domains, many of which may be irrelevant for a given task.

Several approaches for generating alignments (i.e. sets of mappings between ontologies) have emerged [5], that provide different correspondences depending on the method used, the characteristics of the ontologies themselves, and other resources (e.g. knowledge-bases). Thus, as new correspondences are generated, they can be registered with a mapping repository, to facilitate discovery and reuse by other agents at runtime. However, those agents may have different preferences for ontological alignments, based on their ontologies and their tasks, and thus a negotiation mechanism should consider these preferences when searching for possible solutions.

In this paper, we examine the *Meaning-based argumentation* approach proposed by Laera *et.al.* [1], which allows two agents to argue over a set of candidate mappings obtained from a mapping repository. We postulate that *Ontology Modularization* can be used as a filtering mechanism for reducing the size of the ontologies used, and hence the size of the search space. Ontology modularization techniques typically split an ontology into partitions, or produce a subset, an *ontology module*, of the original ontology with respect to a supplied *signature* (i.e. a set of seed concepts). We demonstrate empirically that the number of correspondences that need to be argued over is reduced by an average of 75%, thus supporting the hypothesis that modularization can be used to reduce the cost of the argumentation process. The results also demonstrate that in 41% of the cases investigated, the use of argumentation could be avoided as no satisfactory solution is possible; i.e. where an insufficient number of correspondences exist that could support viable communication. Thus, an agent can avoid costly negotiations with those agents that would ultimately be unable to satisfy a query or task.

The paper is organized as follows: the motivation for this approach and related work is presented in Section 2, followed by Section 3 which presents the

---

[1] The terms *correspondence* and *mapping* are equivalent, and have been used interchangeably within this paper.

Meaning-based argumentation approach. Section 4 introduces ontology modularization and presents the various approaches that can be used to modularize an ontology, whilst Section 4.3 describes how modularization could be used to reduce the search mechanism for suitable alignments produced by the *Meaning-based argumentation*. Modularization as a search reduction mechanism is evaluated in Section 5, and Section 6 presents some concluding remarks.

2   Motivation and Background

Efficient agent communication within open and dynamic environments relies on the agents ability to reach a mutual understanding over a set of messages, where no prior assumptions can be made on the vocabulary used by the agents to communicate. Requests made to other agents should be interpreted through the underlying semantics of the request itself, and thus an agent should resolve any type of mismatch that may exist due to the use of different, but conceptually overlapping ontologies. Early solutions relied on the existence of a shared ontology, or simply assumed that a canonical set of ontology mappings (possibly defined at design time) could be used to resolve ontological mismatches. However, such assumptions work only when the environment is (semi-) closed and carefully managed, and no longer hold in open environments where a plethora of ontologies exist. Likewise, the emergence of different alignment-generation tools [5] has resulted in the existence of different possible alignments between ontologies, whose suitability can vary depending on the agent's tasks, goals and preferences.

A number of solutions have been proposed that attempt to resolve ontological mismatches within open environments [3,1,4]. The work by van Diggelen *et al* [3] dynamically generates a minimal shared ontology, where minimality is evaluated against the ability of the different agents to communicate with no information loss. However, this approach uses a limited ontology model whose expressivity supports only simple taxonomic structures, with no properties and few restrictions other than disjointness and partial overlap. The expressive power of this model is non-standard, in that it does not correspond to any of the OWL [6] flavours[2]. Therefore, its applicability to the augmentation of existing real-world, published, OWL ontologies is limited.

The increased availability of mechanisms for ontology mapping and alignment [5] raises the challenge of discovering a number of different correspondence sets that may be mutually acceptable between two agents. This is essentially a collaborative search problem through the space of possible ontology correspondences between entities within different ontologies. To facilitate this search, a repository of (previously generated) correspondences for overlapping ontologies is required, as well as a mechanism for searching over these correspondences.

---

[2] The authors mention a reformulation of their model using Description Logics (the logical theory underpinning the standard ontology language OWL [6]), but no formal proof of the soundness of this reformulation is provided [3].

Mechanisms supporting the storage and provision of correspondences have already been devised; for example, Laera *et al* [1] postulate the notion of an *Ontology Alignment Server* (OAS), an agent which can supply potential mappings between two agents' ontologies. Various approaches that facilitate collaborative search have also been proposed [1,4]. A simple method might consist of a brute force approach that selects only those mappings whose level of confidence is above a certain threshold specified for each agent. More sophisticated approaches have exploited the use of *argumentation* as a negotiation mechanism to locate mappings that are mutually acceptable by both agents [1,4]. Laera *et al* [1] use argumentation as a rational means for agents to select ontology mappings from a repository [5], based on the notion of partial-order preferences over the different types of correspondences (e.g. structural vs terminological). Their approach assumed the use of OWL as a common ontology language. Dos Santos *et al* [4] proposed a variant on this idea, by representing ontology mappings as disjunctive queries in Description Logics.

The complexity of the search through the space of possible correspondences can, however, become prohibitive when complex negotiation mechanisms such as argumentation are involved, and reach $\Pi_2^{(p)}$-complete [7][3]. This can make the search costly, especially when it is used to establish a common communication vocabulary (thus constituting the initial phase of any communication or transaction). Hence, it is important to identify ways in which the search space can be reduced *before* the argumentation process takes place.

One possible approach would be to reduce the size of the search space, by isolating only the pertinent correspondences that are relevant to some communication. This can be achieved by finding the relevant concepts in the original ontology through *ontology modularization*. Modularization refers to a set of principles and methodologies for either splitting an initial ontology into a number of partitions [8,9], or producing a subset of the input ontology with respect to a supplied signature [10,11,12,13,14,15]. Several different ontology modularization techniques have been proposed, which can broadly be classified as *traversal approaches* [10,11,12,13,14,15], which conditionally traverse the ontology represented as a graph, and *logical approaches*, [10,15] which identify modules that preserve certain logical properties, such as coverage.

In the next sections we introduce the *meaning-based argumentation* approach for dynamically selecting a set of mutually acceptable mappings from all the possible ones, and we provide a survey of ontology modularization approaches.

3   Arguing over Alignments

To better understand how the synergy between modularization and negotiation can be used to efficiently find alignments, we first present the *Meaning-based argumentation* [1], before then describing in the next Section how modularization can be used to reduce the space of all candidate mappings. Agents could then

---

[3] This is the complexity of deciding whether an argument is in every preferred extension of an agent (see Section 3).

argue over this reduced set of candidate mappings (as no rational agent should waste time arguing over possibly irrelevant alignments). The central hypothesis within this paper is that the use of modularization can be used to reduce the search space and consequently the cost of arguing over acceptable correspondences, by reducing the number of alignments, and hence arguments (this hypothesis is explored empirically in Section 5).

3.1   Value-Based Argumentation Framework (VAF)

This paper adopts the framework used by Laera *et al.* [16], which is based upon Bench-Capon's Value-Based Argument Framework (VAF) [17], that introduces the notions of *audience* and *preference values*. An audience represents a group of agents who share the same preferences over a set of values, with a single value being assigned to each argument. The VAF is based on the seminal work by Dung [18]. Dung showed that many forms of non-monotonic reasoning and logic programming are special forms of his argumentation theory.

In Dung's framework [18] attacks always succeed; in essence they are all given equal value. For deductive arguments this suffices, but in our scenario, ontology alignment negotiation, the persuasiveness of an argument could change depending on the audience, where an audience represents a certain set of preferences. One alternative is to use a Value-Based Argumentation Framework (VAF) [17], which assigns different strengths to arguments on the basis of the values they promote and the ranking given to these values by the audience for the argument. Thus, it is possible to systematically relate strengths of arguments to their motivations and to accommodate different audience interests.

Definition 1. *A Value-Based Argumentation Framework (VAF) is defined as $\langle AR, A, \mathcal{V}, \eta \rangle$, where:*

- *$\langle AR, A \rangle$ is an argumentation framework;*
- *$\mathcal{V}$ is a set of k values which represent the types of arguments;*
- *$\eta : AR \rightarrow \mathcal{V}$ is a mapping that associates a value $\eta(x) \in \mathcal{V}$ with each argument $x \in AR$.*

The notion of *audience* is central to the VAF. Audiences are individuated by their preferences over the values. Thus, potentially, there are as many audiences as there are orderings of $\mathcal{V}$[4]. The set of arguments is assessed by each audience in accordance to its preferences. An audience is defined as follows:

Definition 2. *An* audience *for a VAF is a binary relation $\mathcal{R} \subseteq \mathcal{V} \times \mathcal{V}$ whose irreflexive transitive closure, $\mathcal{R}^*$, is asymmetric, i.e. at most one of (v, v'), (v', v) are members of $\mathcal{R}^*$ for any distinct $v, v' \in \mathcal{V}$. We say that v_i is preferred to v_j in the audience $\mathcal{R}$, denoted $v_i \succ_{\mathcal{R}} v_j$, if $(v_i, v_j) \in \mathcal{R}^*$*

This notion allows us to consider that different agents (represented by an audience) can have different perspectives on the same candidate mapping. Thus, the VAF [17] defines what it means for an argument to be acceptable relative to some audience; it is defined as follows:

---

[4] Number of audiences $= |\mathcal{V}|!$.

Definition 3. *Let* $\langle AR, A, \mathcal{V}, \eta \rangle$ *be a VAF, with R and S as subsets of AR, and an audience* $\mathcal{R}$:

(a) *For* $x, y \in AR$, *x is a* successful attack *on y with respect to* $\mathcal{R}$ *if* $(x, y) \in A$ *and* $\eta(y) \not\succ_{\mathcal{R}} \eta(x)$.

(b) $x \in AR$ *is* acceptable *with respect to S with respect to* $\mathcal{R}$ *if for every* $y \in AR$ *that successfully attacks x with respect to* $\mathcal{R}$, *there is some* $z \in S$ *that successfully attacks y with respect to* $\mathcal{R}$.

(c) *S is* conflict-free *with respect to* $\mathcal{R}$ *if for every* $(x, y) \in S \times S$, *either* $(x, y) \notin A$ *or* $\eta(y) \succ_{\mathcal{R}} \eta(x)$

(d) *A conflict-free set S is* admissible *with respect to* $\mathcal{R}$ *if every* $x \in S$ *is acceptable to S with respect to* $\mathcal{R}$

(e) *S is a* preferred extension *for the audience* $\mathcal{R}$ *if it is a maximal admissible set with respect to* $\mathcal{R}$

(f) $x \in AR$ *is* subjectively acceptable *if and only if x appears in the preferred extension for some specific audience.*

(g) $x \in AR$ *is* objectively acceptable *if and only if x appears in the preferred extension for every specific audience.*

(h) $x \in AR$ *is* indefensible *if it is neither subjectively nor objectively acceptable.*

3.2 Argumentation over Ontology Alignments

Laera *et al.* [16] adopt the VAF, allowing agents to express preferences for different mapping types, and restrict the arguments to those concerning ontology mappings allowing agents to explicate their mapping choices.

Definition 4. *An agent,* Ag_i, *is characterised by the tuple* $< O_i, VAF_i, Pref_i, \epsilon_i >$ *where* O_i *is an ontology,* VAF_i *is the Value-based argumentation framework,* $Pref_i$ *is the private pre-ordering of preferences over the possible values,* $\mathcal{V}$, *and* ϵ_i *is the private threshold value.*

Laera *et al.* define the arguments as follows:

Definition 5. *An argument* $x \in AR$ *is a triple* $x = \langle G, m, \sigma \rangle$ *where m is a mapping, G is the grounds justifying the* prima facie *belief that the mapping does or does not hold and* σ *is one of* $\{+, -\}$ *depending on whether the argument is that m does or does not hold*

Laera [19] presents an algorithm for the agents to generate the arguments. The agents will argue for (+) a mapping if it is the agent's most preferred value in $\mathcal{V}$ and the degree of confidence, n, of the mapping is greater than the agents private threshold, ϵ; otherwise the agent will argue against (−) the mapping.

Laera *et al.* [1] also address the notion of attack; x is attacked by the assertion of its negation, $\neg x$, this counter-attack is defined as follows:

Definition 6. *An argument* $x \in AR$ *attacks an argument* $y \in AR$ *if x and y are arguments for the same mapping, m, but with different* σ. *For example, if* $x = \langle G_1, m, + \rangle$ *and* $y = \langle G_1, m, - \rangle$, *x counter-argues y and vice-versa.*

Table 1. The classification of different types of ontological alignment approaches

Semantic	M	These methods utilise model-theoretic semantics to determine whether or not there is a correspondence between two entities, and hence are typically deductive. Such methods may include propositional satisfiability and modal satisfiability techniques, or logic based techniques.
Internal Structural	IS	Methods for determining the similarity of two entities based on the internal structure, which may use criteria such as the range of their properties (attributes and relations), their cardinality, and the transitivity and/or symmetry of their properties to calculate the similarity between them.
External Structural	ES	Methods for determining external structure similarity may evaluate the position of the two entities within the ontological hierarchy, as well as comparing parent, sibling or child concepts.
Terminological	T	These methods lexically compare the strings (tokens or n-grams) used in naming entities, or in the labels and comments concerning entities. Such methods may employ normalisation techniques (often found in Information Retrieval systems) such as stemming or eliminating stop-words, etc.
Extensional	E	Extension-based methods which compare the extension of classes, i.e., their set of instances. Such methods may include determining whether or not the two entities share common instances, or may use alternate similarity based extension comparison metrics.

Furthermore, in [1] a way to instatiate the set of values $\mathcal{V}$ is also provided. These values depend on the methods used to generate the mappings; the possible values of $\mathcal{V}$ are described in Table 1.

The agents can now express, and exchange, their arguments about ontology mappings and decide from their perspective, audience, what arguments are in their preferred extension; but the agents still need to reach a mutually acceptable position with regards to what ontology alignment they actually agree upon. Laera *et al.*define the notion of *agreed* and *agreeable* alignment as follows:

Definition 7. *An* agreed alignment *is the set of mappings supported by those arguments which are in every preferred extension of every agent.*

Definition 8. *An* agreeable alignment *extends the agreed alignments with those mappings supported by arguments in some preferred extensions of every agent.*

Thus, a mapping is *rejected* if it is in neither the agreed nor agreeable alignment. Given the context of agent communication it is rational for the agents to accept as many candidate mappings as possible[16], thus both sets of alignments are considered. The agents should only completely disagree when they want the opposite, indeed, the agents gain little by arguing and not reaching some kind of agreement.

4   Ontology Modularization

Ontology modularization [10,11,12,13,14,15] refers to the process of fragmenting existing ontologies into a set of smaller, and possibly interconnected parts, or *modules*. Broadly speaking, modularization approaches aim to identify the minimal set of necessary concepts and definitions for different parts of the original ontology.

The reasons for modularizing can be different and range from ontology reuse in order to support the work of ontology engineers [12,11,20] to information integration[10], or to support efficient agent communication [21]. Thus, whilst size is often quoted for some modularization techniques, it unsuitable as an objective indicator of the quality of a module or the modularisation approach. This section reviews the different approaches for modularizing ontologies, focussing in particular on module extraction techniques, and presents the different techniques proposed in the literature for evaluating the result of modularization approaches.

An ontology O is defined as a pair $O = (Ax(O), Sig(O))$, where $Ax(O)$ is a set of axioms (intensional, extensional and assertional) and $Sig(O)$ is the signature of O [5]. This signature consists of the set of entity names used by O, i.e., its vocabulary. Ontology modularization is the process of defining a module $M = (Ax(M), Sig(M))$, where M is a subset of O, $M \subseteq O$, such that $Ax(M) \subseteq Ax(O)$ and $Sig(M) \subseteq Sig(O)$. No assumptions beyond this are made here about the nature of a module.

Approaches for modularizing ontologies belong to two main categories: ontology partitioning and ontology module extraction. *Ontology partitioning* is the process of fragmenting an ontology O into a set of (not necessarily disjoint[6]) modules $\mathcal{M} = \{M_1, M_2, ..., M_n\}$, such that the union of all the modules should be equivalent to the original ontology O; i.e. $\{M_1 \cup M_2 \cup ... \cup M_n\} = O$. Thus, a function $partition(O)$ can be formally defined as follows:

$$partition(O) \rightarrow \mathcal{M} = \{\{M_1, M_2, ..., M_n\} | \{M_1 \cup M_2 \cup ... \cup M_n\} = O\}$$

Ontology module extraction refers to the process of extracting a module M from an ontology O that covers a specified signature $Sig(M)$, such that $Sig(M) \subseteq Sig(O)$. M is the relevant part of O that is said to cover the elements defined by $Sig(M)$, therefore $M \subseteq O$. M is also considered as an ontology and could elicit further modules, depending on the signatures subsequently used. Thus, a function $extract(O, Sig(M))$ can be defined as follows:

$$extract(O, Sig(M)) \rightarrow \{M | M \subseteq O\}$$

This paper focusses on ontology module extraction approaches for query answering tassks, since the concept queried can form the basis of the signature used to extract modules. Ontology partitioning approaches are independent from any specific signature used to drive the modularization process, and thus would not reflect a query answering task. The techniques for ontology module extraction in the literature can be further subdivided into two distinct groups: *traversal approaches* and *logical approaches*. Traversal approaches [11,12,13,14] represent the extraction as a graph traversal, with the module being defined by the conditional traversal, which implicitly considers the ontological semantics, of the graph. Logical approaches [10,15] focus on maintaining the logical properties of coverage

---

[5] This definition is agnostic with respect to the ontology language used to represent the ontology, but it should be noted that the modularization techniques detailed in this section assume a description logic representation.

[6] This is in contrast to the mathematical definition of partitioning that requires partitions to be disjoint.

and minimality; as such, they explicitly consider the ontological semantics when extracting an ontology module.

4.1   Traversal Based Extraction

The following approaches perform a traversal based extraction of an ontology module. **d'Aquin *et al*** [11] address the specific task of extracting modules related to components found in a given web page. Their ontology module extraction technique is integrated within a larger *knowledge selection* process. The specific aim is to dynamically retrieve the relevant components from online ontologies to annotate the webpage currently being viewed in the browser. The knowledge selection process comprises of three phases: (i) selection of relevant ontologies, (ii) modularization of selected ontologies and (iii) merging of the relevant ontology modules. The principle used for the extraction of an ontology module (i.e. phase (ii)) is to include all the elements that participate in the definition of an entity, either directly being included in the definition or indirectly (similar to the approach proposed by Seidenberg and Rector [14]). There are two distinct characteristics of this approach:

- **Inferences** are used and computed during the extraction. This is in contrast with other approaches (as is the case with techniques such as Doran *et al* [12]) that assume that an inferred model (including all the derived inferences) is computed prior to the module extraction process. For example, the transitivity of the *subClassOf* edge allows new subclass relations to be inferred in the input ontology.
- **'Shortcuts'** are taken in the class hierarchy by including only the named classes that are the most specific common super-classes of the included classes. This is done by restricting the possible values of the *Least Common Subsumer(LCS)* algorithm [22] to the classes in the ontology.

Doran *et al*. [12] tackle the problem of ontology module extraction from the perspective of an Ontology Engineer wishing to reuse part of an existing ontology. The approach extracts an ontology module corresponding to a single user-supplied concept that is self-contained, concept-centred, and consistent. This approach is agnostic with respect to the language the ontology is represented in, provided that the ontology language itself can be transformed into the *Abstract Graph Model*. A conditional traversal descends down the *is-a* hierarchy from the signature concept; two edge sets are considered: one set of edges to traverse and a second set containing edges that are not traversed. Exceptions to these traversal sets are permitted during the first iteration of the algorithm. For example, when extracting an ontology module from an OWL ontology, `owl:disjointWith` edges are not traversed during the first iteration, but are considered in subsequent iterations (to prevent relevant definitions from being skipped).

Noy and Musen. [13] define the notion of *traversal view extraction*, which defines an *ontology view* of a specified concept, which is analogous to an ontology module. Starting from one class of the ontology being considered, relations from this class are recursively traversed to include the related entities. These relations are selected by the user, and for each relation selected, a depth of traversal (or *traversal directive*) is assigned. This traversal directive is used to halt the traversal of the corresponding relation when the specified depth is reached. A *traversal view* consists of a set of traversal directives. This flexible approach (which was incorporated into PROMPT [23]) allows an Ontology Engineer to iteratively construct the ontology module that they require by extending the current 'view'. However, this can require the Ontology Engineer to have a deep understanding of the ontology that is being used.

We do not consider this approach in our evaluation since it has a high degree of interactivity with the ontology engineer, that can affect the detemination of a module.

Seidenberg and Rector. [14] developed a technique specifically for extracting an ontology module for a given signature, $Sig(M)$, from the Galen ontology. Their technique identifies all elements that participate (even indirectly) to the definition of the signature, or other elements in the extracted module. The algorithm can be decomposed based on the assumption that assuming we have a $Sig(M) = \{A\}$. Firstly the hierarchy is upwardly traversed (analogous to Upper Cotopy defined in [24]), so all of the A's superclasses are included. Next the hierarchy is downwardly traversed so that all the A's subclasses are included. It should be noted that the sibling classes of A are not included. The restrictions, intersection, union and equivalent classes of the already included classes can now be added to the module. Lastly, links across the hierarchy from the previously included classes are traversed; the target of these links are also upwardly traversed.

Whilst the degree of generality for this approach is high (with respect to other ontologies), the focus on GALEN introduces certain features that may be less suitable for other ontologies. For example, result of property filtering can lead to class definitions becoming equivalent, whilst this is not incorrect it does introduce unnecessary definitions that can be transformed into primitive classes.

4.2 Logical Based Extraction

The logical based extraction techniques are based on the notion of conservative extension [25] whereby an ontology module extracted from a given ontology is considered a conservative extension if the entailments regarding the ontology module are captured totally within its signature. More formally Lutz *et al* [25] present the following definition:

Definition 9. *Let T_1 and T_2 be TBoxes formulated in a Description Logic (DL) $\mathcal{L}$, and let $\Gamma \subseteq sig(T_1)$ be a signature. Then $T_1 \cup T_2$ is a Γ-conservative extension of T_1 if for all $C_1, C_2 \in \mathcal{L}(\Gamma)$, we have $T_1 \models C_1 \sqsubseteq C_2$ iff $T_1 \cup T_2 \models C_1 \sqsubseteq C_2$.*

Thus, all the entailments regarding the signature of the ontology module are equivalent to using the ontology module with the ontology it was taken from. Unfortunately, Lutz *et al* [25] also show that deciding if an ontology O is a conservative extension is undecidable for OWL DL. However, Konev *et al* [15] have developed an algorithm, MEX, for extracting conservative extensions from acyclic terminologies formulated in more expressive types of DL ($\mathcal{ALCI}$ or $\mathcal{ELI}$) [7]. Whilst these restrictions limit the use of this approach, it can be successfully applied to large, real world ontologies such as SNOMED CT.

Grau *et al* [10] overcome the limitations of conservative extensions for more expressive description logics by utilizing approximations; they term these modules as locality-based modules. Coverage and safety are the properties that locality-based modules can guarantee, but this is done at the expense of minimality which is also guaranteed by conservative extensions. Coverage and safety [27] are defined in terms of a module being imported by a local ontology ($\mathcal{L}$) as follows:

Coverage. Extract everything the ontology defines for the specified terms. The module O' covers the ontology O for terms from, some signature, X if for all classes A and B built from terms in X, such that if $\mathcal{L} \cup O \models A \sqsubseteq B$ then $\mathcal{L} \cup O' \models A \sqsubseteq B$.

Safety. The meaning of the extracted terms is not changed. $\mathcal{L}$ uses the terms from X safely if for all classes A and B built from terms in X, such that if $\mathcal{L} \cup O' \models A \sqsubseteq B$ then $O' models A \sqsubseteq B$.

Two different variants of locality are described by Grau *et al* [28]. Syntactic locality can be computed in polynomial time, but semantic locality is PSPACE-complete. Syntactic locality is computed based on the syntactic structure of the axiom whereas semantic locality is computed based on the interpretation ($\mathcal{I}$) of the axiom. The issue concerning the syntactic locality is that syntactically different (but semantically equivalent) axioms can be treated differently. For example, Borgida and Giunchiglia [29] raise this issue of the syntactic approximation via the following example; consider the two sets of axioms $\{A \sqsubseteq (B \sqcap C)\}$ and $\{A \sqsubseteq B, A \sqsubseteq C\}$. These axioms are semantically equivalent, but the syntactic difference will effect the extraction process. The syntactic locality also can not handle tautologies, but this is unlikely to affect real world applications as ontologies with tautologies would be considered badly engineered.

4.3 Combining Ontology Modularization and Argumentation

Ontology modularization can be used as a pre-processing step to improve the efficiency of an argumentation framework, when used to search the space of all candidate ontology mappings. When two agents communicate, only the initiating agent (Ag_1) is aware of its task, and consequently, what concepts are relevant to this task. It can therefore select these relevant concepts within the signature of the desired ontology module. The signature of the resulting ontology module can then be used to filter the correspondences, and consequently the number of arguments necessary within the argumentation process. The steps in Table 2

---

[7] The expressivity of a DL is determined by the constructors allowed by the language, such as negation, existential restriction, etc. For more details we invite the reader to refer to [26].

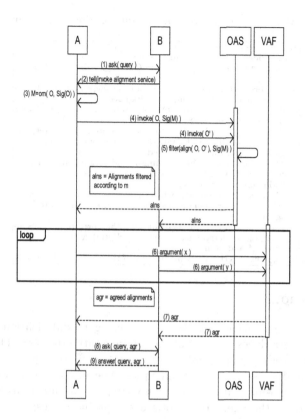

Fig. 1. UML Sequence Diagram of Ontology Modularization and Argumentation

describe this process, whilst Figure 1 depicts the process as a UML Sequence Diagram. It is assumed that two agents, Ag_1 and Ag_2 have ontologies O and O' respectively.

It is assumed that two agents, Ag_1 and Ag_2 have ontologies O and O' respectively.

The set of ontology correspondences are filtered at Step 5 according to the following function:

Definition 10. *A filtering function, filter(), filters the set of candidate mappings prior to argumentation Z into a subset $Z' \subseteq Z$ such that:*

$$filter(Z, Sig(M)) : Z \to Z' \mid \forall m \in Z' , \; m = \langle e, e', n, R \rangle \; and \; e \in Sig(M).$$

Steps 6 and 7 represent a black-box process, which is the argumentation process. Modularization is therefore used to filter the correspondences that are passed to this process. The combination of these two processes reduces the cost of reaching an agreement over the set of correspondences, by reducing the size of the set of correspondences, and hence the number of arguments.

Table 2. Steps involved in Ontology Modularization and Argumentation

1. Ag_1 asks a query, $query(A \in Sig(O))$, to Ag_2.
2. Ag_2 does not understand the query, $A \notin Sig(O')$, and informs Ag_1 they need to use an Ontology Alignment Service (OAS)
3. Ag_1 produces, $om(O, Sig(A))$, an ontology module, M, to cover the concepts required for its task.
4. Ag_1 and Ag_2 invoke the OAS. Ag_1 sends its ontology, O and the signature of M, $Sig(M)$.
5. The OAS aligns the two ontologies and filters the correspondences according to M. Only those correspondences featuring an entity from M are returned to both agents.
6. The agents begin the Meaning-Based Argumentation process, and iterate it, with each agent generating arguments and counter-arguments.
7. The iteration terminates when the agents reach an agreement on a set of correspondences, and this set is returned to both agents.
8. Ag_1 asks a query to Ag_2 but uses the correspondences so that Ag_2 understands, $query(A \in Sig(O) \wedge B \in Sig(O'))$ where A and B are aligned.
9. Ag_2 answers the query making use of the resulting alignment.

5   Evaluation

The aim of the evaluation is to show that using modularization to filter the set of alignments reduces the cost of the argumentation process. The evaluation considers how modularization affects the number of correspondences that are argued over and subsequently agreed upon. The aim is to demonstrate that using ontology modularization prior to invoking the argumentation lessens the effort required by the agent to negotiate acceptable correspondences without compromising the agent's ability to perform its task.

5.1   Evaluation Setup

The ontologies used in the evaluation are listed in Table 3, complete with details of the number of named classes, number of properties and the level of expressivity of the ontology. This is the same set as that available for the OAEI 2007 Conference track[8], with the exclusion of three ontologies[9]. This track has been selected since it is the one with the larger number of real world ontologies, allowing for more pairwise alignments than the other tracks (apart from the benchmark track, that uses artificial ontologies).

To the best of our knowledge, there is no canonical, hand-crafted gold standard for the alignments between the chosen ontologies. To explore the effectiveness of modularization with different alignment techniques and a baseline of valid alignments, the results of the Falcon-AO system[10] were used to provide a *gold standard* in the experiments. Falcon-AO is currently the best performing ontology alignment system, as it provides the best compromise between precision and recall in the alignment task performed for this track.

---

[8] http://oaei.ontologymatching.org/2007/conference/
[9] These ontologies have memory requirements of >1.5GB.
[10] http://iws.seu.edu.cn/projects/matching/

Table 3. Classes, properties, expressivity, and average % reduction in module size for the test datasets

Name	# Cl.	# Prop.	DL expressivity	% Reduction
Cmt	36	59	$\mathcal{ALCIF(D)}$	43
ConfTool	38	36	$\mathcal{SIF(D)}$	28
Crs	14	17	$\mathcal{SHIN}$	39
Edas	104	50	$\mathcal{ALCIF(D)}$	28
Ekaw	77	33	$\mathcal{SHIN(D)}$	34
Sofsem	60	64	$\mathcal{ALCHIF(D)}$	28
Micro	32	26	$\mathcal{ALCIOF(D)}$	14
Pcs	23	38	$\mathcal{ELUIF(D)}$	28
OpenConf	62	35	$\mathcal{ALCIO(D)}$	37
Paperdyne	47	82	$\mathcal{ALCHIOF(D)}$	0
Sigkdd	49	28	$\mathcal{ELI(D)}$	13

The experimental setup consisted of two main tracks:

1. **Builtin** - The possible alignments were determined by using simple textual and structural similarity between concepts and properties; essentially a combination of alignment techniques.
2. **Gold standard** - The possible alignments were those obtained by the Falcon-AO system.

For each track, each ontology has been compared to all other ontologies (excluding itself); for a total of 110 distinct pairs, giving us 220 tests in total. For each pair in the builtin track, the possible alignments have been computed, whilst for the gold standard track the alignments generated by the Falcon-AO system were used. In this evaluation we used Doran *et al*'s approach [12] to modularize the ontologies, as the method has been demonstrated to generate accurate modules for query answering tasks and its performance is comparable to several of the other methods described earlier [30]. The argumentation procedure was started, whereby two agents were created, each one adopting an ontology and using its own preferences. The number of correspondences argued over, broken down into accepted and rejected, was recorded for each test.

The result of the argumentation process between the ontologies when no modularization occurred was used as a baseline result for each pair. Table 3 presents the average reduction in size due to the modularization process; with the overall average being 26.5%. The Paperdyne ontology was not affected by the modularization process as it has a very shallow hierarchy with respect to the number of concepts, and has numerous properties which result in a highly interconnected ontology that is not amenable to modularization.

5.2 Results

The results indicate that ontology modularization has a considerable impact on the number of correspondences that are argued over. On average, this number is reduced by 75% (69% for the built-in and for the gold standard 79%). Figure 2 shows a scatter plot of all the test cases, with the x-axis being the baseline without modularization and the y-axis being that with modularization.

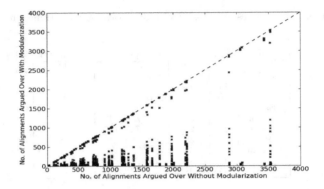

Fig. 2. A scatter plot showing the total number of correspondences argued over without and with modularization

The plot shows that there is a significant number of points where modularization has a considerable effect; it also shows in certain cases it has no effect, the cases where the point lies on the dotted line. Interestingly, and somewhat unexpectedly, there are a number of cases where the modularization (those cases where y is zero) effectively stops the argumentation process from taking place. This is an interesting result as it suggests that the agents are able to identify the cases where without modularization they would produce an alignment that would not help with their task. Thus, it is reasonable to postulate that combining modularization with argumentation should prevent cases where the use of argumentation is redundant.

The experiments identify three cases: those where modularization has no effect, where it reduces the number of correspondences, and where argumentation is redundant. Figure 3 shows the distribution of these three cases as a pie chart. This shows that the case where modularization has an effect (47.1%) is considerably larger than that where it has no effect (11.5%). More interestingly, perhaps, is that in 41.4% of the trials, the agents are stopped from entering an unnecessary argumentation process.

The two pie charts in Figures 4 and 5 show these three types of point split between the two tracks, builtin and gold standard. These show that when using the gold standard (i.e., the set of correspondences that has less noise), the cases where unnecessary argumentation is avoided are greater. Conversely the cases where modularization has no effect are greater in the builtin track. This would seem to suggest that OAS should aim to provide gold standard alignments, but in the likely case that this is not possible, then combining modularization with argumentation would be of benefit.

It is also interesting to see the effect that modularization has on the number of correspondences that are accepted by the argumentation process. Figure 6 shows

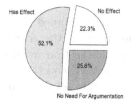

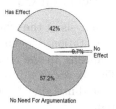

Fig. 3. Pie chart showing three different point types

Fig. 4. Pie chart showing the different point types for the builtin approach

Fig. 5. The different point types for the gold standard approach

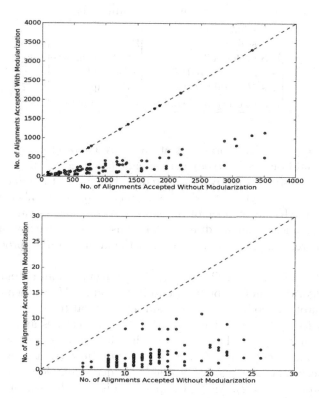

Fig. 6. Two scatter plots showing the number of correspondences accepted without and with modularization: top for the builtin and the bottom for the gold standard

the number of accepted correspondences without using the argumentation process against the number accepted when performing the argumentation process. These graphs support the intuition that since the agents are arguing over fewer correspondences then they eventually *agree* on fewer correspondences.

5.3 Effect on Cost

The analysis of the efficiency of the combined processes of modularization and argumentation depends on the effect on the cost of the combination of these mechanisms, in the remainder of this section we discuss this issue.

The six decision problems of the VAF and their associated complexity [7] are presented in Table 4, where S is a finite set of arguments and H is an argument system.

Table 4. Decision complexity in a VAF

Type of Decision	Complexity
Is S admissible?	P
Is S stable?	P
Is S preferred?	CO-NP complete
Is x in a preferred S?	NP-complete
Has H a stable extension?	NP-complete
Is x in *every* preferred S	$\Pi_2^{(p)}$-complete

All of the above decision problems are used by Laera *et al* [1] for each run of the argumentation over ontology correspondences. Due to this high complexity, there is a substantial motivation to reduce the size of the input; the input being the number of arguments which is correlated to the number of ontology correspondences. If the number of ontology correspondences can be reduced, then fewer arguments can be drawn, and whilst the complexity of the decision problems remains the same, the cost of the argumentation process can be reduced.

Consider the function $om(O, Sig(X))$ that implements an ontology module extraction algorithm and outputs an ontology module M. By definition (Section 4) an ontology module must be a subset or equal to the ontology it was derived from ($M \subseteq O$). If M has p entities, O has n entities and O' – the ontology we are aligning to – has m entities then in the worst case we now have $p \times m$ correspondences, where ($p \times m \leq n \times m$). However, this worst case is unlikely to occur and even less likely when considering ontologies of non trivial size (*i.e.*, whose size $s > 2$). Another implication is that there is an incentive to reduce M as much as possible, whilst ensuring that M is still suitable for the task required.

6 Conclusions

Agents need to reconcile ontological differences, especially within the context of open and dynamic environments where no *a priori* assumptions about the nature of the ontology can be made. Negotiation frameworks (such as the *Meaning-based argumentation* framework), allows agents to negotiate over different ontology correspondences, and identify those alignments that are mutually acceptable.

However, this collaborative search is computationally costly, as the complexity of the decision problems involved range from P to $\Pi_2^{(p)}$-complete. However, *Ontology Modularization* can be exploited to reduce the size of the search space, and hence cost of finding acceptable alignments. The use of ontology modularization as a filter-based pre-processing stage was evaluated empirically, and found to reduce the average number of correspondences (and hence size of the search space) presented to the argumentation framework by 75%, across a number of different ontology pairs. In addition, three patterns emerged: i) where no reduction in size occurred (in 11.5% of cases on average); ii) where the number of correspondences was reduced (47.1%); and iii) where modules of size zero were found (41.4%). We found that this latter case corresponded to failure scenarios; i.e. where the subsequent transaction could fail due to insufficient alignment between the ontologies. Thus, this paper demonstrates that ontology modularization not only reduces the cost of negotiating over correspondences and establishing communication, but can be used to identify cases where negotiation will fail to identify relevant correspondences to support meaningful queries.

References

1. Laera, L., Blacoe, I., Tamma, V.A.M., Payne, T.R., Euzenat, J., Bench-Capon, T.J.M.: Argumentation over ontology correspondences in mas. In: Durfee, E.H., Yokoo, M., Huhns, M.N., Shehory, O. (eds.) AAMAS, p. 228 (2007)
2. Berners-Lee, T., Hendler, J., Lassila, O.: The semantic web. Scientific American 284 (2001)
3. van Diggelen, J., Beun, R.J., Dignum, F., van Eijk, R.M., Meyer, J.J.: Ontology negotiation in heterogeneous multi-agent systems: The anemone system. Applied Ontology 2, 267–303 (2007)
4. dos Santos, C.T., Quaresma, P., Vieira, R.: Conjunctive queries for ontology based agent communication in mas. In: 7th International Joint Conference on Autonomous Agents and Multiagent Systems (AAMAS 2008), Estoril, Portugal, May 12-16, vol. 2, pp. 829–836 (2008)
5. Euzenat, J., Shvaiko, P.: Ontology Matching. Springer, Heidelberg (2007)
6. Patel-Schneider, P.F., Hayes, P., Horrocks, I.: OWL Web Ontology Language Semantics and Abstract Syntax (2004)
7. Dunne, P., Bench-Capon, T.: Complexity in value-based argument systems. In: Alferes, J.J., Leite, J. (eds.) JELIA 2004. LNCS (LNAI), vol. 3229, pp. 360–371. Springer, Heidelberg (2004)
8. Cuenca-Grau, B., Parsia, B., Sirin, E., Kalyanpur, A.: Automatic Partitioning of OWL Ontologies Using E-Connections. In: Proceedings of the 2005 International Workshop on Description Logics, DL 2005 (2005)
9. Stuckenschmidt, H., Klein, M.: Structure-based partitioning of large concept hierarchies. In: Proceedings of the 3rd International Semantic Web Conference, Hiroshima, Japan (2004)
10. Cuenca Grau, B., Horrocks, I., Kazakov, Y., Sattler, U.: Modular reuse of ontologies: Theory and practice. J. of Artificial Intelligence Research (JAIR) 31, 273–318 (2008)

11. d'Aquin, M., Sabou, M., Motta, E.: Modularization: a key for the dynamic selection of relevant knowledge components. In: ISWC 2006, Athens, Georgia, USA (2006)
12. Doran, P., Tamma, V.A.M., Iannone, L.: Ontology module extraction for ontology reuse: an ontology engineering perspective. In: Silva, M.J., Laender, A.H.F., Baeza-Yates, R.A., McGuinness, D.L., Olstad, B., Olsen, Ø.H., Falcão, A.O. (eds.) CIKM, pp. 61–70. ACM, New York (2007)
13. Noy, N.F., Musen, M.A.: Specifying ontology views by traversal. In: International Semantic Web Conference, pp. 713–725 (2004)
14. Seidenberg, J., Rector, A.: Web ontology segmentation: analysis, classification and use. In: WWW 2006: Proceedings of the 15th international conference on World Wide Web, pp. 13–22. ACM Press, New York (2006)
15. Konev, B., Lutz, C., Walther, D., Wolter, F.: Semantic modularity and module extraction in description logics. In: Proceedings of ECAI 2008: 18th European conference on Artificial Intelligence (2008)
16. Laera, L., Blacoe, I., Tamma, V., Payne, T., Euzenat, J., Bench-Capon, T.: Argumentation over Ontology Correspondences in MAS. In: Proc. of the 6th Int. Joint Conf. on Autonomous Agents and Multiagent Systems, pp. 1285–1292 (2007)
17. Bench-Capon, T.: Persuasion in practical argument using value-based argumentation frameworks. Journal of Logic and Computation 13, 429–448 (2003)
18. Dung, P.M.: On the acceptability of arguments and its fundamental role in non-monotonic reasoning, logic programming and n-person games. Artificial Intelligence 77, 321–357 (1995)
19. Laera, L.: Toward shared understanding - an argumentation based approach for communication in open multi-agent systems (2008)
20. Noy, N.F., Musen, M.A.: PROMPT: Algorithm and Tool for Automated Ontology Merging and Alignment. In: Proceedings of the Seventeenth National Conference on Artificial Intelligence and Twelfth Conference on Innovative Applications of Artificial Intelligence, pp. 450–455. AAAI Press/The MIT Press (2000)
21. Doran, P., Tamma, V., Palmisano, I., Payne, T.R.: Dynamic selection of ontological alignments: a space reduction mechanism. In: Twenty-First International Joint Conference on Artificial Intelligence, IJCAI 2009 (2009)
22. Cohen, W.W., Borgida, A., Hirsh, H.: Computing least common subsumers in description logics. In: AAAI, pp. 754–760 (1992)
23. Noy, N.F., Musen, M.A.: The PROMPT suite: interactive tools for ontology merging and mapping. International Journal of Human-Computer Studies 59, 983–1024 (2003)
24. Maedche, A., Staab, S.: Measuring similarity between ontologies. In: Gómez-Pérez, A., Benjamins, V.R. (eds.) EKAW 2002. LNCS (LNAI), vol. 2473, pp. 251–263. Springer, Heidelberg (2002)
25. Lutz, C., Walther, D., Wolter, F.: Conservative extensions in expressive description logics. In: [31], pp. 453–458
26. Baader, F., Calvanese, D., McGuinness, D.L., Nardi, D., Patel-Schneider, P.F. (eds.): The Description Logic Handbook: Theory, Implementation and Applications, Cambridge (2007)
27. Cuenca Grau, B., Horrocks, I., Kazakov, Y., Sattler, U.: Just the right amount: Extracting modules from ontologies. In: WWW 2007, Proceedings of the 16th International World Wide Web Conference, Banff, Canada, May 8-12, pp. 717–727 (2007)
28. Grau, B.C., Horrocks, I., Kazakov, Y., Sattler, U.: A logical framework for modularity of ontologies. In: [31], pp. 298–303

29. Borgida, A., Giunchiglia, F.: Importing from functional knowledge bases - a preview. In: Cuenca-Grau, B., Honavar, V., Schlicht, A., Wolter, F. (eds.) WOMO (2007)
30. Palmisano, I., Tamma, V., Payne, T.R., Doran, P.: Task oriented evaluation of module extraction techniques. In: Bernstein, A., Karger, D.R., Heath, T., Feigenbaum, L., Maynard, D., Motta, E., Thirunarayan, K. (eds.) ISWC 2009. LNCS, vol. 5823, pp. 130–145. Springer, Heidelberg (2009)
31. Veloso, M.M. (ed.): IJCAI 2007, Proceedings of the 20th International Joint Conference on Artificial Intelligence, Hyderabad, India, January 6-12 (2007)

Applying Dialogue Games to Manage Recommendation in Social Networks

Stella Heras, Martí Navarro, Vicente Botti, and Vicente Julián

Department of Information Systems and Computation
Technical University of Valencia
Camino de Vera s/n. 46022 Valencia (Spain)
Tel.: (+34) 96 387 73 50; Fax: (+34) 96 387 73 59

Abstract. Recommendation in social networks is a new area of research that is still in its early beginnings. In this framework, every user can act as an individual recommender for its neighbours in the network. However, social networks are highly dynamic environments where the structure of the network and the information spread across it evolve quickly over time. In these settings, a suitable recommender must be able to manage continuous changes and to provide users with up-to-date and customised recommendations. With this aim, the theory of dialogue games has been applied to manage recommendation dialogues in social networks in this research. As a result, a dialogue game for controlling the interaction between an agent asking for recommendations to other personal agents that are its neighbours in the network has been designed. In addition, a complex decision-making policy based on this game has been developed and tested in a simulation scenario. The results are shown and discussed in this paper.

1 Introduction

As the Internet evolves quickly, the use of social networks as social structures that relate entities (i.e. individuals or organisations) by means of links representing different types of interdependence does it as well. In these networks, people exchange a great deal of information with their neighbours (i.e. other people that are linked with them). Therefore, there is a problem of information overload that results in a need for recommendation systems that help users to reach the information that fits more their preferences [7].

In contrast with the first approaches of centralised recommendation systems, which featured a central recommender entity that has unlimited access to the preferences and profiles of all users of the system, collaborative recommendation among users that have a partial knowledge about others is gaining an increasing interest. The decentralised nature of Multi-Agent Systems (MAS) makes them a very suitable paradigm to develop collaborative recommendation systems. Common features of collaborative recommenders, such as dynamism, partial knowledge, privacy, etc. perfectly fit with the MAS approach. Therefore, recent research in MAS has dealt with recommendation among a set of personal agents that represent users. Most approaches are focused on developing models of trust and reputation in recommender systems [8][10]. In social simulation research, this focus is also the current trend [2]. However, our work copes with other dimension in the area of collaborative recommendation, the problem

P. McBurney et al. (Eds.): ArgMAS 2009, LNAI 6057, pp. 256–272, 2010.
© Springer-Verlag Berlin Heidelberg 2010

of coordinating the interaction between agents to get the maximum profit from the recommendation process. In this paper, we propose the use of a well-known concept of argumentation theory, *dialogue games* [5], as a mechanism to manage recommendation in social networks.

When dealing with the problem of making recommendations in social networks, the high dynamism of the network structure and of the information that is spread across it must be taken into account. Agents' objectives and preferences may change and even, they could not be completely specified when the recommendation process begins. Argumentation provides a useful tool for gathering information to provide agents with a recommendation that better suits their profile. In our model, the best recommendation is selected by using an argumentation dialogue game. Our model allows recommenders to justify their proposals and to persuade other agents to accept their recommendations. Next sections show the formal specification of the dialogue game, propose a dialogue-based decision policy for the initiator of the recommendation dialogue and provide an example of the dialogue game that demonstrates the advantages of using this model for item recommendation in social networks.

2   Argumentation Based Recommendation in Social Networks

The management of recommendation processes in social networks is an ongoing field of research. As pointed out before, argumentation allows recommender agents to justify their recommendations and to persuade other agents to accept them. In addition, by engaging in an argumentation-based recommendation process, agents can also receive feedback from their neighbours to provide better recommendations in the future.

Our aim is to study the advantages of applying dialogue games as a mechanism for modelling the dialogue between agents that share their recommendations in a social network. Dialogue games are interactions between several players where each player moves by advancing locutions in accordance to a set of rules. In MAS, dialogue games have been recently applied as a tool for specifying communication protocols [6] and for evaluating reputation [1]. The application of argumentation techniques to social networks, however, is an innovative area of research.

Our work is based on a general dialogue game, the *Argumentation Scheme Dialogue (ASD)* [9], which extends traditional dialogue games with certain stereotyped patterns of common reasoning called *argumentation schemes*. Concretely, we have instantiated this game by making use of a specific argumentation scheme, the *Argument from Expert Opinion* [11] that captures the way in which people evaluates the opinions (recommendations in our context) of experts (agents with some knowledge about a set of items to recommend). The structure of the scheme is the following:

- *Major Premise:* Source E is an expert in field F containing proposition A.
- *Minor Premise:* E asserts that proposition A (in field F) is true (false).
- *Conclusion:* A may plausibly be taken to be true (false).

Moreover, this scheme also has a set of *critical questions*, which represent the possible attacks that can be made to rebut the conclusion drawn from the scheme and hence, are very useful for coordinating the dialogue:

1. Expertise: How credible is E as an expert source?
2. Field: Is E an expert in the field F that A is in?
3. Opinion: What did E assert that implies A?
4. Trustworthiness: Is E personally reliable as a source?
5. Consistency: Is A consistent with what other experts assert?
6. Backup Evidence: Is E's assertion based on evidence?

Next section describes the dialogue-based recommendation framework proposed.

3 Dialogue Game Protocol

In this paper, we consider a distributed recommendation system consisting of a set of agents that use a social network to ask their neighbours for recommendations about items. Each agent has a preference profile that represents its preferences about the items recommended in the system. In addition, agents have a knowledge database that stores their reviews about the items that they personally know. Therefore, the knowledge is distributed across the network and agents only have a partial view of it (which fits the assumptions of the common algorithms used for social network analysis). *Level-k* recommendations are also allowed and, if an agent receives a recommendation request about an item that it does not know, it propagates the request to their own neighbours. At the end of each recommendation process, the initiator agent gives feedback to the participants about the usefulness of their recommendation.

Furthermore, two measures of social network analysis have been used to provide agents with the information that they need to decide between different recommendations from several neighbours. On one hand, the edges of the social network are directed and weighted with a *local confidence measure* $c_{ij} \in [-1, 1]$ that shows the success of the recommendations that an agent a_i has received from the agent a_j (equation 1).

$$c_{ij} = \frac{\sum_{k=1}^{K} u_{j(k)}}{K} \tag{1}$$

On the other hand, the *expertise degree* e_j of an agent as recommender is calculated by adding the confidence values that all its neighbours have about it (equation 2).

$$e_j = \frac{\sum_{i=1}^{I} c_{ij}}{deg^+(a_j)} \tag{2}$$

In the equations, $u_{j(k)}$ is the usefulness degree of the recommendation k that an agent accepted from its neighbour a_j, K is the total number of recommendations accepted by an agent, I is the total number of neighbours that an agent has and $deg^+(a_j)$ is the *centrality indegree* of a_j (the number of neighbours that have incoming links to this agent). Confidence and expertise degrees are updated at the end of each recommendation process. Note that, although they could be considered subjective and could be risky for an agent to believe them by default, these measures are defeasible and the interaction protocol explained in the next section allows agents to argue about them.

Finally, each agent is assumed to have its own reasoning mechanism for evaluating preferences, matching them with its review database and proposing recommendations. In addition, agents must also know a set of inference rules and the scheme from expert opinion to be able to create arguments. The definition of the individual reasoning mechanisms of agents are out of the scope of this paper. Here, we have focused on formalising the dialogue-based interaction protocol.

3.1 Interaction Protocol Specification

The Dialogue Game Protocol proposed in this paper is a simplification of the ASD game instantiated with the Argument from Expert Opinion scheme. On one hand, the protocol assumes the existence of:

- A finite set of players denoted *Agents*, with elements $\{a_i, a_1, ..., a_n\}$, consisting of the agent a_i that plays the *Initiator* role and starts the dialogue and its neighbours $\{a_1, ..., a_n\}$ in the social network that play the role of recommendations' *proponents*.
- A finite set of items to recommend, denoted *Items*, with elements $\{i_1, ..., i_m\}$. Each item consists of the pair $i = <type, ID>$, where $type$ represents the class of the item (e.g. restaurant) and ID is an unique identifier for each item. Agents can only recommend items if they personally know them.
- A finite set of discrete values that represent the feedback that an agent offers to the dialogue participants about their recommendation, denoted *Usefulness*, with elements *-1: Inappropriate, 0: Useless or 1: Useful*.
- A finite set of variables that represent the agent's preferences when it asks for a recommendation, denoted *Preferences*, with elements $\{p_1, ..., p_q\}$.
- A function *preference:* $P \to F \times V$, which maps each Preference of an agent to a pair $< f, v >$, where f $\in$ Features and v $\in$ Values.
- A function *review: Item* $\to 2^{F \times V}$, which maps each Item reviewed by the agent to a set $\{< f_1, v_1 >, ..., < f_r, v_r >\}$, where f $\in$ Features and v $\in$ Values.
- A function *feedback: Item* $\to Usefulness$, which maps an Item that an agent has recommended to one of the possible values of usefulness.

On the other hand, some variations in the original ASD game have also been included:

- Walton's Strategic Rules have been reformulated as McBurney and Parsons' Commencement and Termination Rules [5].
- For the sake of simplicity, we assume that the fact that an agent asserts a recommendation or an argument commits it to having a reason (inferred from its database of reviews, by social network analysis or from the knowledge acquired during the dialogue) for doing so. Therefore, agents only have propositional commitments either to the last recommendation that they have offered or accepted or to the arguments that they have posed (until they are rebutted). Those commitments are stored in a Dialogue Record *DR* that shows the current state of the dialogue and represents the *commitment stores* [3] of the agents:

$$DR^t = (< a_1, ID_1, \alpha_1 >, ..., < a_n, ID_n, \alpha_n >, d^t) \tag{3}$$

where DR^t stores the identifiers ID_j of the items recommended by each neighbour a_j, the arguments α_j that support each recommendation and the preliminary decision of the initiator to accept $d^t \in \{ID_1, ..., ID_n\}$ as the best recommendation at the step t of the dialogue. Arguments in this model can be reviews about items that justify recommendations or values of confidence or expertise that stand out the recommendation of a specific neighbour from other recommendations.

Finally, the interaction protocol between the agents of the network has been modeled as a formal dialogue game with the components identified by McBurney and Parsons [2]:

- Commencement Rules: The dialogue starts when an agent asks other agents in a social network for a recommendation about an specific item. At that moment, the initiator of the dialogue uses the network to contact their neighbours and send them its preferences about the item. When neighbours have received the recommendation request with the preferences of the initiator, they use their own reasoning mechanisms to match these preferences with their reviews database and offer a recommendation. Eventually, neighbours can decide not to engage in the recommendation dialogue.
- Locutions:
  - Statements: are the permissible locutions in the dialogue and their compounds (propose(Item,Preferences), accept, reject and assert(Data)). Data can be reviews, preferences or arguments, depending on the stage of the dialogue when this locution is stated.
  - Withdrawals: noCommitment(Item) is the locution for withdrawing recommendations.
  - Questions: propose(Item,Preferences)? is used to request recommendations from neighbours. Also, the locution assert({Preferences})? asks the initiator for more information about its preferences when there are some unspecified. Agents are not committed to answering questions.
  - Critical Attacks (CA): the locution pose(CA) poses a critical attack associated with one of the critical questions of the Argument from Expert Opinion scheme. In our model we assume (a) that all agents have some knowledge about the items of the domain and hence, every agent can be considered expert to some extent (Field question); (b) that agents are rational and always propose the recommendation that, using their reasoning mechanisms, fits the preferences of the initiator the most (Opinion question) and (c) that agents are honest and their recommendations and arguments are based on their own reviews and knowledge (Backup evidence question). Thus, permissible attacks to recommendations are: (i) questioning the degree of expertise of the proponent (Expertise question); (ii) demonstrating that the proponent is not personally reliable as recommender (Trustworthiness question) or (iii) demonstrating that the proponent's recommendation is not consistent with the one of other expert with equal or greater degree of expertise (Consistency question). The burden of proof in the case of the Trustworthiness and Consistency attacks falls on the initiator and therefore, if the attack is challenged, it is committed to providing the proponent with arguments that justify those criticisms.

- Challenges: why(locution)?, where locution can be a recommendation proposal or a critical attack, requests arguments that support them.
- Commitment Rules:
  - Before the assertion of the locution propose(Item, Preferences), if proponents have different recommendations that match the preferences of the initiator, they are committed to ask it for specifying those preferences that could stand out a recommendation from the rest.
  - The assertion of the locution propose(Item, Preferences) adds the recommended item to the Dialogue Record and commits the proponent to the assumptions that the game makes about the critical questions of the Argument from Expert Opinion scheme.
  - The assertion of the locution noCommitment(Item), withdraws the recommendation made by the proponent from the Dialogue Record and frees it from all commitments.
  - The assertion of the locution why(propose(Item, Preferences))? commits the proponent of the recommendation either to providing the initiator with a justification about its proposal or to withdrawing it.
  - If a critical attack pose(CA) is challenged, the initiator is committed to providing arguments to justify it.
- Dialogue Rules:
  1. The recommendation process consists of a set of parallel dialogues between the initiator and its neighbours. If neighbours decide to engage in the dialogue, they acquire the role of recommendation's proponents. At each step of the dialogue, the initiator advances (or receives) a locution to (from) one proponent. The initiator centralises the control of the dialogue and proponents do not speak directly between them. However, the initiator can use the information provided by a proponent when it is arguing with another.
  2. The initiator agent opens the recommendation process asking for recommendation proposals with the locution propose(Item, Preferences)?. This can be followed either by a neighbour's request for information about specific preferences (assert(Preferences)?), a recommendation proposal (propose(Item, Preferences)) or, if the neighbour is not interested in engaging in the dialogue, a rejection statement (reject).
  3. When neighbours receive a call for proposals, they can ask iteratively for more preferences (assert (Preferences)?) while the initiator accedes to provide them (assert(Preferences)). The process ends when the neighbour proposes a recommendation and acquires the role of proponent or when it rejects to make the proposal.
  4. The neighbours' locution propose(Item, Preferences) starts the dialogue. Afterwards, the initiator can either challenge the proposal with a request for an argument that supports the recommendation (why(propose(Item, Preferences))?), accept the recommendation (accept) or reject it (reject).
  5. In case a recommendation is challenged, the proponent can answer the challenge either by justifying its proposal or by withdrawing it (noCommitment (Item)). To date, justifications consist basically in showing to the initiator the proponent's review about the item that matches the recommendation request

(assert(Review)). However, if a complex reasoning process to select a specific recommendation among a set had been carried out, this justification could show the rules or the methodology applied to reach to this conclusion.

6. The locution assert(Review) in response to a challenge can be followed by the initiator's acceptance of the recommendation (accept), its rejection (reject) or a critical attack associated with the Argument from Expert Opinion. As pointed out before, possible attacks are: (i) pose(Expertise), (ii) pose(Trustworthiness) or pose(Consistency).

7. Trustworthiness or Consistency attacks can also be challenged by the proponent that receives them (why(pose(Trustworthiness))? and why(pose(Consistency))?). In that case, the initiator is committed to providing an argument that justifies the attack (assert(Argument)).

8. Proponents can answer attacks with the locution assert(Argument), which tries to rebut the attack, or by withdrawing their proposals (noCommitment(Item)).

9. Finally, the initiator can accept the argument of a proponent and choose its recommendation ending the dialogue, preliminary accept its argument but pose again a different critical attack (same attacks to the same proponent cannot be repeated to avoid infinite dialogues) or reject the argument and hence the recommendation (ending the dialogue with this proponent).

– Termination Rules: The initiator agent keeps at every moment the entire control of the recommendation process. The preferences of the initiator do not change during the dialogue and proponents are assumed to be rational and honest. Thus, once a recommendation has been proposed, it cannot be changed. Proponents are only allowed to propose items, to answer challenges and critical attacks and to withdraw their recommendations. The game ends when the initiator has taken a decision among the set of available recommendations, which can happen at any time during the dialogue. Afterwards, the proponents are informed and receive the accept/reject locutions to their recommendations. However, after a maximum time is exceeded, the recommendation partially accepted to this step of the dialogue (i.e. d^t in the Dialogue Record) is taken as the final decision.

3.2 Decision-Making Policies

During the recommendation dialogue, the initiator agent has to make a decision about what recommendation should be chosen from the set of all received recommendations. That decision depends on the *decision policy* that the agent follows during the dialogue. The different policies that an agent can follow determine the decision-making algorithms for the locutions of the dialogue game.

Therefore, following a decision policy based on the *expertise* of the proponents, for instance, the initiator would always choose the recommendation proposed by that proponent with a higher degree of expertise. However, if the initiator agent relies more on its own experience, it could follow a decision policy based on the *confidence* in the recommendations provided by its neighbours during previous dialogues. In that case, the initiator would always choose the recommendation of the proponent that provided it with more useful recommendations. Other basic decision policy could be based on the *frequency* of the proposals received. Therefore, the initiator would choose the most

most frequent recommendation as the best one. In all these policies, a random choice could be made in case of draw. However, they do not allow proponents to argue about the decisions of the initiator and neither allow the initiator to ask proponents for justifications about their recommendations. Thus, basic decision policies do not profit from the dialogical possibilities of the interaction protocol presented in this paper.

In this section, a more elaborated decision-making policy is proposed. By following this policy, agents can argue about recommendations, attacking others' recommendations and persuading the initiator to accept theirs. The main idea is that proponents will always try to persuade the initiator to accept their recommendation. With this aim, every proponent will use all its resources up to rebut arguments supporting other recommendations and to demonstrate that its recommendation is the best. The arguments that a proponent can use to persuade the initiator are different for each challenge or attack that it can receive:

- Challenge about its recommendation: in the current development of our model, the proponent can show its recommendation review, allowing the initiator to compare it with other recommendations.
- Expertise critical attack: the proponent can show its expertise degree. Note that this attack is necessary since, due to privacy reasons, the initiator does not know the expertise degree of its neighbours by default.
- Trustworthiness critical attack: the proponent can challenge the attack. In that case, the initiator is committed to providing the proponent with an argument justifying the attack. There are two possible types of supporting arguments that the initiator can show: (a) a negative confidence degree in the recommendations provided by the proponent to it or (b) a comparison between the confidence degree in the proponent and the one in other neighbour whose recommendations' confidence outperforms the proponent's and that has proposed a different recommendation.

In the former case (a), the argument only refers to the negative proponent's confidence degree from the point of view of the initiator and hence, the proponent can only rebut the attack if a *level-k* recommendation process was performed and the recommendation was actually proposed by one of its own neighbours a_k. In that case, the level-k neighbour's confidence degree c_{pk} (the confidence in the recommendations received by the proponent from its neighbour) could improve the one that the initiator a_i has from the proponent a_p, c_{ip}. The formal definition of this type of rebuttal is shown in equation 4.

$$\begin{aligned} Argument \; AR = c \quad & \left| c_{pk} \; attacks \; c_{ip} \quad iff \right. \\ attacks \subseteq AR \; x \; AR & \left| c_{ip} < 0 < c_{pk} \right. \end{aligned} \tag{4}$$

In the latter case (b), if the proponent has an own negative confidence degree in the recommendations of the other neighbour c_{pn}, it has the opportunity to rebut the argument supporting the other neighbour's recommendation by showing this negative confidence to the initiator. This rebuttal is defined by the attack relation of equation 5.

$$Argument\ AR = (c, \delta, c)$$
$$partial\ ordering\ relation\ \delta = \{<\}$$
$$attacks \subseteq AR\ x\ AR \qquad\qquad (5)$$
$$(c_{pn}, <, c_{in})\ attacks\ (c_{ip}, <, c_{in})\quad iff$$
$$c_{in} - c_{ip} < c_{in} - c_{pn}$$

In addition, if a *level-k* recommendation was performed, the confidence of the proponent on its own neighbour (who has really proposed the recommendation) c_{pk} could outperform both the one that the initiator has about the proponent c_{ip} and the one that it has about the other neighbour c_{in}, as shown in equation 6.

$$Argument\ AR = (c, \delta, c)$$
$$partial\ ordering\ relation\ \delta = \{<\}$$
$$attacks \subseteq AR\ x\ AR \qquad\qquad (6)$$
$$(c_{in}, <, c_{pk})\ attacks\ (c_{ip}, <, c_{in})\quad iff$$
$$0 < c_{ip} < c_{in} < c_{pk}$$

Note that, in case a *level-k* recommendation was carried out and proponents try to persuade the initiator by using arguments of the types shown in equations 4 and 6, the initiator could only be persuaded if it does not have a direct relation with the *level-k* proponent (the initiator does not personally know it).

– Consistency critical attack: likewise, the attack can be challenged and the initiator must provide an argument for supporting it. This argument consist of a comparison between the expertise degree of the proponent e_p and the one of other neighbour that has an expertise degree e_n higher than the proponent's one and that has proposed a different recommendation. In this case, the proponent can rebut the attack if a *level-k* recommendation process was performed and the recommendation was actually proposed by one of its neighbours that has a higher expertise degree e_k than itself and the initiator's neighbour. This argument is specified in equation 7.

$$Argument\ AR = (e, \delta, e)$$
$$partial\ ordering\ relation\ \delta = \{<\}$$
$$attacks \subseteq AR\ x\ AR \qquad\qquad (7)$$
$$(e_n, <, e_k)\ attacks\ (e_p, <, e_n)\quad iff$$
$$e_p < e_n < e_k$$

The attack relations define which arguments are considered valid in this model. Hence, these arguments could persuade the initiator to provisionally accept a recommendation unless other agent poses more attacks. However, the ultimate decision about wether accepting or not a recommendation depends on the initiator's reasoning mechanism. Similarly, the initiator's decision for attacking a specific proponent with certain argument from the set of all available arguments is determined by its internal reasoning design. Moreover, if the proponent agent has several possible arguments to rebut the initiator's critical attack, the decision about which argument should be sent to the initiator depends also on its own reasoning mechanism design.

In addition, proponents do not know which are the other neighbours engaged in the dialogue. Thus, it could happen that an agent tries to rebut a critical attack by sending to the initiator an argument that implies an agent that the initiator personally knows. In that case, the initiator would make a decision and would rely more on its own knowledge or on the experience of the proponent. Furthermore, when an agent that the initiator did not previously know is turned to during the dialogue, the initiator adds it as a new neighbour at the end of the process and reports it the usefulness of its recommendation.

4   Restaurant Recommendation Example

In this section, an example application of the dialogue-based interaction protocol proposed is shown. Let us consider a situation in which an agent wants to reserve a table for a dinner with some friends in Valencia (Spain) and it asks its neighbours in a social network for recommendations. Figure 1 shows a partial view of the social network of the initiator agent a_i. Nodes represent agents and are labelled with their expertise degree $e_j | j = [1..A]$. In what follows, we will refer to neighbour agents as: $a1_l$ (i.e. 1st level neighbour on the left), $a1_c$ (i.e. 1st level neighbour on the centre), $a1_r$ (i.e. 1st level neighbour on the right) and $a2$ (i.e. 2nd level neighbour). Edges $a_j \rightarrow a_k$ represent friendness relationships and are labelled with the confidence degree $c_{a_j a_k}$ in the recommendations received by a_j from a_k.

Moreover, let us suppose that neighbour $a1_l$ has exactly one item review that fits the preferences of the initiator in its reviews database, that neither neighbour $a1_r$ nor

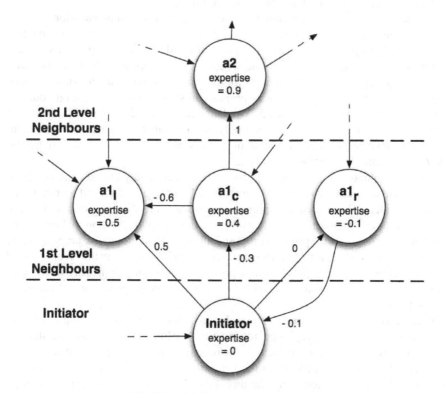

Fig. 1. Partial view of the Social Network

its own neighbours have any suitable item to recommend and that neighbour $a1_c$ has not found any item that matches the initiator's preferences in its reviews and hence, it has started a level-2 recommendation dialogue with its neighbour $a2$. Table 1 shows a partial view of the reviews database of the neighbour $a2$.

Table 1. Reviews Database of the 2nd level neighbour

Item Type	Item ID	Location	Cuisine	Groups
Restaurant	Salita	Valencia	Creative	Yes
Restaurant	Fila	Valencia	Tapas	No
Restaurant	Sarieta	Valencia	Mediterranean	Yes

Table 2 shows a summary of the recommendation dialogue of this example. Note that, as pointed out before, the initiator is looking for a restaurant for a group dinner in Valencia and thus, Preferences = {<Location, Valencia>,<GR, Yes>}. The Dialogue Record DR^t tracks the proposals of each proponent, their arguments and the preliminary decision of the initiator agent for accepting a specific proposal at each step t of the dialogue d^t. Note that. if no more information is provided, the initiator preliminary accepts the proposal of the agent with higher confidence degree from its point of view. In addition, the table also shows the parallel dialogue that $a1_c$ has with its own neighbour $a2$, which is tracked by $a1_c$ in its Dialogue Record DR'^t.

The dialogue starts when the initiator sends a request for recommendations to their neighbours in the social network. Then, neighbour $a1_l$ proposes its recommendation in step 1 and neighbour $a1_r$ rejects engaging in the dialogue in step 2. In steps 2.1 neighbour $a1_c$ propagates the recommendation request to its neighbour $a2$ and, after the necessary steps to answer the request for more information of neighbour $a2$ in steps 2.1 to 4.1, neighbour $a2$ also makes its proposal in step 4.2 and hence, neighbour $a1_c$ propagates it to the initiator in step 5. The latter shows an advantage of our dialogue game protocol, since $a1_c$ is allowed not only to propagate the request for recommendation to its own neighbours, but also to fit its proposal to the initiator's preferences by asking it for more information about them.

When the initiator has received all proposals, it preliminary chooses the one from the proponent with more confidence degree (i.e. $a1_l$) in step 5. If the initiator had used a basic confidence-based decision policy, for instance, the dialogue would end here choosing the recommendation of $a1_l$. However, the complex decision-making policy based on the dialogue game protocol proposed allows the initiator to ask proponents for arguments that justify their recommendations (i.e. their reviews about the recommended items) in steps 6 to 9, taking the maximum profit from the information distributed across the social network. Again, the request for arguments is propagated from $a1_c$ to $a2$ in steps 8.1 to 8.2.

Afterwards, the initiator tries to reject the recommendation of $a1_c$ (the neighbour with lower confidence degree) by posing it a trustworthiness critical attack in step 10. When this attack is challenged in step 11, the initiator shows the argument that supports it in step 12, since its confidence in the recommendations of $a1_c$ (i.e. -0.3) is lower than its confidence in the recommendations of $a1_l$ (i.e. 0.5) and the latter has proposed

Table 2. Restaurant Recommendation Dialogue

Step	Sender	Receiver(s)	Locution	Dialogue Record
0	a_i	$a1_l, a1_c, a1_r$	propose(<Restaurant, ->, Preferences)?	$D_0 = ()$
1	$a1_l$	a_i	propose(<Restaurant, Justo>, Preferences)	$DR^1 = (< a1_l, \text{Justo,->}, d^1 = \text{Justo})$
2	$a1_r$	a_i	reject	...
2.1	$a1_c$	$a2$	propose(<Restaurant, ->, Preferences)?	$DR'^{2.1} = ()$
2.2	$a2$	$a1_c$	assert(<Cuisine, ->)?	...
3	$a1_c$	a_i	assert(<Cuisine, ->)?	...
4	a_i	$a1_c$	assert(<Cuisine, Mediterranean>)	...
4.1	$a1_c$	$a2$	assert(<Cuisine, Mediterranean>)	...
4.2	$a2$	$a1_c$	propose(<Restaurant, Sarieta>, Preferences)	$DR'^{4.2} = (< a2, \text{Sarieta, ->}, d'_2 = \text{Sarieta})$
5	$a1_c$	a_i	propose(<Restaurant, Sarieta>, Preferences)	$DR^5 = (< a1_l, \text{Justo, ->}, < a1_c, \text{Sarieta, ->}, d^5 = \text{Justo})$
6	a_i	$a1_l$	why(propose(<Restaurant, Justo>, Preferences))?	...
7	$a1_l$	a_i	assert({<Location, Valencia>, <GR, Yes>, ...})	...
8	a_i	$a1_c$	why(propose(<Restaurant, Sarieta>, Preferences))?	...
8.1	$a1_c$	$a2$	why(propose(<Restaurant, Sarieta>, Preferences))?	...
8.2	$a2$	$a1_c$	assert({<Location, Valencia>, <Cuisine, Mediterranean>, <GR, Yes>, ...})	...
9	$a1_c$	a_i	assert({<Location, Valencia>, <Cuisine, Mediterranean>, <GR, Yes>, ...})	...
10	a_i	$a1_c$	pose(trustworthiness)	...
11	$a1_c$	a_i	why(pose(trustworthiness))?	...
12	a_i	$a1_c$	assert($(c_{a_i a1_c} = -0.3, <, c_{a_i a1_l} = 0.5)$)	$DR^{12} = (< a1_l, \text{Justo}, (c_{a_i a1_c}, <, c_{a_i a1_l})>, < a1_c, \text{Sarieta, ->}, d^{12} = \text{Justo})$
13	$a1_c$	a_i	assert($(c_{a1_c a1_l} = -0.6, <, c_{a_i a1_l} = 0.5)$)	...
14	a_i	$a1_c$	accept	$DR^{14} = (< a1_l, \text{Justo, ->}, < a1_c, \text{Sarieta}, (c_{a1_c a1_l}, <, c_{a_i a1_l})>, d^{14} = \text{Sarieta})$
15	a_i	$a1_l$	pose(trustworthiness)	...
16	$a1_l$	a_i	why(pose(trustworthiness))?	...
17	a_i	$a1_l$	assert($(c_{a1_c a1_l}, <, c_{a_i a1_l})$)	...
18	$a1_l$	a_i	noCommitment(<Restaurant, Justo>)	$DR^{18} = (< a1_l, -, - >, < a1_c, \text{Sarieta}, (c_{a1_c a1_l}, <, c_{a_i a1_l})>, d^{18} = \text{Sarieta})$
19	a_i	$a1_l$	reject	...
20	a_i	$a1_c, a2$	accept	...

a different recommendation. However, $a1_c$ is able to rebut the attack in step 13, since the difference between the confidence of the initiator in $a1_l$ and the confidence of the initiator in $a1_c$ is lower than the difference between the confidence of the initiator in $a1_l$ and the confidence of $a1_c$ in $a1_l$ (i.e. equation 5, where 0.5 - (-0.3) < 0.5 - (-0.6)). Note that in this case, $a1_c$ could also have used the type of rebuttal shown in equation 6, since a level-2 recommendation was carried out and its confidence degree in $a2$ improves the confidence degree that the initiator has about $a1_c$. However, the attack of equation 5 is stronger, since it does not depend on the potential knowledge that a_i could have about $a2$. Therefore, the argument of $a1_c$ is accepted and the preliminary choice of the initiator changes to the recommendation of $a1_c$ in step 14 (see DR^{14}).

Then, the initiator gives $a1_l$ the opportunity of rebutting again the argument of $a1_c$ by posing it a trustworthiness attack in step 15. After being challenged in step 16, the initiator sends the argument in favour of the recommendation of $a1_c$ to $a1_l$ in step 17. However, $a1_l$ cannot rebut the attack and hence, it must withdraw its recommendation in step 18 (shown in DR^{18}). Finally, all proponents are informed about the final decision of the initiator about their recommendations in steps 19 and 20. At the end of the dialogue, every proponent (even $a2$) will be given the feedback about the usefulness of its recommendation.

Moreover, if $a1_l$ would have an own negative confidence in the recommendations of $a1_c$, it could have rebutted the argument in favour of the recommendation of $a1_c$ in the step 17. In that case, the initiator would have to decide between preliminary accept the recommendation of $a1_l$ and try to find more arguments in favour of the recommendation of $a1_c$ (e.g. by posing an expertise critical attack to both proponents) or definitively rejecting the recommendation of $a1_c$.

5   Evaluation

The complex decision-making policy proposed in section 3.2 has been implemented in JADE (Java Agent DEvelopment Framework, version 3.6) [4] and evaluated in the restaurant recommendation domain under different configuration parameters. In each step of the simulation, a randomly selected initiator agent makes a recommendation request to their neighbours in a social network. Each agent has a list of neighbours to ask (friends) and a database of reviews about restaurants that it personally knows. For fitting our evaluation purposes, the initiator's request can be any restaurant from a file that aggregates all restaurants that appear in the reviews databases of the agents of the social network. Therefore, its level-1 neighbours cannot have a suitable proposal in their reviews database and hence, should propagate the request to their own neighbours to be able to make any proposal.

In order to show the advantages of allowing agents to keep an argumentation dialogue and take the maximum profit from the information spread across the network, the Mean Absolute Error (MAE) (shown in equation 8) of the recommendations received by the initiator when it follows the dialogue-based decision-making policy has been contrasted with the results achieved when following two basic confidence-based and frequency-based policies (see section 3.2 for details) in each round of the simulation:

$$MAE = \frac{1}{n} \sum_{i=1}^{n} |e_i| \tag{8}$$

where $|e_i|$ is a measure of the error made (the distance) between the recommendation received and the original recommendation requested and i is the number of repetitions made for each round of the tests in order to smooth outlayer results and provide them with more robustness.

Moreover, some design assumptions that have been made in this implementation of the dialogue-based decision-making policy are the following:

- Agents recommend restaurants and they all know the range of possible values of the features that characterise restaurants in the system (but reviews with empty values in any feature are also allowed).
- No forced end is considered.
- Proponents always try to ask the initiator for more information about its preferences when they have several available recommendations to propose.
- Initiators always answer questions about preferences.
- The initiator only dialogues with one agent at the same time.
- Agents are honest.
- Only level-2 recommendations are allowed to prevent an exponential increase in propagations and fulfilling deadlines without recommendation proposals.
- The default preference order to pose attacks and make choices between proposals is: first, choosing the proposal of the agent with higher usefulness degree and pose trustworthiness attacks to other proposals (if they exist); in case of drawn, try expertise and consistency attacks; if even then a drawn is reached, make a random choice between proposals.

The first test performed consists in checking the evolution of the accuracy of the recommendations that the initiator agent receives when the number of agents on the social network increases. In this test, each agent has a fixed average of 3 friends with randomly generated initial usefulness degrees and 5 restaurants reviewed per friend and, since the initiator can request any restaurant that appears in one or more of the friends' reviews databases, the dispersion rate of the information present on the social network increases with the amount of agents registered in the network. With this purpose, the number of agents of the social network have been increased by 5 in each round of the test, making 5 repetitions per round to compute the MAE of the recommendations received by the initiator. Figure 2 shows the results obtained.

As expected, all policies achieve similar results when the dispersion rate of the information is low and there are few agents on the network (i.e. 5 agents). However, when the amount of agents increases (i.e. 10 agents) and hence, the dispersion of the knowledge about restaurants also does, the accuracy of recommendations that the initiator agent receives decreases for all policies. Even though, the dialogue-based policy achieves better results and the MAE shows an average tendency to decrease. This is clearly due to its ability to propagate the requests among friends and to ask for more information about the preferences of the initiator when necessary. Furthermore, its results could be even better if more propagations had been allowed. Also, for a number of agents on the network between 10 and 25, the accuracy of the useful-based and frequency-based policies

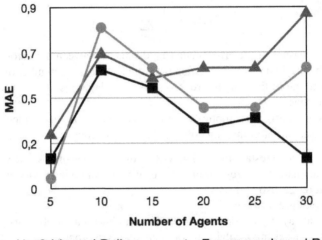

Fig. 2. Accuracy of Recommendations vs. Number of Agents on the Social Network

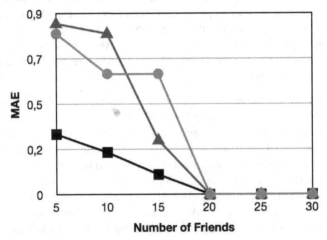

Fig. 3. Accuracy of Recommendations vs. Number of Friends per Agent

tends to decrease and then stabilise, but seems to increase again for a bigger number of agents (i.e. 30 agents). This apparently random behaviour could be motivated by the fact that, in each step of the simulation, a random initiator is selected and the performance of both policies highly depends on the topology of the network. Neither of them allows the initiator to receive recommendations from k-level neighbours and thus, there is a random probability of having a neighbour that has a suitable recommendation to offer.

The second test carried out is aimed at checking the influence on the accuracy of the recommendations received by the initiator agent when its amount of friends increases. Therefore, the number of friends (with randomly generated initial usefulness degrees) for each agent has been increased by 5 in each round, leaving a fixed number of 30 agents on the network, each one with an average number of 5 reviews in their reviews databases and making 5 repetitions per round to compute the MAE of the recommendations received by the initiator. This leads to an increase on the amount of information that the initiator agent can reach in each round. The results are shown in figure 3.

These results show how the MAE of the recommendations received by the initiator agent quickly decreases as the number of friends per agent increases. Obviously, when an agent has more fiends, it has a strongest possibility of having a neighbour with a suitable recommendation to offer. Also, the more information is transmitted in the network, the better the recommendations are. This test shows how the dialogue-based decision-making policy achieves notably better results than the other two basic policies even when agents are linked with few friends. This demonstrates again the power of this complex policy to explore the network and reach to more information than those policies that do not allow dialogue between agents. However, although these benefits could be criticise for having nothing to do with argumentation but with a better transmission of accurate information within a network, note that argumentation is precisely the mechanism that allows this transmission.

6   Summary and Future Work

This paper proposes the use of a dialogue game for modelling the interaction between the agents of a distributed recommendation system on a social network. In addition, a dialogue-based decision-making policy based on this interaction protocol and an example that shows its operation have also been proposed. The model has been implemented in JADE and tested in a restaurant recommendation domain. The preliminary results obtained demonstrate the power of the dialogue-based decision-making policy proposed to retrieve as much information as possible from the social network and hence, to achieve best recommendation results than other basic decision policies. Moreover, further research will study to which extent these results could be even improved if the strong assumption of restricting the propagation of requests only to level-2 friendship relations is relaxed.

To date we assume that agents do not necessarily store the confidence of their recommendations to other agents and the preferences of the initiator in those dialogues. However, this information would be necessary if the system was able to perform multi-item recommendations. It would also imply to consider the Field Critical Question as a possible attack to others' recommendations. By doing so, agents could have different confidence degrees for each type of recommendation performed. Future work will study how agents can specialise themselves in recommending specific items. Moreover, more decision policies and social network analysis measures will be proposed and tested under different evaluation parameters.

Acknowledgements

This work was partially supported by CONSOLIDER-INGENIO 2010 under grant CSD2007-00022 and by the Spanish government and GVA funds under TIN2006-14630-C0301 and PROMETEO/2008/051 projects.

References

1. Bentahar, J., Meyer, J.J.C., Moulin, B.: Securing Agent-Oriented Systems: An Argumentation and Reputation-based Approach. In: International Conference on Information Technology, ITNG 2007, pp. 507–515 (2007)
2. Conte, R., Paolucci, M., Sabater-Mir, J.: Reputation for Innovating Social Networks. In: 4th European Social Simulation Association Conference, ESSA 2007 (2007)
3. Hamblin, C.L.: Fallacies. Methuen, London (1970)
4. Telecom Italia Lab: JADE (Java Agent DEvelopment Framework), version 3.6 (2008), http://jade.tilab.com/
5. McBurney, P., Parsons, S.: Dialogue Games in Multi-Agent Systems. Informal Logic. Special Issue on Applications of Argumentation in Computer Science 22(3), 257–274 (2002)
6. McBurney, P., Parsons, S.: Games that Agents Play: A Formal Framework for dialogues between Autonomous Agents. Journal of Logic, Language and Information 12(2), 315–334 (2002)
7. Montaner, M., López, B., de la Rosa, J.L.: A Taxonomy of Recommender Agents on the Internet. Artificial Intelligence Review, 285–330 (2003)
8. O'Donovan, J., Smyth, B.: Trust in recommender systems. In: 10th International Conference on Intelligent User Interfaces, pp. 167–174 (2005)
9. Reed, C., Walton, D.: Argumentation Schemes in Dialogue. In: Dissensus and the Search for Common Ground, OSSA 2007, CD-ROM, pp. 1–11 (2007)
10. Walter, F.E., Battiston, S., Schweitzer, F.: A Model of a Trust-based Recommendation System on a Social Network. Journal of Autonomous Agents and Multi-Agent Systems, JAAMAS 16(1), 57–74 (2008)
11. Walton, D.: Appeal to Expert Opinion. Penn State Press (1997)

Emotions in Rational Decision Making

Fahd Saud Nawwab, Trevor Bench-Capon, and Paul E. Dunne

Department of Computer Science, The University of Liverpool, UK
{fahad,tbc,ped}@csc.liv.ac.uk

Abstract. Emotions play an important role in human decision making. This often has a beneficial effect, and so it is desirable to explore whether emotions can also play a role in agent decision making. This paper builds on several pieces of earlier work which resulted in a formalization of a model of emotions. We show how, in particular, the emotions of gratitude and displeasure and related emotions can be beneficially integrated into a model of decision making. The model of decision making used is based on a notion of choosing between competing justifications according to the agent's preferences over the social values promoted by the available actions. Emotions of gratitude and displeasure are generated according to whether other agents relevant to the situation support or frustrate the agent's goals and values, and the emotional attitude towards the other agents then influences the ranking of these values, and so affects future choices. The paper summarizes the previous work on which we build, describes the decision making model we use, and explains how emotions are generated and used within that model.

1 Introduction

That emotions do in practice have an influence on human decision making cannot be denied. We should not, however, consider this to be something to be deprecated: if there were no beneficial effects of emotions, it seems unlikely that evolution would have left them with such a widespread role. Damasio [5] writes:

> "Emotions and feelings can cause havoc in the process of reasoning under certain circumstances. Traditional wisdom has told us that they can, and recent investigation of the normal reasoning process also reveal the potentially harmful influence of emotional biases. It is thus even more surprising and novel that the absence of emotion and feeling is no less damaging, no less capable of compromising the rationality that makes us distinctively human and allows us to decide in consonance with a sense of personal future, social convention, and moral principle."

So, what is the beneficial role of emotions, and how might we gain these beneficial effects in agent reasoning? One aspect identified by Damasio and developed in [13] is that emotions can act as heuristics and prevent excessive deliberation. Thus in [13] the authors show how the emotions of hope and fear with respect to plans can be used to determine whether replanning is necessary, or whether

P. McBurney et al. (Eds.): ArgMAS 2009, LNAI 6057, pp. 273–291, 2010.

the current plan can still be followed. There are, however, other sorts of emotion and other roles. In this paper, we will consider the emotions of gratitude, displeasure, like, dislike, joy and distress to show how these emotions can impact on practical reasoning. We argue that these emotions play an important role in social interaction: humans adopt emotional attitudes towards one another, and this seems to play an essential role in developing and maintaining cooperation, and behaving towards one another in a consistent and appropriate way. These emotions also seem to act as tie-breakers to enable a reasoned choice between two alternatives which are equally acceptable on purely rational grounds. We will show how these effects can be realised in a computational model of practical reasoning.

There are several approaches to modeling emotions in artificial agents. One example is the EBDI model built by Jiang et al [7] based on the famous BDI (Belief - Desire - Intention) model of Bratman [4] which incorporates an emotional function into that architecture. Another is that developed by Reilly [12] which aims to express emotions rather than influence decisions. Padgham and Taylor [11] introduced a system that is designed to treat emotions with goal-oriented behaviors trying to model the personality aspect of agents. The work of Steunebrink et al [13], which takes the Ortony, Clore and Collins (OCC) model [10] as its basis, presented a formalization of a number of emotions, and as mentioned above, focused on the use of hope and fear in particular to guide replanning. We will take [13] as our starting point, and show how some of the other emotions impact on the practical reasoning mechanism described in [9].

In Section 2, we will briefly describe the work in emotional agents on which we base our own, and identify the specific emotions on which we will focus. Section 3 will describe the model of decision making we use, and Section 4 will show how emotions can be generated in this model and the ways in which they can influence decision making, using a simple two agent example. Section 5 walks through a more extended example and Section 6 offers some concluding remarks.

2   Emotional Agents

The original psychological basis for the work on which we build is provided by the model of (OCC) [10]. This model, which identifies twenty-two emotions organised into a concise hierarchy, is particularly attractive to those wishing to build computational models as it provides a specification of the conditions which give rise to each distinct emotion in terms of the computationally familiar notions of objects, events and actions. The OCC model includes notions of intensity of emotions, and identifies a number of variables which influence the intensity of the emotions experienced. The OCC model formed the basis of the implementation of a model of emotional agents developed by Reilly [12]. Reilly, whose aim was to construct believable emotional agents, gives a system capable of generating emotions, storing them, and expressing them through behavior. Reilly gives a simplified method of determining intensity, using only a subset of the variables from the OCC model, most importantly the *importance* and *unexpectedness* of the triggering event. Under storage, Reilly includes discussions of, and options for, the mechanisms for combining emotions of a similar type and enabling them to decay over time. Reilly recognises that different combinations and decay mechanisms may be appropriate for different emotions. As far as expression goes, Reilly's focus is on believability and he does not make any strong claims for how it interacts with rationality in decision making. We adopt Reilly's approach to the quantitative aspects of emotions.

The immediate precursor of our approach is the work done by the agents' group at Utrecht e.g. [8,13]. They have provided a formalisation of the emotions of the OCC model, and have shown how hope and fear in particular can play a role in decision making. In [13], the twenty-two emotional fluents of the OCC model are defined. We largely follow their definitions, but subscript states of affairs with the name of an agent where appropriate. We also change the names of some of the emotions: we regard love, hate and anger as suggesting more intensity than is necessary, and so will use *like*, *dislike* and *displeasure* instead.

Definition 1 (Emotional Fluents). The set Emotions is the set of emotional fluents, which is defined as follows:

$$
\begin{aligned}
\text{Emotions} = \\
&joy_i(k_i), & &distress_i(k_i), \\
&hope_i(\pi, k_i), & &fear_i(\pi, \neg k_i), \\
&satisfaction_i(\pi, k_i), & &disappointment_i(\pi, k_i), \\
&relief_i(\pi, \neg k_i), & &fears-confirmed_i(\pi, \neg k_i), \\
&happy-for_i(j, k), & &resentment_i(j, k), \\
&gloating_i(j, k), & &pity_i(j, k), \\
&pride_i(\alpha_i), & &shame_i(\alpha_i), \\
&admiration_i(j, \alpha_j), & &reproach_i(j, \alpha_j), \\
&like_i(j), & &dislike_i(j), \\
&gratification_i(\alpha_i, k_i), & &remorse_i(\alpha_i, k_i), \\
&gratitude_i(j, \alpha_j, k_i), & &displeasurei(j, \alpha_j, k_i),
\end{aligned}
$$

Where i and j are distinct agents, α_i and α_j are actions available to these agents, π a plan of agent i expressed as a sequence of actions, and k is a partial state of affairs, so that k_i is a goal of agent i.

From this definition, we can see that the twenty-two emotions can be divided into eleven pairs. For example, distress is the negative correlate of joy, and so on down the list. We can also note that emotions form a number of distinct types, with respect to their arguments.

- Those relating to a plan: joy, distress, hope, fear, satisfaction, dissatisfaction, relief and fears-confirmed. We will not consider these further as we do not consider plans in this paper.
- Those directed towards another agent. Gratitude and displeasure are directed towards another agent in respect of that other agent's action bringing about or frustrating a state of affairs desired by the emotional agent. Admiration and reproach are also directed towards another agent in respect of that other agent's action, but here there is no connection with the emotional agent's goals. Like and dislike are directed towards another agent, but in

respect of no particular event. Gloating and pity, happy-for and resentment
are directed towards another agent in respect of a state of affairs which need
not be a goal of the emotional agent.
- Gratification and remorse correspond to gratitude and displeasure, but this
  time are directed by the agent towards itself in respect of its own action and
  its effect on the agent's goals.
- Joy and distress, which are experienced when goals are achieved or fail to
  be achieved.

In this paper our focus will be on three pairs in particular: gratitude and displeasure; like and dislike; and joy and distress. In general, terms we are considering
an agent which selects an action hoping to realise some goal. Whether it is successful or not, depends in part on the actions of other agents. Where other agents
cooperate in realising the goal; the emotional agent will feel gratitude towards
them, and conversely, if they frustrate the goal the emotional agent will feel
displeasure. Over a series of actions, gratitude will accumulate into liking and
displeasure into disliking. Similarly a series of successful actions will lead to joy
and unsuccessful actions to distress. Of course, actions giving rise to admiration
and respect will also influence like and dislike, and gratification and remorse will
influence joy and distress. Here, however, we shall consider only gratitude and
displeasure and the emotions influenced by them. Widening the scope into other
related emotions will be left for future work. In the next section, we will present
our model of decision making before going on to explain how the emotions of
gratitude and displeasure are generated in this context.

3   A Model of Agent Decision Making

The model of agent decision making is based on the approach of [1], which has
been further developed in [9]. The approach relies on argumentation techniques:
candidate actions are identified by providing *prima facie* justifications for them
by instantiating a particular argumentation scheme. This justification can then
be critiqued by a set of characteristic counterarguments. The decision is then
made by choosing a defensible set of action justifications. In [9] five steps were
identified:

1. *Formulating the Problem*: A representation of the problem scenario in terms
   of an Action-Based Alternating Transition System (AATS) [14].
2. *Determining the Arguments*: An instantiating of an argument scheme justifying an action in terms of the AATS, and identifying counter arguments
   based on critical questions appropriate to that scheme. A formal description
   of the argument scheme and critical questions can be found in [1].
3. *Building the Argumentation Framework*: The arguments and counter arguments identified in the previous set are formed into a Value Based Argumentation Framework (VAF) [3].
4. *Evaluating the Framework*: The particular value ordering of the agent concerned is now used to identify the preferred extension of the framework for

that agent. This identifies the arguments that withstand the critique from the perspective of the decision making agent.

5. *Sequencing the Actions*: The set of actions justified in the previous step are now sequenced for execution.

Here we are especially interested in the fourth step: our contention is that the emotional state of the agent will affect its ordering of values, and so lead to a preferred extension different from that of an agent unaffected by emotions. We will, now, give some necessary detail of the argument scheme, the AATS, and VAFs.

The particular argument scheme and its associated critiques used in Step 2 was introduced in [2]. The argument scheme to justify an action is as follows:

AS1: In the current circumstances R, action A is justified, since it will bring about new circumstances S, which realise goal G, which promotes value V.

What is distinctive about this scheme is that it distinguishes three aspects of the results of an action: the state of affairs which follows from the action; desirable elements of that state of affairs, the goal, and the reasons why those elements are desirable, the value. Values, which are social values, such as liberty and equality, are central here. Suppose we wish to justify an increase in taxes, then our goal may be redistribution of income, justified by our desire to promote equality, or our goal may be to have more money to spend on national defense, promoting the value of national security. Different justifications will appeal to different audiences, depending on their values and the order in which they priorities them. A fuller discussion of values and their role can be found in [2]. What is important here is that using this scheme associates arguments with values.

In order to generate the arguments, [1] uses a formulation of the problem as an Action-Based Alternating Transition System (AATS). AATS was introduced in [14] in order to represent the effect of a group of agents acting independently in a situation, so that the result of the action of a given agent is dependent on the actions of the other agents concerned. The states of the AATS represent possible states of affairs, and the transitions between them, that is actions composed from the individual actions of the relevant agents. Thus, if two agents can each independently choose one of three actions, there will be nine possible joint actions. Additionally, each of the transitions can be labeled with the values promoted by moving from the source state to the target state. In [1], the argument scheme for justifying actions was formally described by reference to an AATS, as were the possible counterarguments to such a justification. The formal definition of an AATS is given in Definition 2, and the argument scheme AS1 is defined in terms of an AATS in Definition 3. Each transition from the current state which promotes some value can be used to instantiate AS1 and so justifies the agent in performing its component of the corresponding joint action. This justification is, however, subject to counterarguments, and so the result is a set of conflicting arguments, which will justify a range of actions, some of which may be incompatible. These arguments can be ascribed a status by forming them into a Value-Based Argumentation Framework (VAF) [3], an extension of standard Argumentation Frameworks (AF) [6], which are presented in Definitions 4 and

5 below. Whereas, in an AF, attacks always succeed, in a VAF an argument is defeated by its attacker, if that attacker is associated with a value of equal or greater preference. Note that AS1 associates arguments which instantiate it with a value. The agent may now, by applying its preference ordering over values, identify a set of acceptable arguments in the VAF. The actions justified by these arguments will be those that the agent will choose, in the light of its preferences.

Definition 2: AATS. A joint action j_{Ag} for a set of k agents Ag, is a tuple $\langle \alpha_1, .., \alpha_k \rangle$, where for each α_i $(j \leq k)$ there is some $i \in Ag$ such that $\alpha_j \in Ac_i$, the set of available actions for agent i. Sets of available actions are *disjoint*, i.e. $i \neq j \Rightarrow Ac_i \cap Ac_j = \emptyset$. The set of all joint actions for a set of agents Ag is denoted by J_{Ag}, so $J_{Ag} = \Pi_{i \in Ag} Ac_i$. Given an element j_{Ag} of J_{Ag} and an agent $i \in Ag$, i's action in j_{Ag} is denoted by j_i

An AATS is a $(2n+8)$ element tuple S=$\langle Q, q_0, Ag, Ac_1, Ac_n, Av_1, Av_n, \rho, \tau, \Phi, \pi, \delta \rangle$

- Q is a finite, non-empty set of states
- $q_0 = q_x \in Q$ is the initial state
- $Ag = \{1, ..., n\}$ is a finite, non-empty set of agents
- Ac_i is a finite, non-empty set of actions, for each $i \in Ag$ (where we recall that $Ac_i \cap Ac_j = \emptyset$ whenever $i \neq j$)
- Av_i is a finite, non-empty set of values $Av_i \subseteq V$, for each $i \in Ag$
- $\rho : Ac_{Ag} \to 2^Q$ is an action precondition function, which for each (joint) action $\alpha \in Ac_{Ag}$ defines the set of states $\rho(\alpha)$ from which α may be executed
- $\tau : Q \times J_{Ag} \to Q$ is a partial system transition function, which defines the state $\tau(q, j)$ that would result by performing j from state q - note that, as this function is partial, not all joint actions are possible in all states (cf. the precondition function above)
- Φ is a finite, non-empty set of atomic propositions
- $\pi : Q \to 2^\Phi$ is an interpretation function, which gives the set of propositions satisfied in each state: if $p \in \pi(q)$, then this means that the propositional variable p is satisfied (equivalently, true) in state q
- $\delta : Q \times Q \times Av_{Ag} \to \{+, -, =\}$ is a valuation function which defines the status (promoted $(+)$, demoted $(-)$ or neutral $(=)$) of a value $v_u \in Av_{Ag}$ ascribed by the agent to the transition between two states: $\delta(q_x, q_y, v_u)$ labels the transition between q_x and q_y with one of $\{+, -, =\}$ with respect to the value $v_u \in Av_{Ag}$.

Definition 3: Argumentation Scheme AS1 expressed in terms of AATS. The initial state q_0 is $q_x \in Q$; agent $i \in Ag$ should perform α_i, consistent with the joint action $j_{Ag} \in J_{Ag}$ where $j_{Ag_i} = \alpha_i$, so that $\tau(q_x, j_{Ag}) = q_y$, $p_a \in \pi(q_y) \setminus \pi(q_x)$ and for some $v_u \in Av_i$, $\delta(q_x, q_y, v_u) = +$.

Definition 4: Value-Based Argumentation Framework (VAF). VAF is a triple $\langle H(X, A), \nu, \eta \rangle$, where X is a set of arguments, A is a binary relation on arguments, called the attack relation (i.e. $H(X, A)$ is a standard argumentation framework in the sense of [6]), $\nu = v_1, v_2, ..., v_k$ a set of k *values*, and $\eta : X \to \nu$

a mapping that associates a value $\eta(x) \in \nu$ with each argument $x \in X$. A *specific audience*, α, for a VAF $\langle H, \nu, \eta \rangle$, is a total ordering of ν. We say that v_i is preferred to v_j in the audience α, denoted $v_i \succ_\alpha v_j$, if v_i is ranked higher than v_j in the total ordering defined by α.

Definition 5: Admissibility in VAFs. Let $\langle H(X, A), V, \eta \rangle$ be a VAF and α an audience. For arguments x, y in X, x is a successful attack on y (or x defeats y) with respect to the audience α if: $\langle x, y \rangle \in A$ and it is not the case that $\eta(y) \succ_\alpha \eta(x)$. An argument x is acceptable to the subset S with respect to an audience α if: for every $y \in X$ that successfully attacks x with respect to α, there is some $z \in S$ that successfully attacks y with respect to α. A subset R of X is conflict-free with respect to the audience α if: for each $\langle x, y \rangle \in R \times R$, either$\langle x, y \rangle \notin A$ or $\eta(y) \succ_\alpha \eta(x)$. A subset R of X is admissible with respect to the audience α if: R is conflict-free with respect to α and every $x \in R$ is acceptable to R with respect to α. A subset R is a preferred extension for the audience α if it is a maximal admissible set with respect to α.

3.1   Example with Two Agents

In section 5 we give an extended example, but we here use a simpler example. Suppose two colleagues, Teddy and Karen, need to travel from Liverpool to Paris for a conference. They can choose to travel by plane or train. The plane is faster, but the train journey is much more comfortable. Their choice, therefore, comes down to whether they prefer the value of comfort or of speed. There is, however, a third consideration: it is more pleasant to travel in company than alone. The initial state has Karen and Teddy in Liverpool and there are four joint actions, depending on their independent choice of train or plane. These joint actions are:

J1: Teddy plane(Tp) Karen plane(Kp) **J2:** Teddy plane(Tp) Karen train(Kt)
J3: Teddy train(Tt) Karen train(Kt)   **J4:** Teddy train(Tt) Karen plane(Kp)

The transitions will promote the values of Teddy's Comfort (Ct), Teddy's Speed (St), Karen's Comfort (Ck) and Karen's Speed (Sk), and a Pleasant Journey (P). Note that comfort and speed are promoted in respect of particular agents, whereas the pleasant journey is a common good. On the basis of the AATS shown in Figure 1 we can get a number of instantiations of AS1:

A1: Karen travel by train (Kt) to reach q1/q3 to promote her comfort (Ck).
A2: Karen travel by plane (Kp) to reach q2/q4 to promote her Speed (Sk).
A3: Teddy travel by train (Tt) to reach q1/q2 to promote his comfort (Ct).
A4: Teddy travel by plane (Tp) to reach q3/a4 promote his speed (St).
A5: Both travel by train (Kt, Tt) to reach q1 for a pleasant journey(P).
A6: Both travel by plane (Kp, Tp) ro reach q4 for a pleasant journey(P).

These arguments form a VAF as shown in Figure 2, the attack relations representing that a person cannot travel both by train and by plane. First, let us suppose that the agents consider only their own values. Suppose that Karen orders her values $Ck > P > Sk$. For her, A1 will resist the attacks of A2 and

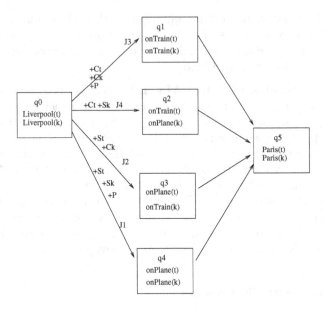

Fig. 1. The AATS of the example

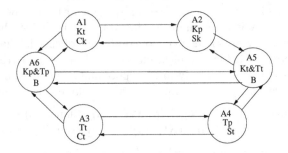

Fig. 2. VAF graph of the example

A6, and in turn defeat them, so that A5 is also justified for Karen, that is her preferred extension is (A1, A5). Thus, Karen will travel by train. But suppose that Teddy orders his values $P > St > Ct$. This preference gives rise to two preferred extensions: (A2, A4, A6) and (A1, A3, A5). Teddy can thus justify traveling by either method. Whereas Karen could ensure that her preferred extension was realised, since it does not matter what Teddy chooses, Teddy needs to predict Karen's actions in order to realise his goals. If he believed that Karen was equally likely to choose the plane and the train, he would choose the plane since $St > Ct$. But if he knows Karen's value order then he should choose the train since he should expect her to choose the train, so that J1 will not occur and choosing Tp will therefore lead to J2 rather than J1, reaching q3 rather than q4 and so failing to promote P.

Note, however, that since A1 subsumes two arguments, Karen's goal can be either q1 or q3. Since she also values P, this makes q1 preferred to q3, so her goal in A1 will be q1. Teddy on the other hand, because his choice is based on A5 or A6, needs to realise q1 or q4 respectively since when Karen's choice leads to q2 or q3 P will not be promoted. In the next section, we will consider how the choices made by Teddy and Karen give rise to emotions, and how these emotions can affect subsequent choices.

4   Gratitude, Displeasure, Like, Dislike, Joy and Distress

4.1   Generation

Recall that gratitude and displeasure are emotions directed by one agent towards another in respect of an action which brings about a state of affairs. This maps very well to the AATS structure in which an agent selects an action to reach a particular state and promote particular values, but is not able to ensure success since the actual state reached, and values promoted, depend on the actions chosen by the other agents involved, the joint action. In so far as the other agent does not allow the desired joint action, the agent will feel displeasure and in so far as it does assist in the joint action being performed, the agent will feel gratitude.

Recall from section 2, that the intensity of emotions depend on how important it is to reach the goal and how unexpected the action is. In our example, suppose first that Karen chooses to travel by train with q1 as her desired state. It is not of vital importance to her whether q1 or q3, the result of other possible joint action when she chooses the train, is reached: both promote her important value of C. For Teddy, on the other hand, it is important that the intended joint action is performed, since the alternative will not promote his important value of P. So if Teddy chooses the plane and Karen the train, both will be displeased with one another, since they had intended to reach a different state, and the value of a pleasant journey is not promoted by the actual joint action. Teddy will feel more displeasure than Karen since he set more importance on promoting P. Suppose, however, that their preferences were known to one another in advance, and that Teddy was well aware of Karen's extreme dislike of flying. Then, Karen's choice should have been expected, and so his displeasure should be reduced to that extent. Teddy's choice is less predictable, since he has two preferred extensions: thus if he chooses the plane, Karen may well feel more intense displeasure with respect to this aspect.

In practice, however, if Teddy knew of Karen's preference, so that he could recognise the train as her only rational choice, Teddy should have performed Tt hoping to reach q1. In this case, both want to reach q1, and this is the state they will reach. They may both feel gratitude towards the other. However, because Kt was entirely expected, and because Ct was less important than the now unrealised St, Teddy's gratitude is likely to be minimal. On the other hand, Teddy's choice was less predictable, and enabled Karen's desired state to be reached, and so she should feel rather more intense gratitude towards him.

We need to make some attempt to quantify importance and unexpectedness. For our current purposes precision is less important than getting the qualitative aspects right: provided importance and intensity move in the right direction, we can explore their effects. We therefore, use a very simple method. More sophisticated methods are also possible, and can be explored in future work, but the following has the correct characteristics.

Let $Audience_i$ be the order given to a set V of n values agent $i = \langle v_n > v_{n-1} > ... > v_1 \rangle$. Let q be a state such that moving from q_0 to promote the set of values $V_v \subseteq V$. Now the *importance* of q to agent i, $importance_i(q)$ will be $\sum_{i=1}^{i=n} v_i$ such that $v_i \in V_v$. Let VAF_0 be the VAF formed by agent i in q_0 and m the number of preferred extensions of VAF_0 with respect to $Audience_i$. Now the unexpectedness of the action of agent i, $unexpectedness_{q_0}(i)$ in q_0 will be $1 - 1 \div m$. Note that when an agent i is considering the expectedness of an action of some other agent j, it will often only be possible to estimate a partial order, increasing the value of m considerably. If there is information available about the probability of an agent choosing an action, that can be used instead of the calculation in terms of preferred extensions.

In our example, the importance of q1 is 5 for Karen and 4 for Teddy, the importance of q2 is 1 for both of them, the importance of q3 is 3 for Karen and 2 for Teddy, and the importance of q4 is 4 for Karen and 5 for Teddy. The unexpectedness of Karen choosing the train in q_0 is 0, of Teddy choosing the train 0.5 and Teddy choosing the plane in 0.5.

Now suppose agent i in q_0 desires to reach q_d and, given the action chosen by agent j, α_j, q_a is the state actually reached. Where $q_d = q_a$, the intensity of $gratitude_i(j, \alpha_j, q_d)$ is $importance_i(q_d) \times unexpectedness_j(q_0)$. If $q_d \neq q_a$, then the intensity of displeasure is $(importance_i(q_d) - importance_i(q_a)) \times unexpectedness_j(q_0)$.

So in the example, the intensities of the emotions experienced are as follows. When both choose the train: Teddy feels neither gratitude nor displeasure, since Karen's action was entirely expected, while Karen feels gratitude to Teddy with intensity 2.5. Where Karen chooses the train and Teddy the plane, Teddy feels no displeasure because Karen's choice was entirely predictable, whereas Karen feels displeasure with intensity 0.5. If both choose the plane, Teddy feels considerable gratitude (5) to Karen, since her action was entirely unexpected. whereas Karen feels only mild gratitude to Teddy (2), since P was of less importance to her. Finally, if Teddy chooses the train and Karen the plane, Teddy feels displeasure towards Karen of 4 and Karen to Teddy of 1.5.

Definition 6: Gratitude and Displeasure. Formally, suppose agent i seeks a state q from the current state q_k to promote value v, ie $\delta(q_k, q, v) = +$. Let $J = \langle a_0, a_1, \ldots, a_n \rangle$ be an *intended* joint action whose effect achieves these, and $J' = \langle a_0, b_1, \ldots, b_n \rangle$ be the *actual* joint action performed. Agent j is *cooperative* w.r.t the joint action J if $b_j = a_j$; otherwise agent j is said to *frustrate* joint action J.

We can now model gratitude and displeasure felt by agent i towards other agents in terms of the outcome of joint action J' relative to the value promoted. We have the following possibilities where performing J' results in the state q'

1. If $\delta\{q_k, q', v) = +$ then $gratitude(i, b_j, g)$ for all cooperative agents.
2. If $\delta\{q_k, q', v\}_\neg = -$ then $displeasure(i, b_j, g)$ for all frustrating agents.

Gratitude and displeasure relate to a single action. In practice, agents will, over time, participate together in many joint actions, each with the potential to evoke gratitude and displeasure. These experiences of gratitude and displeasure will combine, taking into account intensity and decay over time, to form an overall attitude towards the other agent, giving rise to the emotions of like and dislike. Again for illustrative purposes we suggest a very simple mechanism; more sophisticated work can be found in [12].

Let $L_i(j, t)$ be the intensity of like, where $L_i(j, t)$ positive, or dislike, where $L_i(j, t)$ negative, for agent i towards agent j at time t. Let $G_i(j, v, t)$ be the intensity of gratitude felt by agent i towards agent j at t and $D_i(j, v, t)$ be the intensity of displeasure felt by agent i towards agent j at t both with respect to v. Now $L_i(j, t+1) = L_i(j, t) + (G_i(j, v, t) - d_g) - (D_i(j, v, t) - d_d)$, where d_g and d_d are suitable decay factors for like and dislike respectively. In our examples, for simplicity, we will not consider decay, so that like and dislike are only altered by specific experiences.

Similarly the achievement, respectively failure, of the goals will contribute to the overall attitude of the agent, and so contribute to the emotion of joy, respectively distress. We provide a mechanism similar to that for like and dislike.

Suppose there are n other agents in Ag. Let $J_1(v, t)$ be the intensity, with respect to some value v, of joy, where $J_1(v, t)$ positive, or distress, where $J_1(v, t)$ negative, for agent 1 at time t. Let $\sum_{j=2}^{j=n} G_1(j, v, t)$ be the intensity of gratitude felt by agent i towards the other agents at tin respect of v and $\sum_{j=2}^{j=n} D_1(j, v, t)$ be the intensity of displeasure felt by agent 1 towards the other agents at t with respect to v. Now $J_i(v, t+1) = J_i(v, t) + (G_i(j, v, t) - d_g) - (D_i(j, v, t) - d_d)$, where d_g and d_d are suitable decay factors. Again we will, for simplicity, not consider decay further in this paper.

4.2 Influence on Decision Making

In the last section, we indicated how gratitude and displeasure can be evoked in our decision making model, and how over a series of actions these could lead to the emotions of like, dislike, joy and distress. In this section, we will describe how these emotions can impact decision making.

The mechanism by which emotions will influence decisions is by their impact on the value ordering of the emotional agent. Recall, from Section 3 that the crucial element in the decision making model is the preference order which the agent uses to identify the acceptable arguments in the VAF. Had Teddy preferred Speed to a Pleasant journey, he would not have considered using the train, whatever Karen's preferences. Thus, if the emotions are to have an effect, they must produce some change in the preference ordering. Recall, also, that some values are common goods and do not relate to any particular agent, whereas some values are promoted and demoted in respect of a specific agent.

An agent will have some initial value order. In the example, Teddy prefers pleasure to speed and speed to comfort. Thus far, our agents have considered only their own values and have decided independently of one another, but in practice the comfort and speed of Karen should have some importance for Teddy, and the speed and comfort of Teddy some importance for Karen. Suppose that they must come to a joint decision. Their two value orders can be merged on P to give either $Ck > P > Sk > St > Ct$ or $Ck > P > St > Sk > Ct$: plausibly Karen will favor the first and Teddy the second since that resolves the partial order by preferring their own value. Now, because Ck is the most preferred value, and because P is preferred to St, the preferred extension will be (A1, A3, A5), that is they both travel by train. A more interesting situation arises if we suppose that Karen orders her values $P > Ck > Sk$, and we assume that neither have any knowledge of the others preferences, so that each believe that there is an even chance of the other choosing plane or train. Now there are four possible merged orderings.

$$1\text{-}P > St > Ck > Ct > Sk \ , \ 2\text{-}P > St > Ck > Sk > Ct$$
$$3\text{-}P > Ck > St > Ct > Sk \ , \ 4\text{-}P > Ck > St > Sk > Ct$$

With these preferences, the situation is less clear, since there is no clearly preferred value. Order 1 and 2 give rise to (A2, A4, A6) and orders 3 and 4 to (A1, A3, A5). Suppose after some discussion they agree on the train, that is Teddy defers to Karen and they travel by train. The agents now consider the actual joint action, ranking states according to the method given above, that is using their own values. Teddy will feel some displeasure (0.5) towards Karen and Karen will feel gratitude towards Teddy (2.5). Accordingly, Karen will increase her liking for Teddy and Teddy will feel some dislike for Karen. Now our suggestion is that liking will influence the value order *by increasing the priority given to values promoted in respect of the liked agent* or *by demoting the values in respect of the disliked agent.* That is, as Karen's liking for Teddy increases, she is more likely to accept order 1. Similarly, Teddy is less likely to accept orders 2, 3 and 4. Like and dislike must pass some threshold to reorder the values, since otherwise the value order will be too volatile. Different agents may have different thresholds, and there may be different thresholds for different emotions. Suppose the liking of 2.5 is enough to dispose Karen to accept order 1. When the question arises again, they will travel by plane this time. Now the roles are reversed: Karen's liking for Teddy will decrease to 2, whereas Teddy will now like with intensity 2. The liking - disliking is asymmetrical because reaching the unfavored state still realises some of their values. Suppose, however, that 2.5 had been insufficient to get Karen to change her value order, but that Teddy had a very low threshold for dislike. Now Teddy may elevate St above P, and so choose the plane. This will, of course, displease Karen, and a mutual dislike will arise, so that P ceases to be so important for either of them, and they will habitually travel separately. We can see here how liking and displeasure can provide a mechanism for *reciprocation*: when one agent makes a concession to another, the influence of liking on the part of agent who receives the concession and dislike on the part of the agent who makes the concession, influences the value order so that subsequently the roles are reversed. Where reciprocation occurs, mutual liking grows, making it more likely that these agents will value the interests of each other in subsequent decisions (a form of *bonding*). Where reciprocation does not occur, the influence of the value order is to diminish the importance of shared values, giving less importance to the resulting non-cooperation.

Thus far we have considered two agents with competing values relating to themselves. These emotions have a role also where several agents are involved, and the decision maker's own interests are not really of concern: this is typically the case, for example, where a manager is making decisions affecting a group of staff. Here we would expect attitudes of like and dislike to influence the way the manager orders values promoted in respect of his staff. For example, suppose that Teddy and Karen's travel arrangements were decided by their manager rather than by their mutual agreement: an indifferent manager might have the order $(St = Sk) > P > (Ct = Ck)$. Suppose that the manager liked Teddy better than Karen: now his ordering would become $St > Sk > P > Ct > Ck$. Normally, we would expect liking and disliking only to influence the order of the values with respect to particular agents *within* the overall value order. If, however, these emotions become very intense, the effect may be on the *order of values*, rather than merely the ordering of individuals within a value. Intense liking for Teddy might lead the decision maker to prefer Teddy's Comfort to the common good of Pleasure, and intense dislike for Karen might lead to preferring Pleasure to her Speed: $St > Ct > P > Sk > Ck$. At this point it may be that we think the decision making is being distorted to the point of bias: like and dislike have tipped over into love and hate (as they were termed in the original OCC model). Certainly such instances of illegitimate bias abound in human decision making, but we may wish to disallow them in an agent system, and to ensure that a value in respect of a particular agent is not promoted beyond a supposedly preferred value in this way.

We can also consider the effect of joy and distress. It is well known that the best time to ask a person for something is when they are in a good mood. A joyful agent is more likely to be amenable to requests than one experiencing distress. Thus, if the manager agent experiences a lot of joy-evoking events, it may revise its value order so that, for example, Pleasure becomes preferred to Speed. This seems natural: if a lot of time has been saved because Speed has been much promoted, Speed becomes less critical, whereas it may rise in importance if many delays have been suffered. Again, it can be seen that this can have some beneficial effects. A rigid and unchanging value order will lead to one-sided decisions, continually promoting one value at the expense of another. Experiencing joy will mean that a consistent run of success has been achieved, and so the more favored values will have been served. A mechanism which allows attention to be turned to promoting some more neglected value (remember that all the values are legitimate values worthy of promoting and that a different agent could equally well have chosen a different ordering to start with) will often be desirable. Equally, the failure which gave rise to distress might have meant that the values of the decision-making agent were radically out of step with the other agents, and a more cooperative atmosphere may result from some reordering.

In this section, we have described how the emotions of gratitude, displeasure, like, dislike, joy and distress can arise in our decision-making model. We have also discussed how these emotions can influence decisions in ways which correspond to experience of human decision making, and which are likely to have beneficial effects on the decision making of a society of agents. In the next, section we will explore these points further with an extended example involving a manager and several staff.

5   Extended Example

Here our extended example is based on the example used to illustrate the decision making methodology in [9]. Suppose there is an academic Head of Department (HoD) who must make a series of decisions related to his staff. The HoD has four concerns: he wishes to increase the international reputation of the Department, increase the number and quality of the papers written by members of his Department, develop the careers of his staff and, so, enhance their experience, and to keep his staff happy. The HoD thus has four values: two are common goods, Reputation (R) and Publication (P); and two relate to individuals, Experience (E_1, E_2 and E_3) and Happiness (H_1, H_2 and H_3). The HoD will order these values according to his priorities. Suppose that he is most concerned for Reputation, then for Publication, then for Experience and, finally, for Happiness. Suppose also that, initially, the HoD ranks the Experience and Happiness of all his staff equally. The staff will have the values of Experience and Happiness. If they are ambitious and want to further their careers, they will value Experience over Happiness, otherwise they will prefer Happiness to Experience. We have four agents: The Head of the Department (HoD), and three staff (S1, S2 and S3).

We will use a simplified picture of the HoD's job, in which he can ask people to write papers, send them to conferences and give them places on training courses. In response, the members of staff may attend the training or not, may or may not succeed in writing a paper, and, if they go to a conference, may make an impact, enhancing the reputation of the department, or they may remain relatively anonymous. This gives the following actions, and consequent joint actions.

Possible Actions:

$\alpha_1(n)$: HoD Send staff Sn to a conference,
$\alpha_2(n)$: HoD Ask staff Sn to write a paper
$\alpha_3(n)$: HoD Send staff Sn on a training course
$\beta_n, \beta_n\prime$: Staff Sn does well/poorly in the conference
$\gamma_n, \gamma_n\prime$: Staff Sn does /does not write a paper
$\delta_n, \delta_n\prime$: Staff Sn attends /does not attend the training

Possible Joint Actions:

$j1_n : (\alpha_1(n), \beta_n)$, $j2_n : (\alpha_1, \beta_n\prime)$, $j3_n : (\alpha_2, \gamma_n)$, $j4_n : (\alpha_2, \gamma_n\prime)$, $j5_n : (\alpha_3, \delta_n)$, $j6_n : (\alpha_3, \delta_n\prime)$

Next we need to see how values can be promoted. Staff enjoy attending conferences, (irrespective of how they perform), but do not enjoy training courses. Staff experience is promoted by attending training courses. Publication is promoted whenever staff write papers (writing a paper includes getting it accepted), and Reputation is promoted when a member of staff performs well at a conference. Thus: Values (V) are:

R is promoted by $j1_n$ for any n, **P** is promoted by $j3_n$ for any n
H(n) is promoted by $j1_n$, $j2_n$, and demoted by $j5_n$, **E(n)** is promoted by $j5_n$.

We next need to define how emotions will affect the ranking of values for the HoD. Let us suppose that if the particular HoD likes a member of staff he will give more value to the happiness of that member of staff. Dislike will cause him to value the experience of the member of staff less. If the HoD experiences joy, the happiness of his staff will become more important, and the value with respect to which it is felt will diminish in importance, and conversely with distress, it will increase in importance. The effect on the value order of these changes will depend on the particular agent: some agents will be volatile and react to quite small emotional stimuli, whereas others will respond only to strong stimuli. We can represent this by associating initial weight with each value. The ordering of these weights will give the value order, and the difference between adjacent weights will represent the volatility of the agent with respect to those values. Suppose the initial weights, uninfluenced by emotions, for R, P, E and H are r, p, e and h. Now to give the effects of the emotions in our scenario we can say:

$r_{t_n} = r - J(R, t_{n-1})$. That is, the weight of R decreases as joy with respect to R is experienced, and rises as distress is experienced.

$p_{t_n} = p - J(P, t_{n-1})$. That is, the weight of P decreases as joy with respect to P is experienced, and rises as distress is experienced.

$e_{i_{t_n}} = e - J(E, t_{n-1}) + \min(0, L(i, t_{n-1})))$ That is, the value placed on an agent's experience decreases with joy in respect of experience and dislike for the particular agent.

$h_{i_{t_n}} = h + J(R, t_{n-1}) + J(P, t_{n-1}) + J(E, t_{n-1}) + \max(0, L(i, t_{n-1}))$. That is, weight placed on an agent's happiness increases with joy with respect to the other values and liking for the agent.

In what follows we will subscript the values with weights. We want the agent to initially order the values $R > P > (E_1 = E_2 = E_3) > (H_1 = H_2 = H_3)$. We also want the agent to rank R and P quite closely, and E and H quite closely, but to always prefer both R and P to H and E. The weights of P and R must therefore be substantially higher than those of H and E. For illustrative purposes we can use any weights with the correct properties: we arbitrarily choose $r = 240$,

$p = 239$, $e = 7$ and $h = 6$ for our example. Thus the initial Value Order of the HoD, Value Order at t $= 0$ is:

$$VO_0: R_{240} > P_{239} > (E1_7 = E2_7 = E3_7) > (H1_6 = H2_6 = H3_6).$$

The extent of the impact of events on the emotions of gratitude and displeasure depends, as discussed in the previous section, on how unexpected the event is. Since he assumes that his staff are ambitious, the HoD will expect that staff attend training courses when they are offered, will hope that they write a paper, but since this is not easy, recognizes that they may fail. Making a significant impact at a conference is quite unusual, and so the accomplishment of j1 will be rather unexpected. Thus, the HoD will, as opportunity arises, given V_0, try to bring about j1, j3 and j5: j5 is expected, (0.9) j3 is thought likely (0.6) and j1 is very unexpected (0.1).

In this paper, we will only show how emotions will affect the value ordering, the other steps of the decision making process are fully discussed in [9].

Suppose, on taking over, the HoD has the chance to send all three members of staff on training courses. He will do so and expect them to attend. The state reached by $j5_n$ will promote the HoD's fourth most important value (remember the experience of each member of staff is ranked equally, so their position is averaged), and demote his seventh most important value, since the staff do not enjoy the training, giving the state a value of 3, whereas $j6_n$ will have a value of 2. Thus the HoD will feel gratitude with an intensity of 0.3 if a member of staff attends and displeasure with intensity 1.8 if the staff member does not attend.

Suppose S1 and S2 are suitably ambitious and so do attend, but S3 prefers happiness to experience and therefore chooses to miss the course. Because attendance was expected, the HoD will feel a little gratitude towards S1 and S2, but considerable displeasure towards S3. This also means that the HoD will feel distress rather than joy. The HoD emotional state is now:

$$L_{HoD}(S1, 1) = 0.3; L_{HoD}(S2, 1) = 0.3; L_{HoD}(S3, 1) = -1.8; J_{HoD}(E, 1) = -1.2$$

His value order at time 1 then becomes

$$VO_1: R_{240} > P_{239} > (E1_{8.2} = E2_{8.2}) > E3_{6.4} > (H1_{5.1} = H2_{5.1}) > H3_{4.8}.$$

Now the HoD will be inclined to send S1 and S2 to conferences in preference to S3. Next, suppose a conference does occur, to which only two people can be sent. Since the HoD now prefers the happiness of S1 and S2 to S3, he will choose to send them. At the conference, S1 performs very well and impresses a number of leading academics, whereas S2 is an undistinguished participant. Thus j1 is achieved in respect of S1 and j2 in respect of S2. With respect to S1 R and H_1 are promoted. The state reached by S1 has an importance of 10.5 to the HoD. Since the unexpectedness was 0.9, the intensity of gratitude towards S1 is 9.45. With regard to S2, the state reached has importance 5.5 and unexpectedness

0.1: thus the intensity of displeasure towards S2 is 0.55. This gives the HoD emotional state as:

$$L_{HoD}(S1, 2) = 9.75; L_{HoD}(S2, 2) = -0.25; L_{HoD}(S3, 2) = -1.8; J_{HoD}(E, 2) = -1.2; J_{HoD}(R, 2) = 9.5$$

Now the HoD has experienced considerable joy: the success of S1 at the conference leads him to raise the importance of happiness for his staff. Also it lowers the importance of R :

$$VO_2: P_{239} > R_{230.5} > H1_{24.05} > (H2_{14.3} = H3_{14.3}) > E1_{8.2} > E2_{7.95} > E3_{6.4}.$$

Now the new importance of P means that the HoD turns his focus to publication and asks all three staff to write papers. Suppose that S1 and S3 succeed, but S2 is unable to produce a worthwhile paper. The importance of the paper being written was 8, and the importance of failure was 8, since no other values were promoted by reaching the alternative state. Since the unexpectedness of success was 0.4, this gives rise to gratitude with respect to S1 and S3 with intensity 3.2 and displeasure towards S2 with intensity 4.8. The HoD's value emotional state becomes:

$$L_{HoD}(S1, 3) = 12.95; L_{HoD}(S2, 3) = -5.05; L_{HoD}(S3, 3) = 1.4; J_{HoD}(E, 3) = -1.2; J_{HoD}(R, 3) = 9.5; J_{HoD}(P, 3) = 1.6$$

Now S2 has failed to live up to his initial good impression: successive failures have obliterated it. S3 meanwhile has redeemed himself, and is now in favor.

$$VO_3: P_{237.4} > R_{230.5} > H1_{28.85} > H3_{17.3} > H2_{15.9} > (E1_{8.2} = E3_{8.2}) > E2_{1.95}).$$

This is, necessarily, a simplified and somewhat idealised example, but nevertheless it does serve to illustrate some important points. First, we can see that when it comes to ordering agents within a value even quite small changes can have an impact, but something rather significant is required to affect the ordering of the values themselves. Where values are ranked equally, a slight change will make a difference: this is useful in that equally ranked values impede the ability of the decision making approach to reach definite conclusions, meaning that decisions may be arbitrary. Second, we can note that the short-term promotion of happiness by staff 3 when he missed the training course, was not in his long-term interests since, subsequently, he was overlooked for conference attendance. Thus, the mechanism fosters cooperation with the wishes of the HoD. Thirdly, we can see that the effect of joy is to enable a shift in focus: the success of S1 at the conference meant that reputation did not need to be given such a high priority. Finally, the example suggests that some decay on joy may be required: although the short-term shift in focus was desirable, we might prefer to see the standard preferences reasserting themselves after a while.

6   Concluding Remarks

In this paper, we have shown how we can integrate emotions into a rational decision making process by which an agent chooses between alternative courses of action, building on previous work, especially [13] for emotions and [9] for decision making. Whereas [13] focused on the role of hope and fear, however, we have in particular investigated the emotions of gratitude and displeasure, like and dislike, joy and distress. These emotions seem to play a beneficial role in decision making in that:

1. Emotions can motivate choice between actions which seem equally desirable from a purely rational perspective
2. The motivation in 1 provides a mechanism which fosters cooperation, since cooperative agents will be favored over less cooperative agents
3. Emotions provide a mechanism by which an agent can re-evaluate its priorities, avoiding a single-minded pursuit of one goal to the exclusion of other desirable goals.

Although we have described the mechanism, and characterised formally in terms of our decision making model, when these emotions arise, we have only sketched the more quantitative aspects. Currently, we have implemented the decision making model without emotions. Our next step will be to add emotions, so that we can get a better understanding of the acceptable settings for the crucial parameters which govern the intensity of emotions and the extent of its effect on the decisions of the agent.

References

1. Atkinson, K., Bench-Capon, T.J.M.: Practical reasoning as presumptive argumentation using action based alternating transition systems. Artif. Intell. 171(10-15), 855–874 (2007)
2. Atkinson, K., McBurney, P., Bench-Capon, T.: Computational representation of practical arguments. In: Knowledge, rationality and action, pp. 191–240 (2006)
3. BenchCapon, T.: Persuasion in practical argument using value-based argumentation frameworks. Journal of Logic and Computation 13(3), 429–448 (2003)
4. Bratman, M.E., Israel, D.J., Pollack, M.E.: Plans and resource-bounded practical reasoning. Computational Intelligence 4, 349–355 (1988)
5. Damasio, A.: Descartes' Error. G.P. Putnams Sons (1994)
6. Dung, P.M.: On the acceptability of arguments and its fundamental role in non-monotonic reasoning, logic programming. Artificial Intelligence (1995)
7. Jiang, H., Vidal, J.M., Huhns, M.N.: Ebdi: an architecture for emotional agents. In: Proceedings of AAMAS 2007, pp. 1–3. ACM, New York (2007)
8. Meyer, J.J.: Towards a quantitative model of emotions for intelligent agents. In: Emotions and computing (2007)
9. Nawwab, F.S., Bench-Capon, T.J.M., Dunne, P.E.: A methodology for action-selection using value-based argumentation. In: Besnard, P., Doutre, S., Hunter, A. (eds.) Proceedings of COMMA 2008. Frontiers in Artificial Intelligence and Applications, vol. 172, pp. 264–275. IOS Press, Amsterdam (2008)

10. Ortony, A., Clore, G., Collins, A.: The Cognitive Structure of Emotions. Cambridge University Press, Cambridge (1988)
11. Padgham, L., Taylor, G.: A system for modelling agents having emotion and personality. In: Cavedon, L., Wobcke, W., Rao, A.S. (eds.) PRICAI-WS 1996. LNCS, vol. 1209, pp. 59–71. Springer, Heidelberg (1997)
12. Reilly, W.S.: Believable social and emotional agents. PhD thesis, Carnegie Mellon University, CMU (1996)
13. Steunebrink, B.R., Dastani, M., Meyer, J.-J.C.: A logic of emotions for intelligent agents. In: AAAI, pp. 142–147. AAAI Press, Menlo Park (2007)
14. Wooldridge, M., van der Hoek, W.: On obligations and normative ability: Towards a logical analysis of the social contract. J. Applied Logic 3(3-4), 396–420 (2005)

Using Personality Types to Support Argumentation

Ricardo Santos[1,2], Goreti Marreiros[1,3], Carlos Ramos[1,3],
José Neves[4], and José Bulas-Cruz[5]

[1] GECAD Knowledge Engineering and Decision Support Group,
Porto, Portugal
{goreti,csr}@dei.isep.ipp.pt
[2] School of Management and Technology of Felgueiras Polytechnic of Porto,
Felgueiras, Portugal
rjs@estgf.ipp.pt
[3] Institute of Engineering Polytechnic of Porto,
Porto, Portugal
{goreti,csr}@dei.isep.ipp.pt
[4] University of Minho,
Braga, Portugal
jneves@di.uminho.pt
[5] University of Trás-os-Montes e Alto Douro,
Vila Real, Portugal
jcruz@utad.pt

Abstract. Despite the advances in argumentation on group decision negotiation there is a need to simulate and identify the personality of participants. To make participants agents more human-like and to increase their flexibility in the negotiation process in group decision-making, the authors investigated the role of personality behaviours of participants applied to the conflict style theme. The negotiation is made in a bilateral way where both parties are OCEAN participant agents based on the five-factor model of personality (Openness, Conscientiousness, Extraversion, Agreeableness and Negative emotionality).

Keywords: Argumentation, Group Decision Making, Multi- agent systems, Personality.

1   Introduction

Nowadays groups are used to make decisions about some subject of interest for the organization or community in which they are involved. The scope of such decisions can be diverse. It can be related to economic or political affairs like, for instance, the acquisition of new military equipment. But it can also be a trivial decision making as the choice about a holiday destination by a group of friends. Therefore, it may be claimed that Group Decision Support Systems (GDSS) have emerged as the factor that makes the difference one assess the behavior and performance of different computational systems in different applications domains, with a particular focus on socialization. Groups of individuals

P. McBurney et al. (Eds.): ArgMAS 2009, LNAI 6057, pp. 292–304, 2010.

have access to more information and more resources what will (probably) allow reaching better and quicker decisions. However working in group has also some difficulties associated, e.g. time consuming; high costs; improper use of group dynamics and incomplete tasks analysis.

Many of this will take a new dimension if we consider that they will be resolved by a group of individuals, each one with a different type of personality. Our society is characterized by the use of groups to make decisions about some subject of interest for the organization in which they are involved. If we predict the personality of our adversaries we could find the best arguments to be used in the negotiation process in order to reach a consensus or a better decision in the shortest possible time. Personality is one of many individual difference variables that affect group interaction and their outcomes [1]. McRae & Costa [2] grouped a wide array of personality traits into five factors, which they referred to as the Big Five. The Big Five has proven to be the most widely accepted tool for measuring personality, even cross-culturally [3]. The use of multi-agent systems is very suitable to simulate the behaviour of groups of people working together and, in particular, to group decision making modelling, once it caters for individual modelling, flexibility and data distribution [4][5]. Various interaction and decision mechanisms for automated negotiation have been proposed and studied. Approaches to automated negotiation can be classified in three categories [6], namely game theoretic, heuristic and argumentation based. We think that an argumentation-based approach is the most adequate for group decision-making, since agents can justify possible choices and convince other elements of the group about the best or worst alternatives.

Agent Based simulation is considered an important tool in a broad range of areas e.g. individual decision making (what if scenarios), e-commerce (to simulate the buyers and sellers behaviour), crisis situations (e.g. simulate fire combat), traffic simulation, military training, entertainment (e.g. movies). According to the architecture that we are proposing we intend to give support to decision makers in both of the aspects identified by Zachary and Ryder [7], namely supporting them in a specific decision situation and giving them training facilities in order to acquire competencies and knowledge to be used in a real decision group meeting. We claim that agent based simulation can be used with success in both tasks. In our multi-agent architecture model [8] we have two different types of agents: the Facilitator agent and the Participant agent. The Facilitator agent is responsible for the meeting in its organization (e.g. decision problem and alternatives definition). During the meeting, the Facilitator agent will coordinate all the processes and, at the end, will report the results of the meeting to the participants involved. The Participant Agent will be described in detail in the next section.

In this work we are presenting a new argumentation process with the inclusion of the personality using the Five-Factor Model of Personality (FFM) [2]. The personality of our opponents in the negotiation will be identified and used to select the best arguments for that instance.

2   Participant Agent

The participant agent has a very important role in the group decision support system assisting the participant of the meeting. This agent represents the user in the virtual world and is intended to have the same personality and to make the same decision as if it were the real participant user. For that reason we will present the architecture and a detailed view of all the component parts. The architecture is divided in three layers: the knowledge layer, the interaction layer and the reasoning layer (Fig. 1).

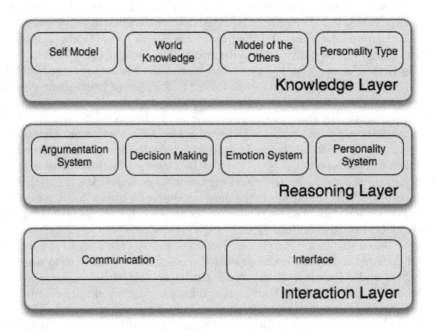

Fig. 1. Participant Agent Architecture

2.1   Knowledge Layer

In the knowledge layer the agent has information about the environment where he is situated, about the profile of the other participants agents that compose the meeting group, and regarding its own preferences and goals (its own profile).

The personality is defined in this layer through the Big Five Inventory (BFI) [9] and available publicly to be used by the other opponent participants.

The information in the knowledge layer has some kind of uncertainty [10] and will be made more accurate along the time through interactions done by the agent. Credibility of the participants and the perception that one user has about the others will be refined along he time in the Model of the Others component.

A database of profiles and history with the groups model is maintained and this model is built incrementally during the different interactions with the system. The community should be persistent because it is necessary to have information about previous group decision making processes, focusing credibility, reputation and past behaviours of other participants.

2.2 Reasoning Layer

The agent must be able to reason based on complete or incomplete information. In this layer the reasoning mechanics is based on the information available in the knowledge layer and on the messages received from other agents through the interaction layer. The reasoning mechanism will determine the behaviour of the agent and allow the acquisition of new knowledge, essentially based on previous experiences.

The reasoning layer contains three major modules:

- The argumentative system that is responsible for the arguments generation. This component will generate persuasive arguments, which are more related with the internal emotional state of the agent, and about what he, thinks from others profiles (including the emotional state).
- The decision making module will support agents in the choice of the preferred alternative. The preferred alternatives are in the self model of the participant agent filtered and sorted by this component.
- The emotional system [4] will generate emotions and moods, affecting the choice of the arguments to send to the other participants, the evaluation of the received arguments and the final decision. The emotions that will be simulated in our system are those identified in the reviewed version of the OCC (Ortony, Clore and Collins) model: joy, hope, relief, pride, gratitude, like, distress, fear, disappointment remorse, anger and dislike (please see [11] for more detail).
- The personality system will identify the personality of the other participants in order to find the best strategy for the argumentation on the negotiation process based on the FFM of personality [19].

2.3 Interaction Layer

The interaction layer is responsible for the communication with other agents and by the interface with the user of the group decision-making system. All the messages received will be sorted, decoded and sent to the right layer based on their internal data. The knowledge that the participant user has about his actions and of the others are obtained through this layer.

3 Argumentation Process

During a group decision meeting, participant agents may exchange the following locutions: request, refuse, accept, request with argument.

- $Request(AgPi, AgPj, \alpha, arg)$ - in this case agent $AgPi$ is asking agent $AgPj$ to perform action α, the parameter arg may be void and in that case it is a request without argument or may have one of the arguments specified at the end of this section.

- $Accept(AgPj, AgPi, \alpha)$ - in this case agent $AgPj$ is telling agent $AgPi$ that it accepts its request to perform α.
- $Refuse(AgPj, AgPi, \alpha)$ - in this case agent $AgPj$ is telling agent $AgPi$ that it cannot accept its request to perform α.

The purpose of the participant agent is to assist the user. For example, in Figure 2, it is possible to see the argumentation protocol for two agents.

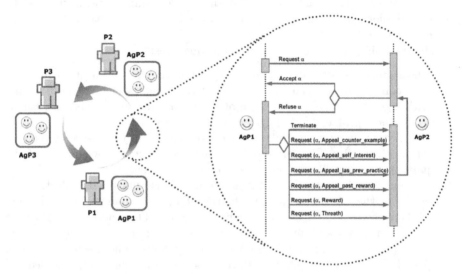

Fig. 2. Argumentation Protocol

This is the simplest scenario, because in real world situations, group decision making involves more than two agents and, at the same time $AgP1$ is trying to persuade $AgP2$, that agent may be involved in other persuasion dialogues with other group members.

Argument nature and type can vary, however six types of arguments are assumed to have persuasive force in human based negotiations [12]: threats; promise of a future reward; appeal to past reward; appeal to counter-example; appeal to prevailing practice; and appeal to self interest [13]. These are the arguments that agents will use to persuade each other.

This selection of arguments is compatible with the power relations identified in the political model: reward, coercive, referent, and legitimate [14].

4   Personality Type Identification

In order to make agents more human-like and to increase their flexibility to argument and to reach agreements in the negotiation process, we updated the previous agent participant model [15] and included the personality system component. Each participant agent its intended to have the same personality as the real participant of the meeting in order to make the same decisions. Personality plays an important role on the behaviors of the participants in a decision meeting. Behaviors are influenced by personalities so that personality refers to sets of predictive behaviors by which people are recognized and identified [16].

Personality is impossible to define succinctly because it means different things to different personality Psychologists. The definition of Personality is not widely consensual but most Psychologists accept that the field of personality is the study of how individuals differ from one another. Personality influences the way people perceives their environment, affects their behaviours and distinguish one from another. The disagreements arise on the best way to conceptualize these individual differences.

Although there is no universally accepted theory of personality the Five Factor Model or OCEAN model [17] is the most widely used in the simulation of human-like computer models. According to this model, the personality of an individual can be defined according to five different traits: openness, conscientiousness, extraversion, agreeableness and negative emotionality, which are explained in [18][19]. Usually, an individual is represented as a combination of these traits possibly with emphasis on one of them. Howard & Howard created a table (table 1) of the personality facets and their different levels [20].

This attributes in the table will later help in the definition of the set of arguments to used in the negotiation process for a specific type of personality.

The FFM will be used in the negotiation process between the participants of a decision meeting. We expect to achieve an improvement of the negotiation process with the selection of the best approach to each type of personality identified. The identification of the personality of each participant its classified using the BFI [9] and fit in one of the themes based on the FFM that we can see on table 2. A theme is a characteristic personality pattern that reflects the combined effect of two or more factors or facets. In the table a plus (+) indicates a score above 55, a minus (-) indicates a score below 45, and a letter without either plus or minus indicates a score in the 45-55 range.

As we can see there are several types of themes based on the FFM for each set of personality types. For the decision making area the themes that could be applied are: the conflict styles and the decision style. We select the conflict style because we will be using the personality in the negotiation process where many disagreements and conflicts arise. The conflict styles theme uses only four of the five factors of the five factor model that are: the agreeableness, the conscientiousness, the extraversion and the negative emotionality. Next we will present some definitions for each one of these factors.

The Agreeableness Factor

Agreeableness is tendency to be a nice person [21]. Agreeableness refers to the number of sources from which one takes ones norms for right behaviour [20].

The Conscientiousness Factor

Conscientiousness is tendency to set high goals, to accomplish work successfully, and to behave dutifully and morally [21]. Furthermore, conscience is the awareness of a moral or ethical aspect to ones conduct together with the

Table 1. Five Factor Model

Level	Low	Medium	High
Factor 1:			
Negative Emotionality	Resilent (N-)	Responsive (N)	Reactive (N+)
N1: Worry	More calm (N1-)	Worried/calm (N1)	More worried (N1+)
N2: Anger	Slow to anger (N2-)	Some anger (N2)	Quick to anger (N2+)
N3: Discouragement	Seldom sad (N3-)	Occasionally sad (N3)	Often sad (N3+)
N4: Self-Consciousness	Seldom embarrassed (N4-)	Sometimes embarrassed (N4)	Easily embarrassed (N4+)
N5: Impulsiveness	Seldom yielding (N5-)	Sometimes yielding (N5)	Often yielding (N5+)
N6: Vulnerabilty	Stress resistant (N6-)	Some stress (N6)	Stress prone (N6+)
Factor 2:			
Extraversion	Introvert (E-)	Ambivert (E)	Extravert (E+)
E1: Warmth	Aloof (E1-)	Attentive (E1)	Cordial (E1+)
E2: Gragariousness	Prefers alone (E2-)	Alone/others (E2)	Prefers company (E2+)
E3: Assertiveness	In background (E3-)	In foreground (E3)	A leader (E3+)
E4: Activity	Leisurely (E4-)	Average pace (E4)	Vigorous (E4+)
E5: Excitement-Seeking	Low need for thrills (E5-)	Occasionally need for thrills (E5)	Craves thrills (E5+)
E6: Positive Emotions	Seldom exuberant (E6-)	Moderate exuberance (E6)	Usually cheerful (E6+)
Factor 3:			
Openess	Preserver (O-)	Moderate (O)	Explorer (O+)
O1: Fantasy	Here and now (O1-)	Occasionally imaginative (O1)	A dreamer (O1+)
O2: Aesthetics	Uninterested in art (O2-)	Moderate interest in art (O2)	Major interest in art (O2+)
O3: Feelings	Ignores feelings (O3-)	Accepts feelings (O3)	Values all emotions (O3+)
O4: Actions	The familiar (O4-)	A mixture (O4)	Variety (O4+)
O5: Ideas	Narrow focus (O5-)	Moderate curiosity (O5)	Broad intellectual curiosity (O5+)
O6: Values	Conservative (O6-)	Moderate (O6)	Open to new values (O6+)
Factor 4:			
Agreeableness	Challenger (A-)	Negotiator (A)	Adapter (A+)
A1: Trust	Skeptical (A1-)	Cautious (A1)	Trusting (A1+)
A2: Straigthforwardness	Guarded (A2-)	Tactful (A2)	Frank (A2+)
A3: Altruism	Uninvolved (A3-)	Willing to help others (A3)	Eager to help (A3+)
A4: Compliance	Aggressive (A4-)	Approachable (A4)	Defers (A4+)
A5: Modesty	Superior (A5-)	Equal (A5)	Humble (A5+)
A6: Tender-Mindedness	Hardheaded (A6-)	Responsive (A6)	Easily moved (A6+)
Factor 5:			
Conscientiousness	Flexible (C-)	Balanced (C)	Focused (C+)
C1: Competence	Unprepared (C1-)	Prepared (C1)	Capable (C1+)
C2: Order	Unorganized (C2-)	Half-organized (C2)	Well-organized (C2+)
C3: Dutifulness	Dutifulness (C3-)	Covers priorities (C3)	Strong conscience (C3+)
C4: Achievement Striving	Casual about success (C4-)	Serious about success (C4)	Driven to succed (C4+)
C5: Self-Discipline	Distractible (C5-)	Mix of work and play (C5)	Focused on work (C5+)
C6: Deliberation	Spontaneous (C6-)	Thoughtful (C6)	Careful (C6+)

urge to prefer right over wrong [22]. Conscientiousness refers to the number of goals on which one is focused [20].

The Extraversion Factor

Extraversion is a trait associated with sociability and positive affect [21]. It refers to the number of relationships with which one is comfortable [20]. High on extraversion: Interest in or behavior directed toward others or one's environment rather than oneself [22].

Table 2. Themes based on the Five-Factor Model [18]

Theme Category & Theme	Components	
Leadership Style	Visionary	O+, A-
	Catalyst	O+, A+
	Troubleshooter	O-, C-
	Traditionalist	O-, C+
Holland Hexagon	Realistic	O-, A-
	Investigative	E-, O+, C-
	Artistic	N+, E+, O+, A-, C-
	Social	N-, E+, A+
	Enterprising	E+, A-, C-
	Conventional	E-, O-, A+, C-
Conflict Styles	Negotiator	N, E(+), A, C(-)
	Agressor	N+, E+, A-, C+
	Submissive	N-, E-, A+, C-
	Avoider	N+, E-, C-
Learning Style	Classroom	N+, E-
	Tutorial	N+, E+
	Correspondence	N-, E-
	Independent	N-, E+
Decision Style	Autocrat	N+, O-, A-, C+
	Bureaucrat	N-, C+
	Diplomat	N-, A, C-
	Consensus	N+, E+, A+, C
Sample Careers	Entrepreneur	E+, O+, A, C+
	Flight Attendant	N+, E+, O+
	Trainer	N(+), E+, O, A+, C
	Sales	N-, E+, O, A, C+

The Negative Emotionality Factor

Negative Emotionality, neuroticism, or need for stability is the trait associated with emotional instability and negative affect [21]. Negative Emotionality refers to the number and strength of stimuli required to elicit negative emotions in a person [20].

After selecting the conflict styles theme we started to select the different set of arguments to be used in each one of the four personality types: Negotiator, Aggressor, Submissive and Avoider.

5   Using Personality to Support the Argumentation Process

In the previous model the argumentation process between two participants consisted in the exchange of arguments that could be accepted or rejected by the parties. The arguments were defined by Sarit Kraus [13] that had natural order of argument power to be sent: Appeal to self interest, Appeal to prevailing practice, Appeal to counter example, Appeal to past reward, Promise of future reward, Threat. With the inclusion of the personality we can specify which arguments can be sent to the different types of personalities identified.

We make a selection of what arguments would be best to be used by the different personalities. This depends on the participants personality type of the conflict Styles theme: Negotiator, Submissive, Aggressor and Avoider.

First we will show for each one of the arguments used in the negotiation process which personality factors and facets have a grater impact on their use.

5.1 Appeal to Self Interest (C=↑, E=↑)

In this case the participant agent that makes a request supported by this argument expects to convince his interlocutor that making action A is of his best interest.

The Conscientiousness (C) and the Extraversion (E) are two important factors for the use of this argument. A very important facet to justify the use of the conscientiousness factor is the C4: Achievement striving. For this facet we can have a participant: casual about success (C4-), serious about success (C4) or driven to success (C4+). Another important facet in the Extraversion is C3 (Assertiveness) where we can have a participant: in background (C3-), in foreground (C3) or a leader (C3+).

It will only be considered the use of this argument in the negotiation with balanced (C) or focused participants (C+), more precisely in foreground (C3) or leaders (C3+).

5.2 Appeal to Prevailing Practice (C=↑, E=↑)

In this case, the participant agent believes that the opponent agent will refuse to perform a request action since it contradicts one of its own goals. For that reason the participant agent sends a request with an argument that it has been accepted the same request made to a third participant agent in the same conditions.

In our opinion the personality factors with more impact in this argument are the Agreeableness and the Negative Emotionality. In the Agreeableness all the facets are important and we will not emphasise any of the attributes from the group. For the negative emotionality the more important facets are N3 (Discouragement) and N5 (Impulsiveness). Depending on the level for the Discouragement it can be seldom sad (N3-), sometimes sad (N3), often sad (N3+) and for the Impulsiveness it can be: seldom yielding (N5-), sometimes yielding (N5) and often yielding (N5+).

This argument will only be considered in the negotiation with the agreeableness level of negotiator (A) or adapter (A+) and with the negative emotionality level of Responsive (N) and Reactive (N+).

The Adapter is prone to subordinate personal needs to those of the group, to accept the groups norms rather than insisting on his or her personal norms contrary to the Challenger that is more self focused. The Negotiator sometimes is a kind of Adapter and other times is more a Challenger but included this level due to the association with N3, N3+, N5, and N5+ facets of the negative emotionality factor.

5.3 Appeal to Counter Example (A=↑)

In this case, the participant agent that makes a request supported by this argument, expect to convey the opponent that there is a contradiction between what he says and his past actions.

In our opinion the personality factor that has more impact in this argument is the Agreeableness. High agreeableness describes someone who is seeking harmony. The best situation is win-win situation.

It will only be considered the use of this argument in the negotiation with the agreeableness level of negotiator (A) or adapter (A+).

5.4 Appeal to Past Reward (C=↑)

In this case the participant agent sends such kind of argument expecting that his interlocutor performs an action based on a past promise.

To use this argument the participant with whom we will perform a request should be trustworthy. The personality factors that are more related to that type of concern is the Conscientiousness. A facet that justifies this factor better for the use of this argument is C3 (Dutifulness) that can be, casual about obligations (C3-), covers priorities (C3) or strong conscience (C3+).

This argument will only be considered in the negotiation with the conscientiousness level of Balanced (C) and Focused (C+).

5.5 Reward (C=↑, =↑)

Like threats we can also have two distinct forms of rewards: If you perform action A I can perform B; and If you do not perform action A I perform B.

In our opinion the personality factors that has more impact in this argument are the Conscientiousness and the Negative Emotionality. For the conscientiousness the facet that justifies the factor better for the use of this argument is C3 (Dutifulness) that can be casual about obligations (C3-), covers priorities (C3) or strong conscience (C3+). For the case of the negative emotionality the more important facet is the N3 (Discouragement) that can be, seldom sad (N3-), sometimes sad (N3) or often sad (N3+).

This argument will only be considered in the negotiation with the conscientiousness level of, Balanced (C) and Focused (C+) and with the negative emotionality level of, Responsive (N) or Reactive (N+).

5.6 Threat (N=↑)

As previously referred, threats are very common in human negotiation, and they can assume two distinct forms: you should perform action A otherwise I will perform action B; and you should not perform action A otherwise I will perform action B.

In our opinion the negative emotionality factor is the more important in the use of this argument. High negative emotionality refers to persons that are bothered by a greater variety of stimuli, and the stimuli do not have to be strong to bother them.

This argument will only be considered in the negotiation with Responsive (N) or Reactive (N+).

6 Personality in Argumentation Process

To resume the previous study of the impacts that personality factors of the FFM have on each one of the arguments that we pretend to use in the negotiation

Table 3. Resume of possible arguments to each personality on the conflicts style

	Appeal to self interest	Appeal to prevailing practice	Appeal to counter example	Appeal to past reward	Promisse of furure reward	Threat
Negotiator	Yes	Yes	Yes	Yes	Yes	Yes
Aggressor	Yes	No	No	Yes	Yes	Yes
Submissive	No	No	Yes	No	No	No
Avoider	No	Yes	Yes	No	No	Yes

process we created a table (Table 3) were we can see all the possibilities. This table and the study is only applied to the personalities of the conflict styles theme.

In order to exemplify the use of the personality in the argumentation process for our multi-agent model [8] we present a diagram (figure 3) with two participant agents (*AgP*1 and *AgP*2) for a general meeting. To explain the diagram we are going to describe the numbered circles (1, 2, 3 and 4).

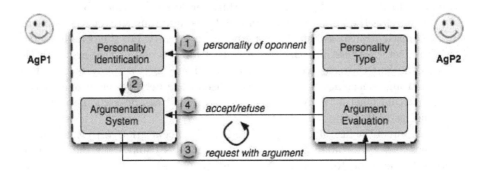

Fig. 3. Participant Agent Architecture

In the diagram we can see two agents (*AgP*1 and *AgP*2) were *AgP*1 would like to make a request to *AgP*2. The more important steps that occur in our model are the following:

1. *AgP*1 receives the personality of *AgP*2 and proceeds to the personality identification component. In this component we will verify if the received information is compatible with previous negotiations with this participant.
2. The personality type is sent to the argumentation system.
3. The argumentation system component selects the possible set of arguments and starts making a request with the weaker argument.
4. *AgP*2 receives the request, evaluates and accepts it or refuses it.

Several iterations can occur in steps 3 and 4, depending on the set of possible arguments to be sent to *AgP*2.

7   Conclusion

This work proposes the inclusion of the personality in the negotiation process of an argument-based decision-making. Each person is unique and has different reactions to the exchanged arguments. Many times a disagreement arises because of the way we began arguing and not because of the content. Our main goal on a decision meeting is to reach consensus where everyone can be satisfied about the result. The principal determinant of a members degree of satisfaction with his or her groups decision is the extent to which the member agrees with the decision [23].

Each participant agent represents a group decision member. This representation facilitates the simulation of persons with different personalities. The discussion process between group members (agents) is made through the exchange of persuasive arguments, built around the same premises stated before.

As future work we will include the emotional component also in the argumentation process.

References

1. Haslett, B.B., Ruebush, J.: What differences do individual differences in groups make? The effects of individuals, culture, and group composition. In: Frey, L.R. (ed.), Gournan, D.S., Pole, M.S. (Assoc. eds.) The handbook of group communication theory and research, pp. 115–138. Sage, Thousand Oaks (1999)
2. McRae, R.R., Costa, P.T.: Validation of the five-factor model of personality across instruments and observers. Journal of Personality and Social Psychology 52, 81–90 (1987)
3. McRae, R.R., Costa, P.T., Del Pilar, G.H., Rolland, J.P., Parker, W.D.: Cross-cultural assessment of the five-factor model: The revised NEO Personality Inventory. Journal of Cross-Cultural Psychology 29, 171–188 (1998)
4. Marreiros, G., Ramos, C., Neves, J.: Dealing with Emotional Factors in Agent Based Ubiquitous Group Decision. In: Enokido, T., Yan, L., Xiao, B., Kim, D.Y., Dai, Y.-S., Yang, L.T. (eds.) EUC-WS 2005. LNCS, vol. 3823, pp. 41–50. Springer, Heidelberg (2005)
5. Davidsson, P.: Multi agent based simulation: beyond social simulation. In: Moss, S., Davidsson, P. (eds.) Proc. of the Second international Workshop on Multi-Agent Based Simulation, pp. 97–107. Springer, New Jersey (2001)
6. Jennings, N., Faratin, P., Lomuscio, A., Parson, S., Sierra, C., Wooldridge, M.: Automated negotiation: Prospects, methods, and challenges. Journal of Group Decision and Negotiation 2(10), 199–215 (2001)
7. Zachary, W., Ryder, J.: Decision Support Systems: Integrating Decision Aiding and Decision Training. In: Handbook of Human-Computer Interaction, ch. VII, pp. 1235–1258. Elsevier Science, Amsterdam (1997)
8. Marreiros, G., Santos, R., Ramos, C., Neves, J., Novais, P., Machado, J., Bulas-Cruz, J.: Ambient intelligence in emotion based ubiquitous decision making. In: Articial Intelligence Techniques for Ambient Intelligence, IJCAI 2007, Hyderabad, India (2007)

9. John, O.P., Srivastava, S.: The Big Five Trait Taxonomy: History, Measurement, and Theoretical Perspectives. In: Pervin, L.A., John, O.P. (eds.) Handbook of personality: Theory and research, vol. 2, pp. 102–138. Guilford Press, New York (1999)
10. Neves, J.: A Logic Interpreter to Handle Time and Negation in Logic Data Bases. In: Proceedings of ACM 1984, The Fifth Generation Challenge, pp. 50–54 (1984)
11. Andrade, F., Neves, J., Novais, P., Machado, J., Abelha, A.: Legal Security and Credibility in Agent Based Virtual Enterprises. In: Collaborative Networks and Their Breeding Environments, pp. 501–512. Springer, Heidelberg (2005)
12. Ortony, A.: On making believable emotional agents believable. In: Trapple, R. (ed.) Emotions in humans and artefacts. MIT Press, Cambridge (2003)
13. OKeefe, D.: Persuasion: Theory and Research. SAGE Publications, Thousand Oaks (1990)
14. Pruitt, D.: Negotiation Behavior. Academic Press, New York (1981)
15. Kraus, S., Sycara, K., Evenchick, A.: Reaching agreements through argumentation: a logical model and implementation. Artificial Intelligence 104(1-2), 1–69 (1998)
16. Salancik, G., Pfeffer, J.: Who Gets Power and how they hold on to it- A Strategic Contingency Model of Power. Organizational Dynamics 5, 3–21 (1977)
17. Marreiros, G., Santos, R., Ramos, C., Neves, J., Bulas-Cruz, J.: ABS4GD: A Multi-agent System that Simulates Group Decision Processes Considering Emotional and Argumentative Aspects. In: AAAI Spring Symposium on Emotion, Personality and Social Behaviour, Stanford, pp. 88–95 (2008)
18. Ghasem-Aghaee, N., Oren, T.I.: Effects of cognitive complexity in agent simulation: Basics. In: SCS 2004, pp. 15–19 (2004)
19. Costa Jr., P.T., McCrae, P.R.: NEO PI-R Professional Manual. Psychological Assessment Resources, Odessa (1992)
20. Howard, P.J., Howard, J.M.: The BIG FIVE Quickstart: An introduction to the five-factor model of personality for human resource professionals. Center for Applied Cognitive Studies, Charlotte (2004)
21. Acton-Glossary, http://www.personalityresearch.org/glossary.html
22. AHD: The American Heritage Dictionary, http://www.bartleby.com/61/86/c0578600.html
23. Miller, C.E.: The social psychology effects of group decision rules. In: Paulus, P.B. (ed.) Psychology of group influence, 2nd edn., pp. 327–355. Lawrence Erlbaum, Hillsdale (1989)

Comparing Argumentation Frameworks for Composite Ontology Matching

Cássia Trojahn[1,2], Paulo Quaresma[1,2], Renata Vieira[3], and Antoine Isaac[4]

[1] Departmento de Informática, Universidade de Évora, Portugal
[2] CENTRIA - Centro de Inteligência Artificial, Universidade Nova de Lisboa, Lisboa, Portugal
[3] Faculdade de Informática, Pontifícia Universidade Católica do Rio Grande do Sul, Brazil
[4] Vrije Universiteit, Department of Computer Science, Amsterdam, Netherlands
cassia@di.uevora.pt, pq@di.uevora.pt, renata.vieira@pucrs.br,
aisaac@few.vu.nl

Abstract. Resolving the semantic heterogeneity problem is crucial to allow interoperability between ontology-based systems. Ontology matching based on argumentation is an innovative research area that aims at solving this issue, where agents encapsulate different matching techniques and the distinct results are shared, compared, chosen and agreed. In this paper, we compare three argumentation frameworks, which consider different notions of acceptability: based on values and preferences between audiences promoting these values, based on the confidence level of the arguments, and based on voting on the arguments. We evaluate these frameworks using realistic ontologies from an established evaluation test case. The best matcher varies depending on specific characteristics of each set, while considering voting on arguments the results are similar to the best matchers for all cases.

1 Introduction

Ontologies have proven to be an essential element in a range of applications in which knowledge plays a key role. Resolving the semantic heterogeneity problem by means of *ontology matching* is crucial to allow the interoperability between such applications. Ontology matching is the process of linking corresponding entities (classes, proprieties, or instances) from different ontologies.

Many different approaches to the matching problem are found in the literature, which have been surveyed from different perspectives in [7]. The distinction between them is accentuated by the manner in which they exploit the features within an ontology. Whereas syntactic approaches consider measures of string similarity; semantic ones consider semantic relations usually on the basis of lexical oriented linguistic resources. Other approaches consider term positions in the ontology hierarchy or instances of the ontologies. However, each category of approaches offers a wide diversity of options.

The matching systems are usually aware that a combination of different techniques are required for dealing with the problem. The different techniques are

P. McBurney et al. (Eds.): ArgMAS 2009, LNAI 6057, pp. 305–320, 2010.
© Springer-Verlag Berlin Heidelberg 2010

then aggregated in a unified process, where the results can be combined varying from a single weighted sum of individual results to automatically learning the best matcher from preliminary results. Moreover, some techniques will perform better than others for specific cases, depending on how well the technique fits the material available. Also, approaches that perform well for a specific case may not be successful in other ones.

An important issue in ontology matching is therefore to find effective ways of choosing among many techniques and their variations, and then combining their results. An innovative approach to solve this problem is to use frameworks of argumentation, where different matchers based on alternative approaches produce distinct matching results (arguments) that must be shared, compared, chosen and agreed. The matchers exchange the arguments and construct their frameworks of argumentation. The preferred extensions of each matcher are then compared in order to identify set of acceptable arguments.

In this paper, we compare three different frameworks of argumentation, Value-based Argumentation Framework (VAF), Strength-based Argumentation Framework (S-VAF), and Voting-based Argumentation Framework (V-VAF). The VAF [2] is based on the classical framework of Dung, aggregating notions of audiences and preferences. The idea of VAF is to relate the arguments in the dispute to the social values represented by their acceptability for given audiences. Both S-VAF and V-VAF frameworks are based on the VAF, in order to effectively combine different audiences. The S-VAF [25] allows to associate to each argument, a confidence value that represents the strength of the argument. Using V-VAF it is possible to manage consensus, i.e., showing that the more often an argument is agreed on, the more chances for it to be valid. This paper extends the work presented in [10], in which we have compared V-VAF and S-VAF by evaluating their application to a range of individual matchers, in the context of a real-world library case.

In this paper, the three frameworks are evaluated using four matching cases of real ontologies, provided by the benchmark track of Ontology Alignment Evaluation Initiative[1] (OAEI). Particularly, the results of each individual matcher is compared with the results of the different frameworks.

The paper is structured as follows. Section 2 introduces the three argumentation frameworks. In Section 3, the argumentation process for ontology matching is described. In Section 4, the experiments are detailed and the discussion on the results is presented. Section 5 comments on related work. Finally, in Section 6, concluding remarks and future work are presented.

2   Argumentation Frameworks

Both S-VAF and V-VAF are development of the VAF, which is based on the classical system of Dung [5]. This section presents the basic notions upon these frameworks rely.

---

[1] http://oaei.ontologymatching.org/

2.1   Classical Argumentation Framework

Dung, observing that the core notion of argumentation lies in the opposition between arguments and counter-arguments, defines an argumentation framework (AF) as follows:

Definition 1. [5] An Argumentation Framework is a pair $AF = (AR, attacks)$, AR is a set of arguments and *attacks* is a binary relation on AR.

$attacks(a, b)$ means that the argument a attacks the argument b. A set of arguments S attacks an argument b if b is attacked by an argument in S. The key question about the framework is whether a given argument $a \in AR$ should be accepted or not. Dung proposes that an argument should be accepted only if every attack on it is rebutted by an accepted argument. This notion then leads to the definition of acceptability (for an argument), admissibility (for a set of arguments) and preferred extension:

Definition 2. [5] An argument $a \in AR$ is *acceptable* with respect to set arguments S, noted $acceptable(a, S)$, if $\forall x \in AR$ $(attacks(x, a) \longrightarrow \exists y \in S, attacks(y, x))$

Definition 3. [5] A set S of arguments is *conflict-free* if $\neg \exists x, y \in S$, $attacks(x, y)$. A conflict-free set of arguments S is *admissible* if $\forall x \in S$, $acceptable(x, S)$. A set of arguments S is a *preferred extension* if it is a maximal (with respect to set inclusion) admissible set of AR.

A preferred extension represents a consistent position within AF, which defends itself against all attacks and cannot be extended without raising conflicts.

2.2   Value-Based Argumentation Framework (VAF)

In Dung's framework, all arguments have equal strength, and an attack always succeeds, except if the attacking argument is otherwise defeated. However, as noted in [15], in many domains, including ontology matching, arguments may provide reasons which may be more or less persuasive. Moreover, their persuasiveness may vary according to their audience. Bench-Capon has extended the notion of AF in order to associate arguments with the social values they advance:

Definition 4. [2] A Value-based Argumentation Framework (VAF) is a 5-tuple $VAF = (AR, attacks, V, val, P)$ where $(AR, attacks)$ is an argumentation framework, V is a nonempty set of values, *val* is a function which maps elements of AR to elements of V and P is a set of possible audiences.

Practically, in [14], the role of value is played by the types of ontology match that ground the arguments, covering general categories of matching approaches: semantic, structural, terminological and extensional. We argue further — and will use later — that any kind of matching ground identified during a matching process or any specific matching tools may give rise to a value. The only limitations are (i) a value can be identified and shared by a source of arguments and the audience considering this information (ii) audiences can give preferences to the values. An extension to this framework, required for deploying argumentation processes, indeed allows to represent how audiences with different interests can grant preferences to specific values:

Definition 5. [2] An Audience-specific Value-based Argumentation Framework (AVAF) is a 5-tuple $VAF_p = (AR, attacks, V, val, valpref_{aud})$ where AR, $attacks$, V and val are as for a VAF, aud is an audience and $valpref_{aud}$ is a preference relation (transitive, irreflexive and asymmetric), $valpref_{aud} \subseteq V \times V$.

$valpref_{aud}(v_1, v_2)$ means that audience aud prefers v_1 over v_2. Attacks are then deemed successful based on the preference ordering on the arguments' values. This leads to re-defining the notions seen previously:

Definition 6. [2] An argument $a \in AR$ defeats an argument $b \in AR$ for audience aud, noted $defeats_{aud}(a, b)$, if and only if both $attacks(a, b)$ and not $valpref_{aud}(val(b), val(a))$. An argument $a \in AR$ is *acceptable* to audience aud with respect to a set of arguments S, noted $acceptable_{aud}(a, S)$, if $\forall x \in AR$, $defeats_{aud}(x, a) \longrightarrow \exists y \in S$, $defeats_{aud}(y, x)$.

Definition 7. [2] A set S of arguments is *conflict-free* for audience aud if $\forall x, y \in S$, $\neg attacks(x, y) \lor valpref_{aud}(val(y), val(x))$. A *conflict-free* set of arguments S for audience aud is *admissible* for aud if $\forall x \in S$, $acceptable_{aud}(x, S)$. A set of arguments S in the VAF is a *preferred extension* for audience aud if it is a maximal admissible set (with respect to set inclusion) for aud.

In order to determine preferred extensions with respect to a value ordering promoted by distinct audiences, *objective* and *subjective* acceptance are defined:

Definition 8. [2,14] An argument $a \in AR$ is *subjectively acceptable* if and only if a appears in some preferred extension for some specific audiences. An argument $a \in AR$ is *objectively acceptable* if and only if a appears in all preferred extension for all audiences.

2.3   Strength-Based Argumentation Framework (S-VAF)

Value-based argumentation acknowledges the importance of preferences when considering arguments. However, in the specific context of ontology matching, an objection can still be raised about the lack of complete mechanisms for handling persuasiveness. Indeed, many matching tools actually output alignments with a strength that reflects the confidence they have in the similarity between the two entities. These confidence levels are usually derived from similarity assessments made during the matching process, *e.g.* from edit distance measure between labels, or overlap measure between instance sets, as in [11]. They are therefore often based on objective grounds.

It is one of our goals to investigate whether considering confidence levels gives better results or not[2]. To this end, we adapt a formulation introduced in [24,26] to consider the strength granted to mappings for determining attacks' success:

Definition 9. A Strength and Value-based Argumentation Framework (S-VAF) is a 6-tuple $(AR, attacks, V, val, P, str)$ where $(AR, attacks, V, val, P)$ is a value-based argumentation framework, and str is a function which maps elements of AR to real values from the interval $[0, 1]$, representing the *strength* of the argument. An audience-specific S-VAF is an S-VAF where the generic set of audiences is replaced by the definition of a specific $valpref_{aud}$ preference relation over V.

Definition 10. In an audience-specific S-VAF, an argument $a \in AR$ defeats an argument $b \in AR$ for audience aud if and only if $attacks(a, b) \wedge (str(a) > str(b) \vee (str(a) = str(b) \wedge valpref_{aud}(val(a), val(b))))$

In other words, for a given audience, an attack succeeds if the strength of the attacking argument is greater than the strength of the attacked one; or, if both arguments have equal strength, the attacked argument is not preferred over the attacking argument by the concerned audience. Similarly to what is done for VAFs, an argument is acceptable for a given audience *w.r.t* a set of arguments if every argument defeating it is defeated by other members of the set. A set of arguments is conflict-free if no two members can defeat each other. Such a set is admissible for an audience if all its members are acceptable for this audience *w.r.t* itself. A set of arguments is a preferred extension for an audience if it is a maximal admissible set for this audience.

2.4   Argumentation Frameworks with Voting (V-VAF)

The previously described frameworks capture the possible conflicts between matchers, and find a way to solve them. However, they still fail at rendering the fact that sources of alignments often agree on their results, and that this agreement can be meaningful. Some large-scale experiments involving several matching tools — as the OAEI 2006 Food track campaign [6] — have indeed shown that the more often a mapping (or correspondence) is agreed on, the more chances for it to be valid.

We have adapted the S-VAF presented above to consider the level of consensus between the sources of the alignments, by introducing the notions of support and voting into the definition of successful attacks. Support enables arguments to be counted as defenders or co-attackers during an attack[3]:

---

[2] Note that as opposed to what is done [24,26], this paper aims at experimenting with matchers that were developed prior to the experiment, and hence more likely to present strength mismatches.

[3] Note that support, as well as attack, is an abstract notion, that depends of the framework instantiation. Also, support and attack relations may be defined independently of each other.

Definition 11. A *Voting Argumentation Framework* (V-VAF) is a 7-tuple *(AR, attacks, supports, V, val, P, str)* where $(AR, attacks, V, val, P, str)$ is a S-VAF, and *supports* is a (reflexive) binary relation over AR. *supports* and *attacks* are disjoint relations.

Voting is then used to determine whether an attack is successful or not. For this paper, we have chosen to test further the most simple voting scheme – the plurality voting system – where the number of supporters decides for success of attacks.

Definition 12. In a *Voting Argumentation Framework (V-VAF)* an argument $a \in AR$ *defeats*$_{aud}$ an argument $b \in AR$ for audience *aud* if and only if
$attacks(a, b) \quad \wedge \quad (\quad |\{x|supports(x, a)\}| > |\{y|supports(y, b)\}| \quad \vee$
$(|\{x|supports(x, a)\}| = |\{y|supports(y, b)\}| \wedge valpref_{aud}(val(a), val(b))) \quad)$.

This voting mechanism is based on simple counting. In fact, as we have seen previously, matchers sometimes return mappings together with a confidence value. There are voting mechanisms which address this confidence information. The first and most elementary one would be to sum up the confidence values of supporting arguments. However, as for the S-VAF, this would rely on the assumption that the strengths assigned by different matchers are similarly scaled, which as we have seen is debatable in practice[4].

3   Argumentation Process

The argumentation process has two main steps: *argument generation* and *preferred extension generation*. First, the matchers work in an independent manner, applying the specific matching approach and generating their alignments (set of correspondences or mappings). A mapping m is described as a 5-tuple $m = (e, e', h, R, s)$, where e corresponds to an entity in the ontology 1, e' corresponds to an entity in the ontology 2, h is one of $\{-, +\}$ depending on whether the mapping does or does not hold, R is the matching relation resulting from the matching between these two terms, and s is the *strength*[5] associated to the mapping. Each mapping m is encapsulated into an argument. An *argument* $\in$ AR is a 2-tuple $x = (m, a)$, where m is a mapping; $a \in V$ is the value of the argument, depending of the matcher generating that argument (i.e, matcher 1, 2 or 3).

After generating their set of arguments, the matchers exchange with each other their arguments – the dialogue between them consists of the exchange of individual arguments. When all matchers have received the set of arguments of the each other, they generate their *attacks* set. An *attack* (or counter-argument)

---

[4] As a matter of fact, in [10] we have carried out experiments with a voting framework that considered these strengths – and was performing some normalization of these. But this did not bring conclusive results.

[5] The *strength* of an argument is defined by the matcher when applying the specific matching approach.

will arise when we have arguments for mapping the same entities but with conflicting values of h. For instance, an argument $x = (m_1,M1)$, where $m_1 = (e,e',+,equivalence,1.0)$, has as a counter-argument an argument $y = (m_2,M2)$, where $m_2 = (e,e',-,equivalence,1.0)$. m_1 and m_2 refer to the same entities e and e' in the ontologies. The argument y also represents an *attack* to the argument x.

When the set of arguments and attacks have been produced, the matchers need to define which of them must be accepted, with respect to each audience. To do this, the matchers compute their preferred extension, according to the audiences and strength of the arguments.

Note that for S-VAF and V-VAF, we choose to have the values $v \in V$ represent different matching approaches used by the agents (i.e., different matching systems). For instance, when three matchers are used, matcher 1 (M1), matcher 2 (M2), and matcher 3 (M3), then $V = \{M1,M2,M3\}$.

Each audience has an ordering preference between the *values*. For instance, the matcher 1 represents an audience where the value *M1* is preferred to the values *M2* and *M3*. The idea is not to have an individual audience with preference between the agents (i.e., matcher 1 is preferred to all other matchers), but to try accommodate different audiences and their preferences. The idea is to obtain a consensus when using different matching techniques, which are represented by different preference between values.

4   Experiments

The evaluation of the argumentation frameworks is carried out focusing on real ontologies portion of the OAEI. Next, the data set is described, the configuration of the matchers is presented, and the results are discussed. The argumentation models are compared with the best matchers for each test case and with the baseline (union of the all individual matcher results).

4.1   Dataset Description

The Ontology Alignment Evaluation Initiative is a coordinated international initiative to establish a consensus for evaluation of ontology matching methods. It organizes evaluation campaigns on the basis of controlled experiments for comparing competitive techniques performances.

A systematic benchmark[6] is provided by the OAEI community. The goal of this benchmark is to identify the areas in which each algorithm is strong and weak. A first series of tests is based on one particular (reference) ontology dedicated to the domain of bibliography. This ontology contains 33 named classes, 24 object properties, 40 data properties, 56 named individuals and 20 anonymous individuals.

We however chose to focus our evaluation on a second series of tests, which is formed by a group of *real ontologies* (tests 301, 302, 303, and 304). We consider

---

[6] http://oaei.ontologymatching.org/2007/benchmarks/

that this would represent a more realistic evaluation scenario, regarding the presentation of several competing approaches. In these tests the reference ontology is compared with four real ontologies: BibTex MIT[7] (test 301), BibTex UMBC[8] (test 302), BibTex Karlsruhe[9] (test 303), and INRIA[10] ontology (test 304).

4.2 Matchers Configuration

The experiments are carried out using the group of OAEI matchers, which had participated of the OAEI Benchmark Track 2007[11]: *ASMOV* ([12]), *DSSim* ([18]), *Falcon* ([9]), *Lily* ([27]), *Ola* ([8]), *OntoDNA* ([13]), *PriorPlus* ([17]), *Ri-MOM* ([23]), *Sambo* ([22]), *SEMA* ([20]), *TaxoMap* ([28]), and *XSOM* ([3]).

DSSim, OntoDNA, PriorPlus, TaxoMap, and *XSOM* are based on the use of ontology-level information, such as labels of classes and properties, and ontology hierarchy, while *ASMOV, Falcon, Lily, Ola, RiMOM, Sambo*, and *SEMA* use both ontology-level and data-level (instances) information.

Considering the techniques used in the matching process, *DSSim, PriorPlus* and *XSOM* are based on edit-distance similarity, where *DSSim* and *X-SOM* combine the string-based approaches with the synonymous relations provided by WordNet[12]. Regarding the structural approaches, several heuristics are used, such as number of common descendants of two classes and the number of similar nodes in the path between the root and the element (*PriorPlus*).

A variety of strategies to combine individual matching techniques is used by the systems. The techniques can be executed in parallel (*DSSim, Falcon, Lily, Ola, PriorPlus, RiMOM, Sambo, XSOM*), or sequentially (*TaxoMap*). To combine the results of these executions, several ways are proposed: weighted formula (*PriorPlus and Sambo*), Dempster's rule of combination (*DSSim*), combination using a feed-forward neural network (*XSOM*), systems of equations (*OLA*), linear interpolation (*RiMOM*), and experimental weighted (*Lily*). *Falcon* executes sequentially a TFIDF linguistic matcher that combines concepts and instances, together a graph-based matcher. *ASMOV* iteratively combines several matchers using a single weighted sum to combine the individual results. Instance-based matchers are commonly based on Naive-Bayes classifiers (*RiMOM*), statistics (*Falcon and SEMA*), or probabilistic methods (*Sambo*).

4.3 Evaluation Measures

To evaluate the alignment quality, we measure precision, recall and f–measure with respect to (manually built) reference alignments provided in the OAEI benchmarks. Such measures are derived from a contingency table (Table 1),

---

[7] http://visus.mit.edu/bibtex/0.1/
[8] http://ebiquity.umbc.edu
[9] http://www.aifb.uni-karlsruhe.de/ontology
[10] http://fr.inrialpes.exmo.rdf.bib.owl
[11] http://oaei.ontologymatching.org/2007/results/benchmarks/
[12] http://wordnet.princeton.edu/

Table 1. Contingency table for binary classification

	manual h = +	manual h = -
output h = +	m_{++}	m_{+-}
output h = -	m_{-+}	m_{--}

Table 2. Individual matcher results

	ASMOV			DSSim			Falcon			Lily			Ola			OntoDNA		
Test	P	R	F	P	R	F	P	R	F	P	R	F	P	R	F	P	R	F
301	0.93	**0.82**	**0.87**	0.82	0.30	0.44	0.91	**0.82**	0.86	0.89	**0.80**	**0.84**	0.70	0.66	0.68	0.88	0.69	0.77
302	0.68	**0.58**	0.63	0.85	**0.60**	**0.70**	0.90	**0.58**	**0.71**	0.82	**0.65**	**0.73**	0.51	0.50	0.50	0.90	0.40	0.55
303	0.75	**0.86**	**0.80**	0.85	**0.80**	**0.82**	0.77	0.76	**0.76**	0.58	0.69	0.63	0.41	**0.82**	0.54	0.90	0.78	**0.84**
304	**0.95**	**0.96**	**0.95**	0.96	0.92	0.94	0.96	0.93	0.95	0.91	**0.97**	0.94	0.89	**0.97**	0.93	0.92	0.88	0.90
Average	0.83	**0.80**	**0.81**	0.87	0.65	0.73	**0.89**	**0.77**	**0.82**	0.80	**0.78**	**0.79**	0.63	**0.74**	0.66	**0.90**	0.69	**0.77**

	PriorPlus			RiMOM			Sambo			SEMA			TaxoMap			XSOM		
Test	P	R	F	P	R	F	P	R	F	P	R	F	P	R	F	P	R	F
301	0.93	**0.82**	**0.87**	0.75	0.67	0.71	0.95	0.69	**0.80**	0.70	**0.75**	0.72	1.0	0.21	0.35	0.91	0.49	0.64
302	0.82	**0.67**	**0.74**	0.72	**0.65**	**0.68**	0.90	0.19	0.32	0.62	**0.60**	0.61	1.0	0.21	0.35	1.0	**0.58**	**0.73**
303	0.81	**0.80**	**0.80**	0.45	**0.86**	0.59	0.90	0.76	**0.82**	0.55	0.80	0.65	0.80	0.24	0.38	0.90	0.73	**0.81**
304	0.90	**0.97**	**0.94**	0.90	**0.97**	**0.94**	0.96	0.89	**0.93**	0.77	0.93	0.85	**0.93**	0.34	0.50	0.96	0.87	**0.91**
Average	0.87	**0.81**	**0.84**	0.71	**0.79**	0.73	**0.93**	0.63	0.72	0.66	**0.77**	0.71	**0.93**	0.25	0.39	**0.94**	0.67	**0.77**

where manual refers to the correspondences in the reference alignment and output refers to the results from the matchers.

Precision (P) is defined by the number of correct automated mappings (m_{++}) divided by the number of mappings that the system had returned ($m_{++} + m_{+-}$). It measures the system's correctness or accuracy. *Recall* (R) indicates the number of correct mappings returned by the system divided by the number of manual mappings ($m_{++} + m_{-+}$). It measures how complete or comprehensive the system is in its extraction of relevant mappings. *F–measure* (F) is a weighted harmonic mean of precision and recall.

$$P = \frac{m_{++}}{(m_{++} + m_{+-})}, \quad R = \frac{m_{++}}{(m_{++} + m_{-+})}, \quad F = \frac{(2 * P * R)}{(P + R)}$$

For all comparative results, a significance test is applied, considering a confidence degree of 95%. The best values are indicated in bold face in the tables below. When there is reference for results *slightly* better, we mean that some true positive mappings are retrieved while some false positive mappings are discarded, however without having so significantly differences in the results.

4.4   Individual Matchers Results

Table 2 shows the results for each OAEI matcher[13], considering values of Precision (P), Recall (R), and F–measure (F).

---

[13] http://oaei.ontologymatching.org/2007/results/benchmarks/ HTML/results.html

Looking for each individual test in terms of F–measure, different groups of best matchers can be ranked:

- Test 301: *ASMOV, PriorPlus, Falcon, Lily,* and *Sambo*;
- Test 302: *PriorPlus, Lily, XSOM, Falcon, DSSim,* and *RiMOM*;
- Test 303: *OntoDNA, DSSim, Sambo, XSOM, ASMOV, PriorPlus* and *Falcon*;
- Test 304: *ASMOV, Falcon, DSSim, Lily, PriorPlus, RiMOM, Ola and Sambo, XSOM,* and *OntoDNA.*

Only PriorPlus and Falcon are in all rankings, but in different positions. In average, PriorPlus, Falcon, ASMOV, Lily, OntoDNA, and XSOM are in the group of the best matchers.

4.5   Baseline and Argumentation Results

The use of argumentation models aims to obtain a consensus between the matchers, improving or balancing the individual results. This section presents the results using VAF, S-VAF, and V-VAF, considering as input the results from the previously described matchers. We compare the results of these frameworks with the baseline – which is composed by the union of all alignments – and with the results of the best matchers.

The argumentation results contain only the arguments objectively acceptable. It means that only the mappings strictly acceptable for all matchers are evaluated. The audiences represent the following complete preference order (pattern), which has been defined according to the individual performance of the matchers (i.e., the best matcher has higher preference, and so on): *ASMOV* audience – ASMOV > Lily > RiMOM > Falcon > Ola > PriorPlus > SEMA > DSSim > XSOM > Sambo > OntoDNA; *Lily* audience – Lily > ASMOV > RiMOM > Falcon > Ola > PriorPlus > SEMA > DSSim > XSOM > Sambo > OntoDNA; and so on. The individual performance is computed by measuring precision and recall of the matcher output against the reference alignment.

Especially for S-VAF, two arbitrary values are used to represent the strength of the counter-argument of a positive mapping, 0.5 and 1.0. The generation of counter-arguments is a step that we implement on top of the positive mappings generated by the matchers. Different values of strength for such arguments can be specified by the user.

Basically, the OAEI matchers produce arguments for positive mappings with strength between 0.8 and 1.0. Using 0.5 as strength for a negative argument will not lead to (many) successful attacks for the positive mappings. Therefore, this results in better values of recall (the majority of the true positive mappings are selected). However, some positive arguments corresponding to wrong mappings are selected as acceptable because generated negative arguments do not lead to successful attacks, resulting in lower precision.

When using a value of 1.0, the positive arguments corresponding to false mappings from the matchers with lower strength are attacked and not selected as

Table 3. Baseline and argumentation results

| | | | | Argumentation | | | | | | | |
| | Baseline | | | VAF | | | S-VAF | | | V-VAF | | |
Test	P	R	F	P	R	F	P	R	F	P	R	F
301	0.46	**0.85**	0.60	1.0	0.13	0.24	0.56	**0.83**	0.67	0.94	**0.78**	**0.85**
302	0.32	**0.72**	0.44	-	0.0	-	0.43	**0.70**	0.53	**0.97**	0.60	**0.74**
303	0.22	**0.86**	0.35	1.0	0.2	0.34	0.42	**0.86**	0.56	0.93	**0.80**	**0.86**
304	0.63	**0.97**	0.76	1.0	0.3	0.46	0.72	**0.97**	0.83	**0.97**	**0.95**	**0.96**
Average	0.41	**0.85**	0.54	0.75	0.16	0.26	0.53	**0.84**	0.65	**0.95**	**0.78**	**0.85**

Table 4. Best argumentation vs. best matcher results

| | Argumentation | Best matcher |
Test	F	F
301	0.85 (V-VAF)	0.87 (ASMOV, PriorPlus)
302	0.74 (V-VAF)	0.74 (PriorPlus)
303	0.86 (V-VAF)	0.84 (OntoDNA)
304	0.96 (V-VAF)	0.95 (ASMOV, Falcon)

Table 5. Best argumentation vs. best matcher results (average for each best matcher)

| | Argumentation | ASMOV | PriorPlus | OntoDNA | Falcon |
Test	F	F	F	F	F
Average	0.85	0.81	0.84	0.77	0.82

objectively acceptable (the false positive mapping is not acceptable for the audience of the true negative mapping). In this way, the precision is better. On the other hand, the resulting recall represents the lowest recall of the matchers. Moreover, a notable problem when using the value 1.0 when one matcher outputs no mapping is that if all others have true positive mappings with strength below 1.0, such true positive mappings are successfully attacked by the negative mappings. So, in this set of experiments, 0.5 is used as strengths for (negative) counter-arguments in the S-VAF.

However, the strength of arguments is an important issue that must be explored in more detail, as well as the preference order, which can have great impact in the results.

Table 3 shows the results of baseline and argumentation, considering the three frameworks.

Tables 4 and 5 show a comparison among the best argumentation model and the best matchers, taking into account the values of F–measure for each case. Best matchers vary for different ontologies – e.g., OntoDNA is the first better matcher for test 303, while it is the last one for test 304.

4.6 Discussion

As expected, baseline produces good values of recall – all true (positive) mappings are retrieved – while precision is lower – all false (positive) mappings are retrieved. By argumentation, false positive mappings can be are filtered out, improving the precision, while true positive mappings are also discarded, reducing the recall.

In average, the V-VAF performs better than VAF and S-VAF. In terms of averaged F-measure, V-VAF slightly outperforms the best matcher (Table 5), while having comparable level of quality in respect to the best matcher, for each test (Table 4). The VAF, since the preferences in the audiences are specified by the individual performance of the matchers, produces high values of precision.

The irregular performance of S-VAF confirms that one cannot fully rely on strengths output by matchers. As we had explained in [10] for motivating the introduction of consensus-based argumentation frameworks, these confidence levels are usually derived from similarity assessments made during the alignment process, and are therefore often based on objective grounds. However, there is no theory or even guidelines for determining such confidence levels. Using them to compare results from different matchers is therefore questionable, especially because of potential scale mismatches. For example, a same strength of 0.8 may not correspond to the same level of confidence for two different matcher. The approach we have taken in V-VAF, which does not rely on strengths, has been confirmed to perform better in our tests.

Analyzing the results of the individual matchers, the consensus achieved by the cooperative models is a balancing between the individual results. Consensus does not improve over every individual result, but instead delivers an intermediary performance, which is close to the one of the best matcher but represents a considerable improvement over the worst matchers.

When comparing our results with the closest state-of-the-art argumentation proposal, namely from [14] (with a report of the results for the four cases used in our paper), better results are obtained by the V-Voting framework.

Using notions of acceptability of arguments based on voting is a more promising option than using quantitative aspects as strengths, especially when a "good" number of matchers is available. Our experiments indeed confirm previous observations in the ontology matching field, according to which mappings that are found by several matchers on a same case are generally more precise.[14] In fact in this paper we have put such observation in practice, by devising a matcher combination framework that can be deployed on top of existing matchers. It is important to notice that even though the implementation we have tested is dependent on a priori knowledge of matcher performance, we claim this dependence to be minimal. First, the "performance knowledge" required just consists of a simple order relation. Second, this preference order is used just when votes do not lead to a choice between contradictory arguments, which limits its application.

---

[14] It is worth noting that we obtain in our experiments results that are way more conclusive than those we previously obtained with much less matchers [10].

Regarding the field of argumentation, in general, in another cases where argumentation is applied, such as law reasoning, using confidence is a reasonable issue to be considered, as well the mechanism of voting, already quoted in the law field, but not at the level of argumentation.

5   Related Work

In the field of ontology argumentation few approaches are being proposed. Basically, the closer proposal is from [15][14], where an argument framework is used to deal with arguments that support or oppose candidate correspondences between ontologies. The candidate mappings are obtained from an Ontology Mapping Repository (OMR) – the focus is not how the mappings are computed – and argumentation is used to accommodate different agent's preferences. Differently from Laera and colleagues, who use the VAF, our approach considers different quantitative issues on ontology matching, such as confidence level and voting on the arguments.

We find similar proposals in the field of ontology negotiation. [21] presents an ontology to serve as the basis for agent negotiation, the ontology itself is not the object being negotiated. A similar approach is proposed by [4], where agents agree on a common ontology in a decentralized way. Rather than being the goal of each agent, the ontology mapping is a common goal for every agent in the system. [1] presents an ontology negotiation model which aims to arrive at a common ontology which the agents can use in their particular interaction. We, on the other hand, are concerned with delivering mapping pairs found by a group of agents using argumentation. [19] describes an approach for ontology mapping negotiation, where the mapping is composed by a set of semantic bridges and their inter-relations, as proposed in [16]. The agents are able to achieve a consensus about the mapping through the evaluation of a confidence value that is obtained by utility functions. According to the confidence value the mapping rule is accepted, rejected or negotiated. Differently from [19], we do not use utility functions. Our model is based on cooperation and argumentation, where the agents change their arguments and by argumentation select the preferred mapping.

6   Concluding Remarks and Future Work

This paper has presented the evaluation of three argumentation frameworks for ontology matching. Using argumentation, it is possible to use the *values* to represent preferences between the matchers. Each approach represents a *value* and each agent represents an audience, with preferences between the *values*. The *values* are used to determine the preference between the different matchers. Based on these notions, extended frameworks using confidence levels and number of supports were also considered. These extended frameworks, respectively, take into account the importance of using arguments with strength, reflecting the confidence the matcher has in the similarity between the two entities (the matching tools actually output mappings with a confidence measure), and the notion of that more often a mapping is agreed on, the more chances for it to be valid.

It is hard to improve the best matcher, especially when there is a large intersection between the individual results. In the experiments carried out, the best individual matcher varies depending on the specific characteristics of each set, while considering voting on arguments the results are similar to the best matchers for all sets.

The results obtained in this paper are more conclusive than the results of our previous paper[10]. First, much more matchers are involved, and their quality is better. We indeed had hinted for these previous experiments the results were inconclusive because there were not enough matchers performing well enough. When one takes more matchers, and the case becomes easier (the library one, as a Dutch one was hard), the proportion of matchers that really fail is lower. This results in less consensus for accepting wrong mappings. In this case voting has really helped, and performs better than baseline and allow for performance close to the best matcher.

An important issue is that we have results similar to the best matcher, but we are aware of the best matcher when obtaining them: in fact this knowledge has been used for the preference order. One possible experiment in the future is thus to check (i) whether a random order achieves good result, or (ii) if an order that is obtained for one test case can achieve good results in another case; and (iii) explore the strength of arguments is a more detail.

References

1. Bailin, S., Truszkowski, W.: Ontology negotiation between intelligent information agents. The Knowledge Engineering Review 17(1), 7–19 (2002)
2. Bench-Capon, T.: Persuasion in practical argument using value-based argumentation frameworks. Journal of Logic and Computation 13, 429–448 (2003)
3. Curino, C., Orsi, G., Tanca, L.: X-som results for oaei 2007. In: Proceedings of the 2nd Ontology Matching Workshop, Busan, Korea, pp. 276–285 (2007)
4. van Diggelen, J., Beun, R., Dignum, F., van Eijk, R., Meyer, J.C.: Anemone: An effective minimal ontology negotiation environment. In: Proceedings of the V International Conference on Autonomous Agents and Multi-Agent Systems, pp. 899–906 (2006)
5. Dung, P.: On the acceptability of arguments and its fundamental role in nonmonotonic reasoning, logic programming and n–person games. Artificial Intelligence 77, 321–358 (1995)
6. Euzenat, J., Mochol, M., Shvaiko, P., Stuckenschmidt, H., Sváb, O., Svátek, V., van Hage, W.R., Yatskevich, M.: Results of the ontology alignment evaluation initiative 2006. In: Shvaiko, P., Euzenat, J., Noy, N.F., Stuckenschmidt, H., Benjamins, V.R., Uschold, M. (eds.) Proceedings of the 1st International Workshop on Ontology Matching. CEUR Workshop Proceedings, vol. 225 (2006), CEUR-WS.org
7. Euzenat, J., Shvaiko, P.: Ontology Matching. Springer, Heidelberg (2007)
8. Euzenat, J., Valtchev, P.: Similarity-based ontology alignment in OWL-Lite. In: Proceedings of the European Conference on Artificial Intelligence, vol. 16, pp. 333–337 (2004)

9. Hu, W., Qu, Y.: Falcon–AO: A practical ontology matching system. Journal of Web Semantics 6(3), 237–239 (2008)
10. Isaac, A., Trojahn, C., Wang, S., Quaresma, P.: Using quantitative aspects of alignment generation for argumentation on mappings. In: Workshop on Ontology Matching (OM 2008) at 7th International Semantic Web Conference, ISWC 2008 (2008) (to appear)
11. Isaac, A., van der Meij, L., Schlobach, S., Wang, S.: An empirical study of instance-based ontology matching. In: Aberer, K., Choi, K.-S., Noy, N., Allemang, D., Lee, K.-I., Nixon, L.J.B., Golbeck, J., Mika, P., Maynard, D., Mizoguchi, R., Schreiber, G., Cudré-Mauroux, P. (eds.) ASWC 2007 and ISWC 2007. LNCS, vol. 4825, pp. 253–266. Springer, Heidelberg (2007)
12. Jean-Mary, Y., Kabuka, M.: Asmov: Ontology alignment with semantic validation. In: Joint SWDB-ODBIS Workshop on Semantics, Ontologies, Databases, Vienna, Austria, pp. 15–20 (2007)
13. Kiu, C.-C., Lee, C.-S.: Ontodna: Ontology alignment results for oaei 2007. In: Proceedings of the 2nd Ontology Matching Workshop, Busan, Korea, pp. 196–204 (2007)
14. Laera, L., Blacoe, I., Tamma, V., Payne, T., Euzenat, J., Bench-Capon, T.: Argumentation over ontology correspondences in mas. In: Durfee, M., Yokoo, E.H. (eds.) Proceedings of the Sixth International Joint Conference on Autonomous Agents and Multi-Agent Systems (2007)
15. Laera, L., Tamma, V., Euzenat, J., Bench-Capon, T., Payne, T.R.: Reaching agreement over ontology alignments. In: Cruz, I., Decker, S., Allemang, D., Preist, C., Schwabe, D., Mika, P., Uschold, M., Aroyo, L.M. (eds.) ISWC 2006. LNCS, vol. 4273, pp. 371–384. Springer, Heidelberg (2006)
16. Maedche, A., Motik, B., Silva, N., Volz, R.: Mafra - a mapping framework for distributed ontologies. In: 13th International Conference on Knowledge Engineering and Knowledge Management, pp. 235–250 (2002)
17. Mao, M., Peng, Y.: The prior+: Results for oaei campaign 2007. In: Proceedings of the 2nd Ontology Matching Workshop, Busan, Korea, pp. 219–226 (2007)
18. Nagy, M., Vargas-Vera, M., Motta, E.: DSSim – managing uncertainty on the semantic web. In: 2nd International Workshop on Ontology Matching, Busan, Korea (2007)
19. Silva, N., Maio, P., Rocha, J.: An approach to ontology mapping negotiation. In: Proceedings of the K-CAP Workshop on Integrating Ontologies (2005)
20. Spiliopoulos, V., Valarakos, A., Vouros, G., Karkaletsis, V.: Sema: Results for the ontology alignment contest oaei 2007. In: Proceedings of the 2nd Ontology Matching Workshop, Busan, Korea, pp. 244–254 (2007)
21. Tamma, V., Wooldridge, M., Blacoe, I., Dickinson, I.: An ontology based approach to automated negotiation. In: Proceedings of the IV Workshop on Agent Mediated Electronic Commerce, pp. 219–237 (2002)
22. Tan, H., Lambrix, P.: Sambo results for the ontology alignment evaluation initiative 2007. In: Proceedings of the Second Ontology Matching Workshop, Busan, Korea, pp. 236–243 (2007)
23. Tang, J., Liang, B., Li, J.-Z., Wang, K.: Risk minimization based ontology mapping. In: Chi, C.-H., Lam, K.-Y. (eds.) AWCC 2004. LNCS, vol. 3309, pp. 469–480. Springer, Heidelberg (2004)
24. Trojahn, C., Quaresma, P., Vieira, R.: An extended value-based argumentation framework for ontology mapping with confidence degrees. In: Rahwan, I., Parsons, S., Reed, C. (eds.) ArgMAS 2007. LNCS (LNAI), vol. 4946, pp. 132–144. Springer, Heidelberg (2008)

25. Trojahn, C., Quaresma, P., Vieira, R.: An argumentation framework based on strength for ontology mapping. In: Workshop of Argumentation, International Conference on Autonomous Agents and Multiagent Systems (2008)

26. Trojahn, C., Quaresma, P., Vieira, R., Moraes, M.: A cooperative approach for composite ontology mapping. In: Spaccapietra, S. (ed.) Journal on Data Semantics X (JoDS). LNCS, vol. 4900, pp. 237–263. Springer, Heidelberg (2008)

27. Wang, P., Xu, B.: Lily: The results for the ontology alignment contest oaei 2007. In: Proceedings of the 2nd Ontology Matching Workshop, Busan, Korea, pp. 179–185 (2007)

28. Zargayouna, H., Safar, B., Reynaud, C.: Taxomap in the oaei 2007 alignment contest. In: Proceedings of the 2nd Ontology Matching Workshop, Busan, Korea, pp. 268–275 (2007)

Author Index